THE PROFESSIONAL PRACTICE SERIES

The Professional Practice Series is sponsored by the Society for Industrial and Organizational Psychology (SIOP). The series was launched in 1988 to provide industrial/organizational psychologists, organizational scientists and practitioners, human resource professionals, managers, executives, and those interested in organizational behavior and performance with volumes that are insightful, current, informative, and relevant to organizational practice. The volumes in the Professional Practice Series are guided by five tenets designed to enhance future organizational practice:

1. Focus on practice, but grounded in science
2. Translate organizational science into practice by generating guidelines, principles, and lessons learned that can shape and guide practice
3. Showcase the application of industrial/organizational psychology to solve problems
4. Document and demonstrate best industrial and organizational-based practices
5. Stimulate research needed to guide future organizational practice

The volumes seek to inform those interested in practice with guidance, insights, and advice on how to apply the concepts, findings, methods, and tools derived from industrial/organizational psychology to solve human-related organizational problems.

Previous Professional Practice Series volumes include:

Published by Jossey-Bass

Published by Guilford Press

Resizing the Organization

Resizing the Organization

Managing Layoffs, Divestitures, and Closings

Maximizing Gain While Minimizing Pain

Kenneth P. De Meuse

Mitchell Lee Marks

Editors

Foreword by Eduardo Salas

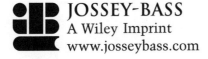

JOSSEY-BASS
A Wiley Imprint
www.josseybass.com

Published by Jossey-Bass
A Wiley Imprint
989 Market Street, San Francisco, CA 94103-1741   www.josseybass.com

Jossey-Bass books and products are available through most bookstores. To contact Jossey-Bass directly call our Customer Care Department within the U.S. at 800-956-7739, outside the U.S. at 317-572-3986 or fax 317-572-4002.

Jossey-Bass also publishes its books in a variety of electronic formats. Some content that appears in print may not be available in electronic books.

Library of Congress Cataloging-in-Publication Data

Resizing the organization : managing layoffs, divestitures, and closings / Kenneth P. De Meuse, Mitchell Lee Marks, editors; foreword by Eduardo Salas.
     p. cm — (The Jossey-Bass business & management series) (The professional practice series)
Includes bibliographical references and indexes.
    ISBN 0-7879-5891-3 (alk. paper)
    1. Downsizing of organizations.   2. Layoff systems.   3. Corporate divestiture.   4. Downsizing of organizations—United States.   5. Layoff systems—United States.   6. Corporate divestiture—United States.   I. De Meuse, Kenneth P. (Kenneth Paul)   II. Marks, Mitchell Lee.   III. Series.
    HD58.85 .R47   2003
    658.1'6—dc21

                                 2002015265

Printed in the United States of America
FIRST EDITION
HB Printing   *10 9 8 7 6 5 4 3 2*

The Jossey-Bass
Business & Management Series

The Professional Practice Series

Contents

Foreword

The corporate world is living through some interesting and challenging times. In today's world, in order to survive or remain competitive, corporations must continue to assess their organizational strategies, structures, and practices. Changing and adapting to external pressures and market shifts is now (and will continue to be) an imperative. It is a must; survival depends on it.

As a consequence, organizations restructure, downsize, reengineer, merge, seek financial protections, or form alliances. This can only be done if organizations remain agile, proactive, fresh, and promote innovative managerial practices. The key to success here seems to be what executives think and do. What actions they take and why. Therefore, executives—while seeking, developing, and executing managerial strategies—must be guided (one would think and want) by sound proven principles of leadership, organizational change, and human resource practices.

This is the focus of *Resizing the Organization*. This book seeks to provide executives with useful insights, tools, guidelines, principles, and lessons learned about organizational transition and change. Kenneth De Meuse and Mitchell Marks have compiled chapters that clearly outline how industrial/organizational psychology can contribute to (and have an impact on) organizational practice. The authors of the chapters provide, in my opinion, very valuable information to executives and human resource practitioners on how to cope, survive, and thrive in the face of external economic and social pressures. These authors collectively give us the good, the bad, and the not-so-good of resizing organizations. De Meuse, Marks, and their collaborators bring us in this volume, a clear illustration of how we (as industrial/organizational psychologists) can contribute to the corporate world. So, well done and thank you.

I believe, on behalf of the SIOP Professional Practice Series Editorial Board, that this volume adds to our collection of how our science can serve practice. We will continue to pursue this goal, and we hope the other volumes to come will do just that. Stay tuned.

October 2002   EDUARDO SALAS
University of Central Florida
Series Editor

Preface

About fifteen years ago at a professional meeting, one of my colleagues shared his current research agenda: how to understand, make sense of, and better deal with layoffs. I privately (and somewhat vocally) mocked him. How had he picked such a time-bound topic? How could someone so insightful focus on issues that executives had already mastered? Why was he not focusing research on the future instead of the past? In the ensuing years, I have regretted my disparaging attitude. Becoming competitive through reshaping the organization is timeless, not time bound. Executives continually thirst for insights to help them become more competitive.

Competition has not gone away. In fact, it has increased. Executives must deal with technology advances, globalization, information ubiquity, customer and employee mobility, legislative and regulatory changes, and economic uncertainty. These new external realities make business more uncertain and challenging than ever before. The evidence of competitiveness abounds:

- Enron, the seventh largest firm in the United States, goes bankrupt in months, leaving employees both out of work and out of economic security.
- Mergers or alliances occur among large global firms in almost every industry. Examples abound: Chrysler and Mercedes Benz; Smith-Kline-Beecham and Glaxco; Citibank and Travelers; General Mills and Pillsbury; and BP and Amoco and Arco and Castrol.
- Traditional firms (like Sears, Dupont, Hewlett Packard, and AT&T) must undergo transformation to survive.
- New firms (among them, Cisco, Microsoft, and Sun) emerge to define and shape new rules of competition.

Today, no firm is safe from the new economic realities that require unending drives to be ever more competitive.

Executives in competitive firms articulate a point of view that defines and shapes industry standards and seeks for a share of opportunity as a strategic agenda. They must also build organizations imbued with capabilities or the ability to deliver on strategic promises. Central to organizational success is productivity, or the ability to do more with less. Much of the productivity gains come from creating lean, focused, agile, and proactive organizations. Executives who identify and instill leading-edge capabilities turn strategy into actions and actions into results. No executive in the public or private sector, in large or small firms, at a plant or division or corporate level, is immune. Executives must respond to new economic realities with innovative strategies and productive organizations.

When I first read work by Ken De Meuse, I was editor of the *Human Resource Management Journal,* and he published an article that challenged some of the orthodoxies inherent in downsizing. He broadened the definition of downsizing from brute layoffs to corporate right-sizing, where executives increase productivity by removing people and fixing work processes. It is wonderful that he has continued and expanded his work. Executives continue to need to know how to grow through product innovation, global expansion, and customer intimacy and yet reduce costs through productivity and process gains. Mitch Marks also has published extensively in the area while maintaining a full-time consulting schedule. He has crafted a nice intersection between research and practice. He was one of the first authors to address the human and cultural aspects of mergers, resizings, and other major transitions and continues to convey insight and innovation into the management of change strategies. He brings the practitioner-scientist model to life by using industrial/organizational psychology theories and concepts to guide management action.

Smart executives in leading companies are learning that right-sizing is not an event but a process. Employees may be asked to leave the firm because of their performance and because of the economic uncertainties that beset firms. In either case, executives must make thoughtful, bold, and caring decisions that increase productivity while maintaining a positive work environment. They must pay attention to employees who stay as well as those who leave; they must discover new ways to deliver work rather than simply removing it; they need to assess strategic choices in downsizing where some units might be reduced or even increased more than others to meet strategic goals rather than across-the-board cuts; and they need to be exemplars of transparency and integrity in the right-sizing process.

During the past decade, executives have learned how to gain competitiveness through productivity while maintaining compassion through caring and contexts. Many of these lessons learned are personal experiences: executives had to close plants, reduce employees, restructure, or exit communities that their organizations had supported. These tough decisions are often a prelude to long-term and viable business results. Trees grow better when pruned, and often organizations grow better after thoughtful but rigorous right-sizing.

As I hear executives struggling with the ups and the downs of economic cycles, I sense that they need innovative and thoughtful tools to get their organization right in both good times and bad. In this light, the issues that I thought were nearly solved were only beginning. Executives will continue to reshape, resize, and renew their organizations. The chapters in this book will inform and focus attention to help make these transitions as effective as possible.

In one company, employees who experienced a reduction in force and then began to grow as the economic cycle returned started a private chant, "happy days are here again," with their new-found success and growth. They felt that downsizing was an event to manage, a managerial action to check off the to-do list. I now believe they were (as I was) wrong. Right-sizing will never end. It is the process of aligning the internal organization to the external realities. As those realities change and strategies are crafted to adapt to them, organizations also must adapt. Executives who accept the new economic realities and master the right-sizing processes will build both competitiveness and compassion in their organizations— competitive because they anticipate and respond and compassion because they learn how to do so in a way that engages employees.

Thanks to the authors of this book for taking some of the mystery out of this complex effort.

October 2002

DAVE ULRICH
School of Business
University of Michigan

This book is dedicated to all the employees and their families who have been resized. Although the experience can be frightening, frustrating, and stressful, a world of opportunity awaits you. We encourage you to take advantage of this opportunity to look for some personal gain along with your pain.

The Authors

Kenneth P. De Meuse is professor of management at the University of Wisconsin–Eau Claire. Previously, he was on the faculties of Iowa State University and the University of Nebraska. De Meuse has served as internal or external consultant for such firms as Union Carbide, AVEX Electronics, Intergraph Corporation, Lucent Technologies, Iowa Power and Light Company, Wausau Insurance, Northern States Power Company, the Internal Revenue Service, and Nestlé USA. Managerial succession planning, employee empowerment programs, team building, employee attitude assessment, strategic planning, and corporate restructuring are some of the consulting assignments he has performed for these companies.

For the past twenty years, De Meuse has been investigating the human side of corporate restructuring and downsizing. More than 100 universities and 150 corporations have contacted him regarding his research work in this area. He has appeared on national television and radio and has been featured widely in the press for his expertise on the impact that corporate transitions have on employees.

He has published numerous articles on employee attitudes and organizational behavior in several leading professional journals. He is coauthor of *The Team Developer: An Assessment and Skill Building Program* (2001). De Meuse is a member of the American Management Association, Academy of Management, Society for Industrial and Organizational Psychology, Human Resource Planning Society, and American Psychological Association. He received his Ph.D. in industrial/organizational psychology from the College of Business at The University of Tennessee.

Mitchell Lee Marks is a consultant to a broad variety of organizations in the United States and abroad. His areas of expertise include corporate culture, team building, organizational effectiveness, management development, executive coaching, senior team development, human resource management, and the strategic planning and implementation of organizational change. He works extensively with firms that are planning and implementing mergers, restructurings, downsizings, and other transitions. He is recognized internationally for developing innovative human resource and cultural approaches to achieving desired business results during transition.

Among his current and past clients are major corporations in the high-technology, financial services, manufacturing, health care, entertainment, government, publishing, consumer products, communications, and not-for-profit sectors.

Reports of Marks's work have been featured in major media. He is the author of *Joining Forces: Making One Plus One Equal Three in Mergers, Acquisitions and Alliances,* and *From Turmoil to Triumph: New Life After Mergers, Acquisitions, and Downsizing* and is coauthor of *Managing the Merger,* along with numerous articles in management and scholarly journals. He has lectured at the Harvard Business School, Smithsonian Institute, and a variety of international business, professional, and academic audiences. A member of the Society for Industrial and Organizational Psychology and the American Psychological Association for nearly twenty years, he received a Ph.D. in organizational psychology from the University of Michigan.

David T. Bastien teaches intercultural communication and intercultural management and ethics in the Master of International Management Program and Organizational Communication at the University of Minnesota. He is a merger and acquisition consultant in private practice and an associate of Waypoint Associates, specializing in corporate judo and competitive intelligence. He has published extensively, especially in the areas of organizational change, mergers and acquisitions, organizational culture, the psychology of social and organizational disruption, leadership, and competitive analysis. He received the Ph.D. from the University of Minnesota.

Thomas J. Bergmann is a professor of management at the University of Wisconsin–Eau Claire. He is the author of *Compensation De-*

cision Making, now in its fourth edition, and has published widely in professional journals. He received the Ph.D. from the Industrial Relations Center of the University of Minnesota.

Scott M. Brooks is executive consultant and director of research and development for Gantz Wiley Research, a consulting firm specializing in employee opinion and customer satisfaction surveys for international corporate clients. In addition to employee survey consulting, he manages the R&D function, which includes oversight of all projects linking employee surveys to customer or business performance measures and develops customized and standard employee and customer survey products based on these linkages. He manages WorkTrends, Gantz Wiley Research's unique database reflecting national trends in employee opinions. He has authored numerous presentations and publications and is a frequent speaker at national conferences and company meetings. He is a member of the Society for Industrial and Organizational Psychology and the American Psychological Association. He received his Ph.D. in industrial and organizational psychology from the Ohio State University.

Anthony F. Buono has a joint appointment as professor of management and sociology at Bentley College. His research and consulting interests focus on the management consulting industry, organizational change, and interorganizational strategies, including mergers, acquisitions, and alliances. He has written and edited seven books, including *The Human Side of Mergers and Acquisitions,* and is the editor of *Research in Management Consulting.* He received the Ph.D. with a concentration in industrial and organizational sociology from Boston College.

Wayne F. Cascio is professor of management and international business at the University of Colorado at Denver. A past president of the Society for Industrial and Organizational Psychology, his most recent book is *Responsible Restructuring: Creative and Profitable Alternatives to Layoffs* (2002). He received the Ph.D. in industrial and organizational psychology from the University of Rochester.

Jeffrey Crandell consults for a global employee assistance program (Ann Clark Associates) and is a certified associate for Lee Hecht

Harrison, a global outplacement training firm. He has been working in the training and human resources field for the past ten years. He began his career working for Goodwill Industries, first developing vocational training programs to help displaced workers find steady employment and then developing and facilitating leadership programs for the staff and management.

Daniel C. Feldman is the James Bradley Distinguished Foundation Fellow at the University of South Carolina Moore School of Business. He is editor of the *Journal of Management,* associate editor of *Human Resource Management,* and consulting editor of *Journal of Organizational Behavior.* He has authored six books and over one hundred articles on career development in organizations, including *Managing Careers in Organizations, Coping with Job Loss: How Individuals, Organizations, and Communities Respond to Layoffs,* and *Work Careers: A Developmental Perspective.* He received the Ph.D. from Yale University.

Emily L. Hause is an assistant professor at Augsburg College. She has consulted with a variety of organizations on managerial assessment, performance appraisal design, and synchronous work group effectiveness. Her publications and presentations have focused on decision making and job attitudes. She received her Ph.D. in industrial and organizational psychology from the Ohio State University and is a member of the Society for Industrial and Organizational Psychology and the American Psychological Society.

Todd J. Hostager is professor of management at the University of Wisconsin–Eau Claire. His research focuses on competitive dynamics following strategic change, perceptions of workplace diversity, and jazz improvisation as a model for cooperation and organizational innovation. He received his Ph.D. in strategic management and organization from the University of Minnesota.

Jill R. Kickul is associate professor of management in the Charles H. Kellstadt Graduate School of Business at DePaul University, where she teaches courses on management and entrepreneurship strategy. Her research interests include psychological contracts and procedural justice. Her work has been published in a number of journals.

Scott W. Lester is an assistant professor of management at the University of Wisconsin–Eau Claire. His research interests include psychological contracts, group potency, and organizational citizenship behavior. He has published research in a variety of management journals, including the *Academy of Management Journal* and the *Journal of Applied Psychology*. He received the Ph.D. in organizational behavior from the University of South Carolina.

Raymond G. Lorenz is operations manager for the Microelectronic Systems Division at 3M Corporation. Prior to that position, he was plant manager for the 3M Eau Claire facility that was acquired from W. L. Gore & Associates, Inc. in 2000. Before the acquisition, he was part of the Gore business development team that established and developed the Advanced Interconnect Products Division. He received the M.B.A. from Villanova University.

Kathryn D. McKee is president of Human Resources Consortia, a consultancy specializing in providing solutions on human resource issues. Prior assignments include senior vice president and regional human resources director for Standard Chartered Bank, senior vice president of human resources at First Interstate Bank Limited, and senior vice president of compensation and benefits at First Interstate Bancorp. McKee is a graduate of the University of California at Santa Barbara and the Anderson School of Management Executive Program. She is certified by the Human Resources Certification Institute and the American Compensation Association.

Philip H. Mirvis is an organizational psychologist whose research and private practice concern large-scale organizational change and the character of the workforce and workplace. He is on the adjunct faculty of the University of Michigan's Graduate School of Business. A regular contributor to academic and professional journals, he has authored seven books, including *The Cynical Americans, Building the Competitive Workforce,* and, with Mitchell Marks, *Joining Forces.* Mirvis is a fellow of the Work/Family Roundtable and Center for Corporate Community Relations and cochair of the board of directors of the Foundation for Community Encouragement. He received the Ph.D. in organizational psychology from the University of Michigan.

Jessica L. Saltz received her B.A. degree in psychology from Emory University and is a doctoral candidate in industrial and organizational psychology at the University of Maryland. Her major research interests focus on organizational change, adaptability at various levels of analysis, and team processes. She is a member of the American Psychological Association, Society for Industrial and Organizational Psychology, and the Academy of Management.

Roger D. Sommer is an adjunct instructor of graduate-level human resources courses for Chapman University and an outplacement consultant with Oi Partners, following over twenty-five years as a human resource executive. He is an author of white papers and articles for the Society of Human Resources Management (SHRM) publications and a former chair of SHRM's national Employment Committee. He earned an M.I.L.R. from Cornell University.

David Ulrich is professor of business administration at the University of Michigan. He has studied how organizations change fast, build capabilities, learn, remove boundaries, and leverage human resource activities. He has helped generate multiple award-winning national databases on organizations that assess alignment between strategies, human resource practices, and human resource competencies. He has published over one hundred articles and book chapters. He serves on the editorial board of four journals, is on the board of directors for Herman Miller, is a fellow in the National Academy of Human Resources, and is cofounder of the Michigan Human Resource Partnership. He has consulted and conducted research with over half of the Fortune 200. In 2001, *Business Week* ranked him as the top management educator in the world.

Ronny Vansteenkiste is vice president of organization development and learning at Seagram, responsible for the development of people at all levels through effective management of individual performance, enhanced teamwork capability, and focus on leadership development and executive coaching. He is a founding member and director of the European Learning Alliance, an alliance of leading management and organization development practitioners in Europe. He received the M.B.A. from the University of Leuven in Belgium.

Jack W. Wiley is president and CEO of Gantz Wiley Research, a consulting firm specializing in employee and customer satisfaction surveys for international corporate clients. He has internationally recognized expertise in linking employee survey results to measures of customer satisfaction and business performance. He has developed WorkTrends, a normative database of employee opinions, has written several articles and book chapters on survey research topics, and has made numerous presentations to professional associations around the world. He is a member of the Society for Industrial and Organizational Psychology, the American Psychological Society, the International Association of Applied Psychology, and the Academy of Management. He received his Ph.D. in organizational psychology from the University of Tennessee.

Nina E. Woodard began her career with First National Bank of Casper, which was part of the First Interstate Banking System in the United States. She worked through various line roles and was promoted to direct the human resource function in that bank. She then joined the official mergers and acquisition teams in Thailand, Indonesia, and Middle East/South Asia. Her most recent assignment is in India, where she advises local human resource teams on cultural integration, employee communication, and change management issues. She is a graduate of the Graduate School of Banking conducted by the Pacific Coast School of Banking at the University of Washington.

Clifford E. Young is a professor and chair and coordinator in the Department of Marketing at the Graduate School of Business, University of Colorado at Denver. His primary work is in marketing research methodology, survey development, and research analysis. He also has experience in selling and sales deployment analysis. He has published articles in a number of journals.

Resizing the Organization

CHAPTER ONE

The Realities of Resizing

Mitchell Lee Marks
Kenneth P. De Meuse

*The most difficult decision any executive has to make is to
reduce the size of the company.*
HENRY SCHACHT, CHAIRMAN AND
CEO OF LUCENT TECHNOLOGIES

Layoffs, divestitures, and closings have become deeply woven into
the fabric of contemporary organizational life. What once were in-
frequent and, in some cases, unheard-of occurrences in most work
organizations have become regularly occurring actions. What once
were managerial reactions to difficult market conditions now have
become proactive tactics for attaining strategic and financial objectives. And what once were poorly managed events that eroded
the psychological relationship between employer and employee
have become, at least in some organizations, opportunities to define or reinforce desired corporate cultures that reflect the realities of today's business environment.

A decade ago, we wrote that transition management—the
leadership and direction of major organizational events—would
become a regular component of the managerial repertoire (De
Meuse, Vanderheiden, & Bergmann, 1994; De Meuse & Tornow,
1990; Marks, 1994; Mirvis & Marks, 1992). At that time, merger and
acquisition activity was on an upswing, major corporations were beginning to make themselves over through restructurings, spin-offs,
and strategic redirections, and large corporations were doing

something they had never done before on a large scale: involuntarily terminating employees through reductions in force and plant closings. We were right. Today, layoffs, divestitures, and closings are found in organizations of every size, in every industry, and just about every geographical location. Transition management and organizational change are so pervasive that courses on the topic are taught in business schools.

A new word, *downsizing*, was coined in the early 1990s to represent the variety of ways in which organizational leaders reduced employee ranks to achieve business objectives. Downsizing occurred through voluntary programs such as early retirement, involuntary dismissals like layoffs, and the displacement of employees through outsourcing. No matter which tactic was used, the underlying objective of downsizing was a one-time reduction in costs to contribute to the achievement of short-term financial objectives (Vanderheiden, De Meuse, & Bergmann, 1999; Morris, Cascio, & Young, 1999).

With this book, we introduce yet another word to summarize a set of organizational transitions: *resizing*. Organizational resizing is the repositioning of employee ranks to achieve a company's strategic objectives. In many ways, organizational resizing is similar to the popularly used term *corporate downsizing*. However, unlike downsizing, resizing does not possess all the negative emotional baggage and the stereotype of corporate decline. Resizing does not necessarily suggest massive job cuts and is not fixed within the decade of the 1990s. *Resizing* is a broad-based term that more accurately reflects the organization of the twenty-first century and its goal of becoming agile, flexible, and proactive. Resizing is primarily strategic in nature (as opposed to financial) and is part of ongoing organizational transformation (as opposed to a one-time-only event). Resizing contributes to executives' intentions of cutting costs, focusing resources, and implementing strategic shifts to capitalize on the ever-changing global marketplace.

The Pervasiveness of Organizational Resizing

Layoffs, divestitures, and closings are affecting organizations of all sizes, in all industries, and across all geographical areas. Huge corporations—including Boeing, Eastman Kodak, General Motors, and Procter & Gamble—have experienced multiple waves of resizing. So have the smallest of work organizations. Over five hundred small dot-com start-ups have announced reductions in force. While key industry sectors such as telecom and manufacturing have experienced a major displacement of employees, resizing also has occurred in the financial services, education, health care, high-technology, and retail industry sectors, among others. During the 1990s, we experienced the longest expansion in U.S. history. Yet we also experienced record numbers of organizational resizing. The companies that have downsized during the past few years reads like a Who's Who among American business (see Exhibit 1.1). Each year during the 1990s, approximately 500,000 jobs were eliminated from the American landscape. In 2001, roughly 2.5 million jobs were cut, shattering the previous record of about 700,000 during 1999 (U.S. Department of Labor, 2002).

What initially was an American phenomenon has transcended national borders. Several European organizations (including Volvo, British Airways, Vivendi, and Alcatel), as well as Asian companies, such as Fuji, Sony, Toshiba, Nissan, and Daewoo, have experienced layoffs, divestitures, and closings in recent years. This downsizing is especially significant given the labor laws, worker councils, and national cultures that traditionally have supported lifelong relationships between employers and employees. In China, for example, mores were at one time so strong that this type of organizational activity was referred to as "taking away someone's rice bowl" (that is, the company would be removing an individual's means of income).

Organizational resizing has become ingrained in contemporary culture. What once was regarded as a stigma has come out into the mainstream of modern life as vast numbers of people have been personally resized or known someone who has gone through a layoff, closing, or divestiture. In many communities, well-publicized "pink slip parties" bring laid-off employees together to socialize, commiserate, and network. Psychologists are forming special therapy sessions and support groups for laid-off employees in San Francisco, Silicon Valley, New York, and other areas with high concentrations of high-tech businesses. And recruiters and job hunters talk openly and matter-of-factly about resizings rather than sidestep or downplay the event when reviewing the applicant's career background.

Exhibit 1.1. The ABCs of Corporate Downsizing.

A	AETNA; Agilent; Amazon.com; AOL Time Warner; Arthur Andersen; AT&T
B	Bell South; Bethlehem Steel; Boeing; Bristol-Myers Squibb; Business Week
C	Charles Schwab; Cisco Systems; Compaq Computer; Corning; Cummins
D	DaimlerChrysler; Dell Computer; Delta Airlines; Disney; Dole Food; Du Pont
E	Eastman Kodak; Eaton; Edison International; Enron; E. W. Scripps
F	FMC; Ford
G	Gateway; General Electric; General Motors; Gillette
H	Hasbro; Hewlett-Packard; Hon Industries; Honeywell
I	IBM; Intel; International Paper
J	John Deere & Company; Johnson Controls
K	Kmart; Knight-Ridder; Kraft
L	Levi Strauss; Lincoln National; Lockheed Martin; Lucent Technologies
M	Marriott; Mattel; Mellon Financial Corp.; Merrill Lynch; Monster.com; Motorola
N	New York Times; Nextel; Nortel; Northeast Utilities; Northwest Airlines
O	Olin; Oracle; Owens-Illinois
P	Pennzoil–Quaker States; Pfizer; Priceline; Procter & Gamble
Q	Qualcomm; Quantum; Qwest Communications
R	Raytheon; Revlon; R. J. Reynolds; Rockwell Automation; Rohm & Hass
S	Sears; Servicemaster; SGI; Sprint; Steelcase; Sun Microsystems; SuperValu
T	3Com; Texas Instruments; Textron
U	United Airlines; Universal; U.S. Freightways
V	Verizon
W	Waste Management; WorldCom; Wyndham International
X	Xerox
Y	Yahoo!; Yellow Trucking
Z	Zales Jewelry

The Dynamics Driving Organizational Resizing

Layoffs, divestitures, and closings are occurring for several reasons. Executive motives appear to range from corporate survival to investor greed. According to John Challenger, president of the outplacement firm Challenger, Gray, and Christmas, "Shareholders rule today. They have all the power. Even if layoffs cause long-term damage, shareholders don't care. They demand instant returns. They always can move their portfolios" (personal communication, 2001). However, a careful examination of the factors influencing resizing indicates numerous dynamics within and surrounding organizations. These dynamics are not unique to American companies.

Globalization

The marketplace for many organizations has expanded from within a region to within a nation to the entire globe. In some industries, only a few Asian, European, and North American competitors will survive consolidations to emerge as global gladiators for market share.

Globalization drives organizational resizing in two distinct ways. First, many organizations react to adverse global economic conditions by eliminating jobs and closing or divesting operations. Whereas in the past, economic downturns in one part of the world may have been relatively isolated, now they affect all regions of the world in the new global economy. Second, some organizations are proactively resizing as a consequence of their mergers, acquisitions, alliances, and joint ventures aimed at broadening their global reach. For example, two automobile manufacturers had separate design centers in North America and Europe, but in an effort to globalize operations following a combination, one was closed.

Globalization also has elevated the saliency of disparate wage rates among countries. For example, it is exceedingly difficult to manufacture computers in the United States, where the average production employee earns more than eighteen dollars an hour when that same computer can be assembled in Mexico, where the average hourly wage is around two dollars (U.S. Bureau of Labor Statistics, 2002). Alternatively, one can look to China, Taiwan,

Korea, or Singapore, all with labor rates and employee benefit packages substantially lower than in the United States, and several other nations around the globe. The ease of transportation and communication enables this intercontinental process to be seamless to the customer. Consequently, job relocation from high-wage countries to low-wage ones is a natural outcome.

Deregulation and Denationalization

As governments continue to deregulate or denationalize industries, private entrepreneurs inevitably look for opportunities to reduce employee populations and close or sell off operations. In the United States, in deregulated industries like air transportation and broadcasting, corporate leaders have responded quickly and aggressively by combining companies, relocating operations, and reducing head counts. The airlines have consolidated into a few large carriers, and most of the nation's radio and television stations are in the hands of a few multimedia communication conglomerates.

Worldwide, deregulation and privatization are transferring the ownership and operations of huge organizations from governments to businesses. Inevitably, this means a delayering of bureaucratic structures. Layers of bureaucracy and managerial excess, built up during years of growth and paternalistic governmental oversight, are being stripped away to reduce overhead and increase organizational responsiveness. Utilities, railroads, and agribusiness are among the industries experiencing a dramatic move toward privatization.

Technological Change

Technology continues to become increasingly more sophisticated and effective in enhancing quality and efficiency in the workplace. Firms are taking advantage of new technologies, from factory automation to information storage, to reorganize work and make it more efficient. Often, though, this comes with a tremendous human price tag. The U.S. steel industry, for example, produced 100 million tons with 577,100 workers in the 1960s. Four decades later, it produces just as much tonnage with fewer than half that number of people. Overall, manufacturing output in the United States is higher than at any other time in its history. At the same time, however, employment in manufacturing has remained flat (Siekman, 2000).

Technological advances enable greater production by fewer people, resulting in the new phenomenon of jobless growth. And the range of employees affected by technology has broadened dramatically. Historically, the positions of lower-level employees were those put at risk by robotics and other forms of automation. However, information technology today is having a tremendous impact on middle management ranks. A desktop computer using decision-support software can do the job of gathering, analyzing, and disbursing information more quickly and, arguably, with more cost-effectiveness than a middle manager. And as technology advances, the skills needed to keep pace with the hardware and software change. For employees at any rank, the shock of job displacement is compounded by the realization that no employer may want the skills they have painstakingly developed over the years.

The Bursting of the Technology Bubble

Concurrent with technological advances came a run-up in the stock prices of technology companies. The stratospheric price-earnings ratios of key technology companies and speculative promises of firms that never came close to turning a profit could not be sustained, however. The meltdown in technology stock prices also affected the broader markets. Investment capital and venture funding dried up. Employee ranks shrank concurrently with share prices. Thousands of people who had short-term hopes of stock bonuses instead found their options underwater and themselves holding pink slips.

The bursting of the technology bubble resulted in huge layoffs in technology firms and, in high-profile cases like Webvan and Pets.com, the complete closing of operations. It also forced senior executives to fixate even more on quarter-by-quarter results rather than build or sustain operations for the long run. Many firms cut employees and closed operations in hopes of short-term lifts to their stock prices.

The Slowing Economy

Obviously, the September 11, 2001, terrorist attacks on the World Trade Towers and the Pentagon had a ripple effect throughout the American economy. However, the end of the great bull market had begun well before this event and affected all industry sectors, not just technology. The September tragedy simply pushed down business spending and consumer confidence that already were in deep trouble. Entire industries, including airlines and hospitality, high tech and telecom, suffered huge losses. Even in organizations not yet directly affected by the economic slowdown, executives took steps to cut costs by eliminating jobs, consolidating and closing operations, and divesting nonstrategic assets.

In many cases, these efforts at resizing were sound, well-thought-out moves. In many others, reductions in forces, closings, and divestitures were more symbolic than substantive. CEOs tried to send a message to Wall Street that they were taking steps to address falling revenues, lowered profit margins, and anemic stock prices—or at least they attempted to stave off the wrath of analysts who wanted action. Yet one-time-only cost reductions do little, if anything, to build sustained momentum for future revenue and income growth (Cascio, 1998; Mishra, 2001; Pfeffer, 1998). And as resizing becomes increasingly commonplace, Wall Street is becoming increasingly unimpressed with nonstrategic cost-cutting maneuvers.

Increasing Costs

Further burdening business leaders are increases in operating costs. Energy costs—including gas, oil, and electricity—skyrocketed during the first few years of the new century. The price of some precious metals rose sharply. Even the cost of milk fat, an essential ingredient in ice cream, jumped 50 percent between 2000 and 2001.

In a stable or growing economy, businesses could pass these price increases on to customers. But in a softening economy, executives instead tend to look at ways to control current costs—or curtail future investments—rather than pass on raw material price increases. Consequently, jobs are cut or hiring is frozen, operations are consolidated or closed, and some functions are outsourced, all in an attempt to enhance short-term cost efficiencies.

Mergers and Acquisitions

Despite the weakening economy, merger mania continues in full force. Depressed stock prices make for some attractive purchases, but most merger and acquisitions activity appears to be prompted by the need to achieve growth objectives rather than by opportunities to pick up corporate bargains. Entire industries have been put into play and reconfigured as one deal prompts a spate of copy-cat mergers. A prime example is the oil industry. BP's 1999 acquisition of Amoco was a careful, strategically sound move that led other companies in the industry, including Exxon and Mobil, Chevron and Texaco, and Phillips and Tosco, to play catch-up.

Thousands of jobs are eliminated as redundant operations are consolidated. In the carefully planned and well-executed pharmaceutical merger between Pfizer and Warner-Lambert, as an example, multiple R&D centers of excellence were rationalized. And many units are divested as companies combine, either because they no longer fit into the strategic mix of the lead company or because they are seen as appeasements to get regulators to bless the deal. Sometimes enormous businesses are divested after acquisitions. Vivendi wanted Seagram's entertainment business when it acquired the company and did not hesitate to sell off its traditional core spirits and wine businesses.

The Unintended Consequences of Resizing

In principle, a resizing should enable an organization to improve its competitiveness without impairing its ability to execute its strategy. In practice, however, a resizing can exact a heavy toll on organizational effectiveness and employee well-being (De Meuse et al., 1994, 1997; Mische, 2001; Morris et al., 1999; Pfeffer, 1998; Vanderheiden et al., 1999). It can also influence customers to flee to competitors and create uncertainty on the part of venders and suppliers (Bastien, Hostager, & Miles, 1996). Entire communities can be adversely affected when companies close plants or significantly curtail operations (Bamberger & Davidson, 1999; Leana & Feldman, 1992).

A Wrenching Experience

A transition that involves the displacement of people is a wrenching experience for all parties, and the norm in most organizations is to get it over with as quickly and quietly as possible. Terminations are painful to execute, and no one wants to stretch out the dirty work. Even the toughest, most bottom-line-oriented executives find it difficult to make cuts. It is one thing to speak abstractly of the need to reduce costs and quite another to make decisions that affect people's lives. Intellectually, senior executives may rationalize that a reduction in force or site closing is necessary to regain or sustain profitability. Emotionally, however, they dread making the cuts. Few CEOs themselves actually let senior staff members go; instead, they frequently pass the burden on to subordinates.

Middle managers are truly that: managers caught in the middle between the conflicting agendas, perspectives, and demands of those at the top and bottom. They feel squeezed. Top-level executives are distant and remote, talking about strategy, planning, and other matters less tangible than middle managers' needs to get products out the door or service quality up amid the turmoil of transition. Meanwhile, lower-level employees are looking for concrete direction and support, but middle managers do not have the direction and support to give them.

Research shows that managers and supervisors have the most impact on making or breaking employees' reactions to a transition (Larkin & Larkin, 1996). Yet in most organizations, they are poorly prepared for their role in implementing transition activities. When an organization offers a voluntary downsizing package, for example, managers and supervisors find themselves in the awkward position of counseling employees on whether to stay or go. No one wants to tell an employee his or her services are no longer needed, even if it is the most humane thing to do when a subsequent wave of involuntary cuts looms. It is especially difficult for managers in organizations engaged in multiple waves of downsizing. The obvious low performers already have been removed, leaving good contributors who have to be shown the door.

After the cuts are made, work team leaders have to accomplish more with fewer resources. Supervisors and managers struggle to maintain productivity with fewer bodies at a time when people are emotionally distraught. Lip-service may be given to how the resizing will result in a leaner, meaner, smarter, and generally more competitive organization. Unfortunately, now no one has the time to think of smarter or better ways of doing things.

Support staff find themselves overwhelmed by the multiple demands placed on them during a resizing. For example, human resource (HR) professionals are staggered by the work load in processing terminations and scheduling outplacement services. Moreover, knowing that their own area, a non-revenue-producing staff function, is likely to be one of the hardest hit preoccupies them. In the meantime, they are burdened by the line of employees outside their door waiting for an HR shoulder to cry on.

In general, resizing threatens the self-esteem and sense of fairness of all employees. People can rationalize layoffs based on performance, as when an employee is repeatedly late to work or fails to meet production standards. However, people cannot rationalize the fact that hard-working fellow employees have lost their jobs because of an economic downturn. Resizing victims blame themselves for not seeing it coming or not doing something to protect themselves. For victims and survivors alike, a resizing eats away at the assumption of fairness in the workplace as they wonder why leadership could not stave off the dreaded event or identify some alternative course of action. Survivors see the human carnage of lost jobs and destroyed careers and wonder, "How could an organization I want to dedicate my life's work to do this to people?"

Finally, some evidence suggests that resizing effects transcend the employees themselves. The impact that job loss has on families and communities initially was reported by Leana and Feldman (1992). Several other researchers now are exploring the effect that parents' job insecurity has on such factors as children's academic performance and social development (Barling, Zacharatos, & Hepburn, 1999; Schmitt, Sacco, Ramey, Ramey, & Chan, 1999). Some families report that elementary school children may revert to thumb sucking and bed-wetting. Overall, research clearly shows that organizational resizing activities affect families and communities.

Psychological Reactions

Some executives like to believe that resizing survivors should be grateful just to have a job in tough economic times; they should be ready to roll up their sleeves and get down to work. The real consequences, however, are very different. Survivors of organizational transitions experience a broad range of psychological and behavioral reactions that begin with rumors of impending events, continue through the weeks and months of transition planning and implementation, and linger long after the dust settles. They have a lasting impact on employees' perceptions of the work organization and expectations for its future (De Meuse, Bergmann, & Lester, 2001). The work of rebuilding after a transition must begin with accepting that there is unintended human and organizational fallout from resizing, understanding these consequences, and acting as proactively as possible to recover from them.

Survivor Syndrome

Symptoms of the layoff survivor syndrome have been well researched and documented over the past decade (Brockner, 1989; Brockner, Wiesenfeld, & Martin, 1995; Greenhalph, 1989). Often, people feel guilty for having been spared, similar to the psychological reaction of children who lose a playmate or sibling in a fatal accident. The survivor responds to the tragedy with extreme guilt and asks, "Why couldn't it have been me?" Survivors also may become depressed at their inability to avert future layoffs or disruptions to their work routine. In the short run, they become distracted from their work responsibilities. Over the long haul, employees who have been through a resizing have considerably less confidence and trust in their employers (Buono & Bowditch, 1989; Marks, 2003; Noer, 1993).

Despite paring down the payroll, leaders of downsized companies find it difficult to realize the increases in productivity and cost savings they had hoped the layoffs would produce. As *U.S. News and World Report* noted, "The survivors of corporate downsizings are like recovering casualties of a lost war—grateful to be alive, but uncertain of what they are living for. Some have found opportunity amid the carnage of fallen colleagues, but others have become deeply distrustful and fearful that they may be next" (Boroughs, 1992, p. 50).

Loss of Confidence in Management

One of the most enduring symptoms of layoff survivor syndrome is the erosion of employee confidence in management. Several factors contribute to this attitude. First, many employees wonder why their leaders did not take action to prevent layoffs or avoid the ugliness of a plant closing. Second, employees do not see how transitions have added any value to the workplace. Outplacement specialists Right Associates surveyed 909 firms that resized and found that 72 percent of the employees still on the job did not think the newly revamped company was a better place to work, and 70 percent felt insecure about their future in the firm. Third, there is a growing sense that management is motivated by greed rather than by concern for customers or employees.

The irony here is that layoffs, closings, and divestitures can be productive tools to enhance organizational effectiveness and profitability and, as a result, job security and quality of worklife. However, the way resizings are implemented and managed often destroys workers' regard and respect for their organizations and leaders (Marks, 2003; Noer, 1997). In one national survey, nearly three-quarters of employees whose companies were not involved in a merger or layoff during the past year reported being confident in the long-term future of their company. In contrast, only about half of employees whose firms had been involved in a merger or layoff were confident about their company's future (Wiley, 1991).

Cynicism and Distrust

A major unintended consequence of resizing has been the growing cynicism of the U.S. workforce. People do not mind enduring some pain if they can see a payoff for it, but this has not been the case in many organizational resizings. Promises that nothing will change during the transition, and of enhanced effectiveness following it, are rarely fulfilled. In many organizations, people see few benefits—for the business or for themselves—resulting from the ordeal.

Poorly managed transitions have a negative not merely a neutral effect on the mind-set of employees. Employees see how departing senior executives have their transition impact softened with the help of generous golden parachutes and how those who stay often have well-endowed employment contracts (Strauss, 2001). People have grown distrustful of their leadership and cynical of opportunities to succeed in their companies. A national study found that 43 percent of working Americans doubt the truth of what management tells them and believe that their companies, given a chance, will take advantage of them (Kanter & Mirvis, 1989).

Decreased Morale

The Laborforce 2000 study of downsizing and restructuring found that morale dropped among surviving employees in six of every ten companies engaged in a downsizing. Interestingly, the drop in morale was the same whether companies downsized for strategic reasons or to contain or control costs (Marks, 1993). Survivors are angry, both at themselves for not seeing trouble before it arrived and at their leaders for exposing people to such stressful treatment. They hurt because the sight of coworkers being dismissed is painful, as is accepting that one's own career dreams have been derailed by downsizings and divestitures. And survivors are frustrated because their ability to get the job done is hampered by the confusion of the resized organization and because they see few signs that things are going to get better any time soon.

Reduced Loyalty

During reductions in force, employers inadvertently hurt most the employees they least wish to alienate: employees who are very loyal to the organization. Most people who join organizations need to feel that they are a part of and contributing to a larger collective. One outgrowth of people's need for group membership is that they expect and want to be treated fairly by the groups to which they belong. Research conducted by a team from Columbia University suggests that if loyal employees believe that layoffs were unfair, their loyalty drops sharply, even more so than that of survivors who are less committed at the onset (Brockner, 1989).

Dismal Outlook

Even for those who breathe a momentary sigh of relief for having retained a job, dismal signs predominate in the resized organization. Survivors feel sad about the past and anxious about the future. People miss their former mentors, coworkers, and other colleagues who may have exited in a divestiture or reduction in force. They miss their former political connections to the powerful decision makers in the organization. When they set their sights on the future, they become further dismayed. All signals point to fewer opportunities for advancement when resizings eliminate traditional career paths. People even see themselves having to work harder just to stay in the same place. Finally, there is less fun on the job. The rhetoric of cost reduction puts a damper on the informal perks and playfulness that many employees enjoy at work.

Loss of Control

What really concerns survivors is the sense that they have lost control over their work lives. They perceive that no matter how well they do their jobs, they could be hit in the next wave of layoffs. The rapid pace of change in today's business world means that one's position, pet project, or potential for advancement could be eliminated at a moment's notice, with no way to counteract it. A middle-level manager from a consumer products company exemplified the control issue when he spoke with us during a interview a year after his company went through a series of resizings:

> I used to think that if I did my job well, completed my projects on time and in fine manner, I would be able to control my fate. That's no longer true. I've seen other managers—people who clearly were good, if not excellent, performers—get the shaft. Now, my track record doesn't count for anything. I'm at the mercy of some bureaucrat at headquarters. I'm no longer the master of my own fate.

While senior executives have the most at stake during a resizing in terms of position, power, pay, and perks, they also have the most control over their situation. They anticipate, conceive, and design the layoffs, closings, and divestitures, as well as arrange for their financial security. Other employees cannot exert control over whether their workplace is being resized, and their sense of lost mastery over their fate extends well beyond the actual event.

Some people perceive that the only way they can regain control over their work situation is to walk away from the organization. A research chemist whose firm had just closed and consolidated R&D units was clear on her plans. She declared, "What is hard work going to get me here? All I have been hearing from this organization is hard work is going to help me keep my job. Well, that's not good enough for me. I was raised in a time when good work was rewarded with an occasional promotion. There was a career path. Now with these layoffs and site closings, there is nowhere to go. Why should I stay here?" Another manager, from a financial services firm, had his plan set for taking back control. He boldly revealed, "Senior management must think they have us by the balls right now, because the job market in our industry is poor. But I can tell you this. At the sight of the first ray of light of an upturn in the economy, I'm walking out of here and not looking back." When surviving employees see the best and brightest performers jumping ship, it reinforces negative feelings and cynical attitudes. And, importantly, it is these highly skilled and creative individuals whom an organization must hold onto to rebound effectively after the resizing.

Behavioral Reactions to Resizing

Employees who survive a resizing often liken their situation to that of a chicken with its head cut off—frantically moving about without any sense of direction or hope for survival. Or they talk about struggling to keep their heads above water. They know what they have to do, but they are weighed down by the burden of a heavy workload with competing demands. Others keep their heads in the sand like ostriches, hoping that the winds of change will blow by them.

Working Harder, Not Smarter

The workload rarely gets smaller when the workforce does. Survivors who return to work following reductions in force face the dismal prospect of being part of the 80 percent of the people who now have to do 100 percent of the work. Everyone is working harder but feeling as though they are accomplishing less. The situation is exacerbated by a likely backlog in the workload carried over from the months preceding the resizing, as people were preoccupied with rumors and gossip and distracted from doing their jobs. Inevitably, work falls through the cracks.

What about the promise of enhanced organizational effectiveness that accompanies the announcement of many organizational resizings? The reality is that no one has time to stop and think of innovative ways to approach work. Work teams or task forces may be convened to identify ways to eliminate non-value-added work. Typically, however, these groups are insufficiently prepared to overcome the group dynamics and individual power plays that can sidetrack team creativity and decision making. When these groups fail to produce enhancements to the workplace, people become more dismayed toward their situation and cynical about the future. Worse yet, when outside consultants are brought in to recommend new ways of approaching work, employees fear the worst and assume this means more job cuts lie ahead.

Meanwhile, there are demands from all directions—superiors, peers, and subordinates—that increase the pressure on transition survivors. "Everybody here is so worried about looking good and wants their work to take top priority," noted a staff analyst in a high-tech company. "My boss says to ask my internal customers if what they need in a week can instead be delivered in ten days. But I'm afraid to do that. It may cost me by being labeled as someone who can't cut it around here."

Lack of Direction

Compounding the sheer volume of work confronting people surviving resizing is a lack of direction in prioritizing which tasks to tackle first. After two regional offices of a health maintenance organization were combined as part of a cost-cutting series of closings, leadership was indecisive regarding the relative merits of aggressively pursuing increases in membership or conservatively maintaining levels of profitability. Middle managers were paralyzed by this lack of direction, waiting to see which way they should lead their work teams. The director of operations expressed this frustration: "Does senior management want us to go out and run up the membership roles, or are they interested in protecting the margin? Either one is fine by me, but someone has got to let me know which way we are going, because I do not want to build an organization that is headed one way and then get chastised because I was supposed to go the other way."

Risk Avoidance

Why wouldn't the operations manager and his peers just step up to the plate and make a decision on their own? The answer is that risk taking plummets following a resizing. Employees are so scared that there is a self-imposed pressure not to make waves or take risks, and just at the time when innovation is needed. Further cuts may be in the offing, and no one wants a blemish on their record that may be used against them when the next list of victims is drawn up. Instead, managers and employees go with what they know, relying on what has worked for them in the past. These are just the behaviors that have gotten the organization in trouble. At the very least, what may have worked in the past is unlikely to work within a new context of changed market, workplace, and social demands.

Political Behavior and Loss of Team Play

Political game playing increases sharply in organizations that have resized. One way people shore up their sense of control is to lobby for themselves. Employees spend time promoting their value to executives and managers, as well as reminding them of any outstanding favors that may be owed. They network with friends and associates from outside the organization—a distraction from getting their work done but an important protective action to take in the event of future layoffs. Coworker relations may become strained as individuals explicitly or implicitly put down their colleagues in an effort to make themselves look better in the eyes of superiors. As uncertainty grows, self-preservation becomes paramount.

Politics prevails also at the group level as work teams look out for themselves. Managers erect barriers between teams, focusing on group results rather than the big picture. In the short run, they conclude that what makes the team look good is more important than what is best for the overall organization over the long haul.

Role Ambiguity

A constant problem interfering with organizational effectiveness following resizing is role ambiguity. Survivors wonder who is responsible for what and whom to go to for which decisions. A lot of time is spent wondering how to prioritize work and how to operate in an environment in which direction is not forthcoming. Individuals reporting to new superiors fret over when to make decisions on their own and when to raise them up to leaders, as well as wondering what detail to provide when communicating. These normal aspects of the learning curve of any new work relationship become sensitive issues within the context of resizing. It is especially frustrating to achievement-oriented people who want to start building a good track record in the resized organization. They hope to make a positive first impression on new superiors, peers, and subordinates, yet they do not always know whom to go to or work with to get the job done right and on time.

Withdrawal

According to Herman Maynard, a former senior manager at Dupont who took early retirement in a reduction in force, these psychological and behavior reactions to resizing have prompted many employees "to withdraw their personal and professional power from their jobs, while making it look like they are still working" (Reynolds, 1992). People's bodies, but not their hearts and souls, show up to work. As executives exhort their employees to boost productivity, improve quality, and be more globally competitive, many workers are responding with a shrug. This psychological turnover is more costly for the organization than actual turnover. Often, these employees are riding out the organizational storm until the next early retirement enticement or enhanced severance pay package is offered. In the meantime, they continue to receive pay and benefits and perform poorly.

Stress and Organizational Resizing

A moderate amount of stress enhances performance, but high levels of stress have a detrimental effect on work productivity and quality. During and after a resizing, people become distracted from doing their jobs. They huddle around coffee makers and water coolers, exchanging the latest rumors. Some employees are at the copying and fax machines, preparing and sending out their resumés. High levels of stress interfere with cognitive processes in intellectual tasks and with the quality of work produced on manual tasks. People respond in robot-like ways instead of thinking creatively or strategically about the situation at hand. One vice president of quality control at an aerospace firm involved in repeated waves of resizing described it as "like waiting for an earthquake— you do not know when the next shocks will be felt, but you know they will be coming. And you do not know if this will be the big one or not."

Sources of Stress in a Resizing

Resizing creates stress for employees in a variety of ways. The loss of someone or something to which people are attached is painful, and it necessitates a period of mourning or depression while they make adjustments in their lives (Kübler-Ross, 1969). The potential for loss abounds in a resizing: people may lose their jobs, coworkers, title, status, or perks. They also may lose less tangible aspects of their work situation, like the opportunity to realize their career aspirations, achievement of their ego ideal, their sense of personal competence, and their identification with what had been regarded as a paternalistic and caring employer.

A key to understanding the stress of resizing is to realize that the threat of loss is as debilitating as actual loss. Whether the threat is to a person's self-esteem or physical person, the resulting stress response is the same. Job insecurity is experienced like job loss. Laying awake at night worrying about losing one's job is as debilitating as losing it. In fact, survivors in companies experiencing multiple waves of resizing report being envious of the victims who lost their jobs; at least they can get on with their lives. Resizing survivors also worry about not fitting into a new company direction or culture, lament about having to prove their worth to new superiors, and agonize over what might happen to their career, all of which produce stress. Importantly, stress is based on subjective perceptions, not objective reality. It matters not what senior leadership intends to do or thinks are opportunities for the future, but what people fear leaders may do and how *they* perceive opportunities in the resized organization.

Next, the frustration experienced when anyone or anything even potentially prevents a person from meeting basic needs or getting what they want is another source of stress. People incur added stress when they feel helpless to do anything about their situation. This is why long hours of work during and following an organizational transition do not necessarily create higher levels of stress. In contrast, a high degree of pressure coupled with a perceived lack of control will cause high anxiety. When people feel their control has been reduced, they wrongly assume that they have lost all control. Frustration is at its worst when a person has little perceived discretion to negotiate deadlines and manage workloads.

Finally, the critical mass of uncertainty in a resizing is a source of stress. The announcement of a reduction in force, closing, or divestiture usually creates more questions than answers. People do not know what to expect, and in today's environment, they generally anticipate the worst. Some may have new duties to master, a new superior and peers to adjust to, and new policies and procedures that alter established—and comfortable—ways of working. For others, there is the more palpable uncertainty about job security and company identity.

Cumulative Effects of Stress

The stress of an event is determined by the amount of change it implies, not necessarily whether the change will be beneficial or detrimental. Marriages and births can be as stressful as divorces and deaths (Holmes & Rahe, 1968). Each event disrupts the status quo, entangles family and friends, and requires that people adapt to new circumstances. Many times, employees perceive resizings as offering both costs and benefits. A reduction in force may be painful but may also lay the foundation for organizational renewal. A divestiture may disrupt current work patterns but also send a business unit to a corporate parent with a better strategic fit and deeper pockets for long-term investment. Thus, even positive changes induce stress.

This point is important to consider because the effects of stress are cumulative. A series of small, seemingly innocuous changes can add up to a large and significant change in a person's eyes. A situation becomes stress inducing when it taxes a person's ability to cope effectively. Unsure of why change is occurring and how it may affect them—and unable to voice their concerns or control their fate—employees' accustomed ways of coping with stress are exaggerated. It is commonplace in organizations engaged in a transition to see people handle stress through the fight-or-flight reaction. Interviews conducted with employees during or soon after resizings are laced with seething indictments of managerial ineptness and examples of strained working relationships across groups. By contrast, lethargy, detachment, and other signs of withdrawal can be found among white-collar professionals whose work keeps them out of political power circuits.

Fight-or-flight reactions should be expected during and after a resizing, but they can be costly. Angry managers cannot work for the common good because they are itching for a fight and will poison the attitudes of their subordinates. Professionals who remain in body but not spirit after the resizing cannot be counted on to contribute fully to fact finding or decision making, but they will surely gripe openly about the resulting decisions.

Stress also takes a toll on well-being. Increased drug and alcohol abuse is common among workers surviving a transition. In one company we were consulting for during a resizing, Valium was the number one prescription drug purchased by employees each of the six months following initial layoffs. Frequently, calls to employee assistance programs skyrocket, and it is common to hear reports of a variety of psychosomatic reactions to stress (for example, trouble falling asleep at night, headaches and back pain, smoking again after having kicked the habit, and increased tension and conflict at home and on the job).

Rates of illness and absenteeism swell at workplaces in transition, and there are plenty of numbers to document the human and financial cost of resizing. At a Fortune 500 firm we studied, incidents of high blood pressure among employees rose from 11 percent in the year preceding a resizing to 22 percent in the year following its announcement. In a study conducted by Northwestern National Life Insurance, 65 percent of employees surveyed reported that they suffered from exhaustion, insomnia, or other stress-related problems; one-third revealed they were close to burnout. Stress saps between $100 and $300 billion annually from the U.S. economy in the form of lost workdays and health care costs related to illnesses like exhaustion, depression, and heart attacks ("Economy Creates More Stress," 1992).

The Saturation Effect

Organizations may operate within a context of ongoing change, continuous improvement, and radical transformation, but people can handle only so much disruption to their accustomed norms (De Meuse & McDaris, 1994). We may be in the Internet age with tremendous technological advances, but the human machine has a breaking point. Over time, people's threshold for dealing with stress, uncertainty, and disorientation is met. Their ability to cope with ongoing change is impaired, resulting in detrimental attitudes, maladaptive behaviors, disappointing performances, and the many other unintended consequences of resizing (Pfeffer, 1998).

A resizing rarely occurs in isolation. Rather, it is part of an ongoing series of real and perceived events that contribute to the cumulative stress experience. Consider a Silicon Valley high-tech firm's history over a two-year period. After rumors of impending change and watching events occurring at other companies in their industry, the firm attempted minor belt-tightening measures to deal with the softening economy and poor financial results. Then the company made a more radical move with a major restructuring of operating units and, for the first time in its history, offered employees a voluntary early retirement program. These activities were followed by the divestiture of a business unit and the consolidation of manufacturing operations, forcing the closing of a plant. With financial results still slumping, the company resorted to an involuntary reduction in force.

As characterized in Figure 1.1, each of these events resulted in the experience of cumulative stress. By the time the involuntary reduction in force was announced, many employees had become numbed by the dizzying course of events. The workforce suffered an intellectual and emotional paralysis brought on by their saturated coping capacity. They were psychologically worn out, unable to take on the responsibilities involved in meeting new challenges, and unwilling to give a good fight.

Shortly after the involuntary reduction in force, the company's leadership team saw a genuine potential for financial growth, organizational success, and individual reward. These executives anticipated that after a long and difficult struggle, victory in an important battle was awaiting at the top of the next hill. They saw

Figure 1.1. The Saturation Effect.

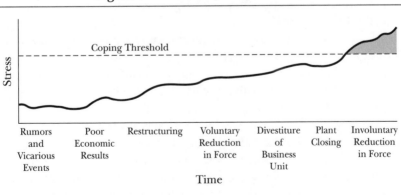

Source: Adapted from Marks (1994, p. 77).

the goal and confidently rallied their troops on the mission at hand. The cry came to charge up the hill and take the prize. However, the troops were neither ready nor willing to charge up the hill. Rather than focus on the opportunity ahead of them, the employees were unable to let go of the pain behind them. Their vision of the target was obscured by the emotional residue of anger, distrust, and depression built up over years of false promises and unmet expectations. Their self-esteem battered and their faith in the organization broken, the troops lacked confidence that they could take the hill. Most significant, they did not see how any personal gain would result from taking the hill. Instead, they fixated on memories of their fallen comrades—the casualties of layoffs and closings and the "walking wounded" whose careers were sidetracked.

Adaptation and Organizational Resizing

To understand why living through a reduction in force, closing, or divestiture—as either a victim or a survivor—can be so debilitating to everyone, it is important to consider the process of psychological adaptation to change and transition. A change can be of two types: continuous change and transformational change. The distinction is based on the extent to which the change requires psychological adaptation.

Two Levels of Change

Continuous change is a path to a known state, with orderly, incremental, and continuous steps. Moving a meeting from a 10:30 A.M. to a 10:00 A.M. starting time is an example of a continuous change. It may cause some disruption and require some adaptation; attendees may have to leave other meetings earlier or reschedule conference calls. Nevertheless, the discrete nature of continuous change lets people know exactly what to expect and allows them to get on with their lives.

A *transformational change,* by comparison, is a path to an unknown state—something that involves many simultaneous and interactive changes. Adopting new ways of thinking, organizing, or conducting activities are examples of this type of deeper, more meaningful, and lasting change. Transformational change poses a break from the past. It involves death and rebirth; existing practices and routines must be abandoned and new ones discovered and developed. A corporate cultural change—perhaps getting people to stop avoiding risk and start embracing the idea of learning from mistakes—is an example of a transformational change. A resizing that prompts a reassessment of deep-seeded perceptions and expectations (for example, "My employer respects and fairly treats all people" or "Hard work is rewarded here with job security") also is a transformational change.

Letting Go of the Old and Accepting the New

For transformational change to occur, a person literally has to let go of the old before accepting the new. People have to abandon old attitudes or behaviors before adopting new ones (Bridges, 1980; Lewin, 1947). This helps explain why transformational change is a much more difficult psychological process than is continuous change. Perhaps the classic example of a transformational change is adapting to the death of a loved one. People who experience the loss of a family member, dear friend, or important colleague do not wake up the next day and get on with their lives. They grieve the loss of their loved one and struggle with accepting new realities. Some people take weeks to go through this natural and normal process, others take months, and still others take years. Some individuals never reach the stage of acceptance. Unlike a continuous change, in which they know exactly what to expect, mourners encounter tremendous uncertainty and insecurity regarding their future. How will they go on living without their loved one? Who will they turn to for support? What will they do when they need assistance normally provided by the deceased? All of this is much more trying on a person's well-being than simply getting to a meeting half an hour earlier.

Ironically, CEOs who resize their companies have had time to let go of the old before accepting the new. Consider the case of the divestiture of a business unit; it takes months to plan a deal, search and select a buyer, and gain government approval for the sale. During this time, executives can come to terms with the fact that the old is being abandoned ("I will no longer be running the largest company in our industry" or "The company I founded in my garage will never abandon its good performers") and contend with new realities ("I am on the path to getting our firm back on sound financial footing" or "Our employees will no longer be weighed down by a money-losing division").

Most individuals, business executives among them, ignore or deny the discontinuous nature of transformational change. That is, they ignore or deny the need to let go of the old before accepting the new. As organizational consultant William Bridges puts it, beginnings start with endings. You do not start the new until you end the old. This takes time, effort, and patience. Bridges (1980) highlights three distinct stages of this transformational process: (1) letting go of the old, (2) dealing with the neutral zone, and (3) accepting the new.

During the first stage, *letting go,* the individual comes to see that the status quo no longer is appropriate for achieving what he or she desires. For example, a person in the midst of an involuntary reduction in force would have to abandon attitudes such as "this is a secure place to work." The second stage, the *neutral zone,* is an ambiguous place in which the old is over but the new has yet to be achieved. That is, you are no longer what you were but not yet what you want to become. The employee will have to take some time to learn by trial and error what behaviors get rewarded in the changing organization. It is truly a difficult period. Many of our clients dub this the "twilight zone": it is dark, scary, and unclear as to what lies ahead. Finally, a new status quo emerges during the third stage of *accepting the new.* People who make it to this stage realize deep, meaningful, and lasting change. The employee not only accepts new attitudes about how tenable job security is in today's work environment, but also adopts behavioral changes such as networking with recruiters from other firms on a regular basis. Employees grow more comfortable with the new reality; externally they are more at ease, and internally they modify their self-image and develop a new sense of self-worth.

Once employees figure out and accept new realities, they make sense out of their new world and grow more comfortable with it. Obviously, adapting to transformational change is much more psychologically taxing and is a much longer process than is adapting to continuous change. Even when change is for the better, people have to cope with uncertainty and the loss of familiar methods and routines. Transformational change implies the loss of the status quo, and that loss must be dealt with before people can fully move on in their work lives.

Unintended Business Consequences of Resizing

The costs of layoffs, closings, and divestitures have been measured in financial as well as human terms. The Laborforce 2000 study of downsizing and restructuring found that most companies surveyed experienced undesirable business consequences. Many companies were not prepared to handle the work that remained after a reduction in force and underestimated the costs required to cover tasks that had been performed by former employees. Some 41 percent of the companies that resized reported a greater need to retrain remaining workers. This finding implies that costs were experienced as a result of taking people off their regular jobs and training them to do additional jobs. One-third of the companies increased the use of temporary workers and consultants, often at a cost higher than the expense of previous employees; a similar number increased the use of overtime. One in every four firms contracted out an entire function (Marks, 1993).

In addition, health care costs incurred by organizations rise for both victims and survivors of resizings. It is easy to see how health care costs can increase for transition casualties. The psychological trauma of losing one's position triggers psychosomatic ailments. Moreover, early retirees have more time on their hands and, as a result, more time to visit a health care provider and ring up expenses. Not so obvious—but equally costly—are increased health care costs for the survivors, who also are subjected to the psychosomatic effects of intense stress on the job. A study of Boeing employees found that individuals who experienced a high degree of emotional stress on the job were more than twice as likely to file back injury claims than other employees (Gaines, 1993). Working harder to cover the tasks of others also results in a higher accident rate. One study of 177 companies found that although the average workforce was cut by only 13 percent over a fifteen-month period, fully one-third of the firms reported an increase in workers' compensation claims. One in five companies said their workers' compensation costs increased between 50 and 100 percent ("A Study of Worker," 1992).

In yet another study, a team of English researchers investigated the physical and emotional health of 764 employees whose organizations were downsizing. They found that employees in work groups experiencing job cuts were more than twice as likely to take sick leave as employees in a cohort work group (Kivimaki, Vahtera, Pentti, & Ferrie, 2000). If survivors perceive there may be another wave of layoffs, they likely will get the annual physical or dental work they have been putting off for the past several years.

As for the impact of resizing on productivity, an American Management Association study found that companies that had resized were as likely to report a decline in productivity as an increase. Fewer than half of the resized firms increased profits after the cuts were made, and one-quarter of them reported a decline in operating profits. In testimony before the Joint Economic Committee of Congress, the study's director concluded, "The after-effects of downsizing are problematic at best and raise the question as to whether the cure is worse than the disease" (Lesly & Light, 1992).

There is a more subtle unintended business consequence of resizing. Recent authors contend that such activities disrupt or damage an organization's ability to learn and adapt to the changing environment because the informal communication networks are adversely affected (Fisher & White, 2000; Lei & Hitt, 1995). Obviously, there is a loss of corporate memory and organizational heritage as long-term employees are terminated. Unless they are carefully managed, many of the more skilled and valuable employees will choose to leave. Consequently, the overall knowledge base in an organization unwittingly can be lowered.

No matter what the economic justification, an organization that chooses to resize as opposed to taking other steps (such as shorter workweeks, forced use of vacation times, or reductions in executive compensation) suffers the stigma of being perceived as a firm that is willing to cast its people aside in the search for profits. There is no doubt that prospective future employees regard a firm like Hewlett-Packard, which historically has been regarded as one of the best places to work in the high-technology industry, less favorably after it engages in involuntary reductions in force than before ever considering such an action. Moreover, there is no doubt that surviving employees at other plants and offices shudder, feeling less secure and less satisfied with their employers when

General Motors announces plant closings. And there is no doubt that future employees who will be acquired by Vivendi as the dynamic firm continues to grow will recall how the French company divested thousands of employees as it picked through acquired Seagrams, retaining the entertainment holdings while casting aside the core spirits and wine business. Ironically, it was the Spirits and Wine Division that generated profits enabling Seagrams to acquire its entertainment units.

The unintended impact of resizing spreads beyond employee ranks and into the perceptions and behaviors of customers as well (Bastien et al., 1996). Customers fret when they hear that a company with which they are doing business is about to lay off employees, close an operation, or sell a unit. They know that employees will be distracted from work, productivity will plummet, and quality will suffer. In fact, many manufacturing firms have gotten to the point where they automatically line up secondary sources when they learn a supplier is anticipating or engaging in a resizing. And when customers have had prior experiences with resizing firms—whether they are large industrial firms receiving raw materials of poor quality or individual consumers fed up with waiting in long lines at a financial institution—they will take their business elsewhere.

Resizing often is a sound and sensible strategy. We are not debating or questioning that point. Rather, our intent is to examine the various ways in which resizing has a direct and indirect impact on organizations and their stakeholders. Our goal is to identify the methods that can be used to minimize the unintended consequences while maximizing the opportunities to use resizing as a stimulus to build a new and better organization for the long haul.

The Healthy Side of Organizational Resizing

Certainly, organizations need to right-size by eliminating unnecessary work, shedding underperforming or nonessential units, and responding to economic, legal, technological, regulatory, and consumer changes. If organizations did not change, they would not remain competitive. Organizational leaders, however, must come to terms with the fact that the way in which they resize their operations affects employee motivation, team performance, and organizational effectiveness.

Resizing does not imply that organizations are malevolent in their actions. In many cases, layoffs, closings, and divestitures are prudent business moves that enhance competitiveness and survivability in the constantly changing business environment. The elimination of jobs at CNN following the AOL Time Warner merger, United Airlines' closing of money-losing stations as firms slashed travel budgets in 2001, and Vivendi's divestiture of a liquor business that was outside its managerial expertise are the kinds of steps that have to be taken to increase the likelihood that the firms, and their many remaining employees, will endure and prosper over the long term.

Resizing can be beneficial for organizations and their people. Companies wallowing in red ink are wise to eliminate a portion— be it 5, 10, or even 20 percent—of the workforce to strengthen the survivability of the vast majority of employees. A serious assessment of workforce apportionment and strategic business mix is an integral component of the organizational introspection needed to rebalance and reposition a firm and its resources to take better advantage of emerging market trends and technological changes.

Transitions also can spark organizational regeneration. A CEO or business unit leader with the right mix of visionary and charismatic leadership skills can rally employees around the notion that the transition is not only a necessary response to business realities, but an opportunity to improve how work is approached and conducted in the organization. Resizing holds the potential to unfreeze the organization and its people, providing a rare chance to change corporate culture dramatically and reinforce a new way of doing things. A middle manager or supervisor can use the unfrozen state as an opportunity to strengthen teamwork, increase effectiveness, and identify and correct impediments to productivity in his or her work group.

Individuals can experience a personal form of renewal as a result of company resizing. Although many employees remain mired in maladaptive responses to the stress and uncertainty of a downsizing or divestiture, others come to recognize that in crisis there is opportunity (Bardwick, 1995). One senior executive who had lost his job in a major organizational restructuring revealed, "When shrubs are transplanted, there is new growth and new life. I know, because it happened to me." Searching out ways to gain from the transition, enlightened employees share three key characteristics. First, they feel in control of things that matter to them. They recognize they cannot manage what is beyond their control and do not even try; instead, they assess the situation and act in the areas they can influence. Second, they feel involved in what they are doing. They see themselves as architects of change rather than as victims of it. Third, they seek challenges, take risks, and look on work with a fresh perspective. These employees recognize that the rules of the game have changed, that there is no business as usual. They see the company's transition as an opportunity to learn new skills, test their ability to cope with stress and uncertainty, and find creative ways to meet work requirements. Savvy employees also will view the transition as an opportunity to reposition their careers or take advantage of new jobs that are created. Organizational resizing enables employees to grasp control of their careers and work lives once again (Noer, 1997).

Unfortunately, using transition as an opportunity for personal growth, team development, or organizational renewal is very much the exception rather than the rule. Reports of layoffs or closings rarely describe productive, regenerating, or even rebalancing outcomes. In contrast, they depict reductions in force, closings, and divestitures as painful, wrenching, and bloody. Worse yet, many resizings fail to achieve desired results, despite the pain that the organizations and their people are put through.

Why Does It Matter How Companies Resize: Why This Book?

Despite the frequency with which they fail to achieve desired financial or strategic objectives and produce unintended consequences, layoffs, closings, and divestitures are here to stay in the managerial repertoire. Chief executive officers, business unit leaders, and other senior executives are regularly and readily going to resize as a step toward achieving their desired organizational visions. As a recent *Fortune* magazine article put it, "Letting employees go in a humane fashion isn't just about finding a way for executives to sleep at night. Bad downsizing, which management experts argue is the norm, is bad business" (Levering & Moskowitz, 2002, p. 61). The purpose of this book, then, is to help executives and their staffs prepare for, implement, and recover from organizational resizings. Our intent is to combine the science of resizing—the insight gained from organizational behavior research—and the practice of resizing—the war stories and lessons learned from practical applications of layoffs, closings, and divestitures—to identify better ways to manage these events.

Accumulating quantitative and qualitative research, as well as case study insights, into resizing is no easy task. The very nature of resizing runs against the grain of conducting sound scholarly research and applying empirically based, conceptually sound methods. A number of varied dynamics account for the difficulty of studying resizing. First, despite the regularity of layoffs and closings, there remains a stigma associated with these events. Executives do not like to boast about their reductions in force or their failed operations and are hesitant to invite in research teams. Second, there is a self-imposed urgency to get on with things. "Get the pain over quickly," say corporate leaders, "rather than let it linger." This approach frequently translates into poor planning and incomplete implementation by practitioners. Third, most layoffs, closings, and divestitures start as highly secretive events. Legal and competitive limitations on communication thwart research opportunities and the application of sound transition management practices.

Yet the stakes are high, and executives, HR professionals, team leaders, consultants, and others can and must do a better job of managing both the victims and survivors of resizing. All the parties involved can benefit from more sophisticated and effective methods for managing resizing efforts. While we can make a humanistic case for why an event that is so disruptive to people's well-being, physical and mental health, and sense of fair play should be carefully managed and executed, the real reason for managing resizings well is to enhance bottom-line business results. How leaders lay people off, close operations, and divest business units has an impact on business results in several key ways:

- *Sending messages to surviving employees.* If surviving employees see that victims were treated respectfully (that is, given adequate notice, provided a safety net of severance pay and extended benefits, and assisted with finding new positions), they are less likely to be distracted from doing their work by worrying about what the future might bring. More than this, if surviving employees perceive that the resizing has occurred for valid reasons and has been well managed, they are less likely to lower their views of their employer. Moreover, organizational productivity is less likely to be adversely affected.

• *Reinforcing or changing a reputation to potential new employees.* Despite a slowdown in the economy, it remains a seller's market on the job front. Excellent performers always are in great demand. One of the ironies of resizing is that nonrevenue producers like corporate training specialists are among the first to go in layoffs. This leaves a workforce with little formal training and adds to the high value of recruits who can enter a workplace and hit the ground running. To be as attractive as possible to potential new employees, organizations will need, at the very least, to minimize the unintended costs of mismanaging resizings and, more positively, to demonstrate that the resizing is part of an overall plan to put or keep the organization on the road toward achieving its desired results.

• *Reducing the likelihood of future lawsuits.* Most employers by now are sensitive to the conditions of advance notification outlined in the Worker Adjustment and Retraining Notification Act. The act took effect in 1988 and has been widely publicized since then. A less familiar legalistic concern is compliance with the Age Discrimination in Employment Act of 1967. This act protects the rights of employees age forty and over. In an effort to maximize the reduction of salary and benefits, senior employees frequently are designated for layoff. When employees perceive that resizing attempts are being managed poorly, it can lead to management distrust, cynicism, and fear. Not only do these conditions cause immediate performance problems, they create a situation ripe for future lawsuits.

• *Creating an opportunity to use the "pain" as a springboard for "gain."* On an individual level, successful psychological adaptation to resizing implies letting go of the old, dealing with the neutral zone, and then accepting the new. On an organizational level, resizing presents the opportunity for renewal by abandoning outmoded perceptions and practices, contending with the trial-and-error learning required to establish new mental models and practices, and settling in on enhanced ways of doing things and expectations consistent with new organizational realities. Resizing provides both substantive and symbolic benefits to the organization. It locks in new and better ways of getting the job accomplished, and it sends a message to employees that there is opportunity and hope in the post-resizing organization.

- *Minimizing the impact on customers and communities.* Resizings have the potential to disrupt life outside the organization as well as within it. The sensitivity that organizations display toward customers and communities in planning and implementing resizing has the potential to minimize the loss of key customers and tighten the relationship with existing ones. Similarly, it has the potential to aid communities and their members during a transition that can have a significant and long-lasting impact on a region's economic health.

Some organizations are taking creative steps to manage resizings in a manner that is consistent with their identities of what it is to be a responsible employer. One particularly innovative case is Endwave, a Silicon Valley company that designs components for broadband wireless systems. Hit hard by the softness that plagued the telecom industry, Endwave conducted a voluntary reduction in force as part of its program to consolidate and transfer manufacturing operations from the Silicon Valley to a less expensive area in early 2001. With key customers like Nortel and Nokia continuing to experience weak demand, Endwave announced its first involuntary reduction in force in July 2001. It took a number of specific steps to minimize the pain of the event, as well as to maximize the gain. Among other activities, it engaged us to conduct a "delivering the bad news" training program to prepare managers and supervisors for the difficult work of alerting good performers, who had stayed through the first wave of voluntary cuts, that they were being let go. More than just a rehearsal for delivering the news, the training program became an opportunity to educate Endwave managers on the psychology of adaptation and transition. It became a forum for managers to express their concerns and to offer support for one another.

Endwave also used the reduction in force as an opportunity to make a positive statement about its culture, its commitment to all employees, and its confidence in its future. In addition to the typical components of severance pay, extension of benefits, and out-placement assistance, Endwave offered laid-off employees stock option grants. As Julie Biagini, Endwave's chief financial officer, stated, "Our company got as far as we did based on the hard work of many people, including those who were asked to leave the company involuntarily in the reduction in force. We believe this company will come back and achieve the operating results and stock share price it is capable of. We want the people who helped start us on this path to share in our success when we achieve it. The stock options are a way for former employees to participate in our renewal whether they come back to work for us in the future or not."

Similarly when the Charles Schwab Corporation announced a 13 percent reduction in force in March 2001, the company offered to pay a $7,500 bonus to any affected employee rehired within eighteen months. In an effort to keep those employees available, Schwab also created a $10 million educational fund, which will pay up to $20,000 in tuition over two years to affected workers. The intent is clear. Charles Schwab wanted to ease the pain of the people who were leaving so when things turned around, those employees would feel favorable about returning. These efforts by Endwave and Schwab demonstrate the essence of the science and practice of resizing: minimizing the pain of an ever increasing event in organizational life while maximizing the gain by using the resizing to enhance all stakeholders' views of the organization and its leadership.

References

Bamberger, B., & Davidson, C. N. (1999). *Closing: The life and death of an American factory.* New York: Norton.

Bardwick, J. M. (1995). *Danger in the comfort zone: From boardroom to mailroom—How to break the entitlement habit that's killing American business.* New York: AMACOM.

Barling, J., Zacharatos, A., & Hepburn, C. G. (1999). Parents' job insecurity affects children's academic performance through cognitive difficulties. *Journal of Applied Psychology, 84,* 437–444.

Bastien, D. T., Hostager, T. J., & Miles, H. H. (1996). Corporate judo: Exploiting the dark side of change when competitors merge, acquire, downsize, or restructure. *Journal of Management Inquiry, 5,* 261–275.

Boroughs, D. L. (1992). Amputating assets. *U.S. News & World Report,* May 4, pp. 50–51.

Bridges, W. (1980). *Transitions: Making sense of life's changes.* Reading, MA: Addison-Wesley.

Brockner, J. (1989). The effects of work layoffs on survivors: Research, theory, and practice. In B. M. Staw & L. L. Cummings (Eds.), *Research in organizational behavior* (Vol. 10, pp. 213–256). Greenwich, CT: JAI Press.

Brockner, J., Wiesenfeld, B. M., & Martin, C. L. (1995). Decision frame, procedural justice and survivors' reactions to job layoffs. *Organizational Behavior and Human Decision Processes, 63,* 59–69.

Buono, A. F., & Bowditch, J. L. (1989). *The human side of mergers and acquisitions: Managing collisions between people, cultures, and organizations.* San Francisco: Jossey-Bass.

Cascio, W. F. (1998). Learning from outcomes: Financial experiences of 311 firms that have downsized. In M. K. Gowing, J. D. Kraft, & J. C. Quick (Eds.), *The new organizational reality: Downsizing, restructuring, and revitalization* (pp. 55–70). Washington, DC: American Psychological Association.

De Meuse, K. P., Bergmann, T. J., & Lester, S. W. (2001). An investigation of the relational component of the psychological contract across time, generation, and employment status. *Journal of Managerial Issues, 13,* 87–101.

De Meuse, K. P., Bergmann, T. J., & Vanderheiden, P. A. (1997). Corporate downsizing: Separating myth from fact. *Journal of Management Inquiry, 6,* 168–176.

De Meuse, K. P., & McDaris, K. K. (1994). An exercise for managing change. *Training and Development Journal, 48*(2), 55–57.

De Meuse, K. P., & Tornow, W. W. (1990). The tie that binds—Has become very, very frayed! *Human Resource Planning, 13,* 203–213.

De Meuse, K. P., Vanderheiden, P. A., & Bergmann, T. J. (1994). Announced layoffs: Their effect on corporate financial performance. *Human Resource Management, 33,* 509–530.

Economy creates more stress. (1992, October 5). *Fortune,* pp. 11–12.

Fisher, S. R., & White, M. A. (2000). Downsizing in a learning organization: Are there hidden costs? *Academy of Management Review, 25,* 244–251.

Gaines, H. (1993, January). Put high priority on job satisfaction. *Executive Excellence,* pp. 8–9.

Greenhalph, L. (1989). Maintaining organizational effectiveness during organizational retrenchment. *Journal of Applied Behavioral Science, 19,* 155–170.

Holmes, T. H., & Rahe, R. H. (1968). The social readjustment rating scale. *Journal of Psychosomatic Research, 2,* 213–218.

Kanter, D. A., & Mirvis, P. H. (1989). *The cynical Americans.* San Francisco: Jossey-Bass.

Kivimaki, M., Vahtera, J., Pentti, J., & Ferrie, J. E. (2000). Factors underlying the effect of organizational downsizing on health of employees: Longitudinal cohort study. *British Medical Journal, 320,* 971–975.

Kübler-Ross, E. (1969). *On death and dying.* New York: Macmillan.

Larkin, T. J., & Larkin, S. (1996, May–June). Reaching and changing front-line employees. *Harvard Business Review,* pp. 95–104.

Leana, C. R., & Feldman, D. C. (1992). *Coping with job loss: How individuals, organizations, and communities respond to layoffs.* San Francisco: New Lexington Press.

Lei, D., & Hitt, M. A. (1995). Strategic restructuring and outsourcing: The effect of mergers and acquisitions and LBOs on building firm skills and capabilities. *Journal of Management, 21,* 835–859.

Lesly, E., & Light, L. (1992, December 7). When layoffs alone don't turn the tide. *Business Week,* pp. 100–101.

Levering, R., & Moskowitz, M. (2002, February 4). The 100 best companies to work for: The best in the worst of times. *Fortune,* pp. 60–90.

Lewin, K. (1947). Frontiers in group dynamics. *Human Relations, 1,* 5–41.

Marks, M. L. (1993). Downsizing and restructuring. In P. H. Mirvis (Ed.), *Building a competitive workforce.* New York: Wiley.

Marks, M. L. (1994). *From turmoil to triumph: New life after mergers, acquisitions, and downsizing.* San Francisco: New Lexington Press.

Marks, M. L. (2003). *Charging back up the hill: Workplace recovery after mergers, acquisitions, and downsizings.* San Francisco: Jossey-Bass.

Mirvis, P. H., & Marks, M. L. (1992). *Managing the merger: Making it work.* Uppper Saddle River, NJ: Prentice Hall.

Mische, M. A. (2001). *Strategic renewal: Becoming a high-performance organization.* Upper Saddle River, NJ: Prentice Hall.

Morris, J. R., Cascio, W. F., & Young, C. E. (1999, Winter). Downsizing after all these years: Questions and answers about who did it, how many did it, and who benefited from it. *Organizational Dynamics,* pp. 78–87.

Noer, D. M. (1993). *Healing the wounds: Overcoming the trauma of layoffs and revitalizing downsized organizations.* San Francisco: Jossey-Bass.

Noer, D. M. (1997). *Breaking free: A prescription for personal and organizational change.* San Francisco: Jossey-Bass.

Pfeffer, J. (1998). *The human equation: Building profits by putting people first.* Boston: Harvard Business School Press.

Reynolds, L. (1992, October). America's work ethic: Lost in turbulent times? *Management Review,* pp. 20–25.

Schmitt, N., Sacco, J. M., Ramey, S., Ramey, C., & Chan, D. (1999).

Parental employment, school climate, and children's academic and social development. *Journal of Applied Psychology, 84*, 737–753.

Siekman, P. (2000, October 2). The big myth about U.S. manufacturing. *Fortune,* pp. 244C–244E.

Strauss, G. (2001, March 20). Forget brass rings—execs grab for gold. *USA Today,* pp. 1B–2B.

A study of worker compensation costs in companies following downsizing. (1992). New York: William M. Mercer.

U.S. Bureau of Labor Statistics (2002, February 14). *Hourly compensation costs in U.S. dollars.* Available on-line: http://www.stats.bls.gov:80/ news.release/ichcc.toc.htm.

U.S. Department of Labor. (2002, April 17). *Mass layoff events and initial claimants for unemployment insurance, January 2001 to February 2002.* Available on-line: http://www.stats.bls.gov/news.release/mmls.t01.htm.

Vanderheiden, P. A., De Meuse, K. P., & Bergmann, T. J. (1999). And the beat goes on: Corporate downsizing in the twenty-first century. *Human Resource Management, 38*, 261–268.

Wiley, J. W. (1991). *A national survey of 2,500 households.* Minneapolis: Gantz-Wiley Research Consulting Group.

CHAPTER 2

Who Moved My Drink? The Preparation for the Closure of Seagram's Spirits and Wine Business
A Personal Experience
Ronny Vansteenkiste

Early in 2000, the popular management parable *Who Moved My Cheese?* was heralded by senior management at the Seagram Spirits and Wine Group (SSWG) as a must-read book. In the book, four characters (two mice and two "little people") were forced to cope with unwanted change. As the story unfolded, the reader vicariously observed all four characters react to change differently (for example, deny it, resent it, embrace it). How could we have imagined how soon the gentle parable was going to become hard reality in our own company? I was vice president of organization development and learning for Seagram and a member of the senior human resource team at that time. I played an active role in planning and preparing the organization for the major transition it was facing.

The views expressed in this chapter are entirely personal and are not intended in any way to represent the opinions of other Seagram Spirits and Wine Group employees or management.

The Business Background

SSWG's journey toward becoming a high-performance company came to an abrupt end when Seagram's chief executive officer, Edgar Bronfman, Jr., sold the company for $23 billion to the French media and utilities company Vivendi in June 2000. The combination of Vivendi and Canal+ with Seagram vaulted it into the top rank of media and entertainment companies in the world, with revenues of $65 billion in 2001 and a market capitalization of $100 billion. This union marked the end of Bronfman's tumultuous decade-long drive to transform the liquor company founded in Canada by his grandfather in the 1920s into a world-class media and entertainment company. It was brought about mainly on the strength of two blockbuster deals—the 1995 acquisition of MCA (owner of Universal Studios) for $5.7 billion and the 1998 purchase of Polygram for $10.4 billion. As part of the deal, Tropicana had been sold to PepsiCo in 1998 for $3.3 billion, and the performance of SSWG had been boosted by a four-year worldwide reengineering and culture change process. For the fiscal year ending June 2000, Seagram's total EBITDA (operating earnings before interest, taxes, depreciation and amortization) was $1.872 billion on revenues of $15.7 billion.

As a consequence of the formation of Vivendi Universal, the world's third largest wines and spirits group was put up for sale because it was considered nonstrategic to the new entertainment and communications powerhouse. The Chateau and Estates Wine Company (Sterling, Mumm, Cuvée, Napa) and the Seagram Beverage Company (Seagram's Coolers) also were put up for sale. SSWG contributed about 35 percent of total revenues and more than 60 percent of operating income in fiscal year 2000 ($602 million) from sales of well-known brands like Chivas Regal, Crown Royal, Seagram VO, Martell, Glenlivet, Captain Morgan, Absolut, and Sandeman. After an intriguing auction process, in which at one time all of the world's top six spirits and wine producers were involved, including Seagram's own management team, Vivendi Universal eventually entered into a $8.15 billion agreement. On December 19, 2000, SSWG was sold to a coalition between Diageo (from the United Kingdom) and Pernod Ricard (from France), two of its fiercest competitors.

Those two drink companies planned to split up the brands. Pernod Ricard acquired six Scotch whiskies, including Chivas Regal and Glenlivet, as well as Martel Cognac and Seagram's Gin. In doing so, it reduced its emphasis on anis and catapulted itself into the third spot in the world's top five distilled spirits marketers and with a better balance in geographical and portfolio terms. Diageo already was the industry leader by far and was strengthening that position by taking Crown Royal and VO Canadian whiskies, as well as Captain Morgan rum. Diageo's main rationale for the deal was to become a focused leader in the alcoholic beverage industry. Both buyers also gained distribution power through the joint acquisition—Diageo predominantly in North America and Pernod Ricard in Latin America, Asia, and North America. However, the deal was disastrous for SSWG's European marketing and sales operations, which were largely going to be decimated. Furthermore, brands in SSWG's long brand tail such as Sandeman, Four Roses Bourbon, and Oddbins were to be auctioned off by the two buying companies.

The irony was that all these events happened at a time when SSWG had posted an all-time record earnings of $5.1 billion in the fiscal year that ended June 2000. Furthermore, SSWG had been enjoying double-digit growth during ten out of the past eleven quarters. From an earnings perspective, SSWG was leading the spirits industry. These great profits had boosted the morale of the employees, who now saw the positive results after five years of culture change. People felt part of a highly streamlined and winning organization with a growing performance discipline. Seagram's top management had been on the deal track for a while, but there never had been any rumors that SSWG was going to be touched. The threat of unloading SSWG sent a shock wave through the organization. Consequently, SSWG's senior management suddenly found themselves faced with the obvious paradox of retaining the talent in order to keep the successful business performance going, while preparing them for an uncertain future with many layoffs. The buying companies were predominantly interested in acquiring new brands, which they could easily integrate in their existing sales and distribution networks. It soon became apparent that only a small number of positions would survive. Managing this balance proved to be a daunting task for several reasons.

A Very Long Period of Uncertainty:
The Breakup Syndrome

SSWG employees had lived through many reorganizations during the past ten years due to a massive reengineering effort that Bronfman had started in the "old Seagram" in 1994. From this time, Bronfman had acquired entertainment assets, signaling that the transformation of Seagram was going to be more fundamental than simply reorganizing inspired by a drive for enhanced performance and effectiveness. A particular psychological aspect played an important role in this transformation. A critical difference between Seagram and Vivendi was that Vivendi was management dominated, whereas Seagram was largely a family company. The wealthy and powerful Bronfman family held about 28 percent of the shares of Seagram. The family business mentality had been particularly prevalent in the spirits business, the origin of Seagram. Typical traits of SSWG's culture had been its inward-oriented focus, formal and top-down communication, multiple layers, arrogance, and a disciplined, dedicated, and committed workforce with high loyalty to the Bronfman family. For a long time, many SSWG employees had felt that they were the masters of the universe in the Seagram empire. However, by 1998, they started to feel increasingly reduced to a position of a money maker, subsidizing the newly acquired entertainment assets (some of which were loss making). Nevertheless, the workforce remained loyal to the Bronfmans for the next few years, because most employees were convinced that they would never sell the spirits and wine business. The Vivendi Universal deal was a major blow to many of the SSWG employees, who felt deeply let down by the Bronfmans, especially in North America, which accounted for 60 percent of the total business and where the strongest growth was being realized.

Following the announcement of the Vivendi Universal creation in June and the SSWG sale by the end of 2000, there arose a hostility and resentment toward the new owners of the company, particularly from the many long-serving employees. Many of the SSWG employees from the senior ranks downward were resentful and angry at what they perceived to be the selling out of the company on the part of Bronfmans. Any communication by the family about the business reasons for the sale was felt to be lacking in empathy and sensitivity. Edgar Bronfman became a target of derision and frustration. There was undoubtedly a lot of projection going on of people's feelings and frustration. Any communication from him about the business reason for the sale was perceived to be lacking in empathy and insensitive to employees. Pointed sarcastic remarks bounced back and forth on Seagram-related chat boards. The idea that something great was coming to an end was very difficult. The task was to channel everyone's strong negative emotions and anxiety into something positive. In most people's minds, somebody had definitely moved their drink, for good.

This anger was fueled in late September 2000 when the *International Herald Tribune* rumored that Bronfman reportedly had opposed the planned buyout of the spirits business by a consortium led by SSWG's management team. The auction of SSWG from September until late December 2000 turned out to be a chaotic and messy affair, highly entertaining for outsiders but not for the SSWG employees. The players in this particular drama were six of the world's largest drinks producers, who found themselves caught up in a six-month bidding war. At stake was the largest portfolio of drink brands ever to be put on sale, giving each of those companies a unique chance to secure leading positions in key categories around the globe, particularly in North America. To the other large group of stakeholders, the SSWG people, it seemed that Vivendi Universal, the investment bankers, and the dealmakers were giving very little consideration to their needs.

SSWG's management team continued to stay together. All of them supported each other in overcoming the disappointment of not being able to carry out their management buy-out. This enabled them to present a united front, sending the message that "we all are in this together" to the organization. They communicated to the organization openly and with credibility about why they had abandoned their buy-out effort and that they now would support the next best solution. The various regional presidents followed up their general communication by discussing the recent happenings face-to-face with their employees. At the same time, the human resource function took a lead role in preparing the organization for transition and made moves to mitigate the sense of impending personal loss.

A Prolonged Pain

One other factor made the emotional roller coaster even more stressful: the date of the close of the deal kept moving. When the deal was announced in December 2000, all parties involved were convinced that they would get regulatory approval in the United States, Canada, and Europe by the end of March 2001. In the hot merger and acquisitions summer of 2001, General Electric saw its deal with Honeywell blocked by the European Union Commission in Brussels. United Airlines received thumbs down in its takeover bid for United Air in the United States. Diageo and Pernod Ricard, in turn, had clearly underestimated the difficulty and the complexity of the transaction and the scrutiny of the Federal Trade Commission in the United States. A transaction directly involving two major competitors head-on and a breakup of a large company is bound to be more complex than some of the other megamergers. Add to this mix the complicated split-up of brands and countries. The use of firewalls (a set of procedures to protect competitor-sensitive data following the closure) was imposed from the start. Nevertheless, all the complexity from a systems and people perspective that comes with such procedures was known in advance. Although the European Union gave its approval in May, the closing date initially slipped to the end of June, then to the first of July, followed by announcements that it was slipping further to the end of July and then August. As I am writing this chapter, it now is tentatively scheduled for the end of October (with possible further delays). Never underestimate the time it takes to clear a deal and the emotional toll it takes on people when they hear conflicting messages all the time, especially when they anticipate that they will not have a job at the end of it.

Preparing the Organization for Transition and Closure

During the fourteen months since the announcement of the intention to sell SSWG, managing and working in SSWG became extremely difficult. We took many initiatives with long- and short-term effects to help the organization and the people get through this transition.

Preparation for the Long Term: An Ongoing Senior Management's Agenda Item

In this day and age of numerous mergers and acquisitions, it always is good management practice to be prepared for them at any time. In the case of SSWG, the positive impact of eight years of continued performance-enhancing actions only now became apparent to its full extent. It had started with five years of intensive reengineering of over forty business processes and deep culture change based on formulating, cascading, and training in the Seagram Values: a customer and consumer focus, quality, innovation, teamwork, respect, and integrity. In addition, the subsequent overhaul of the employee development and management processes proved to be a solid foundation to deal with the breakdown in a more mature way than otherwise would be possible. All of those efforts had culminated in the creation of a vision for "One Team Seagram" and a strong centralized functional matrix organization in 1998. This effort had put the organization back on track, had increased its executional excellence, and had instilled a strong discipline in approaching its business in the organization.

From mid-1994 until late 1997, more than forty cross-functional teams had examined and redesigned every process in the areas of finance, consumer marketing, customer development, order fulfillment, manufacturing, purchasing, information technology, and business planning. These efforts resulted in a more process-oriented company, significant cost reductions, a number of layoffs, a more effective organization, and enhanced business performance. However, process redesign was not sufficient to obtain those results. It went hand in hand with a companywide culture change process initiated by the chief executive officer (CEO) and carried out over a five-year period. During this time, the Seagram Values were formulated, cascaded, and integrated into the way we were doing business and managing our people. This entailed rolling out business-focused values sessions to all employees over a two-year time frame, as well as combined the installation of a 360-degree feedback process for senior and middle managers and a significant change in top leadership positions.

Edgar Bronfman, Jr., had been instrumental in starting the reengineering and values initiatives and oversaw them over a four-year period. The good news for SSWG was that its chief executive, Steve Kallagher, had been the reengineering leader at the onset and consistently and ardently sustained both initiatives in the company. Undoubtedly, those efforts created the nurturing ground for the fundamental change of SSWG that proved to be the ideal foundation to build it into a high-performing company. And though not intended as such, these interventions also created the enabling conditions to see the organization and its people through its ultimate breakup (while being able to maintain focus and business momentum). The basic discipline of creating a quality process staffed by talented people and running it with a deep respect and integrity was certainly rooted in the initiatives of the mid-1990s.

I consider all those change initiatives necessary to be part of any top management agenda on an ongoing basis. It highlights that the best time to prepare for a combination with one or more companies starts a long time before it actually happens so that adequate conditions are created long in advance that will enable a more humane transition.

Medium-Term Preparation: Anticipating the Deal

From the time of the announcement of the intended sale of the company and during the time of the auction, we in the human resource (HR) function embarked immediately on preparing to help the organization through the transition. The senior HR team met and discussed the large number of issues involved in a combination of companies with respect to the organization overall and the individuals. We opted to be proactive rather than wait until it was clear who were the buyers. We agreed on a course of action, starting with the preparation of the HR function. We all knew that fundamentally mergers and acquisitions are a very negative experience for employees, their families, and the communities in which they live. Therefore, in line with the Seagram Values, we were going to try to help our employees through this process with respect and integrity, regardless of who was going to be the new owner of our company. We also realized that our HR professionals had to learn more about combinations and the nature of HR advice and the work it entailed.

A Credible HR Function Takes the Lead

There also was a business reason for the swift HR reaction: we were determined to help senior and line managers maintain focus on the business and stay on track to attain the ambitious business targets that were established. By doing this, SSWG employees would be able to keep themselves busy and gain a sense of achievement, thus somewhat offsetting the feeling of personal loss. We continued to demonstrate that we were attending to the personal and emotional dimension of our employees, while at the same time focusing on achieving the business objectives.

One major condition allowed us to take a lead position. The HR function in SSWG had become one of the strongest functions during the past three years as a consequence of two events: the redesign of the way in which HR management was being handled and the extensive upgrade of the caliber of the HR professionals we employed. A senior team of line managers and HR specialists had reengineered the human development and management processes and accountabilities. The new approach was branded "Team Seagram—You're the business" and provided employees with a framework for development based on ongoing dialogue about goals and performance. It applied five integrated people processes to fundamental business goals. More important, line management owned it. Performance management and talent detection and development were the cornerstones of Team Seagram. The HR function acted as facilitator of the processes and was the custodian of the "People Plan," which addressed the critical people and organization issues at the heart of strategic planning. By mid-2000, the HR function was enjoying an excellent reputation as an influential strategic business partner. SSWG's CEO publicly attributed the outstanding business results of fiscal year 2000 to an important extent to Team Seagram and the efforts of the HR function.

A Catalytic HR Learning Event

In the context of the dramatic changes facing SSWG, the HR function quickly became the best-prepared function and a model for the other functions. The senior HR team decided to design and organize a large-scale three-day learning event for the entire function around the world before any buyer was announced. The communications and legal functions were included because we would be working closely with each other. The event had the following aims:

1. Strengthen the global HR network.
2. Prepare the organization, the HR function, and its individuals for the imminent task at hand.
3. Develop, with the help of some board members and investment bankers, the capability of the function by learning about the business context of the imminent acquisition and the business backgrounds of all possible future partners.
4. Learn from authoritative consultants and other companies that had gone through similar experiences about the dynamics of combining companies and why they often fail.
5. Put a global action plan together for the upcoming six months.

The learning experience was highly interactive and participative. We started by listening to individual concerns, hopes, and fears, as well as allowing them to surface collectively. A key design principle of the conference was to influence the reigning mind-set characterized by a victim syndrome and to help the participants see a different way of approaching an acquisition. We stressed that although one may not be in charge, one can still build an inclusive scenario and offer to co-create a win-win proposition for the new venture in partnership with the buyer. We accomplished this goal through many sessions in which all participants were involved in building future successful scenarios in which they would like to contribute their capabilities. We derived a set of HR principles for dealing with separation, selection, and integration, carefully describing what success would look like. Everything was written in an HR blueprint document for integration, which was shared among the entire HR function. Subsequently, it was passed on to the HR professionals of the buying companies.

We started the conference with a basic discipline of extensive question-and-answer sessions for ourselves that later became the model for communication sessions with line managers. Such sessions were repeated regularly across the globe during the following months whenever management or employee meetings were taking place. At the end of the conference, the HR function had not only enhanced its capability but had unified its understanding of what the function stood for and how we would influence the buyer to co-create the future if it opted to do so. All participants agreed to take the following collective actions:

1. Gear up communications at the local levels as a partnership among the line manager, HR, and communications functions.
2. Provide local teams with an overview of why mergers frequently fail and how to turn them into successful combinations.
3. Answer as many of employee questions as possible in local meetings and road shows.
4. Build or update local, regional, and global human resources databases.
5. Encourage employees to prepare for the impending transition by offering sessions on managing change to increase their understanding of the marketplace and competitors, resumé writing skills, and interviewing skills seminars.
6. Provide regular local and regional communication briefings through the regional HR vice presidents.
7. Identify their HR counterparts at the potential buyers and initiate a telephone call the day after the preferred bidder was announced. (Seventy telephone calls were placed worldwide one day after the announcement of the deal.)

Nine months later, this three-day conference has proven to be a major catalyst for the entire transition process. It built strong confidence and created cohesion in the HR function, which played a lead role in the dialogue with the buyers. We influenced their thinking substantially about HR resourcing principles and helped them to fine-tune their processes for making choices about people and talent integration, staff redundancy, and severance issues. We often found ourselves in a key referee and influencer role during the transition planning, especially in the detailed brand-by-brand and market-by-market approach. The consistent and persistent way in which this was handled within SSWG was a major achievement of the HR learning event.

Short-Term Preparation: When the Heat Is On, All Focus on the People

The feedback from these activities indicated that the long-lasting uncertainty started to cause a significant emotional drain on the staff. Immediately after the HR event, a long series of focused interventions for the individual employees were designed by the organization development team and started to be implemented in December 2000. Most of those events were one-day or half-day sessions with either a practical or a psychological-emotional focus. Included in the former were workshops on resumé writing, interviewing skills, networking, negotiating new work agreements, and career workshops. The last session gave participants an insight into their deeply held career interests and anchors, preferences, and capabilities and how to put these together in a balanced and realistic career perspective.

To provide support at a psychological-emotional level, we offered employees the following:

- Taking-stock sessions in which participants were coached to bring out their areas of strength they can carry forward to a new role, using our 360-degree feedback instrument or other psychometrics.
- Personal coaching for senior executives.
- "Me and Transition" workshops to equip employees with the knowledge, mind-set, and tools to cope with the stress of a transition process and to help them understand their emotions experienced as a result of loss or negative change. Emphasis was placed on developing positive tactics and tools to manage transition and identifying actions for feeling more confident, regaining a sense of control, and remaining productive on the job.
- "Thriving on Change" sessions. Because the most people with the longest service worked in the United States, management in that region expressed a specific need for assisting employees through their career transition with guidance and support. The objective of those work sessions was to work with their employees in identifying and developing the necessary skills and techniques to navigate through the change effectively. We attempted to find new opportunities consistent with their capabilities, interests, and career objectives. It included completing self-assessment exercises and individual coaching follow-up.

Many companies in a merger and acquisition situation tend to offer similar sessions. We went a step further by offering them even before a deal was announced. We continued to do so throughout the organization until the time of closure. The emphasis of the activities shifted over time in line with the evolving reality. We allowed the employees to select the sessions that were most applicable to their specific situations. The leadership initiative LEAP (Leadership Enhancement and Acceleration Process) for employees with high potential was continued but refocused to help people understand their leadership skills in the context of leading change. In parallel, functional training sessions were continued where they had been going on before the announcement occurred. We communicated openly with employees that the prime purpose of all training efforts was now shifting toward furthering their personal capabilities.

Communication

At the learning event, the HR and communications functions had agreed to make a substantial investment in the communication area. This proposal found immediate response from the leaders whose style had become more open over the past three years. In addition to the regular face-to-face meetings organized by line managers and their HR representative, the number of management meetings increased, including numerous question-and-answer sessions in line with the needs of the regions or local organizations. Frequent e-mail messages were distributed. The quarterly company magazine, *Premier,* was discontinued and replaced by *Premier in Brief,* a more regular written update on the sale of SSWG and important developments. This newsletter was published every four to six weeks and answered questions submitted by a feedback button on SSWG's Intranet. An annoying obstacle to speedy communication was that all official messages had to be cleared first by attorneys from all the parties involved. We did not find a satisfactory way around this problem, except for the many face-to-face sessions we conducted.

As the waiting for the closure dragged on, we introduced Radio Seagram—regular telephone broadcasts by the CEO in which all employees could dial in to hear the latest updates. We thereby increased the speed of the messages and found ways to revert to different means of communication. It is a cliché to say that one needs to communicate, communicate, communicate, but it is the truth.

We prided ourselves because our senior management stayed very focused and mostly visible throughout the process. Most leadership groups seem to vanish during a transition like this. In our case, the underlying driver was the strong pride and attachment that the top team continued to hold for their company and what it stood for among its competitors.

Retention

While addressing personal needs and showing respect and understanding to the individual remained important, we believe that money remains one of the best short-term means to secure retention. Consequently, HR created a number of retention schemes to keep the critical talent required to attain the business objectives SSWG's senior management were committed to deliver. Many senior managers feared a massive walkout as soon as the deal was announced. This never materialized; the retention levels stayed remarkably high throughout the period. Almost one year after the announcement of the intended sale, SSWG had only 534 out of its 8,500 employees (6 percent) voluntarily leave. Furthermore, the resignations have been lowest in North America, where we had the largest number of long-serving employees.

Senior management and HR allocated retention funds widely across a broad management population of about 1000 people. The SSWG Focus and Motivation Reward entitled recipients to a full-year bonus after a six-month period; it could be adjusted upward based on strong individual performance. Surprisingly, few resignations occurred after the receipt of this bonus. A complementary special retention scheme also was made available to reward key employees deeper in the organization with lump sums of an average 50 percent of their salary. Within this program, 575 non-bonus-eligible employees were nominated by their country managers and functional heads for being critical to the successful running of the business on a daily basis or essential to closing the sale transaction.

In addition to the retention funds, the senior HR team worked hard on behalf of all SSWG employees to maintain all the normal compensation practices (such as performance bonuses and salary reviews). Understandably, this objective was not always met with great enthusiasm on behalf of the buying companies. These many measures and a generous handling with retention funds provided the necessary boost of morale and kept the employment numbers high until the fall of 2001. They contributed greatly to the record business performance results SSWG delivered at the end of June 2001. If we had been more courageous, we probably should have tried to tailor the retention efforts to individual needs even more. We acted on a very inclusive and generous basis in combination with the many other interventions people could choose. We went some way toward a not one-size-fits-all approach.

Staying with It: Control Your Destiny or Somebody Else Will

It became clear who the two buyers were just before Christmas. SSWG's senior management took the initiative to reach out to them quickly and to start conversations about people. In doing that, strong HR practices that we had built during the past three to four years were leveraged immediately. Our talent and high-potential review process, communication process, and above all the sense of urgency that had become an integral part of our culture all were intact. A series of suggestions regarding resourcing principles and processes was submitted to the buying companies. Early exchange of performance, talent, and resumé information about senior management and those with high potential was well received by the new owners. Based on the robustness of the underlying performance and talent processes, they took the data at face value. Consequently, it became the primary source for their decisions about whom they were going to employ. Throughout the pre-close period, the senior HR team stayed close to what was happening across the company with respect to the decisions about people. We advised the buyers when the practices appeared in conflict between the two buying companies or were not in line with initially agreed principles. Our view was that we had to control the destiny of our employees for as long as we could influence the new owners. We also urged them to communicate the future mission of the overall company and the local organizations to our workforce and helped them organize the necessary road shows in an attempt to improve the confidence in the future.

Lessons Learned: A Personal Reflection

These thoughts and insights from my experience resizing SSWG are entirely subjective but I hope useful:

- *If you cannot escape the organizational change, get into it.* Do not assume an attempt to acquire or merge with your company will not happen. Furthermore, do not think that because you have been acquired, all control is lost. Once a deal has been announced, do not simply sit back and wait for things to happen. A new reality will unfold sooner or later. There is much to be gained by becoming proactive and influencing your own destiny.

- *It is a great opportunity to show your character as both an individual and an organization.* It is a perfect time to answer the question, "What do we stand for?" Unfortunately, all the textbooks on this subject are right: you will encounter some of the worst in human behavior. As the acquirer, it is easy to fall into the superiority trap. It requires great integrity and sensitivity throughout your organization to prevent likely power plays from occurring. Any downsizing, resizing, or closure of a company will happen in a way that is consistent with the organization's culture and underlying values, whether stated or not. In such high exposure times, it is vital that there is a rock-solid core to the organization's reputation. In our case, the six to seven years of investment in cultural change and leadership development paid off. We praised ourselves that one of the ten success criteria for a Seagram leader had been "character counts."

- *Always be in a state of preparation for a possible takeover or combining of companies.* This should be a constant agenda item for senior management. Once it does become reality, both short- and long-term actions will be swiftly required. Mergers, acquisitions, and resizing always will be with us. The way in which you structure your processes and build your culture is critical for the relative smoothness of something that is not smooth at all.

- *Focus on increased retention of top talent.* There are two elements to this point. First, talented people at the top will have much opportunity to influence the new owners. The acquiring company will make decisions about these people first. If they are chosen to stay, they will be able to influence other decisions about people. Second, the talent pool deeper in the organization often occupies roles that are critical to the ongoing success of the business. It is necessary to secure their continued employment and commitment to help the new business reach high performance levels fast. Furthermore, there is evidence that these highly talented people typically are higher in learning agility and faster in dealing with change than other employees.

- *Always be ready to provide rapid follow-up and support after every announcement.* Unfortunately, the human psyche is such that it tends to hear or read all the negative implications in any piece of communication. Morale and motivation can drop quickly if people are left to form their own conclusions. In order to correct potential misconceptions early on, management needs to be available for follow-up dialogue.
- *Use straight talk—and use it often.* You are bound to have to repeat the same message over and over again. As annoying as this may be, you have to do it. Never create illusions. The most honest communication is usually frank.
- *Be ready to manage emotions, and expect to spend a lot of time on this practice.* The emotions around loss or change traditionally have been categorized as some of the strongest stressors. The neurosensory research around emotional intelligence suggests that strong emotional responses from the brain have priority over the more rational side of the brain. When people are forced to live with such extreme emotions for some time, they are likely to develop a strong emotional filter in their mind through which messages are received and which will color the way they normally listen and respond. Managing such a situation requires sensitivity and ongoing care.
- *Help people become aware of their skills and their strengths.* The best help you can give employees with long-lasting effect is to help them assess their job strengths and weaknesses accurately. Money simply is a plaster on the wound; it does not help heal the wound. Always have employees consider redeployment. Even when the new owner has a job to offer, advise your employees to seek other options as well.
- *Telling the truth sometimes appears to be revolutionary in organizations.* Support the managers delivering the message. Most of them, regardless of their seniority, are not trained to give bad news and need special support around the process. In business, most managers resist speaking the plain truth because they think it is going to upset people. They forget that trust can be built only on truth and sincerity. A positive workplace requires unvarnished honesty. Therefore, managers need to be told by their seniors what precisely

is expected from them and given assistance in the form of frequent communication by teleconferencing, briefings, dialogue, and facilitation help from HR.

- *Tailor retention efforts to individual employee needs.* There is no one-size-fits-all retention lure. I recommend that HR professionals try to customize retention programs to the individual employees whom the organization seeks to keep. Some employees will be interested in money only; to others, more flexible practices, such as telework, telecommuting, less travel, a challenging project, or a variable work schedule, may be more appealing. In addition, the employees you want to retain most often are the more talented ones who frequently have more options in the labor market. Consequently, try to demonstrate that you are paying attention to what really matters to them and to what needs they value.

- *Prepare yourself for a long and dirty war in the trenches.* All projected time lines will be incorrect and always will be delayed. Be mentally ready for twice the delay than the one announced at the onset. Also, prepare yourself for an environment of political gamesmanship, self-preservation tactics, and empire building. Organizational change creates uncertainty and ambiguity. Such times bring out the best, but also the worst, in people.

- *Act quickly once the intention for a company sale has been made public.* Insist that senior management roles be dealt with the soonest, so that they can be announced before or, at the latest, at the time of the close of the deal. This approach will provide clarity and direction for the remaining employees. If you do it quickly, the pain is sharp but brief.

- *The best layoff programs show respect for and trust of employees.* As much notice should be given as is reasonably possible before a reduction in force takes place. Employees should be permitted to continue to perform their normal job duties in their regular facilities, with full access to systems and people, enabling them to say good-bye and depart with dignity. Such an attitude can create a positive image of an employer of choice.

- *This is a period of determining times for the HR function.* As a result of four years of ongoing development in our HR function, we now can pride ourselves that it is deeply involved in the business as a true partner to the line. Not wanting to take anything for granted, we saw the breakup of our company as a huge developmental opportunity for our HR professionals despite the adverse circumstances. During such a massive resizing effort, the role of HR is not always clear. Typically, HR is seen as a non-revenue-producing role and is likely to be high on the list of to-be-cut jobs. Moreover, there is an increased workload in the function to process all the personnel changes, often with increasingly fewer people to do the work. At the same time, HR personnel usually are being sought out for emotional support. Despite this challenge that we too had to face, we worked hard immediately after the announcement of the deal to influence the mind-set of our HR staff so that they saw the experience as an opportunity to learn and build competence throughout every phase of the combination. In addition, we found ways to educate senior executives and line managers about the potential pitfalls of mergers and acquisitions. We designed and implemented responsive and adequate interventions to allow the organization to deliver its strategic objectives while at the same time preparing it for its future destiny.

Any HR professional who is faced with resizing issues should respond proactively. Resizing efforts build character, professionalism, competence, and an opportunity for superior performance. These are qualities that are at the top of the list when companies seek to recruit their future strategic HR people.

CHAPTER 3

Another Layoff? A Dot-Com Reality!
My Story
Jeffrey Crandell

Working for an Internet start-up company as a human resources (HR) professional has its highs and its lows. An Internet start-up is a fast-paced and ever-changing environment that forces you to hit the ground running. You learn aspects of your job that you would not have experienced if you were working in a more established or traditional company. The philosophy is that time is money, and growth is the key to success. In this environment, the main responsibility of an HR professional is to hire, hire, and hire. Fill that bubble with talent, and help create an organization that will attract candidates from all over the world.

The Internet bubble has burst. The company I work for was a spin-off of a large media company. Within a year, my company grew from twenty employees to over four hundred. Every department was growing, with three employees seated in one cubicle, facilitating new employee orientations every other day. Days like these make you flex your HR muscle and put everything you have learned about recruiting, benefits, employee relations, and training to the test to make this growing machine roll as smoothly as possible. The one piece missing in the picture was profit. The company was not

---

Jeff Crandell's last day of work at Snowball.com was February 15, 2002.

making a dime in profit and losing millions. The bubble was about to burst.

Less than a year after topping off at over 400 employees, we now are a company with approximately 110 employees. The road getting to 110 employees, like the road to getting to 400 employees, was not an easy one. Nevertheless, it is a road that every HR professional can learn from and may have to go down at some point in his or her career.

One of the challenges that a HR professional has to balance is the desires of the executive staff and board of directors with the needs and rights of employees. When the market changes or revenue declines, the company has to look at its business model and figure out how to cut costs. Staff reduction often is the first area that management considers when attempting to reduce overhead expenses. It is the HR job to make sure that any staff reduction is done legally, fairly, and humanely. It is also the part of the job that is not very pleasant. Concern for people is what made most of us choose HR as a career. We help employees every day in a way that not only affects their work life but their home life as well. Starting a new job is a big milestone. Losing a job can be devastating.

Snowball.com develops and maintains Internet Web sites. Like most other Internet firms, it is only a few years old and grew very quickly and then contracted quickly. It has gone through four layoffs since its height. These reductions were due to shutting down of some on-line networks. The first reduction in force occurred in May 2000. The employees who were let go during this layoff worked directly on those networks. We paid out three months' severance pay to those employees. The second layoff, in October 2000, was primarily a reduction in overall workforce, and cuts were made across the board. About three months later, in January 2001, we implemented an even larger layoff—another across-the-board reduction in force. Employees were given an average of one month's severance pay if they had been employed one year or longer and three weeks if they had been employed less than a year. All of these job reductions were implemented on an involuntary basis. On the morning of the layoff, employees were informed by their respective manager or the director of their division that their job had been eliminated. On average, they were allotted about three hours to pack up their belongings and leave the building. The largest, and probably the most emotional, layoff was the most recent. For months, we experienced a lot of turnover within our company. The job market was hot, and people could go anywhere they wanted. Now, people do not have the same options. Employees are holding on to their jobs, happy to receive a paycheck every two weeks. Consequently, conducting a layoff during these times is even more painful for everyone. Everyone from the executives making the reduction decisions to those employees remaining who have just lost their coworkers and friends feels the pain.

The Layoff

Prior to our most recent layoff, we had 170 employees. We had conducted a few layoffs and had seen reductions in staff through resignations and performance issues. During this time, the HR department was reduced to one employee: me, supporting 170 employees based in San Francisco, New York, and Los Angeles. During the past six months, our vice president of HR resigned. We had to let our recruiter go, and my HR generalist resigned to move out of state. Thus, the chaos within the company had reached the HR department as well. I knew that another layoff was around the corner, because we had a bad quarter and executives were stalling on hiring a replacement for the HR generalist.

The Process

Monday Evening

Late on Monday, the chief financial officer told me that we were going to implement another reduction and that the executive team wanted to do it within a week. The executive team would like the layoff to occur six business days later, on the following Tuesday. Tuesday was selected because we needed the six business days to decide where the cuts in staff would take place and have time to get everything organized.

Wednesday Afternoon: Five Business Days Before the Layoff

After many meetings and discussions with managers, the final number of job reductions was set at fifty-seven. Because we were not giving sixty days' notice of the upcoming reductions to our employees,

I had to be aware of the Worker Adjustment and Retaining Notification (WARN) Act to ensure that we were not violating any laws. The WARN Act states that a company cannot lay off more than fifty employees, or 33 percent of employees per work site where there are more than one hundred employees, without proper notification. Because we were terminating employees from three locations (San Francisco, Los Angeles, and New York), the WARN Act was not an issue. At this point, our attorney okayed our reduction numbers.

Because of the company's current revenue and the stock price (less than one dollar per share at this time), most employees understood their jobs were not very secure. There was a sense within the company that it was just a matter of time before another layoff would be announced. It was not a great working environment. During the previous month, employees had visited my office to inquire about a layoff and voice concerns about their jobs. I made a point of sitting down with the employees to listen to their apprehensions and fears. I told them that there was no layoff planned at the moment, but that every one of us was working in an uncertain environment and that we all should be saving money and carefully planning for the future. Employees know when a company is in trouble.

How a layoff should be conducted always is up for debate. Do you tell people in advance? What day of the week do you let them go? What time during the day? Who should do it? How much time do you give them to pack up their belongings? Do you need security in case someone gets violent? Overall, there is no perfect way of implementing a layoff. The whole process is dismal. Laying people off is something that you never want to get good at doing. The most important thing to remember is that the decisions being made are affecting people and their families. I have found that many executives are afraid of the whole process of downsizing. Often, they make the decisions to lay off staff, but on the day of the layoff, they are nowhere to be seen. They leave the dirty work for middle management and HR professionals to do. I think it is extremely important that top executives are visible and available for every employee during a layoff. It sends a powerful message to employees being let go, as well as employees remaining in the company, that their leadership is not afraid to face their decisions and those individuals affected by them. It is our job as HR professionals to see that employees exit the company in the most professional, respectful, and compassionate way possible. I believe it is imperative that the organization's leadership sees it this way too.

When to Tell People

Thursday Morning: Three Business Days Before the Layoff

The company was reducing staff in some departments by more than one-half. We decided that it made more sense for managers to talk to their employees individually and inform them about the reduction on Thursday morning, three business days before the layoff. This approach would give time to employees who were being let go to give their work to those remaining and give them a few extra days to get their bearings. In addition, managers could check in with employees remaining and make sure they were willing to take on additional tasks. Another major reason we decided to tell people early was that it is nearly impossible to keep an upcoming layoff of such magnitude a secret.

Preparing the Final Packages

Thursday Afternoon: Three Business Days Before the Layoff

Now it is time to kick into administrative overload and prepare the final packages for the exiting employees. It is imperative to be organized and thorough when putting packages together. If all of the paperwork is in order, the day of the layoff will run much more smoothly and you can focus on what is really important: the people. Putting packages together takes time and can be tedious. Here is the process that I followed to make sure I had everything covered.

First Things First

It is imperative that the list of employees being laid off remains confidential, even after the employees have been notified. Typically, the only employees who should be given access to the names are the executives, the hiring manager, the HR manager, and the payroll manager. Payroll has to cut their final checks.

It also is important to examine employee files and check for any special agreements or circumstances. Some employees, depending on their level, may have separation agreements included in their original job offer. Give the final list to the payroll manager, so he or she can cut final and severance checks. Payroll also can provide the dollar amounts of money owed, so that the amount is available for the separation agreement. Also, get employees' current addresses from payroll. Having the information in an Excel spreadsheet makes for a much more efficient process. You can mail-merge data into letters when you are ready.

Finally, it important to determine what company property the employees have been issued (such as cell phones, credit cards, and laptop computers). This information is usually available from the information technology, accounting, or facilities department.

Putting the Packets Together

Buy enough letter-size manila envelopes (one per employee) for paperwork. In addition, buy a sufficient number of small manila envelopes to collect keys, door badges, and cellular phones from each employee. Purchase address labels to go with each of the envelopes. Also, acquire "sign it here" flags to stick on the documents that the employee needs to sign.

The following material belongs in each employee's packet:

1. Change of address form. Put this right at the front of the paperwork. It is very important that you know the employee's current address, and employees feel reassured that the company knows how to contact them in the future.

2. Separation procedures. This document outlines what is in the final package. People who are being let go may be in shock or confusion. This document should guide them through the paperwork and answer their questions.

3. Two copies of their separation agreement. The separation agreement is a legal document that outlines their termination of employment. It should be on company letterhead and needs to be reviewed by an attorney. Once the employee reviews it and agrees to the terms, he or she signs it and returns it to HR.

4. Final paycheck. A final paycheck is given to the employee, along with information describing exactly what is being paid, such as unused vacation time, bonuses, and severance pay.

5. A reminder of any documents that they have signed, for example, a signed proprietary agreement.

6. Information on Consolidated Omnibus Budget Reconciliation Act (COBRA) benefits the employee is entitled to receive. Explain the cost, how to sign up, and other pertinent information. Employees have the right to sign up and pay for their health insurance for a maximum of eighteen months after their termination date.

7. Stock option summary. If the company provides stock options, all employees should receive a statement showing what options they have been granted and their vesting schedule, as well as when they can exercise it.

8. 401(k) rollover forms and tax information. The 401(k) benefits plan administrator should provide these forms. Make sure employees receive them, so they can roll over any 401(k) money they have in their plan.

9. Unemployment brochures and information. You can get this information off the Internet for each state. The information should be easily understood, along with the telephone numbers and locations of local unemployment offices.

10. Employee assistance program brochures. Provide information and telephone numbers for employees who want to talk to a mental health professional about their layoff. Most employee assistance programs provide counseling and referral services.

Once you have all of the documents assembled, customize them by using mail-merge from the information on your Excel spreadsheet. It makes a difference to an employee who was just let go to see a salutation of "Dear Mary" rather than "To terminated employee." These details let employees know that you and the company take this process very seriously. The more customized and professional you can make the documents, the better. The less information you have to get from the employee, the easier the process will go for both of you.

Once the mail-merges are complete, print the documents and assemble the packets. Using the address labels, I printed out the employee's name, department, and location and placed that label on the large envelope packet. I also printed out the name, department, and location, as well as listed any company property the employee had and placed that on the smaller manila envelope. This approach makes it easy for employees to know what they need to turn in to the company and informs them they can do so by just putting it in the envelope.

Coaching the Managers

Every employee responds differently to a layoff. Some are cool and understanding. Some make light of it. Some sob all day. Others get mad and frustrated. Some become vocal, and some shut down. This diversity of responses also is true for the leadership.

When managers have to make choices to cut employees from their staff, it is very difficult and very emotional. They work with these people every day, and in many cases they are like a family. As an HR professional, it is my job to check in with those managers and help them through this process. I coach each manager on how to talk with the employees who are being let go. I usually meet with the manager in my office to discuss their concerns about that specific meeting. I then tell them exactly what I would say to the employee. I remind them to explain to the employee that this termination is not performance related; it is purely a business decision. We review some of the questions that the employee might ask during the meeting. For example, the most common question employees ask is, "Why me? Why am I getting fired?" I reassure the manager that I will be right there to take the ball if the employee gets angry or really upset. I also inform the manager that sometimes we have to let employees vent or simply respect the fact that they may want to say nothing at all. All we can do at this time is tell the employee in the best way that we can, providing as much support going forward as possible. During a large layoff, middle managers often feel as if they have no control. Walking managers through the paperwork that their employees will be receiving not only helps the employee but also gives some control back to the manager. I outline everything the manager needs to review with the employee and then provide this information to them in writing so they have it as a handy checklist.

The Day of the Layoff

Tuesday morning: 9:00 A.M.

By Tuesday morning, the packets are together and ready to be picked up by the managers. We have decided that the managers will hold their meetings with their employees starting at 9:00 A.M. Because I am the only HR professional, I can sit in on only a few of the meetings. The more experienced managers do not need me in their meetings. However, they know where I am if they want me. I have requested a counselor from our employee assistance plan to be on-site. We informed employees that we were paying them through the end of the day, but they could pack their belongings as soon as they wanted and go home. Employees who were not being laid off could take the day off if they were upset or simply wanted to get out of the office for the day. A companywide meeting was scheduled at starting time the next morning.

After the manager had finished meeting with the terminated employee, the employee came to my office as directed, bringing the paperwork. We signed the necessary documents, and I gave them their severance check. They came to my office with scared faces, some with relieved faces, some with no statement, and a handful with tears in their eyes. You cannot predict how people are going to react. Every person has different personal and professional issues that make the specific situation unique. Even in the Internet environment where layoffs have become commonplace, the pain is still very real.

Why I Work in HR

It is difficult to work hard on a project that has a negative result. It is difficult to see the packets that you created in the hands of your friends and colleagues, knowing they may not be able to make next month's rent or mortgage. All I could do at this point was to listen to every employee who came to my office, answering every question they had, no matter how long the answer took. I was amazed at how many laid-off employees came by to see how I was doing. Many came to thank me for orchestrating a process that can be cold and calculated, and making it one of respect and professionalism. The outgoing employees often wanted to shake my hand, say good-bye, or give me a hug. I definitely hugged back.

My job now is to be available for our terminated employees when they call with questions about their COBRA or 401(k), as well as to ensure that existing employees are able to keep moving forward and motivated to come to work. I try to refocus our remaining employees by providing "brown-bag" training sessions on specific topics related to what is going on in the organization. "Time Management," "Coping with Change," and "Stress Management" are some of the sessions we have conducted. We have begun holding employee lunches once a week hosted by our CEO, president, or CFO and allow open discussion to take place between them and every employee attending the lunch.

My primary goal is to help create a work environment that benefits the employee and the goals of the company. Just as we have a responsibility to ensure our employees have a rewarding experience while on the job, we also have a responsibility to make sure each employee exits the job in the most positive way possible. It is something they will remember for the rest of their lives.

When you look back at previous jobs, what you think of first is not what you did every day on that job but the people you did it with. That is why I work in HR. I am fortunate to work with people from all parts of an organization and assist them in ways that they will remember forever.

CHAPTER 4

Contribution-Based Process for Continually Right-Sizing an Organization
Experiences from W. L. Gore & Associates, Inc.

Raymond G. Lorenz

Aligning a company's staffing levels to the needs of the business often is a difficult task, especially when the business is expanding or contracting quickly. To ensure that a business has the right number of employees is hard enough; throw in other critical factors like appropriate skills, motivation, costs, flexibility, timing, and rapidly changing business conditions, and the task becomes daunting. This is the case for many companies, particularly those competing in volatile and rapidly changing industries, such as the dot-coms and other Internet, telecom, and electronic-based organizations. How does a business get the people it needs, when it needs them, and adjust on the fly to the ups and downs of the business or industry it

---

Much of what is described in this chapter is a result of my experiences obtained while working at W. L. Gore & Associates from August 1989 to October 2000. Some of the principles and methods described in this chapter may be extensions or adaptations of what is actually being practiced at Gore today and are offered as suggestions for right-sizing purposes in general.

serves without totally disrupting workforce performance and morale? This chapter presents a model for accomplishing this task that is based on individual employee contributions aligned with business needs.

Contribution-Based Model for Organizational Sizing

W. L. Gore & Associates has an extensive contribution-based organization whose origins date back to the early days soon after the company was founded in Bill and Vieve Gore's basement in 1958. Then, as well as today, Gore employees (called associates) assessed each other's contribution to the success of the enterprise and ranked each other using a peer-to-peer contribution ranking system. This system is based on associates knowing what their coworkers are working on (their commitments), how important this work is to the success of the business (impact of commitments), and what results are being achieved (effectiveness at completing commitments). Associates who are ranked higher than other associates are perceived to be contributing more toward the company's success than their lower-ranking counterparts. All associates are ranked by their teammates and leaders at least once a year, and the resulting lists place everyone in rank order based on contribution, from highest to lowest. The ultimate goal of the contribution assessment process is to develop a contribution-based rank-order list that is accurate and fair to all parties. The process was relatively simple in the early days when the company was small and everyone knew what everyone else was doing. The contribution assessment process gets more complicated as teams and workplace size grow. This is one of the reasons that Gore has kept its teams relatively small, generally fewer than two hundred associates in total.

The primary use of this ranking information is for pay-setting purposes. People are not paid based on seniority or job title at Gore. Rather, pay is based on the contributions the employee is making to the success of the company. Leaders in the organization use the results of the ranking process to ensure that higher contributors are paid more than lower contributors. This is a critical component of the company's overall compensation system and is believed at Gore to be the fairest way to differentiate wages within the organization. Higher contributors have the opportunity to make more money than lower contributors. This philosophy helps avoid salary compression and ensures that associates who are doing great things for the organization are properly rewarded.

A contribution-based compensation system also has a major influence on the staffing levels within the organization. During the hiring process, Gore recruits associates who have the best chance of helping the organization meet its overall business goals and objectives. As business staffing needs change, the contribution needs of the business ultimately will dictate the outcomes of these staffing decisions. The health of the organization will be maintained and improved as associates with high contribution potential are added and individuals with unacceptably low contribution are removed. This process is best practiced on an ongoing basis to ensure overall organizational health and improvement; it may accelerate in times of major business growth or decline.

Diligence at practicing this process on a continuous basis can minimize or dampen the need to change staffing levels in large chunks during major business shifts, especially downturns. Dealing with low contributors and addressing these situations on a consistent basis is a far healthier situation for all associates. Layoffs may be inevitable when business downturns are large and sudden. Nevertheless, systematic and consistent attention to staffing levels using contribution data can reduce these numbers and ultimately result in a more vital organization with higher morale.

Details of the Model

A contribution-based system for staffing is well integrated with the hiring process. A company following this philosophy is constantly seeking individuals who have the skill and talents necessary to be successful within the organization. Ensuring that the company is populated with people capable of making high contributions is critical to the long-term success of the organization. Consequently, the recruiting effort must seek people who are capable of being high contributors within the organization and the business model and requirements it has developed. In addition, the organization needs a process to assess employee contribution for compensation and other reward and feedback purposes. This process must objectively identify low contributors in order for appropriate action, which gives the employee the direct feedback he or she needs to make performance adjustments and improve. It is crucial that low contributors be given prompt and direct feedback. This is not always easy and can result in some uncomfortable conversations. However, good leadership will ensure that this feedback is obtained and delivered in a professional and timely manner. Employees who do not make the necessary improvements eventually will need to leave the company.

Defining Associates' Contributions

Defining associates' contributions is accomplished by the following steps:

1. Define goals (driven by leadership, usually with associate input) and objectives needed to meet business requirements.
2. Determine tasks needed to achieve goals and objectives.
3. Associates make commitments to complete these tasks. People who have the capability, desire, and team and leadership support make these commitments.
4. Associates attempt to complete commitments.
5. A contribution is a function of how effectively commitments are completed and the relative importance (or impact) of the commitments toward achieving the goal or objective.

The tasks and resulting commitments necessary for a team to reach its objectives or goals ultimately are defined and agreed on by teammates or leadership, or both. Determining what tasks and commitments must be made in order to achieve critical goals and objectives is a vital initial step in this process. If the tasks are not properly defined or not performed effectively, wasted effort results. Ensuring that work tasks are appropriate and sufficient is vital. The rest of the process involves getting the right people committed to performing these tasks by ensuring that the individual contributors have the skills, talents, motivation, and necessary resources to complete their commitments successfully in a timely manner. If the tasks and commitments are correct for the objectives at hand and if all contributors successfully complete their commitments, the team is well on its way to achieving the goals set forth due to these contributions.

Contributions are the direct outcomes of people's work. At Gore, for example, people make their own commitments; they are not assigned work. They choose their commitments based on a combination of factors, such as what needs to get accomplished, what skills are needed to do the work, and their own skill level and interests. Associates work with leaders and other associates to help them choose commitments that are right for them and the business overall. Once these commitments are agreed to, an informal contract is made between the associate and the rest of the enterprise. How critical this work is to the success of the business and how well it is completed ultimately determine what the level of contribution the associate makes to the business.

The Contribution Assessment Process

To ensure a healthy organization that is positioned properly to meet the needs of the business from a staffing standpoint, it is important to have a sound system in place for contribution assessment. High contributors need to be recognized and rewarded for their efforts. Because they are making the biggest impact to the success of the business, they must be kept happy and challenged. These are the people the organization must do its best to retain, no matter what it takes. Jack Welch, chief executive officer of GE, stated in the organization's 2000 annual report:

> In every evaluation and reward system, we break our population
> down into three categories: the top 20%, the high-performance
> middle 70%, and the bottom 10%. . . . The top 20% must be loved,
> nurtured and rewarded in the soul and wallet because they are the
> ones who make magic happen. Losing one of these people must be
> held up as a leadership sin—a real failing. . . . The top 20% and
> middle 70% are not permanent labels. People move between them
> all the time [General Electric, 2000, p. 4].

Conversely, lower contributors need to be given direct feedback as to their situation. They need to show improvement since they are prime candidates for replacement. If an organization wants to strengthen itself, it can least afford to keep these employees. In a growing business, these people need to be replaced with those of higher contribution potential. In a flat or declining business, these people are the most susceptible to losing their jobs as productivity improves or business downturns occur. Obviously, they should be given opportunities to improve their situation, but time is of the essence for them to do so. They are the most vulnerable to job loss in a contribution-based organization, especially when times get tough.

Jack Welch takes a clear and direct stand relative to employees in the bottom 10 percent of a company's contribution list:

> The bottom 10%, in our experience, tend to remain there. A Company that bets its future on its people must remove that lower 10%, and keep removing it every year—always raising the bar of performance and increasing the quality of its leadership. Not removing that bottom 10% early in their careers is not only a management failure, but false kindness as well—a form of cruelty—because inevitably a new leader will come into a business and take out that bottom 10% right away, leaving them—sometimes midway through a career—stranded and having to start over somewhere else. Removing marginal performers early in their careers is doing the right thing for them; leaving them in place to settle into a career that will inevitably be terminated is not [General Electric, 2000, p. 4].

This process is easiest when teams are small and everyone knows what everyone else is doing. As teams grow, it is more difficult for participants to know what others are doing, and therefore it lowers the accuracy and the confidence of the assessment. This can be handled by breaking down the participant lists into smaller subgroups based on functional alignment or some other appropriate subgrouping strategy. These techniques and others are useful and effective at handling increasing numbers. Such approaches also complicate the process, making it more difficult to teach and administer. One of the reasons that Gore traditionally has kept its production teams relatively small is to enable associates to know a larger percentage of the workforce. Consequently, the accuracy of the data collected in the contribution assessment process is improved. Rating integrity is vital since the ultimate goal of the contribution assessment is to ensure that the process is fair and accurate.

Staffing Decisions

This contribution-based model is appropriate for making adjustments to staffing levels as the need exists. The model is a useful tool for both internal job movement and increasing or decreasing the overall workforce size. A job opportunity could be filled in this way:

1. The champion for the new job position (the person who defines the need for the new employee) defines requirements of the job and skills needed to meet these requirements.
2. The opportunity is posted for internal candidates to review and consider.
3. Interested and qualified candidates apply.
4. A selection process is used to identify the best available candidate for the job.

The selection process thoroughly analyzes each candidate's previous contributions to the organization using information obtained through personal interviews, information on previous contribution assessments, and performance reviews. Each candidate's suitability for the open position is assessed based on the job and skill requirements of the posting, the candidate's demonstrated skills and previous contributions, and a combination of other factors related to the candidate's future potential, interests, and other factors.

A similar process is followed for filling position openings with external candidates. Typically, this process is conducted only if a suitable internal candidate cannot be identified. The difficulty when selecting external candidates is that the candidate's previous contribution history is not as well defined, accessible, or traceable. Consequently, additional emphasis must be placed on information supplied by the candidate, personal interviews, and reference checking.

When employees need to be removed from the workforce, a contribution-based system is a fair and appropriate process to consider. The system works well for removing individuals who have not demonstrated the minimum contribution requirements for employment: employees who are consistently at the bottom end of the organization's contribution ranking lists and have not responded adequately to direct feedback and developmental opportunities relative to their contribution deficiencies. The organization needs to separate from these unacceptably low contributors in order to remain healthy.

Precisely where an organization draws the line as to what is acceptable and unacceptable contribution varies. Guidelines set by the organization's leadership and any pertinent employment law requirements need to be considered. Where an organization draws this line also may be dictated on the growth expectations for the business, as well as other factors related to workforce skill level and availability. At GE, this line is drawn directly above the bottom 10 percent of the organization. At Gore, anyone whose contribution is low after repeated feedback is in jeopardy. For example, an associate who is hurting the contribution of other individuals or teams as a result of significant absenteeism, tardiness, or any other behavior that could have a detrimental effect on the contributions of others is a serious problem and needs to be corrected quickly. Associates who are consistently at the bottom of the contribution list over multiple ranking periods are likely candidates for layoff during a business downturn.

Staffing Ramp-Ups or Ramp-Downs

Times of ramp-up or ramp-down are particularly challenging for an organization since the workforce size may need to change significantly over short periods of time. When a business is growing rapidly and the workforce needs to expand quickly to support this growth, a philosophy that uses a candidate's previous contributions and behaviors as a basis of predicting future potential is likely a standard practice in many organizations. The challenge is to assemble this information as quickly and completely as possible to make good hiring decisions. Inevitably, mistakes will happen that result in poor contributors' entering the organization, particularly during a heavy ramp-up. To deal with this, the hiring process needs to learn from these mistakes and take action to prevent similar occurrences. Also, an organization would be wise to separate these problem employees from an organization within the initial ninety-day probationary period of employment. Some method of performance feedback that can quantify a new employee's initial contribution, fit, and potential is a useful tool to ensure mistakes are identified and dealt with promptly. These tools should be aggressively used during the initial ninety-day period so sufficient information can be collected for decision-making purposes. In addition, the information collected during this time is excellent feedback for all new employees, so they know exactly how their early contributions are being viewed. This feedback is valuable input that new employees can use to make adjustments in their work or behavior to improve their overall contribution.

When a workforce is too large for the economic condition the company is facing, ramp-down adjustments may needed. This has been the case for many companies in the telecom, electronic, and other related industries throughout 2001 due to industry slowdowns in those markets. Many companies serving these industries had been ramping up capacity and people in the late 1990s and into the year 2000 to support the seemingly unending growth throughout this period. When economic conditions began to worsen in 2001, many companies had to reduce staff quickly. A typical way most companies reduced staff was through a seniority-based layoff system, with layoffs conducted strictly by company service time, lowest to highest. The major problem with this process is that the newest employees may be higher contributors or have a much higher contribution potential than employees who have been with the company a longer time. Consequently, the business potentially could be weakened by the layoff, terminating higher contributors and retaining lower contributors. A contribution-based reduction plan avoids this outcome. In fact, a contribution-based reduction approach could significantly strengthen an organization if it made necessary cutbacks largely from the bottom of the contribution list. This process is fairer than a seniority-based system since it rewards employees for actual contribution, not simply service time. Such a system is good for the business since the higher contributors remain in the organization after the reduction. It is also good for employees because hard work and higher relative contribution are rewarded. A potential pitfall of using contribution data for layoff purposes is that some employees may be unwilling to participate in the assessment process. The fact that these data eventually may be used to terminate a coworker can alienate some individuals.

Conclusion

A critical component for an effective contribution-based system is obtaining a fair and accurate contribution assessment on a regular basis. The process must be kept up-to-date and aligned annually to the organization's size and structure. If employees in the organization believe the contribution assessment process is implemented fairly and is an accurate representation of each employee's relative contribution, it will have value and be supported.

This information can be useful in many ways for an organization and its people. It has great utility in such areas as compensation, personnel development, and contribution feedback and improvement. A company that measures the contribution of its employees also has a useful and effective tool for ensuring the organization's staffing is sufficient and aligned properly with its business needs. As staffing needs change, it provides the information necessary to make adjustments in a fair, timely, and objective manner. In good times, low contributors can be replaced with higher contributors. In more difficult economic times, a business may elect not to replace these lower contributors and let staffing levels decline. This strategy can reduce the possibility of a larger layoff if conditions worsen. At Gore, this tool is used primarily for compensation purposes, but it is also one of the tools used to identify people for layoff or separation in general.

Although there may be pitfalls and challenges in the contribution assessment process and potential concerns from some employees on how the data are used, the benefits far outweigh these concerns. When implemented with fairness and accuracy as guiding requirements, a contribution-based process can be used to continuously right-size an organization, an ongoing approach that is beneficial for all employees and to the business overall.

Reference

General Electric. (2000). *Annual report.* Available on-line: http://www.ge.com/annual100/letter/page4.html.

CHAPTER 5

The Effects of Organizational Resizing on the Nature of the Psychological Contract and Employee Perceptions of Contract Fulfillment

Scott W. Lester
Jill R. Kickul
Thomas J. Bergmann
Kenneth P. De Meuse

For the past decade, organizations have had to cope with a highly competitive and dynamic marketplace. Executives bought other companies, merged with competitors, sold unprofitable divisions, laid off employees, hired contingency workers, and outsourced jobs in an attempt to survive marketplace pressures. As executives have sought to resize their organizations, they also have developed strategies to increase employee commitment and satisfaction. Initiatives such as team building, participative management, and mentoring communicate to employees that they are valuable assets to the organization and should be nurtured and developed. However, at the same time, these organizations engaged in strategies to reduce labor costs such as outsourcing, hiring more part-time and contract labor, and implementing frequent downsizing efforts. An important issue that executives must ponder is what messages their organizational actions are sending to employees. If employees think that organizations view them as expendable, this likely will have an effect on their perceptions of their psychological contract and its fulfillment.

Resizing and the Psychological Contract

The psychological contract refers to employees' beliefs about the mutual obligations between the employee and his or her organization (Rousseau, 1989). These beliefs are based on the perception that employer promises have been made about such matters as competitive wages, promotional opportunities, and job training in exchange for certain employee obligations, such as the giving of their energy, time, and skills (Rousseau & Tijoriwala, 1998). Earlier reviews by Argyris (1960), Levinson, Price, Munden, and Solley (1962), Schein (1965), and Kotter (1973) argue that the psychological contract is conceptually different from a formal contract in that it considers an individual's beliefs of the terms and conditions of an agreement between the individual and the employer. This concept of the relationship between an employee and the organization has been accepted and noted in many different forums, including academic journals (Morrison & Robinson, 1997; Robinson, Kraatz, & Rousseau, 1994), practitioner journals (De Meuse & Tornow, 1990; Ehrlich, 1994; Sims, 1994; Wilhelm, 1994), and management textbooks (Osland, Kolb, & Rubin, 2001; Robbins, 2001).

Kotter (1973) views the psychological contract as an implicit agreement between the employee and an organization that specifies what each is expected to give and receive in the relationship. Without these expectations, neither the employee nor the employer has the incentive to contribute to each other, and the relationship could not endure. Kotter's interpretation of the psychological contract (1973) contrasts somewhat with the conceptualization of Rousseau and colleagues (Rousseau, 1989, 1990; Robinson et al., 1994). Instead of focusing on mere expectations, Rousseau and her colleagues define a psychological contract as an individual's beliefs regarding obligations that arise in the context of a relationship. The employer and employee believe that both parties have made promises to each other, and both have accepted the same terms of exchange (Rousseau, 1989). However, this does not mean that the employee and employer share a mutual understanding of all of the obligational terms within the contract (Robinson & Rousseau, 1994).

While an employee's formal employment contract always is based on a written document, the types of promises contained in an employee's psychological contract typically are communicated in ways that do not involve written documentation. For example, an employee's understanding of the psychological contract may be influenced by oral discussions with managers, recruiters, or other organizational representatives and construed from specific organizational practices and procedures (Rousseau, 1989; Rousseau & Greller, 1994; Rousseau & McLean Parks, 1993; Sims, 1994). Because of the pervasive norms of reciprocity that are part of any exchange agreement between an individual and his or her organization, an individual often expects, seeks out, and creates a psychological contract as a means for understanding and representing the employment relationship with the employer (Shore & Tetrick, 1994).

Organizations can respond to an employee's psychological contract to varying degrees, including (1) going beyond the conditions of the contract, thereby honoring the intent rather than the letter of the contract; (2) complying with the contract and fulfilling all of the conditions and terms; and (3) breaching or violating the agreement between the employee and the organization (Rousseau, 1995). When organizations uphold their side of the psychological contract with their employees, it is more likely that employees will attempt to fulfill their own contractual obligations to the organization (De Meuse & Tornow, 1990; Rousseau, 1989).

Dimensions of the Psychological Contract

At the broadest level, the literature distinguishes between two major components of the psychological contract: transactional and relational, which emphasize different types of exchange relationships between the employee and the employer (Macneil, 1985; Morrison & Robinson, 1997). In a transactional exchange, organizations promise to provide specific monetary remuneration for employee contributions. Therefore, a short-term agreement between the two parties results because the exchange is defined by economic terms, a close-ended time frame has been established, and the scope of the obligations is very narrow. In contrast, the relational component emphasizes a socioemotive interaction between the parties. Relational elements revolve around trust, respect, and commitment developing over time. A relational exchange exists when both parties expect that this relationship will continue on into the future; in other words, it is open-ended, dynamic, and pervasive (Rousseau, 1995). Table 5.1 summarizes the types of promises that make up the relational and transactional components of the psychological contract.

The conceptualization and measurement of the psychological contract has been the subject of recent debate (Rousseau & Tijoriwala, 1998). Most agree that it is multidimensional, yet its components are discussed in a variety of ways. Some recent research has gone beyond the transactional and relational distinction and identified as many as seven separate contract dimensions (Rousseau, 1998; Robinson, 1996). Turnley and Feldman (1998, 2000) have developed additional items that more fully address the extent to which employees feel they have a good employment relationship. These authors also use scales that capture a full range of potential responses to questions regarding psychological contract fulfillment.

Table 5.1. Examples of the Relational and Transactional Components of the Psychological Contract.

Relational (Intrinsic Outcomes)	Transactional (Extrinsic Outcomes)
Opportunities for promotion and advancement	Competitive salary
	Pay for performance
Continuing professional training	Benefits (for example, health care, retirement, vacation)
Meaningful and challenging work	
A job that provides autonomy and control	Stock options
	Flexible work schedule
Participation in decision making	Safe work environment
Freedom to be creative	
Career guidance and mentoring	

In other words, instead of just asking whether a contract obligation was fulfilled, Turnley and Feldman assert that employees should be asked the extent to which it was fulfilled and given the opportunity to report both underfulfillment and overfulfillment.

The Changing Nature of the Psychological Contract

The employee-employer relationship in the old economy was characterized by long-term commitments where growth and compensation came from expanding domestic markets (Kochan, 2001). This psychological contract promoted lifetime employment and loyalty between employee and employer. The new economy is heavily influenced by global economies and demanding international competition. This globalization has rendered regional labor expendable and interchangeable. While employees in the past could rely on their employer to provide stable wages, we now have a dramatically new economy where job security, task assignment, and organizational stability are uncertain (Kochan, 2001). The new psychological contract emphasizes the need for a short-term orientation in the employment relationship (Rousseau, 1995).

Modern organizations are resizing themselves in a variety of ways. Mergers, acquisitions, restructurings, outsourcings, and layoffs all play a prominent role in the current employment landscape. In fact, research has shown that mergers and acquisitions, as well as layoffs, have reached record levels during recent years. Global merger and acquisition activity reached a record $3.5 trillion in the year 2000, an increase of almost 700 percent over the $514 billion of reported merger activity in 1995 ("M&A in 2000," 2001).

With regard to layoffs, in the first quarter of 2001 alone, there were 1,664 mass layoff actions resulting in a loss of 305,227 jobs. This is the highest number of layoff events and job loss in any quarter since the government started collecting the data in 1995 (U.S. Bureau of Labor Statistics, 2001). In addition, over 50 percent of employers believe these reductions in force are permanent, and thus the affected workers have little or no probability of being recalled. The consulting firm Challenger, Gray and Christmas reported that during April 2001, organizations announced 165,564 new job cuts, which is the fifth consecutive month with cuts exceeding 100,000 ("Announced Job Cuts," 2001). During the early 1990s, many experts believed that mass layoffs were a temporary event and eventually employment stability would return to normal. However, each year has seen a constant flow of new layoff announcements. These 2001 figures follow record layoffs in 1999 and 2000, in which all sectors of the economy were represented (manufacturing, retail, service, and now the dot-com companies).

The biggest impact that these resizing strategies have on the changing psychological contract is that they undermine perceptions of long-term job security. Because job security does not appear to be a core tenet of the new employment relationship, employees now are focusing more attention on other inducements, such as autonomy, continuous training, and added responsibilities (Jaffe & Scott, 1998). In general, today's employees want to be empowered and expect to retain their marketability in case their current employment relationship is severed.

Organizational Resizing and Psychological Contract Breach

Morrison and Robinson (1997) define psychological contract breach as the cognition that one's organization has failed to fulfill one or more obligations comprising the psychological contract. This type of breach can cause the employee to have intense attitudinal and behavioral reactions toward the employer (Rousseau & McLean Parks, 1993; Robinson et al., 1994). When breaches or violations occur within an employee's psychological contract, a variety of unfulfilled promises can deprive the employee of desired outcomes and benefits (Robinson & Morrison, 1995; Robinson & Rousseau, 1994).

From an equity theory perspective (Adams, 1965), individuals try to find an equitable balance between what they receive from the organization and their own contributions. When employees perceive that their employer has failed to fulfill promised inducements, they may withhold their own designated contributions by reducing their performance or refusing to engage in expected organizational citizenship behaviors. In one study, Robinson and Rousseau (1994) found that approximately 55 percent of employees believed their psychological contract had been violated by their organization during the past two years. These researchers observed that employee trust and satisfaction were inversely related to violations of the psychological contract. In addition, they found that psychological contract violations were positively related to employee turnover. Finally, their results revealed that careerism moderated the relationship between contract violations and trust, satisfaction, and intentions to remain with the employer. Individuals high on careerism "perceived their current employer as an instrumental stepping-stone up the interorganizational ladder" (p. 249). In other words, the more careerist the employee was, the stronger the relationship was between perceived contract violations and lack of trust in the organization.

Robinson (1996) also investigated the relationships between specific types of contract breaches and employee reactions, attitudes, and behaviors. Robinson examined seven types of employer obligations and promises drawn from Rousseau's measure of psychological contracts (1990). In her research, Rousseau interviewed human resource managers from thirteen engineering, accounting, and manufacturing companies and identified the following seven obligations that are most commonly promised by recruiters and organizations to applicants: (1) promotion and advancement, (2) high pay, (3) pay based on current level of performance, (d) training, (5) long-term job security, (6) career development, and (7) sufficient power and responsibility. Overall, Robinson (1996) found moderate relationships between specific contract breaches and trust, civic virtue, performance, and intentions to remain with the organization. For instance, all of the seven obligations were moderately related to an employee's intention to remain with the organization. Pay based on performance, training, career development, and sufficient responsibility were associated with trust. High pay, training, and career development were related to organizational citizenship behaviors (civic virtue). Promotion and responsibility were associated with actual turnover, and career development was related to job performance.

In the same study, Robinson (1996) found that prior trust in the organization at the time of hiring moderated the association between psychological contract breach and trust eighteen months after employees were hired. Individuals with low prior trust in the organization exhibited lower feelings of trust after a contract breach than did those individuals who had high initial trust in their relationship with their employer. Robinson contended that these findings were consistent with the research on attitude function and cognitive consistency (Eagly & Chaiken, 1993). She argued that individuals with high initial trust are likely to assimilate aspects of an unfulfilled psychological contract into their initial attitude of trust in their employer and thus see a contractual infraction in a positive way. Individuals who have a low level of initial trust are more likely to interpret the unfulfilled promises in an unfavorable manner, thereby confirming their initial attitude regarding the organization.

The measure of trust that Robinson used in this study included items such as, "In general, I believe my employer's motives and intentions are good," "My employer is open and upfront with me," and "I believe my employer has high integrity." These items address a type of trust that McAllister (1995) labels cognition-based trust. Cognition-based trust is grounded in an individual's belief about peer reliability and dependability. It differs from affective trust in that it is not contingent on an individual having a strong emotional attachment with the other party. The establishment of cognition-based trust between employees and organizational leaders will play an important role in the success of resizing strategies, because it will facilitate communication efforts between the two parties.

Employee Responses to Psychological Contract Breach

The first aspect that is likely to have an impact on employees' reactions to psychological contract breach is the level of importance they place on the outcomes that have been breached. The expectancy theory of motivation proposes that employees will be more motivated to perform if they value the outcomes they receive when they perform at a high level. This is the valence component of expectancy theory (Vroom, 1964). Building on this theory, it seems reasonable to expect that an employee will be motivated to make more extreme responses to contract breach when the outcomes that have been violated are extremely important to that individual.

Lester and Kickul (2001) examined which psychological contract obligations employees perceived as being most important and how well employers were fulfilling these obligations. Their findings revealed that employees rated obligations that were more relational in nature (such as open and honest communication, meaningful work, and trust and respect) as most important. Furthermore, they found that many of these more important obligations were the same ones that organizations were finding more difficult to fulfill. As expected, discrepancies between the importance placed on an obligation (by the employee) and the perceived fulfillment of this obligation were significantly related to employees' attitudinal responses. Specifically, larger discrepancies were associated with lower levels of job satisfaction and greater intentions to leave the organization.

Employee Attributions for Psychological Contract Breach

The types of attributions that employees make when they perceive a psychological contract breach has occurred also may influence their responses to breach. Previous theorists have proposed different categories of attributions that individuals may report in the event of a breach.

Rousseau (1995) and Morrison and Robinson (1997) suggest three main reasons that psychological contracts go unfulfilled. First, *reneging* occurs when organizations intentionally and willfully fail to keep their commitments to employees. For example, organizations sometimes engage in layoffs even when they are making sizable profits and members of the top management team are receiving large bonuses. In such cases, individuals are likely to perceive that the organization could have lived up to its prior commitments but chose not to do so.

Second, *disruption* occurs when the organization is unable to live up to its prior commitments due to changing economic or environmental factors. Often, this type of psychological contract breach occurs when the organization is suffering financial hardship or unexpected changes force it to alter existing practices. For example, when an organization's profit margins are shrinking, employees may expect that the organization will implement staff reductions, merge departments, or close units.

Third, *incongruence* occurs when the employee recognizes that there has been an honest misunderstanding regarding the terms or conditions of the employment relationship. In such instances, while employees do not receive what they expected, they recognize the organization perceives that it is living up to its end of the bargain. For example, employees may misunderstand the nature of the organization's profit-sharing plan. Thus, when the organization fails to make its profit target and bonuses are lower than expected, employees may perceive that they have not received all the compensation they expected. However, they may recognize that the organization did not deliberately mislead them and may attribute the breach to miscommunication or their own lack of diligence in finding out exactly what was being offered (Lester, Turnley, Bloodgood, & Bolino, 2002).

Since the psychological contract is based on an exchange relationship, we believe that it is important to include a fourth category of attributional response. We label this category of response *nullification*. Remember that employees offer their contributions to the organization in exchange for the inducements they expect to receive. Thus, there may be cases when the psychological contract has been nullified due to the employee's failure to live up to his or her end of the bargain. Although the self-serving bias makes it unlikely that employees will make this particular attribution very often, it is important to recognize this possibility.

When employees perceive that contract breach occurred because their organization intentionally reneged on its promises, we hypothesize that they will respond more negatively. Conversely, if employees indicate that the cause of psychological contract breach was beyond the organization's direct control, we predict them to be more forgiving of the perceived violation. In an initial study to examine attributions for psychological contract breach, researchers found that employees were more likely to attribute breach to reneging while their supervisors were more inclined to attribute breach to factors outside the organization's control (Lester et al., 2002). Consequently, it is critical that organizations make necessary and relevant information available to employees so that they understand when psychological contract breach has resulted from environmental conditions beyond the organization's control.

Psychological Contract Breach and Employee Perceptions of Justice

Other circumstances that may influence responses to breach include an employee's perception of the underlying reasons and considerations taken by the organization when a breach has occurred. Two such factors are procedural justice and interactional justice (Morrison & Robinson, 1997).

Procedural justice refers to the fairness of the decision-making processes underlying the allocation of outcomes rather than the outcomes themselves (Thibaut & Walker, 1975). Leventhal, Karuza, and Fry (1980) suggested there are at least six procedural rules that individuals use in judging fairness:

1. Procedures that are consistent across individuals and over time (consistency)
2. Decisions that are grounded on good information and informed opinion (accuracy)
3. Opportunities in place that can be used to modify or reverse decisions based on inaccurate information (correctability)
4. Allocation processes that represent the concerns of all important subgroups and individuals (representativeness)
5. Allocation processes that are compatible with prevailing moral and ethical standards (ethicality)
6. No personal self-interest and blind allegiance that may narrow preconceptions (bias suppression)

Any violation by a decision maker or an organization can lead to perceptions of procedural injustice.

Interactional justice deals with how an individual is treated during the enactment of procedures (Bies & Moag, 1986). This form of justice includes whether individuals believe that the reasons underlying a resource allocation decision were clearly and adequately explained to them (Bies, Shapiro, & Cummings, 1988) and whether those individuals responsible for implementing a decision treated them with both respect and dignity (Bies & Moag, 1986; Shapiro, Buttner, & Barry, 1995). An explanation of why interpersonal treatment influences justice judgments can be found in group value theory (Lind & Tyler, 1988). According to this theory, individuals value their relationships with work groups and organizations. When there is a perception of fair treatment, employees may feel that they have a respected and dignified position within the group or organization, thereby heightening their feelings of self-worth. These feelings may be seen in their working relationships with others where they take pride in being a group or organizational member (Lind & Tyler, 1988; Tyler, 1994; Tyler, Degoey, & Smith, 1996).

Organizations are most likely to minimize negative connotations associated with resizing efforts when employees perceive high levels of procedural and interactional justice within their organizations. When this occurs, individuals are more likely to accept the explanations and justifications behind the resizing efforts as legitimate and thereby reason that the organization is reacting in a fair and appropriate manner given the surrounding conditions and circumstances that may be beyond the organization's control (such as a poor economy). However, the absence of adequate justifications or explanations, combined with the loss of an outcome, may imply that an employee is not worthy of respect and is seen as an insignificant organizational member. The employee, in turn, may have strong feelings of anger and blame the organization for being causally responsible for the downsizing activity.

Folger (1993) noted that "exonerating behaviors (ethically responsive and socially desirable) that have no causal implications for outcomes (e.g., advance notice, apologies, timely information, courteousness, considerateness, honesty, and the like; cf., Folger & Bies, 1989) can keep the decision maker from being a target of resentment that increases as the perceived severity of the outcome loss increases" (p. 177). Thus, employees will react more negatively to unfair outcomes when an organization fails to use equitable procedures and conducts itself in an inappropriate manner, that is, when procedural and interactional justice violations have occurred.

Individual Differences and Responses to Psychological Contract Breach

An interesting avenue for additional research includes incorporating individual difference variables as moderators of the relationships between psychological contract breach and negative employee attitudes and behaviors. One such individual difference variable is equity sensitivity (Huseman, Hatfield, & Miles, 1985, 1987; King, Miles, & Day, 1993; Miles, Hatfield, & Huseman, 1989). The equity sensitivity concept goes beyond equity theory by exploring individual differences in how one perceives what is and is not fair. It also examines how these perceptions can have an influence on an individual's reactions to injustices within the workplace. Huseman and his colleagues (1985, 1987) contend that there are three types of individuals who have varying degrees of sensitivity to equity: benevolents, equity sensitives, and entitleds.

Miles, Hatfield, and Huseman (1989) have asserted that the concern for the relationship between the employer and employee and the desire for outcomes differentiates one type of individual from another. At one end of the spectrum are the benevolents, who place their emphasis on the relationship with their employer. At the opposite end of the spectrum are the entitleds, who believe that personal outcomes are of primary importance in dealing with their organizations. In the middle of both benevolents and entitleds are the equity sensitives, who place the same emphasis on having a good employment relationship and achieving desired outcomes. For the three forms of equity sensitivity, it may be interesting to explore how individuals differ in their reactions when their psychological contracts have been breached and both procedural and interactional injustice are present.

Preliminary research suggests that the entitled individual responds more negatively to psychological contract breaches that affect tangible, extrinsic outcomes such as pay and benefits (the transactional component of the contract). Conversely, the benevolent individual tends to react more negatively when promises of autonomy and control, such as relational outcomes associated with a long-term employment relationship, are broken (Kickul & Lester, 2001).

Implications for Managing the Psychological Contract

When management introduces resizing initiatives, employees frequently perceive these transitional periods as highly stressful times. Organizational change often brings with it a sense of apprehension, concern, and uncertainty. This feeling of uncertainty is particularly stressful when employees perceive they have little control over the outcomes that will result from proposed changes or the process that leads to those changes. The rumors that emerge prior to the actual implementation of changes often are far worse than reality, because in the absence of information, employees' perceptions and behaviors are driven by their emotions. Once an organization has decided that resizing is the only feasible response to competitive pressures on the organization, management must identify the specific actions it will implement to maintain a sound psychological contract between the organization and its employees.

We believe that organizations will have a better chance of upholding their psychological contracts and achieving the goals and objectives of their resizing initiative by honestly addressing four key questions:

1. Why is resizing necessary?
2. What processes should be in place to address employee perceptions of justice?
3. How will resizing affect the various positions and responsibilities throughout the company?
4. How will resizing modify the personal outcomes that organizational members will receive?

Communicating this information should greatly increase employee satisfaction and performance levels during (and after) resizing. If the issues are effectively addressed, a more positive psychological contract will exist between the employee and the employer, and resizing efforts will be facilitated.

The Importance of Open Communication

Perhaps the most important component when resizing an organization is to have an effective communication system. When change is implemented, managers obviously are concerned about what types of information need to be communicated to employees to ensure that change activities run as smoothly as possible. A longer-term concern is how human resource practices can be used to ensure open communication persists over time in order for future change initiatives to be effective. Organizations that are successful in their resizing efforts need to have good communication throughout the organization. We describe why communication across multiple levels of the organization is an important part of resizing efforts by introducing the concept of a communication triad. Table 5.2 summarizes how each triad member contributes to effective communication during resizing.

**Table 5.2. Communication Strategies of
Triad Members During Resizing Initiatives.**

Key Organizational Roles	Communication Strategies
Chief executive officer (CEO)	Discuss with all employees why the organizational change initiative was necessary to improve the organization's performance and ability to compete.
	Maintain constant dialogue to answer questions and provide additional input to meet employee expectations and needs.
	Communicate with organizational members about their role in the organization's ability to achieve the leader's vision for the future.
Human resource staff	Monitor employee attitudes and needs to determine when future public forums between the CEO and employees are needed.
	Facilitate many of the resizing benefits provided to employees who are being displaced (for example, schedule outplacement services, coordinate employee severance packages, and provide counseling services).
	Engage in activities such as providing counseling, updates on new compensation packages, and additional job training to those who are remaining with the organization.
First-line supervisors	Serve as the change liaison between top management and employees on a daily basis.
	Provide information and answers to questions that arise as the organizational change effort evolves.
	Correct inaccurate rumors that are traveling along the corporate grapevine.
	Allocate time to respond to questions concerning what is now expected from employees in the organization over the short and long terms.

Due to today's constantly changing business environment, organizations may alter the nature of the psychological contracts they have with their employees. Obligations that the organization previously acknowledged may no longer be fulfilled as previously promised. During these dynamic times, employees become more focused on whether they feel the organization is treating them fairly. In other words, employees take time to process the information being presented to them by the organization and its agents (the supervisors) and assess whether they perceive the change initiatives as necessary responses to a dynamic business environment or violations of psychological contract obligations regarding fairness. Therefore, this is a time where it is important for organizations to communicate more (not less) with their employees.

The employer and employee may not always share a mutual understanding of the psychological contract obligations that are being offered. Open communication is a vital mechanism for increasing the chances of mutual understanding. It is important to remember that whether employees' perceptions of psychological contract breach are accurate does not matter. Perceived breaches still will lead to negative attitudinal and behavioral responses. The development of an effective communication network is an essential element of an organization's resizing strategy.

The Communication Triad

It is important that the organization develop a truly integrative communication team to deal with both employees who are being laid off and those who are being relied on to execute the new organizational strategies. There are three key levels that must be highly involved in this communication process. The chief executive officer (CEO), the human resources staff, and the first-line supervisors all must be sensitive to the uncertainty in this changing environment.

Chief Executive Officer

Although employees may look to their immediate supervisors first when assessing levels of psychological contract fulfillment, they are likely to focus more attention on top executives when making attributions as to why psychological contract breaches are occurring. The CEO's role is to meet with all employees to explain why resizing is necessary and how the action will improve the organization's performance and ability to compete in the marketplace. It is important that the CEO remain visible throughout the change period (De Meuse, Vanderheiden, & Bergmann, 1994). If the CEO is not willing to interact with employees and answer difficult questions during these transitional times, employees are likely to perceive that the organization does not value them. This inference will lead to barriers in the implementation of resizing activities and possibly have a negative effect on perceived psychological contract fulfillment.

Other writers have suggested that in the interest of effective time management, CEOs should communicate only to supervisors and managers (Larkin & Larkin, 1996). Although we acknowledge this may be prudent for routine business activities, it is important for employees to hear directly from executives when major change initiatives are under consideration. Resizing organizations must work hard to gain their employees' commitment to their vision for the organization's future. Often this becomes an issue of leadership. Successful leaders are able to communicate a vision of success to their followers (Conger & Kanungo, 1987). Leaders also can inspire higher performance levels by communicating to each organizational member how he or she will play a pivotal role in the organization's ability to achieve the leader's vision for the future. In other words, organizations need to go beyond merely explaining why resizing and other change initiatives are necessary and communicate why their employees should expect to be successful in the new business environment. If employees comprehend the potential benefits of the changes, they will be more likely to perceive that they have been treated justly. These perceptions of procedural and interactional justice will lead to higher levels of psychological contract fulfillment and increase organizational commitment.

Human Resource Staff

Resizing organizations must have a good idea of where they want to go and ensure to the best of their ability that they will be able to convince employees that this new direction is desirable for all parties involved. First, organizations need to gather information concerning what psychological contract obligations employees perceive as being most valuable. Probably the best way to do that is to gather feedback from an employee survey. In essence, organizations need to know what employees want if they hope to retain and motivate the key people in their workforce. Understanding what employees value most will allow an organization to be more prudent in the implementation of its resizing efforts, because organizational leaders will be better equipped to minimize the number of employees who perceive serious psychological contract breaches.

The organization must constantly monitor the changing need structure of its employees. This process should be tied to the strategic direction of the organization. Human resource managers need to be aware that as the strategic direction of the organization changes, the operational design of the total reward package and its method of implementation (performance assessment) also must change in order to increase the likelihood that it will satisfy the needs of employees. By looking at all of the total reward dimensions (for example, pay, benefits, and employee development), the organization may be able to satisfy the needs of a larger number of employees during resizing.

In addition, human resource managers are facilitators for many of the resizing benefits provided to employees who are being displaced, as well as to employees who remain with the organization. For example, the human resource staff should schedule outplacement services, coordinate employee severance packages, and provide counseling services to assist layoff victims. To respond to the needs of surviving employees, the human resource staff should engage in activities such as providing counseling, updates on new compensation packages, and additional job training.

When there have to be changes in the psychological contract, employers should seek to modify it in terms that are reflective of the new employment conditions. Both procedural and interpersonal remedies may be used to reduce some of the adverse consequences that may arise for the organization when changes to the psychological contract are made (Morrison & Robinson, 1997; Rousseau, 1995). Remedies to reestablish a relationship may include instituting communication mechanisms that inform employees how decisions are made and implementing procedures that allow employees to challenge or appeal job decisions made by the firm. Human resource managers should ensure that employees understand how the organization is trying to meet their multiple needs. In addition, they should give employees the opportunity to express any new changes in their expectations of what they believe their organization should provide to them. By focusing on their needs, in conjunction with organizational capabilities and resources, the manager may enable the company to retain key talent.

First-Line Supervisors

First-line supervisors are an integral part of a successful change initiative, because they serve as the change liaison between top management and employees on a daily basis (Larkin & Larkin, 1996). Although companies are very cognizant of the detrimental impact of layoffs on those who lose their jobs, they often forget about the struggles of those who remain with the organization. Noer (1993) labels these struggles "layoff survivor sickness" and identifies the debilitating symptoms that may accompany this sickness, such as anger, guilt, fatigue, stress, anxiety, and fear. Noer recognizes a major reason for the long-term suffering of layoff survivors is that they feel violated by changes in the psychological contract.

Employees are dependent on supervisors to provide information and answers to questions that arise as resizing evolves. By keeping employees informed, these individuals can increase the likelihood that employees will view the changes in a more positive light. Managers need to be sensitive about correcting inaccurate rumors traveling along the corporate grapevine and set aside time to respond to questions concerning what is now expected for the company in the short term and the long term.

Social Accounts During Resizing Efforts

From a theoretical perspective, social accounts have been defined as managerial justifications used to explain the actions undertaken by an organization and its representatives (Sitkin & Bies, 1993; Rousseau & Tijoriwala 1999). These social accounts are intended to address employees' questions concerning who is responsible for the actions taken, what the motives are for the action, and how unfavorable this action might be for employees (Sitkin & Bies, 1993). Previous research has demonstrated that social accounts can play an important role in facilitating a variety of desirable outcomes, such as helping to socialize new employees into an organization, managing conflict among a wide variety of parties (Sitkin & Bies, 1993), and avoiding retaliatory behaviors when employee pay has been cut or budget proposals have been rejected (Greenberg, 1990; Bies & Shapiro, 1988).

Cobb and Wooten (1998) discuss why social accounts may have a significant effect on perceptions of fairness and consequently perceptions of psychological contract fulfillment in the midst of organizational change. They conclude that "social accounts can address the full range of justice issues that emerge in change" (p. 77). The full range of justice issues are distributive justice, procedural justice, and interactional justice. Distributive justice deals with the fairness of the outcome itself (such as job loss during a downsizing), procedural justice addresses the fairness of the procedures that guided the action (such as what the layoff criteria were and how they were determined), and interactional justice is the extent to which employees were treated with respect and dignity (for example, whether managers were empathetic when informing layoff victims of their job loss). Because social accounts can address all these issues, they are versatile and powerful justice interventions (Cobb & Wooten, 1998).

Managers who effectively use social accounts during change initiatives are more likely to convince their followers that the changes taking place are fair, because they were caused by matters beyond the organization's control (mitigating responsibility), implemented in order to facilitate the achievement of shared goals (exonerating motives), or far more desirable than any of the other feasible alternatives (reframing; Sitkin & Bies, 1993). In summary, reactions to changes in the psychological contract will be more positive when social accounts are taken at face value.

Human Resource Practices That Increase the Likelihood of Resizing Success

Previous research has demonstrated the adverse consequences of a poorly implemented downsizing effort. Negative effects can range from financial losses to reductions in employee morale and satisfaction to increased absenteeism and turnover (Mishra & Spreitzer,

1998; De Meuse, Bergmann, & Vanderheiden, 1997). In recent studies that have examined the longitudinal effects of downsizing on an organization's financial performance, the results are inconclusive. There is a lack of strong data to support the belief that downsizing will solve the financial woes of an organization (Cascio, 1998; De Meuse et al., 1994; Vanderheiden, De Meuse, & Bergmann, 1999). Downsizing is only one type of resizing strategy. Nevertheless, this strategy highlights the reality that organizations can no longer promise lifetime employment. Figure 5.1 summarizes and illustrates the value and importance of the human resource strategies discussed in this section as they relate to resizing and the psychological contract.

Figure 5.1. The Value and Importance of Human Resource Strategies During Resizing.

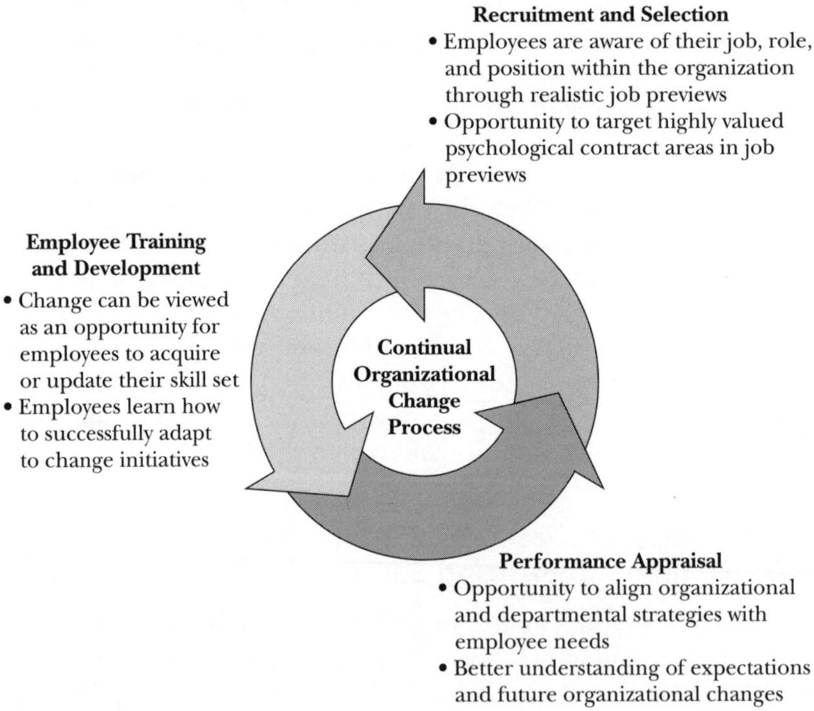

Recruitment and Selection
- Employees are aware of their job, role, and position within the organization through realistic job previews
- Opportunity to target highly valued psychological contract areas in job previews

Employee Training and Development
- Change can be viewed as an opportunity for employees to acquire or update their skill set
- Employees learn how to successfully adapt to change initiatives

Continual Organizational Change Process

Performance Appraisal
- Opportunity to align organizational and departmental strategies with employee needs
- Better understanding of expectations and future organizational changes

Employee Training and Development

Without the promise of job security, employees frequently conceptualize other inducements they receive from the organization as part of the organization's total rewards system. Employee training and development is a key facet of this reward system (Bergmann & Scarpello, 2001). Employees expect that if they do not have job security with the new psychological contract, their employer should at least guarantee that it will provide them the training needed to maintain their marketability (Jaffe & Scott, 1998). Although future employment may not be with their current employer, the employee will have a positive perception of the employment relationship because the employer is assisting the employee in two important ways. First, organizations allow the employee to view change as an opportunity by ensuring that they are able to acquire and update their skill sets. Second, organizations enable the employee to learn how to adapt to resizing initiatives successfully.

In the context of downsizing, a critical piece to managing layoff survivors effectively is to communicate what, if any, changes to their jobs will occur as a result of the downsizing. In addition, management must allay their fears by providing training programs to employees who will experience significant changes in their responsibilities. If employees are confident that they can be successful in the resized organization, they will not be as inclined to resist the change. Resizing efforts also can bring about new opportunities for employees. A crucial aspect of managing a resizing process is to make sure that the remaining employees are clearly informed of the opportunities that exist in the changed work environment (Brockner, 1992).

Performance Appraisal

Supervisory and managerial personnel within organizations should receive guidance on giving employees adequate explanation of all job and role changes. Many of these recommendations may be integrated within the performance appraisal process where employee expectations can be aligned with organizational and departmental strategies and objectives. Roles and responsibilities that are defined and delegated in conjunction with an employee's needs and development may provide them with additional motivation and encouragement toward the common goals of the organization.

For example, supervisors should assess how their subordinates' needs and values may have changed during the year. Relational aspects of the employment relationship, such as relations with coworkers, growth and development issues, and work-family aspects, should be examined within the context of the performance appraisal process. Rewarding employees' contributions in terms of their needs and expectations may give them additional incentive to achieve their job and role requirements, as well as engage in organizational citizenship behaviors (Organ, 1988).

Recruitment and Selection

Given that employee attitudes and behaviors are generally negative following a psychological contract violation, organizations may want to reexamine policies and practices that directly influence how employees formulate and create a psychological contract. One practice that can be applied to manage promises that the organization makes is to give realistic information (such as realistic job previews; Wanous, 1980). This information should be made salient to employees throughout their tenure in the organization, beginning during the recruitment and selection process.

From an organizational cost-saving perspective, the implementation of realistic job previews can be quite substantial. In a recent meta-analysis, Phillips (1998) found that employees who were given realistic job previews prior to hiring were less likely to leave the organization. Given these findings, organizations should reevaluate their recruitment policies and procedures and ensure they allow the applicant to fully understand the type of job, work group, organization, and employment relationship they are entering. The costs associated with using realistic job information are minimal and could be used by a business to reduce turnover, as well as increase employee satisfaction and performance (Wanous, 1980; Phillips, 1998).

Furthermore, organizations may enhance their ability to fulfill psychological contract obligations by targeting highly valued psychological contract areas in their job previews. In other words, recruiters could gather information about an employee's most valued outcomes (early in the process) and then specifically address what the candidate can expect in that area of the employment relationship. If the company is confident in what it can offer in that area, the chances of a successful relationship are good. On the other hand, if an employee prioritizes outcomes that the organization will have difficulty providing, the organization may be better off not to hire that individual.

Conclusion

At the most basic level, organizations have responded to competitive pressures by implementing business strategies (like resizing) that alter the nature of the psychological contract between the organization and its employees. As the psychological contract continues to be transformed, employees frequently perceive their organization as failing to live up to its psychological contract obligations. Resizing efforts make employees more likely to perceive that the relational or socioemotive component of the psychological contract has been violated (Cavanaugh & Noe 1999; De Meuse, Bergmann, & Lester, 2001). Relational elements of the psychological contract focus on the benefits of a long-term relationship built on trust, respect, and loyalty. For many employees, resizing denotes a violation of their expectations of job security. For others, it means a violation of the expectation that organizational members will be treated with respect. These perceptions carry major implications for organizations, since recent research suggests that the relational component of the psychological contract contains obligations that employees value most (Lester & Kickul, 2001). If organizational leaders do not address these perceived psychological contract breaches, their organizations are likely to suffer detrimental consequences. Previous research has demonstrated that psychological contract breach can adversely affect employee attitudes and behaviors (Robinson, 1996; Robinson & Rousseau, 1994).

Fortunately, organizational change and psychological contract breach do not have to be inescapably tied to one another. Management can take a number of steps to reduce the occurrence or magnitude of perceived psychological contract breach. Most of these steps revolve around efforts to improve the communication occurring among executives, human resource staff, supervisors, and the employees who may be affected the most by the changes.

Organizations must build norms of open, honest, and ongoing communication.

Resizing organizations cannot avoid resistance to change completely. Organizations that have made the effort to build cognition-based trust over time with their employees will be more successful in dealing with employee concerns during times of organizational change and likely will face less opposition to the resizing effort. The reason that cognition-based trust has a significant effect on the success of change efforts is that it influences the employees' willingness to accept the social accounts given by organizational leaders. Organizations that are suffering from low levels of cognition-based trust likely will encounter more difficulty in managing their resizing efforts, because change agents within the organization lack credibility. By improving communication networks and more closely aligning human resource practices with organizational strategies, these organizations will build trust. In so doing, they will possess greater capabilities for achieving resizing objectives because their employees will perceive higher levels of psychological contract fulfillment.

References

Adams, J. S. (1965). Inequity in social exchange. In L. Berkowitz (Ed.), *Advances in experimental social psychology* (pp. 267–299). Orlando, FL: Academic Press.

Announced job cuts hit record high in April. (2001, May 3). *USA Today.*

Argyris, C. (1960). *Understanding organizational behavior.* Homewood, IL: Dorsey Press.

Bergmann, T. J., & Scarpello, V. (2001). *Compensation decision making.* Fort Worth, TX: Dryden Press.

Bies, R. J., & Moag, J. S. (1986). Interactional justice: Communication criteria of fairness. In R. J. Lewicki, B. H. Sheppard, & M. H. Bazerman (Eds.), *Research on negotiation in organizations* (pp. 43–55). Greenwich, CT: JAI Press.

Bies, R. J., & Shapiro, D. L. (1988). Voice and justification: Their influence on procedural fairness judgments. *Academy of Management Journal, 31,* 676–685.

Bies, R. J., Shapiro, D. L., & Cummings, L. L. (1988). Causal accounts and managing organizational conflict: Is it enough to say it's not my fault? *Communication Research, 15,* 381–399.

Brockner, J. (1992). Managing the effects of layoffs on survivors. *California Management Review, 34*, 9–28.

Cascio, W. F. (1998). Learning from outcomes: Financial experiences of 311 firms that have downsized. In M. K. Gowing, J. D. Kraft, & J. C. Quick (Eds.), *The new organizational reality: Downsizing, restructuring, and revitalization* (pp. 55–70). Washington, DC: American Psychological Association.

Cavanaugh, M. A., & Noe, R.A. (1999). Antecedents and consequences of relational components of the new psychological contract. *Journal of Organizational Behavior, 20*, 323–340.

Cobb, A. T., & Wooten, K. C. (1998). The role social accounts can play in a "justice intervention." In R. W. Woodman & W. G. Passmore (Eds.), *Research in organizational change and development* (Vol. 11, pp. 73–115). Greenwich, CT: JAI Press.

Conger, J. A., & Kanungo, R. N. (1987). Toward a behavioral theory of charismatic leadership in organizational settings. *Academy of Management Review, 12*, 637–647.

De Meuse, K. P., Bergmann, T. J., & Lester, S. W. (2001). An investigation of the relational component of the psychological contract across time, generation, and employment status. *Journal of Managerial Issues, 13*, 102–118.

De Meuse, K. P., Bergmann, T. J., & Vanderheiden, P. A. (1997). Corporate downsizing: Separating myth from fact. *Journal of Management Inquiry, 6*, 168–176.

De Meuse, K. P., & Tornow, W. W. (1990). The tie that binds—has become very, very frayed! *Human Resource Planning, 13*, 203–213.

De Meuse, K. P., Vanderheiden, P. A., & Bergmann, T. J. (1994). Announced layoffs: Their effect on corporate financial performance. *Human Resource Management, 33*, 509–530.

Eagly, A. H., & Chaiken, S. (1993). *The psychology of attitudes.* New York: Harcourt Brace Jovanovich.

Ehrlich, C. J. (1994). Creating an employer-employee relationship for the future. *Human Resource Management, 33*, 491–501.

Folger, R. (1993). Reactions to mistreatment at work. In J. K. Murnigham (Ed.), *Social psychology in organizations: Advances in theory and practice* (pp. 161–183). Upper Saddle River, NJ: Prentice Hall.

Folger, R., & Bies, R. J. (1989). Managerial responsibilities and procedural justice. *Employee Rights and Responsibilities Journal, 2*, 79–90.

Greenberg, J. (1990). Organizational justice: Yesterday, today, and tomorrow. *Journal of Management, 16*, 399–432.

Huseman, R., Hatfield, J., & Miles, E. (1985). Test for individual perceptions of job equity: Some preliminary findings. *Perceptual and Motor Skills, 61*, 1055–1064.

Huseman, R., Hatfield, J., & Miles, E. (1987). A new perspective on equity theory: The equity sensitivity construct. *Academy of Management Review, 12,* 222–234.

Jaffe, D. T., & Scott, C. D. (1998). Rekindling work commitment and effectiveness through a new work contract. In M. K. Gowling, J. D. Kraft, & J. C. Quick (Eds.), *The new organizational reality: Downsizing, restructuring, and revitalization* (pp. 185–205). Washington, DC: American Psychological Association.

Jones, F. F., Scarpello, V., & Bergmann, T. J. 1999. Pay procedures—What makes them fair? *Journal of Occupational and Organizational Psychology, 72,* 129–145.

Kickul, J., & Lester, S. W. (2001). Broken promises: Equity sensitivity as a moderator between psychological contract breach and employee attitudes and behavior. *Journal of Business and Psychology, 16,* 191–217.

King, W., Miles, E., & Day, D. (1993). A test and refinement of the equity sensitivity construct. *Journal of Organizational Behavior, 14,* 301–317.

Kochan, T. A. (2001). How to update employment and labor policies for the twenty-first century workforce and economy. *Perspectives on Work, 3,* 12–17.

Kotter, J. P. (1973). The psychological contract: Managing the joining-up process. *California Management Review, 15,* 91–99.

Larkin, T. J., & Larkin, S. (1996, May–June). Reaching and changing front-line employees. *Harvard Business Review,* pp. 95–104.

Lester, S., & Kickul, J. (2001). Psychological contracts in the twenty-first century: An examination of what employees value most and how well organizations are responding to these expectations. *Human Resource Planning, 24,* 10–21.

Lester, S. W., Turnley, W. H., Bloodgood, J. M., & Bolino, M. C. (2002). Not seeing eye to eye: Differences in supervisor and subordinate perceptions of and attributions for psychological contract breach. *Journal of Organizational Behavior, 23,* 39–56.

Leventhal, G. S., Karuza, J., & Fry, W. R. (1980). A theory of allocation preferences. In G. Mikula (Ed.), *Justice and social interaction* (pp. 167–218). New York: Springer-Verlag.

Levinson, H., Price, C. R., Munden, K. J., & Solley, C. M. (1962). *Men, management, and mental health.* Cambridge, MA: Harvard University Press.

Lind, E. A., & Tyler, T. R. (1988). *The social psychology of procedural justice.* New York: Plenum Press.

M&A in 2000: Fast start . . . fading finale. (2001, January 4). [Thomson Financial Quarterly League Table.] Available on-line: http://www.tfsd.com/home.asp.

Macneil, I. R. (1985). Relational contract: What we do and do not know. *Wisconsin Law Review*, 483–525.

McAllister, D. J. (1995). Affect- and cognition-based trust as foundations for interpersonal cooperation in organizations. *Academy of Management Journal, 38,* 2449.

Miles, E., Hatfield, J., & Huseman, R. (1989). The equity sensitivity construct: Potential implications for worker performance. *Journal of Management, 15,* 581–588.

Mishra, A. K., & Spreitzer, G. M. (1998). Explaining how survivors respond to downsizing: The roles of trust, empowerment, justice, and work redesign. *Academy of Management Review, 23,* 567–588.

Morrison, E. W., & Robinson, S. L. (1997). When employee feels betrayed: A model of how psychological contract violation develops. *Academy of Management Review, 22,* 226–256.

Noer, D. M. (1993). *Healing the wounds: Overcoming the trauma of layoffs and revitalizing downsized organizations.* San Francisco: Jossey–Bass.

Organ, D. W. (1988). *Organizational citizenship behavior.* San Francisco: New Lexington Press.

Osland, J. S., Kolb, D. A., & Rubin, I. M. (2001). *Organizational behavior: An experiential approach.* Upper Saddle River, NJ: Prentice Hall.

Phillips, J. M. (1998). Effects of realistic job previews on multiple organizational outcomes: A meta-analysis. *Academy of Management Journal, 41,* 673–690.

Robbins, S. P. (2001). *Organizational behavior.* Upper Saddle River, NJ: Prentice-Hall

Robinson, S. L. (1996). Trust and breach of the psychological contract. *Administrative Science Quarterly, 41,* 574–599.

Robinson, S. L., Kraatz, M. S., & Rousseau, D. M. (1994). Changing the obligations and the psychological contract. *Academy of Management Journal, 37,* 437–452.

Robinson, S. L., & Rousseau, D. M. (1994). Violating the psychological contract: Not the exception but the norm. *Journal of Organizational Behavior, 15,* 245–259.

Rousseau, D. M. (1989). Psychological and implied contracts in organizations. *Employee Responsibilities and Rights Journal, 2,* 121–139.

Rousseau, D. M. (1990). New hire perceptions of their own and their employer's obligations: A study of psychological contracts. *Journal of Organizational Behavior, 11,* 389–400.

Rousseau, D. M. (1995). *Psychological contracts in organizations: Understanding written and unwritten agreements.* Thousand Oaks, CA: Sage.

Rousseau, D. M. (1998). The "problem" of the psychological contract considered. *Journal of Organizational Behavior, 19,* 665–671.

Rousseau, D. M., & Greller, M. M. (1994). Human resource practices: Administrative contract makers. *Human Resource Management, 33,* 385–401.

Rousseau, D. M., & McLean Parks, J. (1993). The contracts of individuals in organizations. In L. L. Cummings & B. M. Staw (Eds.), *Research in organizational behavior* (pp. 1–43). Greenwich, CT: JAI Press.

Rousseau, D. M., & Tijoriwala, S. A. (1998). Assessing psychological contract: Issues, alternatives and measures. *Journal of Organizational Behavior, 19,* 679–695.

Rousseau, D. M., & Tijoriwala, S. A. (1999). What's a good reason to change? Motivated reasoning and social accounts promoting organizational change. *Journal of Applied Psychology, 84,* 514–528.

Schein, E. H. (1965). *Organizational psychology.* Upper Saddle River, NJ: Prentice-Hall.

Shapiro, D. L., Buttner, E. H., & Barry, B. (1995). Explanations: What factors enhance their perceived adequacy? *Organizational Behavior and Human Decision Processes, 55,* 23–40.

Shore, L. F., & Tetrick, L. E. (1994). The psychological contract as an explanatory framework in the employment relationship. *Trends in Organizational Behavior, 1,* 91–107.

Sims, R. R. (1994). Human resource management's role in clarifying the new psychological contract. *Human Resource Management, 33,* 373–382.

Sitkin, S. B., & Bies, R. J. (1993). Social accounts in conflict situations: Using explanations to manage conflict. *Human Relations, 46,* 349–370.

Thibaut, J., & Walker, L. (1975). *Procedural justice: A psychological analysis.* Mahwah, NJ: Erlbaum.

Turnley, W. H., & Feldman, D. C. (1998). Psychological contract violations during organizational restructuring. *Human Resource Management, 37,* 71–83.

Turnley, W. H., & Feldman, D. C. (2000). Re-examining the effects of psychological contract violations: Unmet expectations and job dissatisfaction as mediators. *Journal of Organizational Behavior, 21,* 25–42.

Tyler, T. (1988). What is procedural justice? Criteria used by citizens to assess the fairness of legal procedures. *Law and Society Review, 22,* 301–355.

Tyler, T. (1994). Psychological models of the justice motive: Antecedents of distributive and procedural justice. *Journal of Personality and Social Psychology, 67,* 580–863.

Tyler, T., Degoey, P., & Smith, H. (1996). Understanding why the justice of group procedures matters: A test of the psychological dynamics of the group-value model. *Journal of Personality and Social Psychology, 70,* 913–930.

U.S. Bureau of Labor Statistics. (2001, May 17). *Extended mass layoffs in the first quarter of 2001* [News release]. Available on-line: http://www.bls.gov/mlshome.htm.

Vanderheiden, P., De Meuse, K., & Bergmann, T. (1999). And the beat goes on: Corporate downsizing in the twenty-first century. *Human Resource Management, 38,* 261–268.

Vroom, V. H. (1964). *Work and motivation.* New York: Wiley.

Wilhelm, W. R. (1994). Guest editor's note: The employment contract. *Human Resource Management, 33,* 323–324.

Wanous, J. P. (1980). *Organizational entry: Recruitment, selection, and socialization of newcomers.* Reading, MA: Addison-Wesley.

CHAPTER 6

The Impact of Corporate Downsizing on Employee Fulfillment and Organizational Capability

Jack W. Wiley
Scott M. Brooks
Emily L. Hause

A new wave of holistic models of organizational performance has emerged during the past decade. These models share a common framework that explicitly acknowledges the interrelationships among management strategy and leadership practices, employee satisfaction, customer satisfaction, and the financial outcomes for a business firm. Models such as the Service-Profit Chain, Balanced Scorecard, and High Performance Model provide explanations of how organizations become successful; these models help organizations understand, track, and manage their resources. This chapter focuses on a key message of these models: carefully selected employee opinions are leading indicators of future business success. In other words, we suggest that promoting a performance-oriented work environment today will generate greater bottom-line performance tomorrow.

Corporate downsizing is a technique designed to promote organizational success by reducing labor cost, generally an organization's largest expense. Many authors (Cascio, 1998; Vanderheiden, De Meuse, & Bergmann, 1999) have questioned the general success of layoffs in achieving these goals. Indeed, as De Meuse, Bergmann, and Vanderheiden (1997) and Lester and De Meuse (1998) and others illustrate, badly managed layoffs are associated with negative employee opinions and negative implications for financial performance. Armstrong-Stassen (1994) points out that the impact of downsizing on survivors may well be a key element in determining long-term organizational survival. Given these findings, it is the purpose of this chapter to examine how holistic models of organizational performance can help us more effectively understand and manage the impact of layoffs on organizations. More specifically, if certain employee characterizations of the workplace predict success, how do layoffs affect those critical employee opinions?

Models of Organizational Performance

One holistic model of organizational performance, based on a rigorous review of multiple case studies, is the Service-Profit Chain (Heskett, Jones, Loveman, Sasser, & Schlesinger, 1994). Analyzing data from several different services industries, these researchers closely examined the connection of internal management practices, employee satisfaction and loyalty, productivity, value, customer satisfaction and loyalty, growth, and profit. The model they developed to describe these relationships comprises a cause-and-effect series of sequential links: internal service quality practices lead to employee satisfaction, which leads to employee loyalty and productivity, which leads to externally perceived value, which leads to customer satisfaction and loyalty and ultimately to sales growth and profit.

The Service-Profit Chain was subsequently tested at Sears (Rucci, Kirn, & Quinn, 1998). The authors, using a time-series research design, present strong evidence regarding how improvements in employee opinions (descriptions of their work environment as measured through employee surveys) drive specific levels of increase in customer satisfaction, which in turn generate specific levels of revenue growth (see Figure 6.1).

Figure 6.1. The Employee-Customer-Profit Chain at Sears.

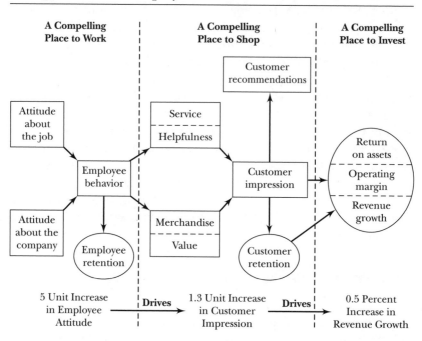

A Compelling Place to Work | **A Compelling Place to Shop** | **A Compelling Place to Invest**

It is clear from the description provided that Rucci et al. (1998) relied on measurement systems focused on the extent to which key elements of Sears's management strategy were successfully operationalized and visible for all three critical stakeholder groups: employees, customers, and investors. The authors concluded that management's strategic focus was working. In other words, the more compelling Sears became as a place to work, the more compelling it became as a place to shop. As sales and revenue grew and store profits increased (as a result of increased customer satisfaction and loyalty), the more compelling Sears became as a place to invest.

Another model of organizational performance that has received significant attention in recent years is the Balanced Scorecard (Kaplan & Norton, 1996a, 1996b), a method for translating management strategy into action. It produces a measurement system that reflects a management team's hypotheses and beliefs about how a set of interrelated variables interacts over time to produce business success. Within this framework, certain variables are leading indicators that predict success; others are lagging indicators that indicate actual performance levels after the performance has occurred. The balanced scorecard contains four perspectives: financial, customer, internal business process, and learning and growth (see Figure 6.2).

The financial objectives serve as the focus for the objectives and measures on all other scorecard perspectives. The idea is that every measure selected for the balanced scorecard should be part of a link of cause-and-effect relationships, culminating in improved financial performance. The customer perspective enables a company to identify and measure the value proposition it will deliver to targeted customers and market segments. The internal business perspective identifies the processes that are most critical to achieving the objectives from the customer and shareholder perspectives. Fundamentally, the learning and growth perspective is posited as the enabler of achieving ambitious objectives in the other three perspectives. In other words, this perspective is viewed as containing the drivers of the outcomes for the other perspectives.

While the Service-Profit Chain and Balanced Scorecard Models are derived from a series of intensive case studies, another holistic model of organizational performance emerged primarily on the basis of larger-scale quantitative studies. Wiley (1996) reviewed previously published empirical studies that examined the relationship between how employees describe their work environment and the relative performance of those work environments from both customer and financial perspectives. Wiley summarized this research and captured the main findings in the High Performance Model (previously referred to as the Linkage Research Model; see Figure 6.3). This model provides a comprehensive framework for integrating all previously published linkage research. It suggests that the more present and visible certain organizational and leadership

Figure 6.2. Balanced Scorecard Framework for Translating Strategy into Operational Terms.

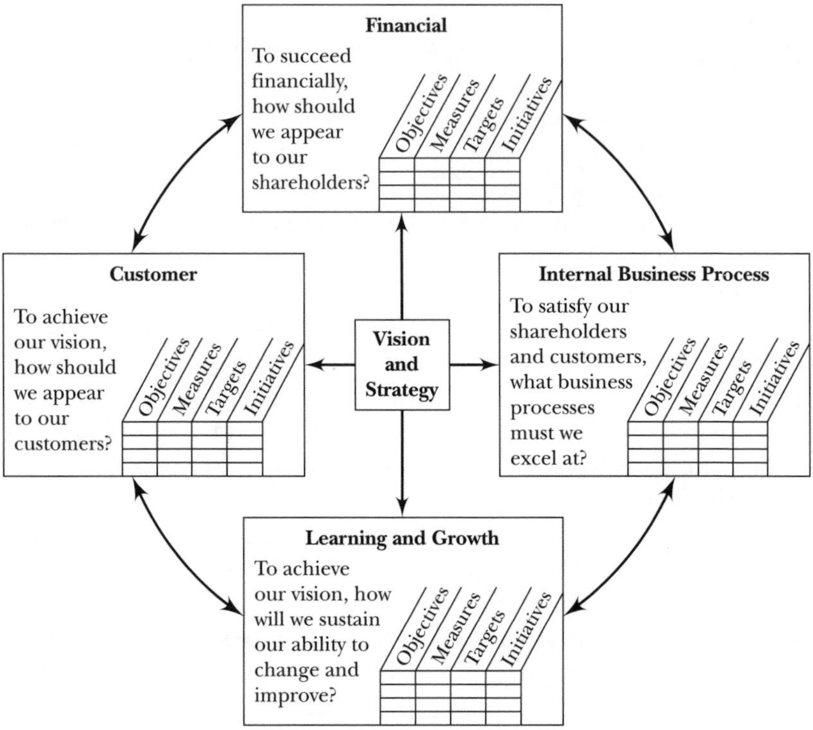

practices are in a work environment, the more energized and productive the workforce is. In turn, the more energized and productive the workforce is, the greater are the satisfaction of customers and the stronger the long-term business performance of the organization.

The model is built around the following conclusions drawn from a summary of linkage research studies:

Figure 6.3. The High Performance Model.

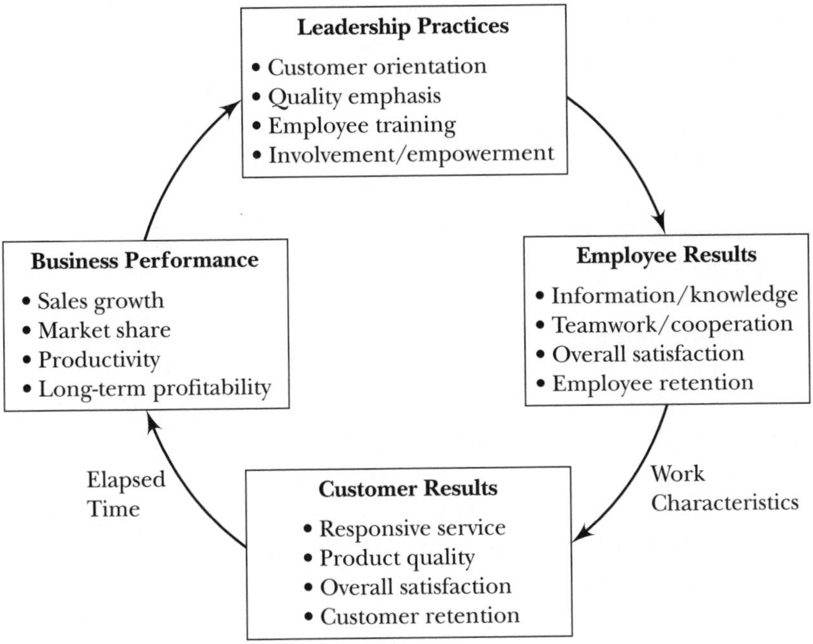

Leadership Practices

- Customer orientation
- Quality emphasis
- Employee training
- Involvement/empowerment

Business Performance

- Sales growth
- Market share
- Productivity
- Long-term profitability

Employee Results

- Information/knowledge
- Teamwork/cooperation
- Overall satisfaction
- Employee retention

Elapsed Time

Customer Results

- Responsive service
- Product quality
- Overall satisfaction
- Customer retention

Work Characteristics

Source: Wiley (1996). © Gantz Wiley Research.

- Employee and customer satisfaction are strongly and positively linked.
- A leadership value system, easily observed by employees and emphasizing customer service and product quality, is fundamental to this linkage.
- Specific practices that the organization and its managers derive from this value system include providing employees with the support, resources, and training required to perform their jobs effectively; involving them in decisions that affect their work; and empowering them to do what is necessary to meet customer objectives and expectations.
- Employee retention is positively related to customers' satisfaction with the quality of service they received.

- Quality and customer satisfaction have long-term positive relationships with customer retention, market share, and profitability.
- Certain practices that increase short-term sales and profits may do so at the expense of employee and customer satisfaction.
- Investment in practices that support quality and employee and customer satisfaction is a long-term business strategy, not a quick-fix solution.
- As the leadership value system over time continues to be regarded as the foundation for achieving higher customer satisfaction and stronger business performance, it becomes self-reinforcing.

Wiley and Brooks (2000) provided a subsequent review of the linkage research literature that added support for the original model. In their review, they also provided three new case studies and, blending those results with the previous research, developed a taxonomy of the characteristics of the high-performance organization. This taxonomy describes in greater clarity and detail, based on descriptions provided by employees, how high-performing units differ from low-performing units.

These new models of organization performance share a common framework that explicitly acknowledges the interrelationship between management strategy and leadership practices, employee satisfaction, customer satisfaction, and the financial consequences for a business firm. There are several reasons why and how this is relevant to a discussion of corporate downsizing, all of which are inherent in these complementary models of organizational performance:

- Downsizing is a tool focused on improving financial performance (generally short term; Cascio, 1998).
- Employee opinions of the work environment are leading indicators of customer satisfaction and long-term business performance (Wiley, 1996).
- Downsizing has a negative impact on how favorably employees characterize their work environment and increases their intention to resign voluntarily (De Meuse & Tornow, 1990).

The remainder of this chapter documents the impact of layoffs on key employee opinions. This research draws on an ongoing multi-decade program of research tracking employee opinions across the United States.

The WorkTrends Database

To examine the impact of layoffs on key employee opinions, we analyzed selected subsets of the WorkTrends survey database. WorkTrends is an ongoing survey program conducted annually by Gantz Wiley Research of Minneapolis, a customer and employee survey research consulting firm. The database was created and is maintained to allow clients of Gantz Wiley Research to compare results of employee surveys conducted within their organizations to a representative and valid external database.

Each year of WorkTrends data is gathered by a survey measuring worker opinions on a broad variety of workplace topics. Subjects participating in the survey are drawn from a random sample of adult workers in the United States. The sample is stratified according to key U.S. census demographics, including age, income, and geography. Surveys are administered in paper-and-pencil form and completed by the principal wage earners of a household, with the requirement that the respondents are full-time employees of organizations employing one hundred or more employees. The WorkTrends database has been used previously as the source of information about worker opinions in the United States. The most recent publication drawing on WorkTrends is *The Changing Nature of Work* (National Research Council, 1999), which examines macrolevel trends in the U.S. economy and uses WorkTrends to complement economic, sociological, and demographic data.

The subsets of the WorkTrends database analyzed for the purposes of this chapter are the years 1990, 1994, 1996, and 2000. In each of these years, 10,000 surveys were administered. The number of respondents in 1990, 1994, 1996, and 2000 were, respectively, 4,055, 5,887, 6,203, and 5,630, representing response rates of, respectively, 41 percent, 59 percent, 62 percent, and 56 percent.

In addition to being asked to express their opinions on a broad variety of workplace topics, respondents to the WorkTrends survey are asked to provide a yes or no answer to the question: "My organization has laid off employees in the last 12 months due to a downturn in business." For the four years under consideration, the percentage of employees who reported working in an organization that had downsized were 34 percent (1990), 36 percent (1994), 35 percent (1996), and 21 percent (2000) (see Table 6.1). It is interesting to note that in the early and mid-1990s, the percentage of organizations laying off employees was relatively stable. In the year 2000, at the height of the economic cycle in the United States, layoff activity was, according to WorkTrends data, at a fifteen-year low. This would correspond to broad-scale economic data reflecting that the unemployment rate also was at its lowest point in decades.

**Table 6.1. Employees Reporting Recent
Layoffs by Industry, 1990–2000.**

Industry	1990	1994	1996	2000	Totals
Heavy manufacturing	59%	48%	48%	39%	48%
Electronics and computer manufacturing	50	54	52	34	48
Light manufacturing	53	38	44	35	42
Retail/wholesale trade	33	29	29	18	27
Health care services and products	24	37	39	23	32
Government/public administration	18	27	28	9	21
Communication services/utilities	27	47	42	20	35
Transportation services	36	33	28	17	28
Banking and other financial services	44	42	34	26	36
Business services	44	53	33	22	37
Education	23	26	26	11	22
Totals	34%	36%	35%	21%	32%

Source: Gantz Wiley Research, WorkTrends survey program.

Table 6.1 provides the percentage of downsizing activity by major industry type. Employees who report the highest levels of downsizing activity tend to work in manufacturing industries (heavy, electronic and computer, light). Employees who report the lowest levels of downsizing activity tend to work in government/ public administration and education.

Impact of Downsizing on Employee Fulfillment

Since well before the advent of *Fortune* magazine's "Best Places to Work" rankings, many organizations have made it a goal to be a fulfilling place to work. Each organization might have its own definition of what this means—from employer of choice or engagement to more traditional and understood constructs of job satisfaction or commitment. However defined, it is widely acknowledged that layoffs can have a profound impact on an employee's quality of work life. This chapter describes one approach to defining fulfillment and delineates how downsizing affects organizations' efforts to promote it.

For this research, our definition of employee fulfillment is consistent with traditional concepts of psychological contracts, as well as popular notions of employer of choice. Specifically, an employee is fulfilled when, in return for work performed, he or she receives sufficient value back from the organization. To answer the question of what employees value, the annual surveys described in the previous section have frequently included the open-ended question, "As an employee, what is the one thing you want most from the organization for which you work?" Written comments are transcribed and rigorously coded according to the methods described by Hause, Wiley, and Lunsford (1997).

From the mid-1980s through the 1990s, the responses from approximately 70 percent of over 30,000 employees responding to this question can be sorted into five categories: (1) fair compensation (including pay and benefits), (2) psychological recognition, (3) career development, (4) job security and stability, and (5) interesting work (Hause & Wiley, 1996). Analyses performed by Hause and Wiley, as well as those performed subsequently on later survey iterations, demonstrate that these issues are remarkably stable across industry, organization size, job type, gender, and other organizational and personal demographics.

Based on this program of research, quantitative scales have been developed to measure each of these topics. Table 6.2 provides sample items for each of these scales, plus a range of Cronbach's alpha reliability coefficients for the multiple years of survey iterations included in this research.

Negative relationships between downsizing and employee relations (De Meuse et al., 1997) have been established. The current analyses add an examination of the following core questions:

Table 6.2. Employee Fulfillment Scales.

Scale	Number of Items	2000 Alpha	Sample Items
Career Development	3	.82	How satisfied are you with your opportunity to get a better job in your company?
			How satisfied are you with the opportunity for career development at your company?
Recognition	3	.84	My performance on the job is evaluated fairly.
			How satisfied are you with the recognition you get for the work you do?
Fair Compensation	4	.83	How do you rate the amount of pay you get on your job?
			How do you rate your total benefits program?
Security/Stability	2	N.A.[a]	How do you rate your company in providing job security for people like yourself?
			I have confidence in the future of my company.
Interesting Work	4	.87	I like the kind of work I do.

[a]For this two-item scale, the correlation is .57, $p < .001$.

- To what extent is there an impact of layoffs on the fulfillment of employees surviving within the organization?
- What elements of employee fulfillment, again for employees surviving layoffs, are most affected by downsizing?
- How stable are these relationships over time?

In essence, analyses compared the employee fulfillment scales listed in Table 6.2 across layoff and nonlayoff samples. Although the content of the annual surveys changes somewhat from year to year, these five scales are completely intact for the years used in these analyses: 1990, 1994, 1996, and 2000.

Table 6.3 presents the means of all five scales for each of the years included for the overall sample, as well as by layoff and non-layoff samples. Given the large sample sizes, all differences are significant at the $p \leq .001$ level. Thus, the eta statistic is provided as a measure of association (interpreted in this case similarly to a correlation). Several conclusions are apparent.

Employees within organizations recently experiencing layoffs feel significantly less fulfilled. All findings are remarkably consistent across time. Clearly, a sense of security and confidence in the future of the organization is the issue most affected by layoffs. This reflects that the major concern of employees during this time of organizational stress has to do with the uncertainty of both whether they will have jobs in the future and whether the organization will emerge from the business context prompting layoffs in the first place. Although previous research has demonstrated that perceptions of security and stability are important to layoff survivors (Armstrong-Stassen, 1994; Brockner, Grover, Reed, & Dewitt, 1992), these data indicate that they are the most important factor.

Although the size of the impact is notably less, the category demonstrating the second strongest impact of layoffs is career development. While career growth within a company clearly is secondary to ensuring one still has a job, an employee's sense of longer-term development opportunities is disrupted by layoff activity.

Armstrong-Stassen (1994), Brockner, Grover, and Mauritz (1988), and others have found that supervisor recognition can help to increase organizational commitment and retention among layoff survivors. In addition, Brockner et al. (1992) found that layoff survivors whose jobs became more interesting (based on a self-report) increased their work effort over employees whose jobs did

Table 6.3. Employee Fulfillment
by Layoff Activity, 1990–2000.

Scale	1990	1994	1996	2000
Career Development	3.17	3.14	3.12	3.18
No layoffs	3.27	3.26	3.23	3.24
Layoffs	2.97	2.92	2.92	2.96
Difference	.30	.34	.31	.28
F-value	97.63	172.76	144.70	82.53
p-value	.00	.00	.00	.00
Eta	.15	.17	.15	.12
Recognition	3.36	3.30	3.30	3.32
No layoffs	3.42	3.38	3.40	3.37
Layoffs	3.23	3.15	3.14	3.15
Difference	.19	.23	.26	.22
F-value	40.80	81.94	102.60	52.38
p-value	.00	.00	.00	.00
Eta	.10	.12	.13	.10
Fair Compensation	3.40	3.40	3.35	3.34
No layoffs	3.46	3.44	3.38	3.38
Layoffs	3.30	3.33	3.27	3.17
Difference	.16	.11	.11	.21
F-value	30.32	21.06	23.76	58.89
p-value	.00	.00	.00	.00
Eta	.09	.06	.06	.10
Security/Stability	3.67	3.44	3.41	3.64
No layoffs	3.92	3.69	3.64	3.79
Layoffs	3.20	3.01	2.97	3.11
Difference	.72	.68	.67	.68
F-value	588.48	690.79	674.93	551.90
p-value	.00	.00	.00	.00
Eta	.36	.33	.31	.30
Interesting Work	3.97	3.92	3.96	3.92
No layoffs	4.02	3.99	4.01	3.97
Layoffs	3.86	3.82	3.85	3.76
Difference	.16	.17	.16	.21
F-value	39.60	64.02	63.12	59.52
p-value	.00	.00	.00	.00
Eta	.10	.10	.10	.10

Note: Means are based on five-point scales (agreement, satisfaction, or good-poor). Higher means reflect more favorable responses. Sample sizes range from 4,236 to 6,876.

not. These findings, coupled with the data presented here, highlight the importance of these factors for layoff survivors.

Interestingly and consistently, the category least influenced by layoff activity is fair compensation. While some companies (such as Seagram; see Chapter Two) have had success using money as a short-term means to bolster retention following layoffs, these data suggest that satisfaction with pay and benefits, although important, is not influenced nearly as much by layoff activity as are job security and opportunities for career development.

Impact of Downsizing on Leading Indicators of Organizational Performance

If we accept the argument that certain selected employee opinions are leading indicators of organizational performance, a logical next step for organizations wishing to improve performance is to leverage employee input to help diagnose problems and promote best practices. Organizations with recent layoff activity should be no exception. Indeed, when layoffs occur, organizations commonly are also experiencing other stresses, such as falling market share, significant restructuring, or the challenge of merging two or more corporate cultures and value systems. This would make it even more important to attend to information sources that could be used to leverage higher performance.

The High Performance Model provides a structure for tracking how employee opinions relate to customer satisfaction and business results (Wiley, 1996; Brooks, 2000; Wiley & Brooks, 2000). Table 6.4 describes the eight scales defined by this model: four leadership practices (Customer Orientation, Quality Emphasis, Employee Involvement, and Employee Training) and four employee results (Information/Knowledge, Teamwork/Cooperation, Overall Satisfaction, and Employee Retention). With those scales, Table 6.5 presents how employees characterize these practices and their results differently for organizations with recent layoffs compared to those without. (Note that these employee opinion measures are available only for the 2000 data set.)

Focusing on only the overall 2000 column, a few conclusions are apparent. First, all topics are significantly less favorable for organizations with recent layoffs. This result suggests that downsizing organizations find it harder to create a favorable climate for

Table 6.4. High Performance Model Scales.

Scale	Number of Items	2000 Alpha	Sample Items
Orientation/ Information	4	.83	Customer problems get corrected quickly.
			We regularly use customer feedback to improve our work processes.
Quality Emphasis	4	.84	Where I work, we set clear performance standards for product/ service quality.
			Where I work, we are continually improving the quality of our products and services.
Employee Involvement	4	.83	In my company, employees are encouraged to participate in making decisions that affect their work.
			When employees have good ideas, management makes use of them.
Employee Training	4	.86	Overall, I am satisfied with the on-the-job training I have received.
			New employees receive the training necessary to perform their jobs effectively.
Information/ Knowledge	4	.79	I get enough information about how well my work group is meeting its goals.
			Senior management gives employees a clear picture of the direction our company is headed.
Teamwork/ Cooperation	4	.68	The people I work with cooperate to get the job done.
			When there are problems in my work group, they get corrected quickly.
Overall Satisfaction	4	.84	I am proud to tell people I work for my company.
			Considering everything, I am satisfied with my company as a place to work.
Employee Retention	1	N.A.	I am seriously considering leaving my company within the next 12 months. *(reverse scored)*

Table 6.5. High Performance Model by Layoff Activity: Industry Comparison.

Scale	Overall 2000	Financial Services	Health Care	Retail
Leadership Practices				
Customer Orientation	3.68	3.88	3.73	3.92
No layoffs	3.72	3.99	3.77	3.96
Layoffs	3.53	3.58	3.60	3.73
Difference	.19	.41	.17	.23
F-value	62.52	22.36	7.64	10.35
p-value	.00	.00	.00	.00
Eta	.10	.26	.10	.12
Quality Emphasis	3.55	3.77	3.59	3.68
No layoffs	3.60	3.88	3.64	3.70
Layoffs	3.40	3.46	3.40	3.56
Difference	.20	.42	.24	.14
F-value	56.23	22.58	13.57	3.29
p-value	.00	.00	.00	.07
Eta	.10	.26	.13	.07
Employee Involvement	3.36	3.59	3.38	3.40
No layoffs	3.40	3.69	3.44	3.42
Layoffs	3.20	3.28	3.18	3.32
Difference	.20	.41	.26	.10
F-value	54.17	18.72	14.10	1.23
p-value	.00	.00	.00	.27
Eta	.10	.23	.13	.04
Employee Training	3.40	3.60	3.44	3.38
No layoffs	3.44	3.70	3.51	3.40
Layoffs	3.23	3.31	3.20	3.31
Difference	.21	.39	.31	.09
F-value	58.25	14.15	19.16	.77
p-value	.00	.00	.00	.38
Eta	.10	.21	.16	.03

Note: Means on a five-point scale; higher is more favorable. Sample sizes range from 5,943 to 6,369 for the overall sample, 340 to 361 for financial services, 829 to 879 for health care services, and 717 to 766 for retail.

Table 6.5. High Performance Model by Layoff Activity: Industry Comparison, Cont'd.

Scale	Overall 2000	Financial Services	Health Care	Retail
		Employee Results		
Information/				
Knowledge	3.21	3.52	3.21	3.31
No layoffs	3.25	3.64	3.27	3.33
Layoffs	3.04	3.18	2.98	3.19
Difference	.21	.46	.29	.12
F-value	65.44	22.72	17.48	2.45
p-value	.00	.00	.00	.12
Eta	.11	.26	.15	.06
Teamwork/				
Cooperation	3.32	3.53	3.24	3.26
No layoffs	3.36	3.59	3.30	3.28
Layoffs	3.21	3.36	3.05	3.21
Difference	.15	.23	.25	.07
F-value	38.97	6.36	14.93	.83
p-value	.00	.00	.00	.36
Eta	.08	.14	.14	.04
Overall				
Satisfaction	3.79	3.89	3.82	3.76
No layoffs	3.87	4.02	3.89	3.81
Layoffs	3.51	3.53	3.75	3.54
Difference	.36	.49	.34	.22
F-value	196.32	26.80	23.96	11.00
p-value	.00	.00	.00	.00
Eta	.18	.29	.17	.13
Employee				
Retention	3.67	3.52	3.65	3.50
No layoffs	3.77	3.69	3.76	3.57
Layoffs	3.26	3.05	3.28	3.17
Difference	.51	.54	.48	.40
F-value	134.68	13.62	18.04	8.20
p-value	.00	.00	.00	.00
Eta	.16	.21	.16	.11

Note: Means on a five-point scale; higher is more favorable. Sample sizes range from 5,943 to 6,369 for the overall sample, 340 to 361 for financial services, 829 to 879 for health care services, and 717 to 766 for retail.

customer service and performance than do other organizations. Indeed, as Lewin and Johnston (2000) and others describe, performance is critical following downsizing, and this necessitates keeping survivors' attitudes and behaviors from having a negative impact on productivity, quality, and customer service. Second, although most effect sizes are fairly consistent, Overall Satisfaction and Employee Retention show the greater negative impact from layoff activity. This finding suggests that overall morale issues (summary attitudes) are more affected by downsizing than are the more specific and targeted topics, which are the values or practices within the model that are the stronger predictors of customer satisfaction and business results (for example, climate for service and other enabling factors indicated by the Leadership Practices; Schneider, White, & Paul, 1998; Wiley & Brooks, 2000). Although job cuts disrupt employees' abilities to get work done, it seems that the overall emotional impact is even greater. Given the literature showing the impact of work attitudes and emotions on job performance in times of layoff, these emotional disturbances should not be underemphasized.

In order to explore this issue further, the results were analyzed across industries. In general, gaps in opinions between layoff and nonlayoff groups were consistent among eleven industry categories. Said differently, the impact of downsizing is more the same than different. Nevertheless, some interesting differences did emerge. To highlight these, results for three service industries—financial services, health care, and retail—also are included in Table 6.5. These industries were chosen because the importance of customer service is recognized to be high across each of these industries (making the High Performance Model especially relevant); they represent 2000 layoff rates that could be characterized as high (financial services), medium (health care), and low (retail) according to Table 6.1; and the causes and context of downsizing generally would be different (for example, mergers and acquisitions in financial services versus store closings in retail).

Table 6.5 demonstrates, when looking across industries, that the effect of layoffs can vary dramatically depending on the context. Whereas the impact for retail shrinks to insignificance for many topics, the impact for financial services increases correspondingly. While involving, training, and communicating to employees are essentially unchanged in retail environments, they become more of a struggle for financial service organizations undergoing downsizing. Interestingly, it is in the Leadership Practices (the topics most related to getting the work done) where the differences between financial services and retail are greatest. Thus, all downsizing efforts are not made equal (Mellor, 1992). The increased scope, magnitude, restructuring, and resultant uncertainty surrounding financial services layoffs appear to impede employee efforts to get things done more so than the typically decentralized and localized store closings in clear command-and-control retail environments.

Special Retention Analysis

Because retention of key employees always is a concern, special comparisons were conducted regarding employee retention. A single item measuring intentions to leave one's organization is available across multiple years of the WorkTrends survey, dating back to 1985. This item is the best predictor of future turnover (Griffeth, Hom, & Gaertner, 2000) and is an accepted predictor of actual turnover. As such, its inverse, employee retention, is a valuable indicator of retaining talented staff. Table 6.6 presents the results for Employee Retention. From the effect sizes, one can see that the impact of layoffs on intentions to quit is relatively stable across the fifteen years of the sample. However, there is a slight increase in the strength of the relationship in 2000, driven by the decline in employees' interests in staying with recently downsized organizations. In fact, the intention to stay with the company is at a historic low for this group. Consequently, it seems a reasonable conclusion that the external market forces (historically low unemployment rates during this period) increased an employee's job opportunities, resulting in increased mobility, with more employees intending to act on their dissatisfaction and leave their respective organizations.

Conclusion

Downsizing is an organizational effort aimed at managing the cost of human resources. How layoffs are managed has broad-reaching implications for the success of the shrunken organization. Never-

Table 6.6. Turnover Intention by
Layoff Activity, 1985–2000.

	1985	1990	1994	1996	2000
Employee Retention	3.55	3.60	3.66	3.65	3.67
No layoffs	3.69	3.73	3.79	3.76	3.77
Layoffs	3.31	3.35	3.42	3.44	3.26
Difference	.38	.38	.37	.28	.56
F-value	39.02	77.05	103.69	82.01	134.68
p-value	.00	.00	.00	.00	.00
Eta	.13	.14	.14	.12	.16

Note: Mean on a five-point scale; higher is more favorable. Sample sizes range from 2,499 (in 1985, with half the 10,000 outbound sample of later years) to 6,393.

theless, the analyses of a longitudinal sample of companies permit us to draw several conclusions:

• Despite changing economic conditions, the impact of layoffs is remarkably consistent across the past decade. Even during particularly challenging economic times, essentially the same pattern of results emerges.

• The largest impact is on the employee's sense of job security and stability. The implication is clear: the number one concern of employees surviving layoffs is the need for reassurance regarding their future with the company. Although organizations are often in no position to make promises, communicating clearly with the most highly valued employees about their importance to the company's future may be a more effective (and financially prudent) retention strategy than special monetary bonuses.

• Related to future security concerns, a tertiary concern of employees is their opportunities for future career growth. Beyond knowing that they will be employed tomorrow (or even that the company will exist tomorrow), employees have a heightened need to see promising growth outlooks for themselves.

• In general, an organization's climate for performance is hampered by layoff activity, although this effect is clearly moderated by the type and nature of downsizing. Some types of layoffs (for example, those in the retail industry) leave comparatively less impact on the characteristics of the work environment. Other types of layoffs (such as those in the financial services industry) are clearly more disruptive of maintaining a clear orientation toward the customer and bottom-line results.

• Although there can be differences in the impact of layoffs on support to get the work done, they do have a universal dampening effect on morale and overall satisfaction. And not far behind lowered satisfaction, in terms of the negative impact of downsizing, is an increasing intention to leave the organization.

• Although the impact of downsizing on employee opinions is stable across time, there are a few exceptions to this rule. Specifically, the impact on employee retention and fair compensation fluctuates between various annual samples of the WorkTrends surveys. This finding makes sense because these are the two topics most closely tied to external marketplace conditions, and thus most likely to vary with the state of the current economy (such as unemployment and inflation).

Overall, the most significant theme for employees is one of future perspectives: Will I have a job? Will the company succeed? Will I have developmental opportunities?

The message from this research should not be that the adverse repercussions resulting from layoffs mean that downsizing is an imprudent tool to manage organizational health. Indeed, in extreme circumstances, downsizing can be a mandatory step to short-term survival. However, a greater understanding of longer-term implications, such as the ones documented here, can help executives more effectively manage downsizing efforts in order to maximize their benefits.

References

Armstrong-Stassen, M. (1994). Coping with transition: A study of layoff survivors. *Journal of Organizational Behavior, 15,* 597–621.

Brockner, J., Grover, S., & Blonder, M. (1988). Predictors of survivors' job involvement following layoffs: A field study. *Journal of Applied Psychology, 73,* 436–442.

Brockner, J., Grover, S., Reed, T., & Dewitt, R. (1992). Layoffs, job insecurity, and survivors' work effort: Evidence of an inverted-U. *Academy of Management Journal, 35,* 413–424.

Brooks, S. M. (2000, August). *Diagnosing the value chain: A summary of linkage research dynamics.* Paper presented at the 2000 Academy of Management Meeting, Toronto, Canada.

Cascio, W. F. (1998). Learning from outcomes: Financial experiences of 311 firms that have downsized. In M. K. Growing, J. D. Kraft, & J. C. Quick (Eds.), *The new organizational reality: Downsizing, restructuring, and revitalization* (pp. 55–70). Washington, DC: American Psychological Association.

De Meuse, K. P., Bergmann, T. J., & Vanderheiden, P. A. (1997). Corporate downsizing: Separating myth from fact. *Journal of Management Inquiry, 6,* 168–176.

De Meuse, K. P., & Tornow, W. W. (1990). The tie that binds—has become very, very frayed! *Human Resource Planning Journal, 13,* 203–213.

Griffeth, R. W., Hom, P. W., & Gaertner, S. (2000). A meta-analysis of antecedents and correlates of employee turnover: Update, moderator tests, and research implications for the next millennium. *Journal of Management, 26,* 463–488.

Hause, E. L., & Wiley, J. W. (1996, April). *What do employees want most from their organizations?* Paper presented at the Eleventh Annual Conference of the Society for Industrial and Organizational Psychology, San Diego, CA.

Hause, E. L., Wiley, J. W., & Lunsford, S. (1997, April). *What stands in the way of quality products and services?* Paper presented at the Twelfth Annual Conference of the Society for Industrial and Organizational Psychology, St. Louis, MO.

Heskett, J. L., Jones, T. O., Loveman, G. W., Sasser, W. E., & Schlesinger, L. A. (1994). Putting the service-profit chain to work. *Harvard Business Review, 72,* 164–174.

Kaplan, R. S., & Norton, D. P. (1996a). *The Balanced Scorecard: Translating strategy into action.* Boston: Harvard Business School Press.

Kaplan, R. S., & Norton, D. P. (1996b). Using the Balanced Scorecard as a strategic management system. *Harvard Business Review, 76,* 75–85.

Lester, S. W., & De Meuse, K. P. (1998, August). *The effect of mergers and acquisitions on the psychological work contract.* Paper presented at the American Psychological Association Convention, San Francisco.

Lewin, J., & Johnston, W. (2000). The impact of downsizing and restructuring on organizational competitiveness. *Competitiveness Review, 10,* 45–55.

Mellor, S. (1992). The influence of layoff severity on post layoff union commitment among survivors: The moderating effect of the perceived legitimacy of a layoff account. *Personnel Psychology, 45,* 579–600.

National Research Council, Committee on Techniques for the Enhancement of Human Performance: Occupational Analysis. (1999). *The* changing nature of work: Implications for occupational analysis. Washington, DC: National Academy Press.

Rucci, A. J., Kirn, S. P., & Quinn, R. T. (1998, January–February). The employee-customer-profit chain at Sears. *Harvard Business Review*, 83–97.

Schneider, B., White, S. S., & Paul, M. C. (1998). Linking service climate and customer perceptions of service quality: Test of a causal model. *Journal of Applied Psychology, 83*, 150–163.

Vanderheiden, P. A., De Meuse, K. P., & Bergmann, T. J. (1999). And the beat goes on: Corporate downsizing in the twenty-first century. *Human Resource Management Journal, 38*, 261–268.

Wiley, J. W. (1996). Linking survey results to customer satisfaction and business performance. In A. I. Kraut (Ed.), *Organizational surveys* (pp. 330–359). San Francisco: Jossey-Bass.

Wiley, J. W., & Brooks, S. M. (2000). The high performance organizational climate: How workers describe top-performing units. In N. M. Ashkanasy, C.P.M. Wilderom, & M. F. Peterson (Eds.), *Organizational culture and climate* (pp. 177–191). Thousand Oaks, CA: Sage.

CHAPTER 7

Financial Consequences of Employment-Change Decisions in Major U.S. Corporations, 1982–2000

Wayne F. Cascio
Clifford E. Young

In a previous study, Cascio, Young, and Morris (1997) used data from the Standard & Poor's (S&P) 500 between 1980 and 1994 to examine 5,479 occurrences of changes in employment in terms of two dependent variables: profitability (return on assets) and total return on common stock (price appreciation plus dividend yield). The fundamental question that they addressed was whether corporate downsizing improves financial performance in the year of the event and in the two subsequent years following the implementation of changes in employment.

In brief, they found that companies that engaged in pure employment downsizing did not generate significantly higher returns on assets or stock returns than the average companies in their own industries. However, companies that combined employment downsizing with asset restructuring generated higher returns on assets and stock returns than firms in their own industries.

The study examined in this chapter uses the same methodology as the previous one but extends the previous study by considering a much larger sample: all occurrences of employment changes in the

Standard & Poor's 500 from 1982 to 2000. The larger sample size therefore provides a more stable estimate of the results reported in the previous study. As a basis for putting the current study into perspective, we first provide a broad framework for the study of employment changes and then return to the more specific framework that we used to carry out our study.

The Downsizing Juggernaut Continues

The job churning in the labor market that characterized the 1990s has not subsided. If anything, its pace has accelerated. Indeed, the free-agent mentality that characterized the late 1990s is over. Layoffs are back, and with a vengeance. In 2001, there were 1.96 million announced layoffs, and new ones seem to be announced every day ("Shadow of Recession," 2002). Most of the layoffs are announced by medium- and large-sized companies, and they involve white-collar, college-educated employees (Newby, 2001). Small companies, especially small manufacturers, tend to resist layoffs because they are trying to protect the substantial investments they made in finding and training workers (Ansberry, 2001).

In many cases, the same firms that are laying off employees are hiring new ones, presumably with the kinds of skills needed to execute new strategies. According to the American Management Association's annual survey of its member companies, 72 percent of the firms that eliminated jobs in the previous twelve months said they also had created new positions ("Hire Math: Fire 3, Add 5," 2000). The surveyed companies were predominantly mid-size and large-size firms that employ fully 25 percent of the American labor force.

Foreign firms operating in the United States are also announcing many layoffs. Such firms now account for about 6 percent of the U.S. workforce and an estimated 15 percent of manufacturing employees (Pearlstein, 2001). The flexibility to hire and fire that characterizes U.S. labor laws, as compared to laws, customs, and union contracts in Western Europe and Japan, may account for many of the workforce reductions. As an example, consider Alcatel SA, the large French telecommunications company. Recently, it spent $17 billion to buy its way into the North American market with a string of premium-priced acquisitions. When the telecom bubble burst in early 2001, Alcatel lost little time in closing some of its newly acquired plants and laying off five thousand of its U.S. employees, or slightly more than one in four. Back home in Europe, however, it was a different story. The head of the company's union held out the possibility of a nationwide strike to protest the company's strategy of "catering to the financial world at any price." To date, Alcatel has managed to sell only one of its European plants and to cut a modest four thousand jobs from a European workforce of seventy thousand, or about one in seventeen workers (Pearlstein, 2001).

Layoffs are not limited to the United States. Japan has been especially hard hit, with high-profile firms such as Mazda, NEC, Hitachi, and Sony cutting deeply (Shirouzu, 2000; "Sony's Shake-Up," 1999; "Worst-Case Scenario," 2001). Such massive corporate and personal disruption once again raises important questions about the long-term benefits of strategies that emphasize reductions in the workforce. Although the quest for improved economic performance is undoubtedly a key driving force behind managerial decisions to implement layoffs, it is by no means the full explanation for such actions.

Alternative Theoretical Perspectives on the Study of Employment Changes

At the outset, it is important to distinguish organizational downsizing from organizational decline. According to Freeman and Cameron (1993), downsizing is an intentional, proactive management strategy, whereas decline is an environmental or organizational phenomenon that occurs involuntarily and results in erosion of an organization's resource base. Employment downsizing, the intentional reduction of employees, focuses exclusively on layoffs. In contrast, *workforce reductions* (what we call *employment-change decisions*) is a broader term that includes early retirements and voluntary severance programs in addition to layoffs (Wayhan & Werner, 2000). DeWitt (1998) pointed out that early scholarly work focused on downsizing as a strategy to be used when organizations are in decline, but in recent years it also has become common for organizations to use the same strategy to improve their performance, even when they are doing well (McKinley, Mone, & Barker, 1998).

Much of the growing literature on downsizing, workforce reductions, or employment-change decisions has focused on the effects of this strategy on organizations and their employees. At the level of individuals affected by these changes, scholars have examined effects on employees who lose their jobs (Leana & Feldman, 1992; Leana, 1996) as well as those who survive layoffs (Armstrong-Stassen, 1998; Brockner, 1988; Brockner & Wiesenfeld, 1996; Mishra & Spreitzer, 1998).

On a more macrolevel, researchers have studied the impact of employment changes on learning organizations (Fisher & White, 2000), changes in organizational structure (DeWitt, 1993; McKinley, 1992), and financial outcomes (Cascio, Young, & Morris, 1997; De Meuse, Vanderheiden, & Bergmann, 1994; Vanderheiden, De Meuse, & Bergmann, 1999; Wayhan & Werner, 2000; Worrell, Davidson, & Sharma, 1991). Explicitly or implicitly, in much of the research cited, researchers have adopted an economic perspective to explain the occurrence of downsizing (McKinley, Zhao, & Rust, 2000). This perspective assumes that downsizing is caused by a search for productivity and efficiency, whether in response to organizational decline or as a means to enhance profitability when the corporation is performing well. It also assumes that decision makers understand the relationship between downsizing and future financial performance, so that downsizing can be used as a rational, predictable tool for manipulating that performance (McKinley et al., 2000).

The fact that scholars do not find consistent relationships between downsizing and financial performance (De Meuse, Bergmann, & Vanderheiden, 1997; Wayhan & Werner, 2000) suggests that the causal factors driving downsizing may be more complex than a purely economic perspective can explain. Two other perspectives that have been proposed are the institutional perspective and the sociocognitive perspective (McKinley et al., 2000; McKinley & Scherer, 2000). The institutional perspective holds that downsizing is impelled by social conventions that define it as "good" or "effective" management. The sociocognitive perspective argues that managers have an incentive to simplify their cognitive domains and to converge quickly on a mental model that defines the "truth" about problems or issues they are facing, such as downsizing. This process creates order for the manager even in the absence of empirical evidence that the interpretation the manager is adopting is valid. As long as the manager's interpretation is plausible, it furnishes an adequate platform for action (Weick, 1995).

We note these alternative perspectives in an effort to convey the breadth of research activity in this area. Ours is but one perspective from which the study of employment changes can be addressed. The remainder of this chapter focuses on the economic perspective of downsizing, specifically on the economic consequences of employment-change decisions. We recognize that the economic perspective by itself does not tell the full story, but we hope that the large-scale research described will contribute to firmer conclusions about the relationship between changes in employment and financial outcomes for corporations. To help guide our research, we developed a conceptual framework of the relationship between employment costs and financial performance.

Employment Costs and Financial Performance

A fundamental assumption is that firms seek to operate efficiently with minimum costs and choose to downsize in order to decrease their employment costs. This implies that management thinks that the firm's goals (output, revenue, earnings) can be attained with fewer employees.

Firms that have the greatest need to cut employees will be those that are not performing well (those for whom costs are greatest and returns are least). Firms that are doing well do not need to cut employees, but may choose to do so anyway in an effort to boost their financial performance. Employment downsizing will be seen as a way to improve performance by cutting employment costs. However, one might expect that several factors could mitigate the presumed benefits of downsizing. Among these would be mediating variables such as employee stress, as well as attitudes and behaviors of the surviving employees in response to the downsizing. Lack of procedural justice in the workforce reduction process (Elovainio, Kivimaki, & Helkama, 2001), coupled with feelings of guilt and negative attitudes toward the organization ("survivors' syndrome," Brockner, 1988), could potentially counteract the cost-cutting benefits of the workforce reduction process. Nevertheless, the extent to which companies have been able to improve their performance over time with employment downsizing remains an empirical question, and that is the primary focus of this chapter. A fundamental issue is the nature of financial performance and how to measure it.

A standard measure of the financial performance of a firm is return on assets (ROA), measured as operating income before depreciation, interest, and taxes (OIBDP) divided by total assets (AT). Others who have examined the financial performance of the firm in response to managerial actions (Kaplan, 1989; Healy, Palepu, & Ruback, 1992; Ofek, 1994), focused on OIBDP/AT as a measure of the cash flow return on assets before and after the event they were studying. Any changes in the performance of the firm that result from employment downsizing should show up in the ROA measure. It can be shown that ROA may be expressed as:

$$\text{OIBDP}/\text{AT} = [(\text{SALES}/\text{EMP})(\text{EMP}/\text{AT})] \, [(1-\text{CGS}/\text{SALES}) - (\text{SGA}/\text{SALES}) + (\text{DEPRECIATION}/\text{SALES})]$$

where SALES/EMP denotes sales per employee, EMP/AT measures the use of labor relative to invested capital, CGS denotes cost of goods sold, and SGA denotes selling, general, and administrative expenses. Thus, ROA reflects the level of employment by way of the following firm-level financial performance ratios: production cost (CGS/SALES), administrative cost (SGA/SALES), employee productivity (SALES/EMP), and employees to capital (EMP/AT). Costs of labor normally are included in CGS and SGA.

In addition to financial performance, as reflected in cost ratios and ROA, management is interested in stock performance. This index is the ultimate performance measure from the shareholders' point of view. Consequently, as in Worrell et al. (1991), we used stock returns as a measure of performance for evaluating the benefits of employment downsizing.

Some of the earliest explorations of stock market efficiency (Ball & Brown, 1968; Watts, 1978) showed that news regarding a firm's earnings is reflected quickly in stock prices. Hence, changes in employment that increase (decrease) earnings or cause investors to expect higher (lower) future earnings should lead to changes in stock prices.

Our study seeks to determine whether companies that have engaged in major employment downsizings have been able to improve their financial performance as measured by ROA and total returns on common stock. To do so, we tested the following two null hypotheses:

HYPOTHESIS 1: Changes in employment have no effect on profitability in the year of the employment change and in the two succeeding years.

HYPOTHESIS 2: Changes in employment have no effect on return on common stock in the year of the employment change and in the two succeeding years.

Our null hypotheses are phrased in terms of the dependent variables, profitability (return on assets) and total return on common stock. However, it is important to note that other studies that have attempted to assess the financial consequences of workforce reductions have used different dependent variables, such as growth in sales and market capitalization (Wayhan & Werner, 2000). Thus, although researchers may use the same higher-order construct (financial performance) to express the nature of their studies, that construct may be operationalized very differently across studies. It is important to keep this fact in mind when attempting to compare results across research investigations.

Method

The Sample

We examined the set of management decisions about employment levels made by all companies included in the S&P 500 over the eighteen-year period 1982-2000. If there were no missing data and the same companies were included in the S&P 500 every year, each company would be included in the sample in each of the eighteen years, and we would have 9,000 occurrences. We used 1982 data to set the reference change in employment. We also used 1999 and 2000 to establish financial returns in years $t+1$ and $t+2$. Thus, we have a total of potentially 8,000 employment-change cases. Due to missing financial data in many of the cases, 6,418 cases were available for analysis in all three years. A total of 497 out of 500 companies had some data in every year of the analysis. The remaining 3 companies had data in seventeen of the eighteen years.

In the original sample, COMPUSTAT defined the S&P based on the year the study was conducted, 1995.[1] This study uses the S&P 500 based on the year 2000. Thus, there are some differences in the composition of the S&P 500 between the two studies. In each study, however, there is a consistent use of the same companies throughout the time periods we examined using a repeated measures design.

We obtained data from the May 2001 S&P COMPUSTAT CD-ROM database (Standard & Poor's, 2000), which contained complete data through year-end 2000. We extracted data on individual companies for the years 1982 through 2000 to investigate the impact of changes in the number of employees on the financial performance of firms in the year of the event and the two succeeding years.

The primary variable of interest in this study was the change in employment from one year to the next, as reported in the COMPUSTAT database. Over the period of the study, some companies increased their levels of employment, others decreased their levels of employment, and many did both at various times. Moreover, some changed their levels of employment through hiring and layoffs, while others reported employment changes that must have resulted from purchasing or selling plants or divisions. For example, suppose a firm reports a 10 percent reduction in employment from time 0 to time 1. That reduction in employment could be due to a decision to lay off employees without any reduction in assets or a decision to sell off unprofitable plants or divisions. The former set of circumstances represents a pure employment downsizing, and the latter represents employment downsizing with divestiture. Each of these scenarios might have a different impact on the performance variable being considered. For example, the market might react differently over time to a divestiture than it does to a pure employment downsizing. By considering changes in employment relative to changes in assets, we can take account of most of the effects of changes in these two variables.

To control for the varying impacts of employment increases or decreases and for changes due to pure employment changes versus asset acquisitions or divestitures, we classified each firm into one of seven mutually exclusive categories in each period of the study:

Employment downsizers: Companies where the decline in employment is greater than 5 percent and the decline in plant and equipment is less than 5 percent. There were 657 occurrences, or 10.2 percent of the total, in this category.

Downsizing by reducing assets (asset downsizers): Companies with a decline in employment greater than 5 percent and a decline in plant and equipment that exceeds the change in employment by at least 5 percent. There were 93 occurrences, or 1.4 percent of the total, in this category.

Combination employment and asset reduction (combination downsizers): Companies that reduce the number of employees by more than 5 percent but do not fit into either of the other two categories. There were 224 occurrences, or 3.5 percent of the total, in this category.

Stable employers: Companies with changes in employment between plus or minus 5 percent. The modal number of occurrences fell in this category. There were 2,770 occurrences, or 43.1 percent of the total, in this category.

Although our focus is on downsizing, we also categorized companies based on their employment growth, defining three more categories relating to employment upsizing:

Upsizing by acquiring assets (asset upsizers): Companies with an increase in employment of 5 percent or greater and an increase in plant and equipment that exceeds the change in employment by at least 5 percent. There were 1,094 occurrences, or 17.0 percent of the total, in this category.

Employment upsizers: Companies where the increase in employment is greater than 5 percent and the increase in plant and equipment is less than 5 percent. There were 409 occurrences, or 6.4 percent of the total, in this category.

Combination employment and asset increase (combination upsizers): Companies that increase employment more than 5 percent but do not fit into either of the other upsizing categories. There were 1,172 occurrences, or 18.3 percent of the total, in this category.

Comparing these results to those from our 1995 analysis, we find some notable differences in the nature of the data. In the current sample, there are substantially more companies in the upsizing categories. We think this is due to the inclusion of the current set of S&P 500 companies for all years. Companies are included in the S&P 500 because of their size and financial contribution to the market. Companies that are in the current index now but were not in the index in prior years most likely are included because of their growth (that is, increases in the number of their employees or in the value of their assets).

We recognize that our classification of companies as downsizers, upsizers, or stable employers is somewhat arbitrary. For stable employers, we chose ±5 percent, relative to a base year, as a cutoff point. We considered 3 percent and 10 percent as alternative limits, but concluded that using ±3 percent would include in the downsizing categories too many companies that could have reduced their employment that much merely through attrition and not through a conscious downsizing decision. On the other hand, using ±10 percent would exclude from the downsizing categories many larger companies that had announced and implemented downsizings that were quite large in terms of the absolute numbers of employees affected.

The Data

We extracted data on individual companies for the years 1982 through 2000 to investigate the impact of changes in the number of employees on the financial performance of firms in the year of the downsizing event (year 0) and the two succeeding years (years 1 and 2). For each company, we collected measures of profitability and stock return, along with industry-aggregate measures of each of the variables. Measures of industry-aggregate variables are defined in the COMPUSTAT User's Guide (2000). The specific variables that we used are listed below with the same acronyms as used in the COMPUSTAT CD-ROM database:

Number of employees (EMP)

Operating income before, depreciation, interest, and taxes (OIBDP)

Plant and equipment (PPENT)

Total assets (AT)

Dividends on common stock (DVPSX)

Price of common stock, end-of-year close (PRCC)

For each event-year in the study period, 1983 through 1998, we calculated the change in employment as the ratio $REMP_0 = EMP_0/EMP_{-1}$, where the subscripts denote the year, with the event year being 0, and -1 the prior year. The subscripts 1 and 2 denote the first and second years following the year of the employment-change event. If employment data were unavailable for the year of analysis and the prior year, we excluded the company from the sample for that year. In addition, we calculated the change in plant and equipment as the ratio $RPENT = PPENT_0/PPENT_{-1}$, to measure the extent to which capital assets were acquired or divested in the event year.

To measure the improvement or decline in profitability, we calculated differences in ROA from the base period, $t = -1$, to periods $t = 0$, 1, and 2 as:

$$\Delta ROA_t = OIBDP_t/AT_t - OIBDP_{-1}/AT_{-1}$$

The return to the stockholders surrounding the change in employment was equal to the dividend yield plus price appreciation in each one-year period, ending in time periods 0, 1, and 2:

$$\text{Stock return} = (PRCC_t - PRCC_{t-1} + DVPSX_t)/PRCC_{-1}$$

We used industry-aggregate variables to generate industry-adjusted measures for the performance ratio by subtracting the corresponding industry ratio from the company ratio. As with the direct measures of company performance, we calculated the industry performance-change measures relative to the performance in time period -1. For performance measures relative to the industry, the empirical question is, "Are companies doing any better or worse relative to their industries than they were in time period

−1?" With respect to the stock return, by subtracting the industry-average stock return, we are implicitly factoring out the return on stocks with the same level of systematic market risk (beta), because firms in the same industry typically have about the same level of market risk.

After conducting our analysis on the overall set of data from 1992 to 2000, we conducted a second analysis, limiting our data to 1995 through 2000. Because we have the data from 1994 as prior-year data, we have event-year data from 1995 through 1998 and post-event data for 1999 and 2000.

Results

Table 7.1 shows the average percentage change in employment for each of the categories of companies. The first data column is the change in the percentage of employees in the event year (year 0) measured from the base year (year −1). The second and third columns are the employment changes in years 1 and 2. The numbers in parentheses beneath the changes are the standard deviations of the percentage employment changes for the samples in each category. The number of occurrences in the sample in each category is indicated as n below the category name. Among the three categories of downsizing occurrences, the (weighted) average decline in employment in year 0 was −13.0 percent, and the average increase in employment among the three categories of upsizers was 27.8 percent. The downsizing companies exhibited a very small average increase in employees in years 1 and 2, with the result that by the end of year 2, their average employment level was still 7.8 percent below its level at the end of the year prior to downsizing. The upsizing companies exhibited large increases in employment, not only in the event year but also in years 1 and 2. For the sample as a whole (all seven categories combined), the average number of employees increased by 9.65 percent in the event year.

It is apparent from Table 7.1 that the largest changes in employment, either up or down, occurred in conjunction with restructuring that combined changes in employment with changes in assets (combination downsizers and upsizers). Among the downsizers, the greatest declines in employment occurred among companies that also disposed of assets (combination and asset downsizers).

Table 7.1. Change in Employment by Employment-Change Category, 1982–2000 (percentage).

Employment-Asset-Change Category	Year 0	Year 1	Year 2
Employment downsize ($n = 657, 10.24\%$)	−10.87 (7.02)	1.83 (19.45)	3.38 (19.95)
Combination downsize ($n = 224, 3.49\%$)	−20.30 (15.69)	1.67 (24.04)	2.92 (21.79)
Asset downsize ($n = 93, 1.45\%$)	−16.86 (11.66)	5.16 (36.77)	7.75 (32.69)
Stable employment ($n = 2,770, 43.13\%$)	0.27 (2.67)	3.97 (30.93)	4.23 (32.84)
Asset upsize ($n = 1,094, 17.03\%$)	28.08 (45.01)	22.49 (52.33)	20.10 (46.07)
Combination upsize ($n = 1,172, 18.25\%$)	32.35 (59.95)	17.31 (39.35)	16.26 (40.50)
Employment upsize ($n = 409, 6.37\%$)	13.98 (18.64)	10.71 (25.34)	11.46 (37.91)

Similarly, the largest increases in employment occurred among the companies that had substantial additions to their assets (combination and asset upsizers).

Profitability

If the policy of adjusting the workforce is successful, it should increase the productivity of employees and reduce costs, resulting in an increase in the profitability of the firm, as measured by ROA. Figures 7.1 through 7.4 summarize the ROA for the combined years 1982 through 2000, industry-adjusted ROA for 1982 through 2000, ROA for 1995 through 2000, and industry-adjusted ROA for 1995 through 2000.[2] Figures 7.1 and 7.3 show the time trend of ROA obtained by adding the successive mean changes in ROA to the base year. Figures 7.2 and 7.4 show the industry-adjusted ROA obtained by adding the successive mean changes in industry-adjusted ROA to the base year.

Figure 7.1. Return on Assets, 1982–2000.

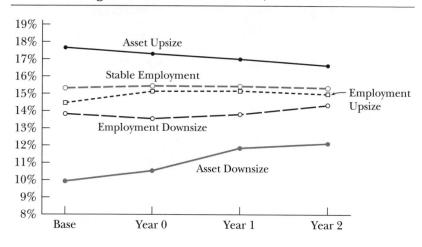

Figure 7.2. Industry-Adjusted Return on Assets, 1982–2000.

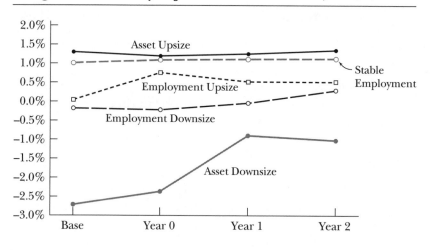

Figure 7.3. Return on Assets, 1995–2000.

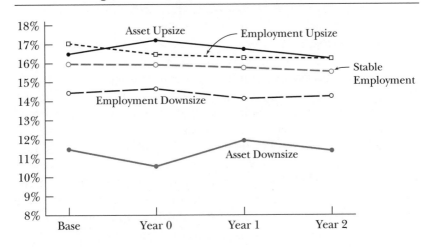

Figure 7.4. Industry-Adjusted Return on Assets, 1995–2000.

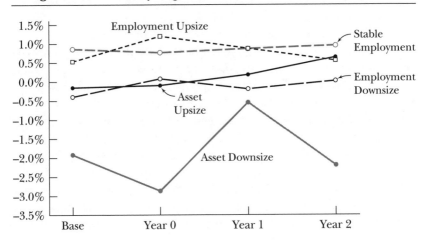

For the eighteen-year period 1982–2000, the downsizers were, on the average, less profitable in the base year and in years 0, 1, and 2 than either the upsizers or the stable employers. The downsizers had a (weighted) average return on assets of 13.26 percent, as compared to 16.64 percent for the upsizing categories, and 15.33 percent for stable employers in the base year. In addition, the downsizers compared less favorably with their industries in the base year, with an average industry-adjusted return on assets of −1.4 percent, as compared to the upsizers, whose average industry-adjusted return was +1.3 percent and stable employers at +1.0 percent. Relative to the base year, the ROA of the employment downsizers declined in years 0 and 1 and rose slightly in year 2. By the end of year 2, the change in ROA for employment downsizers continued to be lower than that for stable employers, but it was higher (significantly so) than that of their industries. By the end of year 2, the asset downsizers showed a statistically significant increase in their profitability, relative to stable employers and also relative to their industries. However, asset downsizers still trailed both comparison groups.

A similar picture emerges for ROA and industry-adjusted ROA from 1995 to 2000 (see Figures 7.3 and 7.4). Beginning with the base year and continuing through the event year (year 0) and years 1 and 2, employment and asset downsizers were consistently less profitable than either the stable employers or the upsizers.

To test whether there was a systematic relationship between profitability and the change in employment, we regressed, for the total sample and for each category, the change in ROA (from year −1 to year 0) against the employment-change ratio (REMP), with the asset-change ratio (RAT) also included as an independent variable to account for variations in asset policies. With all categories combined (6,351 occurrences for which we had complete data), there was a significant, positive coefficient for REMP. Because REMP is increasing with additions to employment, a positive coefficient means that firms with the larger increases (or smaller declines) in employment had the larger increases in return on assets. When we performed regressions for each category separately, the REMP coefficient was insignificant for all but the asset upsizers, for which it was significantly positive. This finding indicates that for companies in that group, those with the largest acquisitions exhibited the largest increases in ROA. The relationship between RAT and ROA generally was negative. The R^2 coefficients for the regression equations were generally quite small, with values around 2 percent. They were statistically significant only because of the large sample sizes used in the analyses.

Stock Return

The final judgment as to the effectiveness of a management action is whether it can generate stock returns that are attractive to investors. Figures 7.5 through 7.8 show the mean annual returns on common stock for 1982 through 2000, the industry-adjusted mean annual return on common stock for 1982 through 2000, the mean annual returns on common stock for 1995 through 2000, and the industry-adjusted mean annual return on common stock for 1995 through 2000.

The pattern of results is similar for both cumulative total returns from 1982 to 2000, as well as for industry-adjusted cumulative total returns from 1995 to 2000. Figures 7.5 and 7.7 show cumulative total returns over both time periods. There appear to be three groups. The first is the stable employers and the downsizers (employment and asset). Their total returns on common stock are

Figure 7.5. Return on Common Stock Cumulative from Beginning of Event Year, 1982–2000.

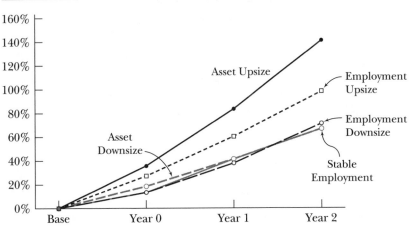

Figure 7.6. Industry-Adjusted Return on Common Stock Cumulative from Beginning of Event Year, 1982–2000.

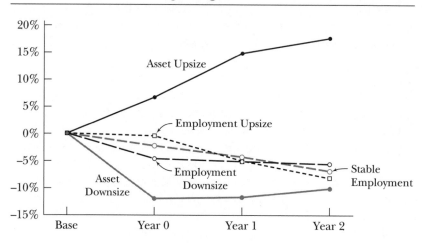

Figure 7.7. Return on Common Stock Cumulative from Beginning of Event Year, 1995–2000.

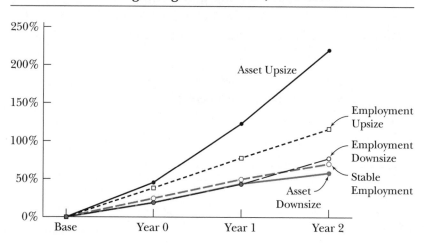

Figure 7.8. Industry-Adjusted Return on Common Stock Cumulative from Beginning of Event Year, 1995–2000.

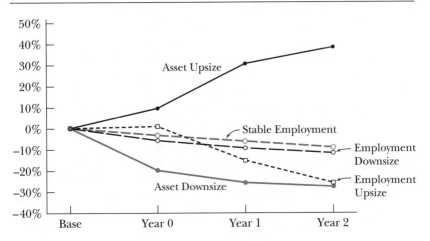

very similar throughout all of the time periods that we examined. The second group, which generated returns significantly higher than returns in the first group, is the employment upsizers. Asset upsizers (group three) generated the highest returns.

What is the total compound return that would have been earned by the end of period 2 from an investment at the start of year 0 in a portfolio of companies in each category that earned the annual returns shown for years 0, 1, and 2? For each $1.00 invested in the employment downsizers, the investor would have $1.72 at the end of year 2. For each dollar invested in the employment upsizers, the investor would have $1.99 by the end of year 2, and for each dollar invested in the asset upsizers, the investor would have $2.42 by the end of year 2. In addition, the asset upsizers generated cumulative stock returns that were significantly higher than those of their industries: an average of 18 cents higher by the end of year 2. No other employment asset-change category would have generated returns that were significantly higher than those of their industries.

Note that employment downsizers had a significantly lower mean return than stable employers in the year of the downsizing

(14.71 percent versus 18.91 percent). Both groups generated equivalent mean returns in years 1 and 2. None of the downsizing categories exhibited returns significantly different from those of their industries after the event year. However, asset upsizers generated higher returns than their industries (statistically significantly so in years 0 and 1). Figure 7.6 presents the cumulative industry-adjusted return from investing in a portfolio of companies in each category, starting at the beginning of the year of downsizing.

We used linear regression to test the relation between stock returns and change in employment (REMP), with the change in assets (RAT) included as a moderating variable. For the whole sample (6,351 occurrences for which we had complete data), there was no significantly positive coefficient for REMP. Within categories, for asset upsizers there was a significant negative relationship between REMP and stock returns, indicating that stock returns declined for larger asset acquisitions.

With respect to null Hypothesis 2 that changes in employment do not improve the firm's stock returns, the results are clear. For all categories of downsizers (employment, combination, and asset), there is no evidence to reject the null hypothesis and state that they outperformed either the stable employers or their industries. All three categories of upsizers (employment, combination, and asset) did yield higher cumulative stock returns than the stable employers. The regression results also provide no support for rejection of the null hypothesis because for the sample as a whole, firms that had greater increases (or lower declines) in employment did not generate higher stock returns.

Discussion

We developed and tested two hypotheses. Null Hypothesis 1 stated that changes in employment do not generate higher profitability (ROA) in the year of the employment change and in the two succeeding years. Over the eighteen-year period from 1982 to 2000, the results were clear. All categories of downsizers generated lower returns on assets than either stable employers or upsizers in the year prior to the announcement of the layoffs, in the year in which the layoffs occurred, and in the two subsequent years. This conclusion held on an industry-adjusted basis as well. However, in years

1 and 2, the asset downsizers showed improvements in returns on assets that were significantly higher than those of stable employers and also higher than those of their industries. We conclude that while some categories of downsizers improved their profitability through downsizing, this effect is not sufficiently consistent across categories to justify rejection of the null hypothesis.

The results of the regression of the change in ROA on the change in employment provided further support for this conclusion. Firms with larger increases (or smaller declines) in employment had larger increases in their returns on assets, although that effect was very small. The same pattern of results held for the time period 1995 to 2000.

Hypothesis 2 stated that there is no effect of changes in employment on total return on common stock in the year of the employment change and in the two succeeding years. Figure 7.5 shows that for the 1982-to-2000 time period, only two categories of companies consistently and significantly yielded higher total returns on their common stock than stable employers: the asset and employment upsizers. However, on an industry-adjusted basis, only the asset upsizers yielded returns that were significantly higher than those of all other groups, including stable employers (see Figure 7.6).

The cumulative total return by the end of year 2 for a $1 investment was $1.69 for stable employers. For asset upsizers, it was $2.42, and it was $1.99 for employment upsizers. In contrast, it was $1.72 for employment downsizers and $1.72 for asset downsizers. The same overall pattern of results held for the 1995 to 2000 time period, as Figures 7.7 and 7.8 demonstrate.

In terms of Hypothesis 2, we reject the null and conclude that some types of restructuring, namely, asset upsizing and employment upsizing, do produce significantly higher returns on common stock, especially by year 2 after the restructuring. However, on an industry-adjusted basis, this conclusion holds only for asset upsizers.

These results suggest that downsizing strategies, either employment downsizing or asset downsizing, do not yield long-term payoffs that are significantly larger than those generated by stable employers. The latter group includes those companies in which the complement of employees did not fluctuate by more than ±5 percent. This conclusion differs from that in our earlier analysis of the data from 1982 to 1994. In that study (Cascio et al., 1997), we concluded that some types of downsizing, namely, asset downsizing, do yield higher ROAs than either stable employers or their industries. However, when the data from 1995 to 2000 are added to the original 1982-to-1994 data, a different picture emerges. That picture suggests clearly that at least during the time period of our study, that it was not possible for firms to "save" or "shrink" their way to prosperity. Rather, it was only by developing their businesses (asset upsizing) that firms outperformed stable employers as well as their own industries in terms of profitability and total returns on common stock.

Managers of publicly owned firms have an obligation to run them as efficiently as possible. Even if these firms are large and stable, managers should be searching for ways to improve profitability, including adjusting their workforces. Yet what is striking about the results of the downsizings is the negligible impact on firm profitability relative to the size of the layoffs. The employment downsizers reduced their workforces by an average of 5.66 percent by the end of year 2. Although they did increase their returns on assets slightly (1/2 of 1 percent), their profitability never exceeded that of stable employers that did not downsize. Relative to their industries, they were able to attain an ROA that was only 3/10 of 1 percent above their industry average by the end of year 2. The combination downsizers reduced their workforces by 15.71 percent by the end of year 2, yet showed profitability results that were little better than those of the employment downsizers.

What are the implications of this study? Senior managers are under considerable pressure from their stockholders to improve financial performance. They often try to do this by cutting costs or restructuring assets. Many managers have accepted employment downsizing as a strategy for cutting costs in a manner that is tangible and predictable. Does such cost cutting translate into higher profits? Our research, performed at the firm level rather than at the level of the strategic business unit, has not produced evidence that downsizing firms were able generally and significantly to improve profits or cumulative returns on common stock. However, the evidence indicates that upsizing firms were able to please their stockholders, and asset upsizers generated stock returns that were superior to those of their industries in every year after the base year.

Given these results, we conclude that downsizing may not necessarily generate the benefits sought by management. Managers must be very cautious in implementing a strategy that can impose such traumatic costs on employees, both on those who leave as well as on those who stay (Cascio, 1993, 2001; De Meuse et al., 1997). Management needs to be sure about the sources of future savings and carefully weigh those against all the costs, including potential increased costs associated with subsequent employment expansions.

Employment Downsizing and Flexibility

This study did not directly address the issue of flexibility. However, it is probably true that many firms increased their strategic flexibility by thoughtful downsizing and asset restructuring. Many sharpened the focus of their business by divesting business units that did not fit with their mission. Others eliminated excess employees and cut costs to improve their competitiveness.

However, there is a paradox in the attempt to make a company lean and mean, while maintaining the flexibility to be nimble. In order to be nimble, a company must have the flexibility to take advantage of emerging prospects. To a great extent, flexibility depends on the firm's having some excess capacity, or slack. For example, in order to increase production when demand increases, a manufacturing firm needs to have some excess production capacity in its plants, and to take advantage of new investment opportunities, it needs unused financial resources. This need for excess capacity applies at least as much to its people as it does to its physical plant or financial resources. Even if the firm has the physical and financial resources, its ability to make productive use of those resources will be constrained by its human resources. Simply put, it needs the people to implement its plans, expansions, and investments, particularly in the increasingly service- and information-dominated U.S. economy. Consequently, it may be advantageous to maintain human resources even in slower periods in order to support flexibility.

Implications for Decision Makers

Decisions about restructuring deserve the same diligent analysis as any important capital investment decision. That is, the same methods of capital investment analysis can and should be applied to the firm's hiring and firing decisions as are applied to the decisions to acquire or divest a plant or division. Firms should evaluate the present value of the cash flows associated with the decision over the full course of the business cycle and over the entire life of the decision. With respect to layoffs, this should take account of the cost savings in the short run, net of severance payments and outplacement costs (typically 10 to 15 percent of the salaries of professionals and senior executives), as well as the costs of possibly having to rebuild the workforce at a later date.

Notes

1. COMPUSTAT provides aggregate, total data for each industry based on its Standard Industrial Classification code. Our industry ratios are the ratios of the industry-aggregate variables. If the number of companies in the industry is small or the data are unavailable, COMPUSTAT does not produce the industry-aggregate data. Stock returns for the industry are equally weighted portfolios of the companies in the industry SIC group.

2. The tables from which these data are extracted are not included to conserve space. They are available by request from the authors. In addition, for clarity, figures do not show results for the combination downsizers and the combination upsizers.

References

Ansberry, C. (2001, July 6). Private resources: By resisting layoffs, small manufacturers help protect economy. *Wall Street Journal,* pp. A1, A2.

Armstrong-Stassen, M. (1998). The effect of gender and organizational level on how survivors appraise and cope with organizational downsizing. *Journal of Applied Behavioral Science, 34,* 125–142.

Ball, R., & Brown, P. (1968, Autumn). An empirical evaluation of accounting income numbers. *Journal of Accounting Research,* 159–178.

Brockner, J. (1988). The effects of work layoffs on survivors: Research, theory, and practice. In B. M. Staw & L. L. Cummings (Eds.), *Research in organizational behavior* (Vol. 10, pp. 213–255). Greenwich, CT: JAI Press.

Brockner, J., & Wiesenfeld, B. M. (1996). An integrative framework for explaining reactions to decisions: Interactive effects of outcomes and procedures. *Psychological Bulletin, 120,* 189–208.

Cascio, W. F. (1993). Downsizing: What do we know? What have we learned? *Academy of Management Executive, 7,* 95–104.

Cascio, W. F. (2001, October). *Strategies for responsible restructuring.* Keynote address presented at the National Manpower Summit, Singapore.

Cascio, W. F., Young, C. E., & Morris, J. R. (1997). Financial consequences of employment-change decisions in major U.S. corporations. *Academy of Management Journal, 40,* 1175–1189.

De Meuse, K. P., Bergmann, T. J., & Vanderheiden, P. A. (1997). Corporate downsizing: Separating myth from fact. *Journal of Management Inquiry, 6,* 168–176.

De Meuse, K. P., Vanderheiden, P. A., & Bergmann, T. J. (1994). Announced layoffs: Their effect on corporate financial performance. *Human Resource Management, 33,* 509–530.

DeWitt, R. L. (1993). The structural consequences of downsizing. *Organization Science, 4,* 30–40.

DeWitt, R. L. (1998). Firm, industry, and strategy influences on choice of downsizing approach. *Strategic Management Journal, 19,* 59–79.

Elovainio, M., Kivimaki, M., & Helkama, K. (2001). Organizational justice evaluations, job control, and occupational strain. *Journal of Applied Psychology, 86,* 418–424.

Fisher, S. R., & White, M. A. (2000). Downsizing in a learning organization: Are there hidden costs? *Academy of Management Review, 25,* 244–251.

Freeman, S. J., & Cameron, K. S. (1993). Organizational downsizing: A convergence and reorganization framework. *Organization Science, 4,* 10–29.

Healy, P., Palepu, K., & Ruback, R. (1992). Does corporate performance improve after mergers? *Journal of Financial Economics, 31,* 135–175.

Hire math: Fire 3, add 5. (2000, March 13). *Business Week,* p. 28.

Kaplan, S. (1989). The effects of management buyouts on operating performance and value. *Journal of Financial Economics, 24,* 217–254.

Leana, C. R. (1996, April 14). Why downsizing won't work. *Chicago Tribune Magazine,* pp. 15–18.

Leana, C. R., & Feldman, D. C. (1992). *Coping with job loss: How individuals, organizations, and communities respond to layoffs.* San Francisco: New Lexington Press.

McKinley, W. (1992). Decreasing organizational size: To untangle or not to untangle? *Academy of Management Review, 17,* 112–123.

McKinley, W., Mone, M. A., & Barker, V. L. III. (1998). Some ideological foundations of organizational downsizing. *Journal of Management Inquiry, 7,* 198–212.

McKinley, W., & Scherer, A. G. (2000). Some unanticipated consequences of organizational restructuring. *Academy of Management Review, 25,* 735–752.

McKinley, W., Zhao, J., & Rust, K. G. (2000). A sociocognitive interpretation of organizational downsizing. *Academy of Management Review, 25,* 227–243.

Mishra, A. K., & Spreitzer, G. M. (1998). Explaining how survivors respond to downsizing: The roles of trust, empowerment, justice, and work redesign. *Academy of Management Review, 23,* 567–588.

Newby, A. (2001, July 23). White-collar blues. *Fortune,* pp. 98–110.

Ofek, E. (1994). Efficiency gains in unsuccessful management buyouts. *Journal of Finance, 46,* 637–654.

Pearlstein, S. (2001, August 6). Foreign firms' layoffs hit home for U.S. workers. *Washington Post,* pp. A1, A8.

"Shadow of recession"; available at www.cbsmarketwatch.com; retrieved February 9, 2002.

Shirouzu, N. (2000, January 5). Leaner and meaner: Driven by necessity— and by Ford–Mazda downsizes, U.S.-style. *Wall Street Journal,* pp. A1, A10.

Sony's shake-up. (1999, March 22). *Business Week,* pp. 52, 53.

Standard & Poor's. (2000). *Standard & Poor's research insight.* New York: McGraw-Hill.

Vanderheiden, P. A., De Meuse, K. P., & Bergmann, T. J. (1999). And the beat goes on: Corporate downsizing in the twenty-first century. *Human Resource Management Journal, 38,* 261–268.

Watts, R. (1978, June-September). Systematic "abnormal" returns after quarterly earnings announcements. *Journal of Financial Economics,* 127–150.

Wayhan, V. B., & Werner, S. (2000). The impact of workforce reductions on financial performance: A longitudinal perspective. *Journal of Management, 26,* 341–363.

Weick, K. E. (1995). *Sensemaking in organizations.* Thousand Oaks, CA: Sage.

Worrell, D. L., Davidson, W. N. III, & Sharma, V. M. (1991). Layoff announcements and stockholder wealth. *Academy of Management Journal, 34,* 662–678.

Worst-case scenario. (2001, March 26). *Time,* pp. 54–57.

CHAPTER 8

Resizing and the Marketplace

The Response of Customers and Competitors to Reorganization

David T. Bastien
Todd J. Hostager

A critical element of organizational performance is the behavior of competitors and customers. Ultimately, it is the customers of any company who determine its success or failure. A major problem for almost any organization undergoing a resizing change is that its revenues drop, sometimes dramatically (Hughlett, 1997; Kover, 2000; Waters, 1997). Furthermore, in competitive contexts, competitors of the changing organization can have an important impact on the patronage of the changing organization's customers (Bastien, 1994; Bastien, Hostager, & Miles, 1996; Grubb & Lamb, 2000).

The other chapters in this book have established that resizing efforts are frequently marked by a discrete set of performance characteristics: downturns in short-term productivity, upswings in unwanted employee turnover, upswings in production errors, downturns in revenues and in market share, and the unwillingness or inability of strategic decision makers to anticipate these markers. Each of these markers can have a serious impact on customers, making a customer's patronage more expensive in a number of ways. Customers of any competitive enterprise always have choices, and their patronage decisions do not involve stakes as high as those faced by employees, managers, or shareholders of the resizing company. In other words, when customers face changing or unhappy contact people, defective products or poor service, slowed delivery or changes in delivery terms, or any other new customer routine, it may be easier and cheaper to change vendors.

Over the years of research on resizing changes in all their varieties, little attention has been focused on customers' reactions to resizing change and the competitive response to resizing by rivals. In some measure, this inattention is due to the difficulty in gathering data directly from customers. For example, resizing companies are reluctant to allow researchers access to their customers, rivals are equally reluctant, and the customers often are difficult to identify and access. This has resulted in only a few studies in addition to the case data and anecdotal data in the literature.

In this chapter, we explore the reactions of customers and competitors to resizing change as explained in the literature and as is visible in the press. Then we present a study of customer and competitor behavior in a resizing context, and integrate the literature with the study results to develop a set of guidelines for resizing managers who are trying to maintain revenues and market share while resizing.

The Literature on Customers and Competitors of Resizing Firms

Most of the other chapters in this book have looked at resizing as downsizing, but many other strategies involve resizing as well. For instance, mergers and acquisitions (M&As) and reorganizations frequently are justified by the notion that administrative costs can be decreased while increasing production, operational, or distribution capacity. In other words, the downsizing dimension of resizing is embedded in a growth dimension. Thus, the organizational performance dynamics associated with M&As, reorganizations, automation, and downsizing as described in the literatures relating to those strategies must be outlined, especially those dynamics likely to have some impact on customers.

First, it is often noted that the process of implementing resizing change is where many problems occur. Marks and Mirvis

(1985) identified a pathological syndrome (see Table 8.1) that is more or less universally observed in M&As, downsizing, and other forms of resizing changes. This syndrome focuses on internal dynamics, including high levels of personal uncertainty about expected performance and behavior; increased attention to behavior of the top management; increased needs for communication and information with a tendency toward worst-case rumor generation in the absence of hard information; and strong resentment of the behavior of the acquiring organization's managers. On an organizational

Table 8.1. Common Responses
to Mergers and Acquisitions.

Responses at the Individual Level	*Responses at the Organizational Level*
Personal uncertainty about expected performance and behavior	Tendency toward rumor mills in the absence of hard information, with the rumors carrying worst case prophecies
Increased needs for receiving communication and information, combined with a decreased willingness to give information	Levels and units isolate themselves from horizontal and vertical communication channels inside the organization, leading to information constipation
Heightened attentiveness to communication from higher organizational levels, especially from the acquiring company management	High rates of unwanted turnover among employees and managers, especially on the acquired side
Simultaneous fight-or-flight response by employees and managers	Generalized decline in organizational performance manifest by decreased earnings, profits, and productivity
Resistance to change	
Culture shock	
Focus on personal security rather than organizational goals	
Job searches by acquired company employees and managers	
Cultural differences reported as a source of hostility and conflict, including resentment of acquiring company managers	

Source: Based on Bastien, 1989.

level, these same studies noted the following common phenomena: (1) a tendency not to pass news of problems either up or down; a tendency among top management on both sides not to communicate with their respective organizations about the resizing; (2) a tendency toward high rates of unwanted turnover; (3) conflict within the acquired organization or between the participating organizations, often quite intense; and (4) a tendency toward a decrease in earnings and productivity (Cameron, Whetten, & Kim, 1987; Cascio, 1998; Cascio, Young, & Morris, 1997; De Meuse, Vanderheiden, & Bergmann, 1994; Vanderheiden, De Meuse, & Bergmann, 1999).

A number of other authors have confirmed and expanded on this change syndrome (Bastien, 1987, 1989; Buono & Bowditch, 1989; Burke & Nelson, 1998; Campbell, Goold, & Alexander, 1995; Cascio, 1993, 1995; Geneen & Bowers, 1999; Jick, 1985; Leana & Feldman, 1992; Marks, 1994; Noer, 1993; Sirower, 1997; Zweig, Kline, Forest, & Gudridge, 1995). Bastien, McPhee, and Bolton (1995), in examining a reorganization of a municipal government following the election of a new mayor, found that the syndrome as described by Mirvis and Marks (1986) exemplified the dynamics in their reorganization case. O'Neill and Lenn's study of middle managers in a downsized organization (1995) revealed high levels of anger, resentment, resignation, anxiety, and cynicism. Blundell (1978) interviewed government employees whose staff had been downsized and reorganized and found that fear and uncertainty about the future produced declines in productivity.

Many authors have pointed out that organizational culture is an important source of problems in resizing efforts (Ambrose, 1998; Bastien, 1989, 1994; Cartwright & Cooper, 1996; Clemente & Greenspan, 1998; Galpin & Herndon, 1999; Haspeslagh & Jemison, 1991; Lajoux, 1997; Marks, 1994; Marks & Mirvis, 1998; Mirvis & Marks, 1992). They have reported that the process of change not only creates a negative effect in the changing organization but also involves a slowdown of organizational and operational process that must affect customers. Furthermore, the process of change generates errors, again affecting customers. Cameron, Freeman, and Mishra's study of downsizing in the U.S. automobile industry (1991) revealed widespread implementation efforts and decreased levels of quality, productivity, and effectiveness.

Changes such as M&As (and restructurings, downsizings, and strategic alliances) are often responses to outside pressures to increase the size or the short-term profitability of a company quickly. Acquiring company executives see M&As as a quick way to increase the size of their empires, please the stock market, and improve their standing with their boards of directors. Acquired company executives see M&As as a way to generate the resources they need quickly to expand or provide protection from a hostile takeover. Managers on both sides see an M&A as a route to expressing their personal ambitions and press executives to make an acquisition (Bastien, Hostager, & Miles, 1996; Haspeslagh & Jemison, 1991). Finally, outside advisers (financiers, accountants, attorneys, and so forth) also press for acquisitions to take place since these parties profit from their advice being taken (Mirvis & Marks, 1992).

Of course, growth is not the reason for downsizing or restructuring. Rather, the goal typically is to maintain revenue size while dramatically cutting costs. Executives see the downsizing as a way to please shareholders (Cascio, 1998; Cascio et al., 1997). Retained managers see the change as a way to eliminate their personal rivals while they show how lean and mean they can manage. Accountants are able to generate many billable hours advising executives on where to make cuts (Downs, 1996).

There are four common problems with this decision-making process. First, the process generally happens so quickly that the managerial implications of the proposed changes are rarely thought through (Mirvis & Marks, 1992; Zuboff, 1989). The process of actually making organizational changes is much more complex and difficult than the process of deciding on what changes to make. In fact, many times the decisions may not even be implementable (Jemison, 1986; Jemison & Sitkin, 1986).

Second, there usually are interpersonal conflicts left hidden in order to get the basic decision made. For instance, Zuboff (1989) noted in cases of automation that midlevel managers and executives have fundamentally different reasons for automating and fundamentally different expectations of the outcome. In M&As, the acquirer and acquiree often have fundamentally different reasons for entering into the deal and have fundamentally different expectations of how it will be implemented: acquiring executives believe that since they bought the other, they should manage it, while the acquired company managers believe that since they know how to run their business, they ought to be given the resources to run it. If these conflicts are addressed early, the deal will appear less attractive. Consequently, the bargaining parties keep the conflict hidden.

Third, customers are not considered in the process. Certainly, the abstraction of market share is, but pre-resizing customers are not; only the idealized benefits to the changing company are. The analysis process reduces customers to market quantities such as market share and revenues. Moreover, the resizing decision is based on the assumption that the changes will not negatively affect customers' continued patronage. In fact, Bastien (1994) found that at least 10 percent of an acquired company's customers will look for new vendors simply as a result of the acquisition announcement, and subsequent changes are likely to affect customers adversely. Researchers of the downsizing process noted similar customer dynamics (Cascio, 1993; Leana & Feldman, 1992; Marks, 1994; Noer, 1993).

Fourth, executive hubris ("overbearing pride or presumption, arrogance"; *American Heritage Dictionary,* 1994) also is a driving force behind a resizing effort (Roll, 1986). Mirvis and Marks (1992) observed that the pressures in the resizing decision process lead executives to think of themselves as infallible. Outside advisers and their subordinates use flattery to convince them of the wisdom of their strategic change decisions. As one investment banker put it, "It's my job to convince my clients that it's their destiny to own and control other companies." As a result, executives often are so unprepared for implementation problems that they not only misinterpret information contrary to their expectations and have no contingency plans, but sometimes they simply refuse to believe that there are problems even when company data clearly suggest that there are.

These factors may lead to unrealistically high expectations for the outcomes of a resizing initiative. In the case of M&As, these expectations may lead acquiring companies to justify paying premium prices for firms (Bastien et al., 1996). In the case of strategic alliances, they may lead to the expectation of unrealistically quick return on investment and justify taking resources from a core business to devote to the alliance. In the case of automating, they may lead to unreasonable expectations of immediately lowered cost and error rates. And in the case of downsizing, they may lead to expectations of unrealistically high-cost reductions (Byrne, 1999; Cascio, 1998; Cascio et al., 1997; De Meuse et al., 1994).

The resizing decision process occupies a great deal of managerial attention and makes it difficult for executives to pay attention to the daily conduct of business. Executives become increasingly isolated from their organizations (Cameron et al., 1987). When it is time for implementation, new decision-making demands exacerbate the problem, and executives remain isolated during the implementation phase (Bastien, 1987, 1989; Jemison, 1986; Jemison & Sitkin, 1986; Haspeslagh & Jemison, 1991). Midlevel managers also tend to isolate themselves from each other and cease communicating horizontally or vertically during the implementation phase (Cameron et al., 1987). Since they see the organizational change as either a threat or a means of realizing their personal ambitions, they are reluctant to let executives know of operational problems that are surfacing in implementation (Mirvis & Marks, 1986, 1992).

Managerial isolation creates a form of information constipation in a merging, downsizing, or restructuring organization (Bastien et al., 1996; Cameron et al., 1987), which in turn generates two important elements of the resizing syndrome: rumors become the basis of action in the absence of hard, official information, and a fight-or-flight response emerges to the change among staff of the changing organizations. Rumors proliferate as employees attempt to define their new situation without adequate information and support from their isolated managers. Employees use horizontal channels of information to make sense of the situation and speculate about the managerial motives behind the M&A.

Consistent with Shibutani's seminal study of rumors (1966), these rumors frequently are worst-case scenarios that include visions of an impending disaster and negative attributions of the motives behind the resizing effort (Marks & Mirvis, 1985; Mirvis & Marks, 1986; Bastien, 1987). Employees may find it demoralizing to have to rely on rumor mills for information (Shibutani, 1966). Rumor mills also may exact a toll on productivity: Bastien et al. (1995) found that employees facing the uncertainty of major organizational change spent up to 20 percent of their time seeking and discussing unsanctioned information.

Negative, pervasive rumor mills contribute to a flight-or-fight mentality among employees and managers. Two common indexes of flight are post-M&A increases in job search activity and turnover (Bastien, 1987, 1989, 1994; Marks & Mirvis, 1985; Mirvis & Marks, 1986, 1992). As job searches yield successful results for a few, others follow, creating added task demands for employees who remain behind. Critical organizational functions may seriously suffer since organizations often do not have redundant talent, and the best talent often is the first to leave. For example, Bastien et al. (1995) noted a case in which the person who designed the firm's computer network left early in the implementation process, and none of the remaining employees were capable enough to adapt the system to the organization's new needs.

While the flight response is in full swing, managers and employees fight the M&A by mobilizing resistance to the changes that the merger is rumored to bring and by mobilizing political opposition to the decision makers themselves. This fight side of the reaction usually takes the form of culture clash and culture conflict (Bastien, 1992; Marks & Mirvis, 1985; Mirvis & Marks, 1986). Sometimes employees and managers mobilize attempting to dominate the postchange scene, in the hopes that their values and practices will dominate (Cameron et al., 1987). Sometimes the same employees and managers are no longer certain of work standards or the future of the organization, so they cease to be aggressive and proactive in their execution and pursuit of regular daily business.

Both the substantive requirements of organizational change and the flight-or-fight response of personnel create a substantially increased workload and burnout for remaining employees and managers, exacerbating the problems with managerial isolation (Brockner, 1988). In this context, daily production suffers. Production declines, errors increase, and delivery schedules suffer (Bastien, 1989; Bastien et al., 1995; Cameron et al., 1991; Mirvis & Marks, 1986). Remaining employees become increasingly uncertain and demoralized, and they may take their negative affect out on customers (Burke & Nelson, 1998; Cameron et al., 1987; O'Neill & Lenn, 1995).

As a result of implementation process problems, the ability to perform and deliver to customers declines. Customer dissatisfaction mounts, leading some to switch to other vendors. Customer losses contribute to higher levels of employee uncertainty and an escalating bailout of personnel. Customer losses also encourage isolated managers to mandate cost-cutting measures that further amplify the dysfunctional change syndrome (Bastien, 1994). Remember that the resizing decision was predicated on the assumption of stable or increasing revenues.

This alienation of customers is a critically important aspect of the change syndrome. Customers are the source of revenues and the object of all competitive action regardless of context. Bastien (1994) observed that when an organization goes through the disruption of resizing change, not only are customers alienated but competitive rivals also can get into the act. He observed that when competitive rivals become aware of uncertain and dissatisfied customers, they might decide to capitalize on this dissatisfaction and uncertainty by trying to attract the resizing company's customers. Furthermore, he noted that these same rivals might become aware of dissatisfied employees and try to recruit them away from the resizing company. This is especially important since customers in many instances take their patronage to whatever company where a particular sales or contact person works, thereby further increasing the loss of customers and their revenues.

A vicious cycle is called a positive feedback loop in scientific parlance (Maruyama, 1963; Masuch, 1985; Weick, 1979). Bastien (1994) observed a positive feedback loop operating in M&As between organizational change and customer loss—the more change, the more loss, and the more loss, the more change—and a positive feedback loop operating between a rivals' marketing efforts and customer loss in the M&A: the more a rival tries to get customers away from the merging company, the greater the customer loss is for the merging company, and the more the customer loss, the greater is the marketing effort. Bastien noted that these two loops are connected through the customer, leading to the model shown in Figure 8.1.

On the basis of these findings, we make the following predictions:

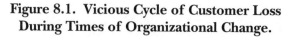

Figure 8.1. Vicious Cycle of Customer Loss During Times of Organizational Change.

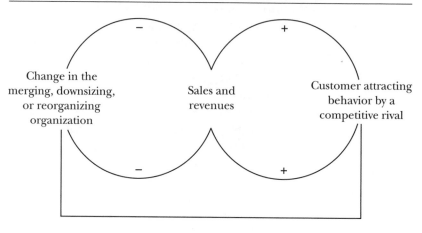

PROPOSITION 1: Competitors with the explicit purpose of taking customers and revenue from the resizing company will be more successful than competitors that are not intentionally pursuing these customers and revenues.

PROPOSITION 2: Successful efforts by a competitor at attracting customers and revenue from the resizing company will lead to further efforts by the competitor.

An important aspect of vicious cycles is that once they start, they are self-reinforcing and very difficult to stop (Maruyama, 1963; Masuch, 1985; Weick, 1979). In fact, they tend to accelerate over time. Consequently, in the cases of downsizing, M&As, and other reorganizations, executives become isolated after the change decision is made. This leads to poor daily management, which leads to uncertain and unhappy employees, which leads to customer dissatisfaction and revenue loss, which leads to isolated executives' making more change decisions to adjust to lower-than-expected revenues (Bastien et al., 1996; Cameron et al., 1987; Grubb & Lamb, 2000). Of course, this starts the loop again.

Bastien et al. (1996) observed that customers of a resizing company would change vendors in three identifiable waves. In the first wave, news of the resizing triggers high levels of uncertainty among employees (Cameron et al., 1987; Marks & Mirvis, 1992). The news may come in the form of a formal announcement or rumors (Bastien, 1989). This uncertainty leads to an increase in turnover as some managers and employees leave to find a more stable organization (Buono & Bowditch, 1989; Marks & Mirvis, 1985, 1998). Productivity drops as the remaining managers and employees try to understand their new situation and keep up with increased workloads (Marks, 1994).

News of the resizing generates customer uncertainty about the changing company's performance, quality, service, and prices (Bastien, 1994; Cameron et al., 1987). Loss of revenues result as customers reduce their uncertainty by switching to vendors that are not resizing. Bastien (1994) found that vendor switching is more likely if a customer had a prior negative experience with another resizing company. Customers may even change from a resizing vendor simply because they do not approve of the resizing effort. Bastien also reported an instance when a customer's purchasing policies allowed it to do business with the smaller pre-M&A companies but prevented it from doing business with the larger post-M&A entity. Moreover, he noted that features of the post-M&A organization may discourage some pre-M&A customers from continuing their patronage. In one case, the merger of a barbershop and beauty parlor alienated some of the existing clientele, who would not tolerate the coed nature of the new business. The initial loss of customer revenue from a resizing may be as high as 10 percent (Bastien, 1994; Hughlett, 1997; Waters, 1997). Based on these findings, we predict that:

PROPOSITION 3: Successful efforts by a competitor at attracting customers and revenue from the resizing company will be tied to the announcement of the resizing change.

The second wave of customer loss emerges when the details of the resizing implementation plan become public. For instance, if resizing involves changing product lines, delivery schedules, payment routines, service schedules, contact personnel, or almost any other change affecting customers, these changes will remove the incentive for patronage of some customers who might not respond to the first-wave announcements; the changes, though, may be necessary for the resizing company to achieve its goals. In other words, the very changes on which the resizing effort is predicated may alienate some customers. Importantly, this wave of customer loss, like the first wave, may not be anticipated by the resizing company decision makers (Bastien et al., 1996).

The third wave of customer loss occurs during the resizing implementation process. As managers and employees attempt to change, errors occur and inefficiencies emerge. The resizing syndrome comes into play in this wave more than in the first two waves, and customer dissatisfaction can become greater. As managers become overloaded and fail to recognize the problems with employees, these employees start to take out their frustration on customers as they increase their job searches. When flawed products and services are delivered, customers may increase their efforts at finding other vendors. Competitive rivals may recognize the opportunities and increase their marketing and employee recruitment efforts. The losses of customers and revenues in this wave are more a function of problems in management than are the first two (Bastien et al., 1996; Grubb & Lamb, 2000). Accordingly, we predict that:

PROPOSITION 4: The degree of success by a competitor at attracting customers and revenue from the resizing company will depend on the extent to which the competitor is knowledgeable about the internal processes unfolding within the resizing company.

PROPOSITION 5: The degree of success by a competitor at attracting customers and revenue from the resizing company will depend on the extent to which the competitor is knowledgeable about the resizing company's customers.

PROPOSITION 6: The degree of success by a competitor at attracting customers and revenue from the resizing company will depend on the extent to which the competitor is successful in recruiting employees from the resizing company.

With these propositions from the literature specified, we will outline a study of customers and competitors in a corporate acquisition, one of the several resizing strategies under study in this book.

A Case Study in Resizing

In order to examine the resizing propositions, an organizational case is required with access to information regarding customer and competitor perceptions of the resizing, customer and competitor responses to the resizing, and outcomes of the responses for competitors, customers, and the merging company. The banking industry is particularly well suited to these requirements, since performance (outcome) data for competitors and merging companies are publicly available. The Federal Reserve publishes comprehensive quarterly performance data for all banks, credit unions, and savings and loans doing business in the United States. To expedite access to information on resizing perceptions and responses by customers and competitors, a locally well-known bank merger was selected by the researchers.

This case involved the acquisition of a moderate-sized, multi-branch, single-state bank by a large, multistate, regional bank headquartered in a neighboring state. Since banks can expand in a state only through the use of a state-granted charter and since performance is published at the state charter level, data were available at the state charter (rather than at the corporate) level. Performance data on two key indicators, deposits and loan growth, were obtained for periods before and after the acquisition announcement:

Preacquisition deposits (acquiring bank charter)	$1,603,199,000
Preacquisition deposits (acquired bank charter)	$864,870,000
Preacquisition deposits (combined)	$2,468,069,000
Postacquisition combined deposits (combined)	$2,159,038,000
Deposit growth	($309,031,000)
Deposit growth percentage	(12.52 percent)

Overall, the merged bank lost $309,031,000 in deposits over this period, with a deposit growth rate of -12.52 percent. During this same period, a cohort of twenty-seven community banks was tracked. Community banks were identified through membership in the Independent Bank Association of America. The combined deposit growth among these community banks was $356,225,000, with an average growth rate of 13.37 percent.

Loans are the second key indicator of bank performance:

Preacquisition loans (acquiring bank charter) $1,797,918,000
Preacquisition loans (acquired bank charter) $ 618,097,000
Preacquisition loans (combined) $2,416,015,000
Postacquisition combined loans (combined) $2,276,562,000
Loan growth   ($139,453,000)
Loan growth percentage   (5.77 percent)

In total, loan volume at the merged bank dropped by $139,453,000, with a loan growth rate of –5.77 percent. During the same period of time, among the twenty-seven community banks in the cohort, loan volume increased by $329,412,000, with an average loan growth rate of 18.8 percent. These data document an overall growth in deposits and loan volume among the cohort institutions that exceeds the losses experienced by the merged bank. However, both deposits and loans are considerably affected by the substantial amounts displaced through these losses. A review of the performance of the twenty-seven community banks reveals that several of these banks increased both deposits and loans at rates substantially above average, several others performed above the average in one of the two indicators but near average in the other, while most performed at or below average in both indicators. Of course, this implies that some of these firms were very effective at competing with the merged bank, others were somewhat effective, while the remainder appear not to have improved their positions at all despite the huge amounts of deposits and loan demand in this market.

The sample for this exploratory study was selected from the frame of twenty-seven community banks operating in the same geographical areas as the branches of the acquired bank. Several credit unions and branches of other large regional banks operated in the same area, but they were excluded from the sampling frame due to the presence of confounding factors that made it difficult to attribute their performance outcomes to merger perceptions and responses.

Of the twenty-seven banks in the frame, managers and executives at ten banks agreed to participate in the study. All respondents were either chief executive officers or vice presidents of marketing, and all were in a position to make strategic and competitive decisions. Of the ten participating banks, five performed at or below the local industry average in both deposit and loan growth during the period of the case, one performed above the local industry average in loan growth but not in deposits, one performed above the local industry average in deposits but not in loan growth, and three performed substantially above average in these two indicators during the same period. Thus, five of the ten organizations represented in the sample did not notably profit from the merger, whereas the remaining five were successful or very successful at gaining deposits and new loans from former customers of the merged bank.

After the managers and executives agreed to participate, interviews were scheduled with them, patterned after the protocol used by Bastien (1989), in which the interviewer asked the respondent to remember the first time he or she became aware that the merger was about to take place. The respondents were asked about their emotional reaction to the news, the reactions of those around them, and their action decisions at the time. Subsequently, they were asked to reconstruct their perceptions of the situation as it emerged over the next six months. A question guide was developed to ensure that responses to all of the propositions from the literature were attained. The interviewer maintained notes of each interview. Following each interview, responses to the hypotheses were categorized according to bank performance (poorer-than-average performance on both indicators, better than average in one but not both, and better on both indicators). Furthermore, the form of the interviews allowed the researcher to explore other areas, which also were coded by bank performance category.

Results

The results for the case study are summarized in Table 8.2. As this table indicates, the first proposition was fully supported. None of the respondents representing banks in the unsuccessful no-growth category perceived any opportunity whatsoever in their rival's merger. Two of these respondents reported that since they were pursuing a geographical and neighborhood strategy and there were no branches of the merged bank in their neighborhoods, they saw no opportunity for attracting customers' deposits or loans from the merger. These results show that when competitors do not perceive an opportunity to take customers and revenue from a merging rival, they will not experience above-average growth in deposits and loans. Competitors that perceive a rival's merger as a growth opportunity and act to exploit this opportunity will experience above-average increases in deposits and loans. Respondents from all of the banks performing in the above-average category reported that the merger was viewed as an opportunity and that actions were taken to reap the benefits provided by this opportunity. For example, one of the most successful competitors started from another city and opened a branch in the core area of the merging bank.

Interviews with respondents representing the five successful banks yielded some modest but interesting findings for Proposition 2. One of the successful competitors had a preexisting program in place for attracting customers from merging bank. The most successful of the competitors pursued the tactic of recruiting staff from the merging bank, yet had no formal program for obtaining new customers. They did not try any additional tactics despite the success in attracting new customers as a result of hiring staff away from the merging bank. One moderately successful competitor implemented initial plans to attract depositors and lendees and was successful by its own standards. However, it did not know how to expand on this success and did not pursue any further efforts. The respondent for the other moderately successful competitor reported that the process of keeping up the pressure by experimenting with new competitive tactics was personally very satisfying and profitable, and experimented with several new tactics (advertising) over the months of the merger integration. Thus, although Proposition 2 was not strongly supported by the case data, the interviews yielded some interesting findings regarding the differential effects of various tactics used by the more successful competitors.

Proposition 3 focused on marketing activities triggered by the announcement of the rival's merger. The resizing itself as a general and broad activity was the trigger for all five of the community banks' exceeding industry averages in at least one of the indicators. However, no specific change event was triggered following marketing action. As noted, one of the successful competitors did

Table 8.2. Support for the Propositions.

	Level of Support		
	Strong	Moderate	Weak
Proposition 1: Competitors with the explicit purpose of taking customers and revenue from the resizing company will be more successful than competitors that are not intentionally pursuing these customers and revenues.	√		
Proposition 2: Successful efforts by a competitor at attracting customers and revenue from the resizing company will lead to further efforts by the competitor.		√	
Proposition 3: Successful efforts by a competitor at attracting customers and revenue from the resizing company will be tied to the announcement of the resizing change.			√
Proposition 4: The degree of success by a competitor at attracting customers and revenue from the resizing company will depend on the extent to which the competitor is knowledgeable about the internal processes unfolding within the resizing company.	√		
Proposition 5: The degree of success by a competitor at attracting customers and revenue from the resizing company will depend on the extent to which the competitor is knowledgeable about the resizing company's customers.	√		
Proposition 6: The degree of success by a competitor at attracting customers and revenue from the resizing company will depend on the extent to which the competitor is successful in recruiting employees from the resizing company.	√		

employ new marketing tactics, but the timing of these activities was not tightly coupled to the merger announcement.

Proposition 4 focused on competitors' knowledge of the situation-specific details regarding what was unfolding inside the merging rival bank. This proposition received strong support in the case study. Respondents from three of the five successful competitors were former employees of the merging banks and claimed to have kept close personal and social contact with employees at the merging bank. In each case, they reported hiring people away from the merging bank. Indeed, for the most successful competitor, almost all new staff members came from the merging bank, and in the moderately successful competitors, at least one merging bank former employee was hired (in addition to the informant). These employees arrived armed with valuable knowledge about the merging bank, including merger integration problems, dissatisfaction among the remaining employees, and insight into which customers were open to changing banks.

Proposition 5 received fairly strong support. One hallmark of community banks is their pride in knowing their customers well. Indeed, respondents for nine of the ten banks reported a high level of awareness of current customers and a strong orientation toward meeting their banking needs. However, the key factor underlying Proposition 5 was knowledge of the resizing company's customers, not one's own customers. Based on the interviews, none of the banks in the unsuccessful category focused on learning about the customers of the merging bank. In contrast, respondents from three of the successful competitors had high levels of current knowledge about customers of the merging bank and expressed a strong concern that the interests of these customers would not be well served by changes implemented at the merging bank. One method they used to obtain knowledge about these customers was to recruit employees from the merging bank. All respondents in the growth category reported directly targeting their marketing efforts to customers of the merging banks.

Proposition 6 received very strong support. Among the five community banks in the unsuccessful category, there were no successful attempts at recruiting employees from the merging bank. Among the moderately successful competitors, one executive-level employee in each bank was a former employee at the merging bank. In one case, the hiring was not linked to the competitor's merger, but in the other it was. Among the very successful competitors, there was much heavier reliance on employees hired from the merging bank. While these competitors certainly were not blind to the customer- and company-related knowledge that these employees could bring, in all cases the respondents asserted that they hired the employees first and foremost because of the known job-related competencies of the employees. All respondents from the successful competitors reported being very cautious about using information provided by these employees, making certain that they remained on the good side of both the law and banking ethics.

Discussion

These data are rich in implications for practice and further research. First, the strong support for Proposition 1, with its focus on perceiving and purposively acting on competitive opportunity, is very important. Bastien et al. (1996) suggested that there always is a windfall of customers changing their patronage in response to a merger and that this windfall could be randomly distributed across all rivals or could go mostly to a limited subset of rivals, depending on whether the rivals recognized the opportunity and acted purposively to exploit them. Certainly in this case, only competitors that recognized the opportunity to attract dissatisfied employees and customers from the merging bank realized above-average growth in deposits and loans. In contrast, the competitors that were blind to this opportunity failed to reap the windfall of benefits.

Two other propositions received strong support in this case study: Proposition 5 examining the level of knowledge about customers of the resizing company and Proposition 6 investigating success in recruiting staff from the resizing company. These findings are not surprising, since all three propositions relate to and underscore the importance of customers. The strong support for Proposition 5 is nearly as striking as the support for Proposition 1. All five of the high-growth competitors focused primarily on the customers of the merging bank and their discomfort with the newly merging bank. For example, one of the case informants had left the acquired bank early in the preacquisition period because

"I just didn't feel I could offer my customers the service they deserved." This person still knew some of the acquired bank customers and knew what issues these customers were anxious about. This information allowed the competitor to develop specific marketing plans focusing directly on themes of customer unhappiness. The other informants also personally knew many acquired bank customers and were aware how they reacted to the resizing changes.

The first strategic challenge for a competitor of a resizing company is to clearly understand what it will take to keep all of its own current customers. The next challenge is to determine the sources of customer dissatisfaction in the resizing company and to provide products and services that target their unmet needs, restoring satisfaction and gaining new customers in the process. Knowing your own customers and knowing your rival's customers is important to competitive success in the context of a rival's merger or acquisition. In this particular case, customer knowledge came from personal sources—people personally known to either the case informants or others in their organizations. Bastien et al. (1996) noted several other methods of securing this information, but in this case, personal knowledge of customers was most effective. Much of this personal knowledge of customers and their concerns with the newly merged bank came through former employees of the merging bank hired by the successful competitors. A reliance on employees coming from the resizing bank is the third strongly supported proposition. In all five no-growth banks, no employees were hired from the merging bank, and in all five of the high-growth banks, there was such hiring.

All of the successful competitors were aware (mostly through personal contacts) of customer and employee dissatisfaction with the merging banks and believed that bank mergers often offer rivals opportunities. However, none of the respondents was aware of the merger syndrome (including both customer loss and employee dissatisfaction) as a predictable and general phenomenon. Furthermore, none indicated that they timed their competitive moves according to announcements of merger change. Thus, the poor support for Proposition 3 (timing of competitive activity with announced changes in the resizing company) could simply be a reflection of the inattention to the integration moves of the merging bank that would naturally stem from not knowing what to look for, or it could be that timing is not as critical as Bastien et al. (1996, 1997) believed it to be. If the inattention comes from not knowing about the merger syndrome, then there may have been many opportunities missed even by the high-growth rivals. From the data in this study, there is no way of knowing.

Taken together, data from this study and from Bastien et al.'s earlier research (1996, 1997) suggest some potentially powerful ways in which the perceptual framing of a competitive situation appears related to the motivations operating in the situation. Figure 8.2 presents a competitive framing matrix illustrating some differences in how competitors might perceive a rival's resizing effort.

Figure 8.2. Competitive Framing Matrix.

| | | Perceived Opportunity | |
		No	Yes
Perceived Threat	No	**Q1: STRATEGIC INDIFFERENCE** Focus = Business as usual; no change in attention Strategy = Stay the course; no change of actions Problems = Blind to competitive growth opportunities and threats to the firm's own customer base	**Q2: OPPORTUNISM** Focus = Firm's attention shifts outward (external focus) Strategy = Offense; growth at the expense of the resizing rival Problems = Firm may lose some of its own employees and customers to the resizing rival
	Yes	**Q3: THREAT** Focus = Firm's attention shifts inward (internal focus) Strategy = Survival and defense; protecting the firm's existence against the onslaught of a resizing rival Problems = Blind to competitive growth opportunities provided by the resizing rival; threat rigidity restricts the firm's range of responses to the rival	**Q4: GUARDED OPPORTUNISM** Focus = Heightened attention inward and outward (intensified internal and external focus) Strategy = Combined offense and defense; grow at the expense of the rival while protecting the firm's own base of employees and customers Problems = Simultaneous focus on growth and protection may prevent full exploitation of competitive growth opportunities

This matrix provides a basic framework for summarizing the results of the resizing competitor research to date, linking these findings to existing research on perceptions of opportunities and threats and their implications for competitive actions and outcomes, and identifying some additional avenues for further research.

Respondents from five of the banks in the study reported they did not see the rival's merger as an opportunity or a threat. These banks occupy the first quadrant (Q1) in Figure 8.2, manifesting a position of strategic indifference toward the rival's merger. Why did these community banks adopt a frame of indifference toward the rival's change? Research on strategic groups suggests one possibility (Fiegenbaum & Thomas, 1995; Olusoga, Mokwa, & Noble, 1995; Reger & Huff, 1993): respondents perceived the resizing rival as occupying an entirely different strategic group, comprising larger regional or national banks. According to this research, firms pay more attention to actions made by close rivals within their own group or cognitive category and less attention to more distant rivals perceived as occupying a different group. This belief may include actions in the form of mergers, acquisitions, downsizings, and other approaches to resizing the firm. For example, some of the community banks in this study might have viewed the rival's merger as an action taken by a firm located in an entirely different strategic group, an action with little direct impact on the conduct and consequences of their own business, prompting a frame of strategic indifference.

Further research is needed in order to explore the role and impact of perceived strategic groups on the framing of competitive situations. One implication of this study is that it identifies a form of strategic myopia. Focusing too much attention on rival firms and too little attention on customers can block companies from seeing the full range of opportunities and threats presented by a particular competitive situation. For example, firms strategically indifferent to resizing in a perceptually distant rival run the risk of not seeing opportunities for gaining new customers from the resizing rival, as well as threats of losing their current customers to the resizing rival. One pitfall of strategic group mapping and other forms of competitor analysis is that executives may focus too much attention on similarities and differences that exist at the level of rival firms, blinding competitors to opportunities and threats clearly visible through an analysis of similarities and differences at the level of customers.

Other factors may have played a role in producing the strategic indifference of the five community banks. Cognitive research suggests that managers develop habitual ways to interpret and act on experience (Axelrod, 1972; Fiske & Taylor, 1991). Managers facing new or unique situations are less confident of their cognitive frames or schemas, resulting in a more active scanning of the environment and the potential for seeing new opportunities and threats. But managers facing familiar or recurring situations are more confident in their schemas, leading to a more passive scanning of the environment with a bias toward information search and analysis that confirms the status quo (Fiske & Taylor, 1991; Higgins & Bargh, 1987). Given the widespread and substantial history of resizing in the banking industry, it is entirely possible that respondents at the strategically indifferent banks were inclined to see the rival's merger as simply business as usual, applying this routinized competitive frame without actively scanning the environment for new opportunities and threats.

Respondents at the remaining five more successful community banks perceived the merger as an opportunity. Accordingly, they are located in the second quadrant (Q2), representing a position of opportunism toward the rival's change. As this study demonstrates, banks adopting an opportunistic frame on the situation saw the merger offering growth opportunities. They were motivated to reap the benefits of these opportunities and were rewarded for their competitive insights and efforts with above-average increases in deposits and loans. This finding shows that being in the right place at the right time may be necessary to take advantage of competitive opportunities presented by a resizing rival, although it is not sufficient to harvest the full range of these opportunities. Conscious and purposive action, coupled with proper market positioning, yields the best competitive gain in the context of a resizing rival. Due to their focus on individualized friendly service to customers, community banks are inherently well positioned to reap the benefits of a resizing regional or national bank.

The case reported by Bastien et al. (1996) illustrates the remaining two quadrants in the competitive framing matrix. In this study, the initial framing of the situation by the competitor of merging banks was based on fear, uncertainty, and a view of the merger as a threat. Once the competitor began to reap some benefits from the merging company, the fear-based emotional frame on the merger as a threat became a more rational cognitive frame on the merger as a competitive growth opportunity. In adopting this new frame on the situation, the CEO of the competitor (also a community bank) adopted a much more aggressive strategy and tactics. Several new types of action intended to identify and approach the merging rivals' customers and employees were taken.

A more simplistic framing of a rival's merger as mere opportunity (Q2) may blind the competitor to potentially debilitating threats to the competitor's own customer base, resulting in below-average performance outcomes or even losses. In contrast, a more simplistic framing of the merger as a mere threat (Q3) may blind the competitor to the significant growth opportunities presented by the merger or may lead to an increased likelihood of strategic inaction similar in form to that observed in the case of threat or rigidity (Ocasio, 1995; Staw, Sandelands, & Dutton, 1981). Existing research suggests that when the resizing rival is comparatively large in size, the threat aspect will become salient and will lead competitors to focus their attention on a more restricted range of responses, including increased commitment to an established course of action (Dutton & Jackson, 1987; Greve & Taylor, 2000; Ocasio, 1995; Staw, 1981).

One implication of the matrix is that framing a rival's resizing as both a threat and an opportunity (Q4) should result in motivations both to protect one's own company and exploit the opportunity presented by the resizing rival. A related implication is that these motivations should be expressed in actions focused on reducing threats to one's own base of employees and customers, as well as actions aimed at reaping benefits from the rival's resizing. Thus, in quadrant 4, the competitor's attention is in two directions: toward its own organization, employees, and customers and toward the resizing rival, its employees, and its customers. Companies adopting the more simplistic framing of a rival's merger as a threat (Q3) are characterized by threat-related motivations and actions focused on protecting the firm and its existing complement of employees and customers. For organizations adopting the framing of the resizing solely as an opportunity, we should see opportunistic motivations and actions focused mostly on how to exploit the resizing firm and its employees and customers.

With regard to performance outcomes, firms in quadrant 2 may experience growth at the expense of the resizing rival, but they run the risk of losing their employees and customers to the rival or to other competitors. Firms in quadrant 3 may protect their employee and customer base, but they run the risk of experiencing below-average growth since they are not attempting to exploit merger-based growth opportunities. Businesses in quadrant 1 run both of the above risks and are likely to experience below-average growth. Companies in quadrant 4 have the greatest chance to protect their own employee and customer base while reaping the benefits of above-average growth at the expense of a rival's resizing effort.

Implications for Resizing Organizations

This study provides some important implications for both managers and competitors of resizing companies. First, resizing company managers must be mindful of the growth opportunities afforded their competitive rivals by their own efforts. Rivals of resizing firms must be aware of these opportunities, as well as be ready to take purposive action to exploit them. Second, resizing managers and competitors must recognize that customers are the key to reaping the benefits flowing from a resizing effort. Although it is important to focus attention on customers of a resizing company and understand the nature and sources of their patronage, it also is critical for rivals of the resizing company to not take their eye off the ball with regard to current customers.

Another clear implication is that employees of the resizing organization are the primary source of customer satisfaction or dissatisfaction. Thus, resizing company managers need to be careful in their planning to understand and appreciate the effects of the resizing efforts on their employees, especially employees in customer contact positions. Competitors, for their part, should be open to hiring employees from the resizing rival in order to strengthen their own base of technically competent workers, expand their knowledge regarding which customers of the resizing firm are dissatisfied and why, and reap the benefits of new customers who are loyal to the employees recruited from the rival. For example, hiring bank tellers, clerks, and loan officers from a merging rival was the primary way banks in our study increased their customer base.

One of the more interesting findings of our study is that the most successful competitor hired staff from the merging bank but did not develop or implement a formal, systematic, or planned program to secure new customers from the merging bank. For managers in firms competing with rivals engaged in resizing efforts, this study suggests that although plans to gain new customers may be effective, an equally effective approach might be to focus their time and attention on hiring some competent but dissatisfied employees from the resizing rival. For resizing managers, the clear implication is that it is important to understand the competitive implications of losing employees to their competitive rivals.

A final implication of the study relates to the concept of strategic differentiation and its impact on the distribution of benefits from a rival's resizing. Community banks pursue fundamentally different banking and customer strategies than do large regional or national banks. Due to their emphasis on customer-focused service, targeting individuals, families, and small- to medium-sized business customers, community banks are well positioned to restore lost satisfaction among customers disenfranchised by merger-related changes commonly imposed by large regional and national banks. In the context of this study, the very points of differentiation defining the customer strategy of community banks placed them in a good position to attract dissatisfied customers from the newly merged bank. In short, they were in the right place at the right time. What separated the high-growth from the moderate- and no-growth banks was a combination of their occupying a good position of strategic differentiation, knowing it, and purposively acting on it. One practical challenge implied in this approach is the need for competitors to assess the degree to which their current strategic definition or niche places them in an opportune position for restoring lost satisfaction to customers disenfranchised by a rival's resizing effort.

There are several specific implications for planners and managers in resizing companies:

- Your customers will notice and will be affected by the resizing, mostly negatively. Be prepared for their reactions, be prepared to reevaluate your plans in the light of this, and be prepared to increase your marketing and sales actions to compensate for the inevitable loss of customer confidence.

• Your employees are the key to the ultimate success or failure of the resizing effort. Carefully consider how they will react to the resizing effort. Be prepared to identify employees whom you must retain if you want to maintain revenues and do whatever is necessary to keep them. You also must be prepared to treat departing employees as well as possible; if you treat them carelessly, they likely will come back to haunt you.

• Your competitive rivals are out there ready to take away customers and employees, and you must be ready to thwart their efforts. Be prepared to pay much more attention to your competitors than you would during more stable times.

Executives in rivals of resizing companies should be aware of the following implications:

• The managers in the resizing company most likely will be occupied by their internal focus on implementing the resizing and thus probably will not be paying much attention to customer satisfaction.

• Resizing company employees will be available for hiring. Be prepared to increase your staffing levels so that you can add already trained employees to your workforce. Remember that customer contact employees will come to you with their own fan clubs of disaffected customers of the resizing company.

References

Ambrose, D. (Ed.). (1998). *Healing the downsized organization: What every employee needs to know about today's new workplace.* New York: Random House.

American Heritage Dictionary. (1994). Boston: Houghton Mifflin.

Axelrod, R. M. (1972). *Framework for a general theory of cognition and choice.* Berkeley: Berkeley Institute of International Studies, University of California.

Bastien, D. T. (1987). Common patterns of behavior and communication in corporate mergers and acquisitions. *Human Resource Management Journal, 26,* 17–33.

Bastien, D. T. (1989). Communication, conflict, and learning in mergers and acquisitions. In A. H. Van de Ven, H. Angle, & M. S. Poole (Eds.), *Research on the management of innovation* (pp. 367–396). New York: HarperCollins.

Bastien, D. T. (1994). A feedback loop model of post-acquisition performance: Customers and competitors. *Management Communication Quarterly, 7,* 46–69.

Bastien, D. T., Hostager, T. J., & Miles, H. H. (1996). Corporate Judo: Exploiting the dark side of change when competitors merge, acquire, downsize, or restructure. *Journal of Management Inquiry, 5,* 261–275.

Bastien, D. T., Hostager, T. J., & Miles, H. H. (1997). Reply: Bullish on thoughtful criticism, bearish on Hitt and Serpa's commentary. *Journal of Management Inquiry, 6,* 35–39.

Bastien, D. T., McPhee, R., & Bolton, K. (1995). A study and extended theory of organizational climate: A structurational approach. *Communication Monographs, 62,* 132–151.

Blundell, W. E. (1978, August 17). As the axe falls so does productivity of grim U.S. workers. *Wall Street Journal.*

Brockner, J. (1988). The effects of work layoffs on survivors: Research, theory, and practice. In B. M. Staw & L. L. Cummings (Eds.), *Research in organizational behavior* (Vol. 10). Greenwich, CT: JAI Press.

Buono, A. F., & Bowditch, J. L. (1989). *The human side of mergers and acquisitions: Managing collisions between people and organizations.* San Francisco: Jossey-Bass.

Burke, R. J., & Nelson, D. (1998). Mergers and acquisitions, downsizing, and privatization: A North American perspective. In M. K. Gowing, J. D. Kraft, & J. C. Quick (Eds.), *The new organizational reality: Downsizing, restructuring, and revitalization.* Washington, DC: American Psychological Association.

Byrne, J. A. (1999). *Chainsaw: The notorious career of Al Dunlap in the era of profit-at-any-price.* New York: HarperBusiness.

Cameron, K. S., Freeman, S. J., & Mishra, A. K. (1991). Best practices in white-collar downsizing: Managing contradictions. *Academy of Management Executive, 5,* 57–73.

Cameron, K. S., Whetten, D. A., & Kim, M. U. (1987). Organizational dysfunctions of decline. *Academy of Management Journal, 30,* 126–137.

Campbell, A., Goold, M., & Alexander, M. (1995). The value of the parent company. *California Management Review, 38,* 79–97.

Cartwright, S., & Cooper, C. L. (1996). *Managing mergers, acquisitions and strategic alliances: Integrating people and cultures.* Boston: Butterworth-Heinemann.

Cascio, W. F. (1993). Downsizing: What do we know? What have we learned? *Academy of Management Executive, 7,* 95–104.

Cascio, W. F. (1995). Whither industrial and organizational psychology in a changing world of work? *American Psychologist, 50,* 928–939.

Cascio, W. F. (1998). Learning from outcomes: Financial experiences of 311 firms that have downsized. In M. K. Gowing, J. D. Kraft, & J. C. Quick (Eds.), *The new organizational reality: Downsizing, restructuring, and revitalization* (pp. 55–70). Washington, DC: American Psychological Association.

Cascio, W. F., Young, C. E., & Morris, J. R. (1997). Financial consequences of employment-change decisions in major U.S. corporations. *Academy of Management Journal, 40,* 1175–1189.

Clemente, M. N., & Greenspan, D. S. (1998). *Winning at mergers and acquisitions: The guide to market focused planning and integration.* New York: Wiley.

De Meuse, K. P., Vanderheiden, & P. A. Bergmann, T. J. (1994). Announced layoffs: Their effect on corporate financial performance. *Human Resource Management, 33,* 509–530.

Downs, A. (1996). *Corporate executions: The ugly truth about downsizing–How corporate greed is shattering lives, companies, and communities.* New York: AMACOM.

Dutton, J. E., & Jackson, S. E. (1987). Categorizing strategic issues: Links to organizational action. *Academy of Management Journal, 12,* 76–90.

Fiegenbaum, A., & Thomas, H. (1995). Strategic groups as reference groups: Theory, modeling and empirical examination of industry and competitive strategy. *Strategic Management Journal, 16,* 461–475.

Fiske, S. T., & Taylor, S. E. (1991). *Social cognition.* New York: McGraw-Hill.

Galpin, T. J., & Herndon, M. (1999). *The complete guide to mergers and acquisitions: Process tools to support merger and acquisition integration at every level.* San Francisco: Jossey-Bass.

Geneen, H., & Bowers, B. (1999). *Synergy and other lies: Downsizing, bureaucracy, and corporate culture debunked.* New York: Griffin.

Greve, H. R., & Taylor, A. (2000). Innovations as catalysts for organizational change: Shifts in organizational cognition and search. *Administrative Science Quarterly, 45,* 54–80.

Grubb, T. M., & Lamb, R. B. (2000). *Capitalize on merger chaos: Six ways to profit from your competitors' consolidation on your own.* New York: Free Press.

Haspeslagh, P. C., & Jemison, D. B. (1991). *Managing acquisitions: Creating value through corporate renewal.* New York: Free Press.

Higgins, E. T., & Bargh, J. A. (1987). Social cognition and social perception. In *Annual Review of Psychology* (Vol. 38, pp. 369–425). Palo Alto, CA: Annual Reviews.

Hughlett, M. (1997, March 11). Purchase of American tests Firstar:

Milwaukee bank loses deposits, executives. *Saint Paul Pioneer Press,* pp. 1E, 6E.

Jemison, D. B. (1986). *Strategic capability transfer in acquisition integration* (Research Paper No. 913). Stanford, CA: Stanford University.

Jemison, D. B., & Sitkin, S. B. (1986). Corporate acquisitions: A process perspective. *Academy of Management Review, 11,* 145–163.

Jick, T. D. (1985). As the axe fails: Budget cuts and the experience of stress in organizations. In T. A. Beehr & R. S. Bhagat (Eds.), *Human stress and cognition in organizations: An integrated perspective* (pp. 83–114). New York: Wiley.

Kover, A. (2000, February 21). Big banks debunked. *Fortune,* pp. 187–194.

Lajoux, A. R. (1997). *The art of M&A integration: A guide to merging resources, processes, and responsibilities.* New York: McGraw-Hill.

Leana, C. R., & Feldman, D. C. (1992). *Coping with job loss: How individuals, organizations and communities respond to layoffs.* San Francisco: New Lexington Press.

Marks, M. L. (1982). Merging human resources: A review of the current research. *Mergers and Acquisitions, 17,* 38–44.

Marks, M. L. (1994). *From turmoil to triumph: New life after corporate mergers, acquisitions and downsizing.* San Francisco: New Lexington Press.

Marks, M. L., & Mirvis, P. H. (1985). Merger syndrome: Stress and uncertainty. *Merger and Acquisitions, 20,* 50–55.

Marks, M. L., & Mirvis, P. H. (1998). *Joining forces: Making one plus one equal three in mergers, acquisitions, and alliances.* San Francisco: Jossey-Bass.

Maruyama, M. (1963). The second cybernetics: Deviation-amplifying mutual causal processes. *American Scientist, 51,* 164–179.

Masuch, M. (1985). Vicious circles in organizations. *Administrative Science Quarterly, 30,* 14–33.

Mirvis, P. H., & Marks, M. L. (1986). Merger syndrome: Management by crisis. *Mergers and Acquisitions, 21,* 70–76.

Mirvis, P. H., & Marks, M. L. (1992). *Managing the merger: Making it work.* Upper Saddle River, NJ: Prentice Hall.

Noer, D. (1993). *Healing the wounds: Overcoming the trauma of layoffs and revitalizing downsized organizations.* San Francisco: Jossey-Bass.

Ocasio, W. C. (1995). The enactment of economic adversity: A reconciliation of theories of failure-induced change and threat-rigidity. In L. L. Cummings & B. M. Staw (Eds.), *Research in organizational behavior* (Vol. 17, pp. 287–331). Greenwich, CT: JAI Press.

Olusoga, S. A., Mokwa, M. P., & Noble, C. H. (1995). Strategic groups, mobility barriers, and competitive advantage. *Journal of Business Research, 33,* 153–164.

O'Neill, H. M., & Lenn, J. (1995). Voices of survivors: Words that downsizing CEOs should hear. *Academy of Management Executive, 9,* 23–34.

Porter, M. E. (1987). From competitive advantage to corporate strategy. *Harvard Business Review, 65,* 43–59.

Reger, R. K., & Huff, A. S. (1993). Strategic groups: A cognitive perspective. *Strategic Management Journal, 14,* 103–124.

Roll, R. (1986). The hubris hypothesis of corporate takeovers. *Journal of Business, 59,* 197–216.

Shibutani, T. (1966). *Improvised news: A sociological study of rumor.* Indianapolis, IN: Bobbs-Merrill.

Sirower, M. L. (1997). *The synergy trap: How companies lose the acquisition game.* New York: Free Press.

Staw, B. M. (1981). The escalation of commitment to a course of action. *Academy of Management Review, 6,* 577–587.

Staw, B. M., Sandelands, L. E., & Dutton, J. E. (1981). Threat-rigidity effects in organizational behavior: A multi-level analysis. *Administrative Science Quarterly, 26,* 501–524.

Vanderheiden, P. A., De Meuse, K. P., & Bergmann, T. J. (1999). And the beat goes on: Corporate downsizing in the twenty-first century. *Human Resource Management Journal, 38,* 261–268.

Waters, J. (1997). Quaker is launching an expensive nationwide promotional campaign reintroducing diet Snapple. *Crain's Chicago Business, 20,* 4–5.

Weick, K. E. (1979). *The social psychology of organizing* (2nd ed.). Reading, MA: Addison-Wesley.

Zuboff, S. (1989). *In the age of the smart machine: The future of work and power.* New York: Basic Books.

Zweig, P. L., Kline, J. P., Forest, S. A., & Gudridge, K. (1995, October 20). The case against mergers. *Business Week,* pp. 122–130.

CHAPTER 9

The Impact of Layoffs on Family, Friendship, and Community Networks

Daniel C. Feldman

The mass layoffs that began occurring during the oil crisis of 1973 reawakened interest in the effects of unemployment, an interest that had generally been dormant among social science researchers since the Great Depression. The restructurings that occurred in the wake of the World Trade Center and Pentagon terrorist attacks in 2001 once again made rising unemployment an important social issue after a decade of remarkable economic growth.

Not surprisingly, the greatest amount of research attention has been given to the laid-off workers themselves: the emotional upheaval they experience (Jahoda, 1982; Kessler, Turner, & House, 1988; Shamir, 1986), how they cope with their new circumstances (Leana & Feldman, 1994; Kinicki & Latack, 1990), and how layoffs affect their performance on subsequent jobs and long-term attitudes toward careers (Feldman, 1996; Feldman & Leana, 2000).

The consequences of restructuring for organizations themselves also have received considerable attention from researchers and practitioners alike. The evidence suggests that organizations often do not yield the productivity gains they expect from downsizing because of losses in product and service quality, lost opportunities to develop new markets, and increased litigation costs

(Cascio, 1998; De Meuse, Vanderheiden, & Bergmann, 1994; Greenhalgh, Lawrence, & Sutton, 1988; Sutton, Eisenhardt, & Jucker, 1986). In addition, some productivity losses are attributable to the reactions and behaviors of coworkers who survive the downsizings. These survivors often experience feelings of guilt and anxiety, are sometimes overwhelmed by the additional amount of work for which they are now responsible, and frequently view their employers as unjust and unfair in their dealings with workers (Brockner, 1990; Brockner, Grover, Reed, DeWitt, & O'Malley, 1987; Fisher & White, 2000; Noer, 1993). Thus, the negative effects of layoffs and downsizing are experienced not only by those who are let go but also by those who remain.

The broader effects of downsizing on family members, friends, and communities have received considerably less attention. Early research suggested that layoffs have negative consequences in terms of spouse abuse (Justice & Justice, 1976), relationships with children (Newman, 1988), withdrawal from friends (Leana & Feldman, 1992), and urban decay (Hoerr, 1988). However, these results were found mainly in studies where the research sites had experienced unemployment rates over 10 percent and entire communities were in enormous distress (for example, Michigan after auto plant shutdowns, Pittsburgh after the steel mills closed, and Cape Canaveral after the *Challenger* disaster). The effects of downsizing on family, friendship, and community networks in less dire circumstances have not yet been comprehensively examined.

This chapter examines the consequences of downsizing and plant closings on the spouses and children of laid-off employees, their friends, and the communities in which they reside; the moderating factors that determine how strong the impacts of organizational restructuring are on each of these four groups; and the effectiveness of corporate assistance programs in repairing any collateral damage created by layoffs for those in employees' networks outside work.

Impact of Job Loss on Spouses of Laid-Off Workers

Plant closings, divestitures, and downsizing have an enormous impact on the spouses of laid-off employees.

Consequences of Layoffs for Spouses

There are five negative outcomes for spouses of laid-off employees (see Table 9.1):

- Deterioration of the marital relationship itself (marital discord, separation, divorce)
- Changes in the standard of living (loss of income, decreases in savings and spending)
- Changes in labor force participation for the spouse (need to enter the workforce or work longer hours)
- Changes in family dynamics (problems with children, changes in distribution of power within the marriage)
- Geographical mobility (the need to move under duress to find new employment or to a less expensive community)

Deterioration of the Marital Relationship

The evidence on the impact of layoffs for the marital relationship is mixed. In terms of divorces and legal separations, there is no strong evidence that layoffs lead to formal dissolutions of marriages (Leana & Feldman, 1992, 1994). Part of the reason for this finding may be that the divorce rate in the United States is already high; the divorce rate for laid-off employees would have to be extremely high to be significantly greater than that of the population in general. Moreover, because layoffs cause financial hardship, unhappy couples may be unable to support two households in divorce when they can barely support one in unemployment.

Empirical data on increases in spousal abuse as a result of job loss are sparse at best. Although there is some qualitative evidence on the increased incidence of verbal abuse during unemployment (Justice & Justice, 1976; Newman, 1988, 1993), it is difficult to measure physical abuse rates reliably, since law enforcement officials typically estimate that spouse abuse is an underreported crime. Also, in several cases, spouse abuse may have occurred before the layoff and continued after unemployment; that is, the abuse might have intensified in frequency or severity but was not caused by the layoff.

Changes in Standard of Living

Probably the most direct negative consequence of layoffs for marriages is a decline in the standard of living. Depending on the

Table 9.1. Consequence of Layoffs to Outsiders.

Consequences

For spouses

Deterioration of marriage (for example, divorce, separation)

Decreases in standard of living (for example, loss in income, decreases in spending)

Changes in labor force participation (for example, start work, increase work hours)

Geographical mobility (for example, to find new job or cheaper community)

For children

Difficulty concentrating in school and lower academic performance

Exposure to negative information about work and a decreased work ethic

Increased social problems with peers (for example, hostility and withdrawal)

Decreases in economic well-being (for example, increased work hours, decreased college attendance)

For friends

Negative changes in affect and mood of the relationship

Decreased financial resources with which to pursue leisure activities

Decreased contact and intimacy of friendships

For communities

Increases in local unemployment rates

Loss of community tax revenues

Declines in real estate values

Decreases in corporate citizenship behavior

current wages of the other spouse and current savings, loss of work can mean depletion of savings and dramatic decreases in the standard of living. Particularly when layoffs are widespread in a community, layoffs can lead to bankruptcy, home foreclosures, and tremendous scaling back of expenditures. Although the most dramatic of these negative consequences (bankruptcy and home foreclosure) typically occur in less than 10 percent of households, that figure is not negligible (Leana & Feldman, 1992).

Not surprisingly, the layoff of one partner increases the need for the other spouse to start working, work longer hours, or take on a second job. Particularly if the laid-off spouse is the major breadwinner, the other spouse may have to increase his or her labor force participation to make ends meet (Hochschild, 1989, 1997).

Although the increases in spouses' labor force participation rates have received the most attention in the unemployment literature, less research has been conducted on spouses' loss of valued activities as child care providers and homemakers. Newman (1993) found, for instance, that many wives of laid-off workers genuinely enjoyed their roles as mothers and homemakers. For them, having to work outside the home was not only a matter of taking jobs in which they had little interest, but also a matter of losing time for roles they cared for deeply.

Changes in Family Dynamics

When spouses of laid-off employees are forced back into the labor market or into increased hours of work, they start contributing a greater proportion of the earnings to the family and hence feel entitled to more power in how that money was spent. This often shifts the dynamics of power in the family, particularly in families where the husbands had been the major decision makers about family finances. Women gain more power in how decisions are made in the family, and that power largely sustains itself even after spouses became reemployed (Goode, 1994).

Another dynamic that can occur in the aftermath of layoffs is resentment about the sharing of household duties. As women take up the slack in terms of earning money outside the household, they often hope that their husbands will take up the slack in terms of household chores and child rearing—and are frequently disappointed in the amount and quality of effort their husbands make in return. Thus, newly employed or increasingly employed women perceive they are working a "second shift" when their husbands are barely working one (Hochschild, 1989).

Need to Relocate Geographically

Another negative consequence many spouses experience as the result of their partners' layoffs is the need to relocate geographically. In some cases, couples have to move to get new employment; where layoffs are widespread in any given community, moving geographically may be one of the few ways out of the predicament of unemployment (Brett, Stroh, & Reilly, 1993; Leana & Feldman, 1995a, 1995b; Stroh, 1999). In other cases, couples may move to different communities because the cost of living there is lower. For example, it is not unusual to see out-migration from large urban areas experiencing high unemployment rates to more rural areas, where the costs of housing are much cheaper (Feldman & Bolino, 1998).

Such movement may be economically rational, but it can often be psychologically traumatic. Particularly for couples who have spent their entire lives in one community or whose extended families live in that community, moving far away for employment opportunities is a wrenching experience. Couples such as these are moving away from their social support networks at exactly the time when they need them the most (Eby, Allen, & Douthitt, 1999). Thus, while the duration of the marriage may not directly suffer in the aftermath of layoffs, the quality of the marriage relationship may indeed deteriorate.

Moderating Factors

Not every spouse will experience all of the disruptions identified, and not every spouse will experience those disruptions with the same intensity and sense of deprivation. Surprisingly little research has been conducted on moderating factors in the reactions of outsiders to downsizing; what research has been conducted in this area has focused almost exclusively on the reactions of survivors (the coworkers of laid-off employees) (Brockner, 1990). We consider factors that we believe are likely to have an impact on the degree to which spouses of laid-off employees experience these reactions (see Table 9.2):

- Percentage of family income earned by the laid-off employee
- Salience of the breadwinner role to the laid-off employee
- Number of dependent children in the family
- Life stage of the spouse
- Personality characteristics of the spouse

Table 9.2. Moderating Factors on Reactions to Organizational Restructuring.

Moderating Factors

For spouses

Percentage of family income earned by the laid-off employee

Salience of the family breadwinner role status to laid-off employee

Number of dependent children in the family

Life stage of spouse

Personality traits of spouse

For children

Age of the child

Degree of disruption to daily routines

Community wealth (for example, local unemployment rates)

Quantity and quality of part-time work experiences

For friends

Basis of friendship (for example, work versus nonwork)

Length of friendship

Level of community affluence

For communities

Diversity of the local economy

Physical distance to communities with greater employment opportunities

Degree of state and federal governmental assistance

Community redevelopment efforts on the part of local business leaders

Percentage of Family Income Earned by Laid-Off Employee

The amount of disruption to the spouse is likely to be moderated by the percentage of family income earned by the laid-off employee. When the laid-off employee is the sole wage earner, the disruption will be greatest. In contrast, when the laid-off employee is a "trailing spouse" or makes substantially less than 50 percent of the family income, the disruption caused to spouses by layoffs is likely to be much more muted (Eby et al., 1999).

Salience of the Breadwinner Role to the Laid-Off Employee

Recent research suggests that the amount of disruption that laid-off employees experience in unemployment may be partially due to the salience of the breadwinner role to them. When laid-off employees keenly feel their responsibility to be the major breadwinners in the family, the loss of unemployment is crushing financially and emotionally (Eby et al., 1999).

In contrast, when the laid-off employee does not highly identify with the role of major family breadwinner, job loss results in much less depression, anxiety, and frustration. In turn, the spouse is likely to suffer fewer negative spin-off effects as well. When the salience of the breadwinner role status to the laid-off employee is low, the negative emotional consequences for the spouse will be tempered, too.

Number of Dependent Children

The number of dependent children in the household may moderate the relationship between unemployment of one spouse and negative outcomes for the other. For example, when an unemployed worker has several children under age eighteen still living at home (particularly children not yet in high school), a spouse who is forced into more hours of work is likely to suffer the greatest sense of deprivation. Younger children need more parental supervision and more emotional support, and after-school day care arrangements and backup plans have to be made.

When a laid-off worker has only one or two children, the disruption to the spouse may be lower. Fewer children mean less financial drain on family financial resources and less difficulty in arranging for day care and after-school activities as well. Although this question has not yet been directly addressed, it may be the age of the youngest child rather than the number of children that makes the most difference here. A very young child may make even part-time employment for the spouse much more difficult to obtain and to sustain.

Life Stage of Spouse

Previous research on layoffs suggests that the life stage of an employee influences how negatively he or she responds to unemployment and how quickly he or she bounces back (Leana & Feldman, 1992, 1995a, 1995b). In general, that research suggests that mid-career employees and those in middle age experience layoffs most negatively and take longer to get reemployed. They often perceive themselves as too old to get retrained and too young to consider retirement. Moreover, they often experience age bias in getting reemployed in comparable jobs (Feldman & Leana, 2000).

Here, we suggest that the life stage of spouses may also influence the extent to which they experience negative spin-off effects from their partners' layoffs. Specifically, middle-aged spouses are likely to experience the layoffs of their partners most severely. Middle-aged spouses (especially those who have been out of the workforce for twenty years) may not have sufficient skills, or sufficiently updated skills, to obtain well-paying jobs easily (Newman, 1993). In contrast, younger spouses have more energy and flexibility to start (or restart) their careers, while older spouses may need to work only part-time for a few years until their partners become eligible for pension or social security benefits (Feldman, 2000; Feldman & Turnley, 2001).

Personality Characteristics

There is some evidence that personality traits may work to mitigate the negative consequences of layoffs on spouses. For instance, "hardiness" refers to the ability of individuals to overcome barriers to goals and persevere in the face of adversity (Kobasa, 1979). Those who are psychologically hardy are more likely to be able to maintain their equanimity in the face of major stressful life events such as job loss (Leana & Feldman, 1992). The work of Barrick and Mount (1991) suggests that some of the "Big 5" personality traits (extraversion, agreeableness, openness to experience, neuroticism, and conscientiousness) may also help temper negative reactions to spousal unemployment. For example, openness to experience and agreeableness are related to positive attitudes toward job searching, and extraversion and conscientiousness are related to success in landing job offers (Boudreau, Boswell, Judge, & Bretz, 2001; Bretz, Boudreau, & Judge, 1994).

Impact of Unemployment on Children

Recent research by Barling and his colleagues (Barling, Dupre, & Hepburn, 1998; Barling, Rogers, & Kelloway, 1995; Barling, Zacharatos, & Hepburn, 1999) suggests that children are more cognizant of the employment problems that their parents face than their parents realize and that layoffs create a distinct set of negative consequences for children too (see Table 9.1).

Consequences of Layoffs for Children

There are four important consequences that downsizing can have on children of laid-off employees:

- Difficulty concentrating on studying and lower academic performance
- Exposure to more negative information about work and a decreased work ethic
- Increased social problems with peers (hostility, withdrawal)
- Decreases in economic well-being, resulting in either increased work hours while still a student or lower enrollment rates in college

Poorer Academic Performance

Layoffs of parents can result in lower academic performance (as assessed by grades) for at least two key reasons. First, layoffs can require students to engage in more hours of part-time work, which detracts from their level of school achievement (Barling et al., 1995; Greenberger & Steinberg, 1986). Second, job loss can lead to more friction in the household, making it more difficult for students to concentrate and focus on their school work (Loughlin & Barling, 1998; Steinberg, Fegley, & Dornbusch, 1993).

Decreased Work Ethic

Another negative consequence of layoffs for children is a decline in their work ethic. For example, children may identify highly with the parent who loses a job and may feel a sense of injustice vicariously.

As a result, those children may lower their own levels of aspiration, since they now perceive the connection between hard work and job security to be much more tenuous (Loughlin & Barling, 1998; Shanahan, Finch, Mortimer, & Ryu, 1991). In general, it appears that teenagers are most negatively affected by their parents' job loss in terms of aspiration levels; teenagers are highly impressionable, and individuals typically form their work values and career aspirations during this time period (Goffredson, 1981; Krosnick & Alwin, 1989; Loughlin & Barling, 1998).

Increased Social Problems with Peers

Another unfortunate negative spin-off effect of layoffs is a decrease in the quality of children's relationships with friends and peers. Particularly in small communities and particularly among teenagers, layoffs and job loss may become widely known throughout a child's friendship and school networks. Sometimes experiencing shame and embarrassment vicariously through their parents, children of laid-off workers become more withdrawn and uncommunicative with their friends (Barling et al., 1999). In addition, teenagers may provoke fights with their friends as a means of justifying their distancing themselves from their peer group (Newman, 1988, 1993).

Decreases in Economic Well-Being

The most palpable negative consequence of layoffs for children is a decrease in economic well-being. At the most superficial level, layoffs often require families to cut back on vacations and toys. For teenagers, parental unemployment can mean decreases in the amount of discretionary spending on clothing, eating out, movies, mall shopping, and recreation.

Parental unemployment often results in increased pressure on teenagers to start working part time or to increase the number of hours they already work (Stern, Stone, Hopkins, & McMillion (1990), and increased work hours can result in lower levels of academic achievement in school. Although there is little evidence that working as a teenager is linked to delinquency (Gottfredson, 1985), there is also little evidence that working as a teenager systematically builds character either (Stern et al., 1990). Although some percentage of a teenager's income does go, directly or indirectly, into supporting the nuclear family, a large percentage of teenagers' income is used to support discretionary purchases, such as telephones, cars, and entertainment, for themselves (Greenberger & Steinberg, 1986).

National data indicate that teenaged children from families with less family income are less likely to enroll in college or continue on to graduate school. Of teenagers whose parents' income was less than $20,000, only 37 percent completed a bachelor's degree within five years of high school graduation. In contrast, 61 percent of children from families with incomes of $60,000 or more completed a bachelor's degree within the same time frame (National Center for Education Statistics, 1998). It appears, then, that wealthier parents not only raise their children's aspiration levels, but also are more likely to pay for their children to go to college on a full-time basis.

Moderating Factors

Not every child of laid-off parents experiences all of these negative consequences of downsizing, nor does every child experience these negative consequences with the same intensity. Little empirical research has been conducted on potential moderating variables. Based on research in allied areas, we consider four factors that are likely to exacerbate (or mitigate) the negative fallout that downsizing has for children of laid-off workers (see Table 9.2):

- Age of the child
- Degree of disruption to daily routines
- Community wealth (for example, local unemployment rates or importance of affluence to status with peers)
- Quantity and quality of their own part-time work experiences

Age at Time of Layoff

In general, the effects of layoffs appear to be stronger on older children and teenagers than they are on young children. Older children are more likely to understand the employment problems that their parents are discussing and are more likely to be asked to cut back their spending or increase their work hours. In addition, older children and teenagers are more likely than their younger siblings to suffer awkwardness with peers and teachers, since older children are more aware of what goes on in families other than their own (Harvey, 1999; Kokko & Pulkkinen, 2000).

Degree of Disruption to Daily Routines

Analogous to the discussion of spouses, how much children are adversely affected by layoffs will be exacerbated, or lessened, by the amount of disruption to daily routines that their parents' layoffs cause. For children from one-parent households whose sole wage earner is unemployed, the degree of disruption of daily routines is likely to be immense, particularly if unemployment continues for several months or more and the family is forced to relocate geographically or change residences. In contrast, for children whose laid-off parent is not the major wage earner or whose unemployment lasts only several weeks, the degree of disruption to daily routines may be minimal. As is the case for laid-off workers themselves (Kinicki & Latack, 1990; Leana & Feldman, 1992), the degree of disruption in daily routines is likely to be a major determining factor in how much stress children of those workers experience.

Community Wealth

It is also likely that the wealth of the community will influence the extent to which a parent's layoff has negative consequences for the child's psychological well-being. For example, in communities where unemployment is widespread and conspicuous consumption by teenagers is low, there is less likely to be any stigma attached to being the child of an unemployed parent. In contrast, in communities that are affluent and in which children are partially evaluated by their peers on the display of material wealth, the discomfort teenagers feel because of a parent's unemployment is likely to be much greater (Newman, 1988, 1993).

Quantity and Quality of Part-Time Work

The evidence suggests that both the quantity and quality of part-time work will moderate the extent to which children of laid-off workers experience negative outcomes as a result of a parent's unemployment (Barling et al., 1995; Barling et al., 1999). In terms of hours worked, the research suggests that the longer the hours worked per week, the greater are the negative consequences for teenagers; this is particularly true when work hours exceed twenty per week (Greenberger & Steinberg, 1986). Long work hours are often negatively associated with high school grades and subsequent enrollment in, and completion of, college degree programs.

Furthermore, the quality of part-time work has a strong moderating impact. In particular, students who work at nonmenial jobs alongside responsible adults are likely to have more positive attitudes toward work in general, and those attitudes are likely to carry over to school settings (Barling et al., 1995). In contrast, when students work in menial service jobs in "teenage ghettos," their work habits and career aspirations are likely to suffer (Greenberger & Steinberg, 1986).

Impact of Job Loss on Friends of Employees

Downsizing has an impact on friends of laid-off employees and the quality of laid-off employees' relationships with their friends. In this discussion, we will be primarily focusing on the nonwork friends of laid-off employees rather than coworkers or survivors in the workplace.

Consequences of Layoffs for Friends

Relative to the other networks being examined in this chapter, the consequences of layoffs for friends from outside work have received the least attention. However, extrapolating from previous research on survivors and other related studies, there appear to be three potential negative consequences of layoffs for friendship networks (see Table 9.1):

- Changes in affect and mood in the relationship
- Decreased financial resources with which to pursue leisure activities
- Decreased contact and intimacy of friendships with laid-off employees

Changes in Affect and Mood of Relationship

The negative consequences of layoffs for employees themselves have been well documented; laid-off workers are more likely to experience depression, mood swings, anger, irritability, and frustration (Leana & Feldman, 1994, 1995a, 1995b). As a result of these changes in affect and mood, friendships with laid-off employees may become more negative in tone or more fragile.

People may try to give social support to their friends who have been laid off but be rebuffed. Alternatively, friends may become frustrated and angry themselves when their repeated attempts to provide emotional support appear to be futile. Friends might feel as if they have to walk on eggshells for fear of inadvertently upsetting those who have lost their jobs (Shellenbarger, 2000).

Decreased Financial Resources for Leisure

One of the most visible and sudden changes in a worker's spending habits in the wake of layoffs is a decrease in discretionary spending on leisure activities. Because of this change in spending habits, friendships that were sustained by shared leisure pursuits, particularly relatively expensive ones, may become more strained. For example, a friendship that is largely based on taking overseas vacations together, shopping, eating out at good restaurants, or going to the theater will likely be disrupted by the inability of one friend to pay or to keep up. Offering to pay for a laid-off friend can prove expensive or seem patronizing; engaging in the leisure activity without the friend can seem hurtful or exclusionary.

Decreased Contact and Intimacy

As a result of the changes in mood and affect and the diminished financial resources, it is likely that the frequency and intimacy of contacts between laid-off employees and their friends will decline. Withdrawal from social relationships is a common symptom of mild depression, and for many laid-off workers, withdrawal from friends is a typical reaction. Moreover, because people tend to avoid situations that make them feel unsure of what to say and do, over time individuals may lessen their contacts with their friends who have been laid off.

The range of topics that friends often discuss with each other may become more restricted in range. For example, it is less likely a friend would discuss his or her own work problems (or even work accomplishments and successes) with someone who recently lost a job. With increased discomfort and decreased topics for conversation, not only the quantity but also the quality of contacts between friends can suffer.

Moderating Factors

Friendship relationships are differentially vulnerable to disruptions caused by layoffs and unemployment. Three moderating variables are most critical to examine in this context:

- The basis of the friendship (work based or nonwork based)
- The length of the friendship
- The level of community affluence

Basis of the Friendship

Friendships vary on the bases on which they are founded and sustained. Friendships that are work based would be more likely to suffer after layoffs than friendships that are not work based. If an employee's closest friends are survivors rather than victims of layoffs or current business associates, maintaining contact after the work-based relationships have ended may become increasingly awkward. Not only will the laid-off worker no longer have daily contact with these business friends, but the number of topics in which they share an interest might decline as well.

In contrast, friendships based on having grown up together, gone to school together, living in the same neighborhood, or enjoying the same leisure activities may be more likely to survive a layoff. Similarly, friendships based on church activities and participation in community organizations may be less affected by the unemployment of one of the friends. Work was not the initial basis for the friendship, and lack of work need not necessarily be the reason for its termination.

Length of Friendship

The negative effects of layoffs on friendships may be tempered by the length of the friendship: the negative effects of layoffs on friendships will be greater the shorter the length of time two individuals have been friends.

When two individuals have been friends for years and have a shared history of positive and negative experiences together, layoffs are less likely to interrupt or disrupt a relationship. Indeed, old friends may be better at understanding a laid-off worker's feelings and be better at providing social support to him or her. A new friendship may not be strong enough to weather the emotional demands that a laid-off employee may put on it.

Community Affluence

Analogous to the effects on children, the disruption that unemployment causes to friendships will probably be moderated by the affluence of the community in which individuals live. In cities and towns where residents are not particularly wealthy and sustaining an expensive lifestyle is not critical to being integrated into the community, layoffs may not have particularly harsh effects on the quality of friendships. In affluent communities where friendships are partially sustained by shared enjoyment of expensive homes, hobbies, and travel, layoffs are much more likely to curtail the quantity and quality of contacts between friends (Newman, 1988, 1993).

Impact of Restructurings on Communities

If the layoffs of the past thirty years have taught us any lesson, it is that high unemployment can have profound negative consequences for communities, including escalating cycles of poverty. When corporations experience business declines and pay fewer taxes, citizens lose their jobs and pay fewer taxes, communities have fewer revenues to support the unemployed and to maintain the same quality of public schools and public services, fewer new businesses are interested in relocating to communities in this kind of distress, and there is less local business leadership to sustain community spirit and to revitalize the local business environment.

Consequences of Layoffs for Communities

We consider the four most significant negative consequences that layoffs can have for the communities in which they occur (see Table 9.1):

- Increases in local unemployment rates
- Loss of community tax revenues
- Declines in real estate property values
- Decreases in corporate citizenship behavior

Increases in Local Unemployment Rates

The most direct effect of layoffs on communities is an increase in local unemployment rates (Kaufman, 1995; Leana & Feldman, 1992; Opdyke & Barta, 1998). These higher rates are typically associated with a wide variety of social problems, most notably increased crime rates, high school dropout rates, and strains on public services like welfare (Hoerr, 1988).

Loss of Community Tax Revenues

Corporate layoffs have a variety of negative collateral consequences for communities as well. Chief among them is loss of tax revenues that the local community derives from local businesses and citizens. Companies that are downsizing are experiencing business declines and as a consequence are generating less tax revenue for local communities, since most local corporate taxes are based on business profits. Because layoffs increase local unemployment rates, they decrease the amount of local income taxes citizens pay, too (Downs, 1995; Noer, 1993).

Declines in Real Estate Values

Corporate downsizing has adverse consequences for both commercial and residential property values. When corporations have wide-scale layoffs, they often close plants or other facilities. As a result, increases in the supply of available commercial real estate drive down the prices sellers and leasers of commercial real estate can command for their properties. In addition, a large number of subcontractors and suppliers locate near major clients and rely heavily on those corporations to survive. As major corporations decline, these secondary companies also experience layoffs and facility closings, dampening the local commercial real estate market even further (Galuszka & Dallas, 1998; Leana & Feldman, 1992).

Layoffs can have drastic consequences for residential real estate markets as well. Many laid-off workers sell their homes, either to relocate to other communities or move into less expensive housing. Thus, the local residential real estate market can be flooded with homes on the market, driving down the prices sellers can command for their houses. At the same time, losses of jobs in the community mean that fewer newcomers will be joining the ranks of home buyers and fewer people will be looking for more expensive homes as "move-up" buyers (Feldman & Bolino, 1998). Thus, just as the supply of existing homes is increasing rapidly, the demand for homes is declining sharply (Dutton, 1997; Galuszka & Dallas, 1998).

Decreases in Amount of Corporate Citizenship Behavior

One of the least discussed aspects of layoffs in communities is the loss of major corporate citizens. It is not unusual for leaders of the largest corporations in communities to be actively involved in community affairs. In some cases, this involvement entails major financial contributions to cultural and charitable institutions, such as museums, schools, and hospitals. In other cases, key corporate executives spearhead local initiatives to recruit new businesses to communities, organize local philanthropic enterprises like the United Way, and lead community efforts to improve local school systems or the environment. When major corporations close down, it is not only the loss of tax revenues that communities miss, but also the loss of critical community leadership (Altman, 1998; Dutton, 1997; Harrison, 1999).

Moderating Factors

Communities have varied dramatically in their success in recovering from plant closings, divestitures, and corporate restructurings. Some communities continued to languish with high unemployment (Flint, Michigan, is an example), while other communities ultimately recovered from widespread downsizing (Pittsburgh, Pennsylvania, for instance). Here we identify four key moderating factors critical to understanding this variation (see Table 9.2). Although they do not eliminate the negative consequences of layoffs for communities in which they occur, they can temper the extent to which communities suffer financially from high unemployment and can shorten the length of time communities experience these adverse consequences:

- Diversity of the local economy
- Physical distance to communities with greater employment opportunities
- Degree of state and federal government assistance
- Community redevelopment efforts on the part of local business leaders

Diversity of the Local Economy

The negative effects of plant closings and downsizings on communities are lower to the extent the local economy is diversified. If a community is basically a one-employer town, the effects of layoffs will be devastating. For example, in many Pennsylvania steel towns in the 1970s and 1980s, the closing of the steel mills spelled financial ruin for entire communities (Leana & Feldman, 1995a, 1995b; Galuszka & Dallas, 1998).

Diversification of the local economy helps mitigate against the adverse effects layoffs and facility shutdowns can have on communities. For instance, Pittsburgh itself, while clearly hurt by the decline of the steel industry, was better able to weather its problems because of a more diversified economy (including major hospital centers, universities, and transportation hub facilities).

Diversification itself does not guarantee protection from the effects of layoffs. Winston-Salem, North Carolina, had a diversified set of corporate headquarters, but in a period of a few months, Planters, USAirways Group, R. J. Reynolds, and Sara Lee Corporation all announced major layoffs. Nonetheless, Winston-Salem's diversified economy has helped keep its unemployment rate below 4 percent (Greene & Brooks, 1997).

Physical Distance to Other Communities

Another moderating factor is the distance to other communities with more robust economies and employment prospects. For example, when mass layoffs occur in communities where there are no nearby employment opportunities, the ability of the unemployed to obtain new jobs without major relocation or retraining is severely constrained. This was frequently the situation facing blue-collar workers in small midwestern towns, which were largely dependent on local steel and auto manufacturing plants for employment. In contrast, the negative effects of layoffs in New Jersey were attenuated by access to replacement jobs in the greater New York and Philadelphia labor markets (O'Regan & Quigley, 2000).

State and Federal Governmental Assistance

Some of the adverse consequences of layoffs on communities can be partially mitigated by state and federal governmental assistance programs. For instance, state governments can increase welfare subsidies to communities suffering high unemployment rates to ensure that education, health care, and other social services continue to be adequately delivered to citizens. Where unemployment is widespread throughout the country, the federal government can extend the time laid-off workers can collect unemployment benefits from twenty-six to fifty-two weeks. (Such an effort was made after the World Trade Center and Pentagon attacks in 2001.) Although these assistance programs do not directly change the unemployment rate, they do help lessen the extent to which communities suffer major financial and social disruptions (Leana & Feldman, 1995a, 1995b).

Community Redevelopment Efforts

There is some evidence that community redevelopment efforts can temper the negative consequences of widespread layoffs, too. For example, in Winston-Salem during the early 1990s, local business leaders and government officials put up $1 million to start Winston-Salem Business, an industrial recruiting organization. At least in its initial efforts, this group was able to attract Pepsi Cola to its community (Greene & Brooks, 1997). Joint business-government task forces in several southeastern states, including Tennessee and South Carolina, have actively lobbied auto manufacturers to open facilities in their communities. As a result of these efforts, large manufacturing facilities for Saturn and BMW have opened in these states and revitalized struggling municipalities.

Corporate Assistance Programs

The literature on job loss suggests that corporate assistance programs can help employees and their families cope in two ways: problem-focused coping (eliminating the source of the stress itself) and symptom-focused coping (decreasing the amount of emotional distress those affected by the job loss experience) (Feldman & Leana, 1994; Kinicki & Latack, 1990). Innovative human resource practices like early retirement incentives decrease the need for as many layoffs, and therefore eliminate the source of the stress itself (the unemployment) for more families. Humane layoff procedures help decrease the amount of anger and frustration employees feel and, by extension, the amount of anger and frustration to which spouses, children, and friends of laid-off employees are exposed (De Meuse, Bergmann, & Vanderheiden, 1997; Marks & Mirvis, 1998; Vanderheiden, De Meuse, & Bergmann, 1999).

We approach how corporations can ameliorate the negative consequences of downsizing for the families and friends of laid-off employees and the communities in which they reside from two directions. First, we consider the ways in which corporations can assist laid-off employees and in so doing indirectly help the spouses, children, and friends of unemployed workers, too. Very rarely, if ever, do organizations directly intervene in the relationships of an employee with his or her spouse, children, and friends in the wake of downsizing. Instead, corporations may provide assistance to laid-off workers that substantially decreases the secondary negative effects unemployment has on family members and friends.

Then we consider the ways in which corporations can directly mitigate the negative consequences of downsizings for the communities in which they operate. With thoughtful corporate citizenship, companies can lessen the extent to which communities suffer the financial and social costs of unemployment. We consider each of these two types of corporate assistance next (see Table 9.3).

Assistance to Laid-Off Employees

A wide variety of corporate assistance programs have been investigated in terms of how effective they are in decreasing the negative effects of job loss on employees themselves (Feldman & Leana, 1994; Marks, 1994). The practices most frequently examined in this regard have been:

**Table 9.3. Corporate Assistance Efforts
to Laid-Off Employees.**

Assistance for Laid-Off Employees	Assistance for Communities
Advance notification, severance pay, and extended benefits	Partnerships with other community businesses
Outplacement, retraining, and counseling services	Partnerships with unions and employee stock ownership plans
Innovative staffing practices and layoff procedures	Partnerships with public sector organizations
Humane layoff procedures	Donations of property in kind

- Advance notification
- Severance pay and extended benefits
- Outplacement services
- Retraining
- Counseling services
- Innovative staffing practices that decrease the need for layoffs
- Humane procedures for announcing and implementing layoffs

Although these interventions are not designed to have a direct impact on the experiences of family members and friends, they can decrease the amount of anxiety and depression laid-off employees experience themselves and therefore mitigate the degree of collateral damage experienced by others in laid-off employees' networks.

Advance Notification, Severance Pay, and Extended Benefits

Advance notification, severance pay, and extended benefits all help the families of laid-off employees weather the short-term negative effects of downsizing on family finances. When employees are given advance notification of plant closings or layoffs, they can start readjusting their standard of living before unemployment hits. Advance notice also gives laid-off workers more lead time to find new employment, possibly lessening the amount of time they are unemployed (Leana & Feldman, 1992). Moreover, it can help employees avoid making large financial commitments in the near term, such as buying a new home, purchasing a new car, or starting a family. Indeed, in 1992, federal legislation (in the form of the Worker Adjustment and Retaining Notification Act) was passed to guarantee workers sixty days' advance notice of large-scale layoffs in their plants and companies.

Severance pay and extended benefits allow unemployed workers to support their families' basic financial needs and continue health care coverage, a benefit frequently dropped without such corporate assistance. Even where organizations do not provide such compensation to laid-off employees, many unions (like the United Steel Workers) are deeply committed to extending such coverage to their members. Indirectly, then, these interventions also lessen the degree to which families experience financial distress after downsizing (Feldman & Leana, 2000; Morris, Cascio, & Young, 1999).

Outplacement, Retraining, and Counseling Services

Although outplacement services may not significantly decrease the amount of time workers are unemployed, they may be very instrumental in improving the quality of replacement jobs obtained. Outplacement helps recently downsized employees get organized for a thorough job search, prepare or update their resumés, refresh their interview skills, network with potential employers, and learn new techniques for locating job leads, such as using on-line recruiting services (Feldman & Leana, 2000). Many corporations are now hiring outside consulting firms (like Drake Beam Morin) to provide these outplacement services rather than providing such services in-house. These outplacement firms provide different levels of assistance to downsized employees, depending on the beneficence of the terminating organization and the hierarchical position of the employees who were let go. For instance, top-level executives are often given six months of outplacement assistance that includes one-on-one counseling, while lower-level managers are more likely to receive three months of outplacement assistance and receive counseling in groups.

Similarly, retraining helps laid-off workers in declining occupations and industries obtain new skills to improve employment prospects elsewhere. For example, corporations like General Electric have partnered with local community colleges to prepare their laid-off workers for other employment opportunities nearby. Among other types of assistance, GE has bused workers in shifts to out-of-town job fairs and has provided funds to laid-off employees from its Employee Venture Fund to help them launch new businesses (Feldman & Leana, 1994; Knowdell, Branstead, & Moravec, 1994).

Many organizations have also included counseling services as part of their outplacement packages or retraining efforts. In some cases, employees have received counseling to get them psychologically ready to change careers or move geographically to get new employment; Stroh's Brewery and IBM have provided these services. In other cases, employees have received counseling to help sustain their psychological energy through the inevitable disappointments and setbacks that job hunting entails. For instance, pilot studies with one thousand participants from State of Michigan unemployment compensation offices have shown positive results from these counseling activities (Vinokur, van Ryn, Gramlich, & Price, 1991). Participants who received this counseling were significantly more likely to be reemployed than their control group counterparts, more likely to get reemployed in their own primary occupations, more likely to get permanent jobs rather than temporary work, and more likely to get reemployed at close to the wages they received on their previous job. Moreover, the gains derived from the program at one month and four months after the counseling were also evident two years later (Vinokur et al., 1991).

The secondary effects of these corporate assistance programs for families are twofold. First, they give unemployed workers some structure to the day and structured support from peers and counselors. Consequently, employees who have lost their jobs may suffer less depression and anxiety, thereby helping sustain the psychological well-being of their spouses, children, and friends as well. Second, although these programs may not decrease the amount of time unemployed, they appear to be instrumental in improving the quality of replacement jobs. Thus, employees who use these services are less likely to end up underemployed in low-paying, dead-end jobs, again buffering spouses and children from long-term financial distress (Feldman, 1996; Schmitt, Sacco, Ramey, Ramey, & Chan, 1999).

Innovative Staffing Practices and Layoff Procedures

The quality of human resource management at the downsizing firm can help buffer the families and friends of laid-off employees from some of the worst aspects of layoffs. If companies use innovative staffing practices, such as voluntary redeployment, early retirement incentives, and job sharing, they may be able to decrease the number of employees who lose their jobs altogether. In addition, if layoffs are implemented in private and in considerate ways, the amount of anger laid-off employees experience may be lower (Brockner, 1990; Brockner et al., 1987; Marks, 1994). IBM has been particularly notable in its efforts to find alternatives to layoffs and to announce layoffs in professional ways (Greenhalgh et al., 1988).

Assistance to Communities

The act of downsizing or closing a facility altogether has obvious negative consequences for a community. However, there are ways corporations can downsize or exit communities that lessen the long-term negative consequences of cutbacks and departures (Feldman & Leana, 1994; Knowdell et al., 1994). Here we consider four kinds of assistance in particular (see Table 9.3):

- Partnerships with other community businesses
- Partnerships with unions and other employee organizations
- Partnerships with public sector organizations
- Donations in kind (such as gifts of property and buildings) to the communities involved

Partnerships with Other Community Businesses

Firms that are laying off workers or closing plants can work with other community businesses to lessen the economic and social disruptions downsizing can create. For example, Body Shop formed an innovative partnership with departing employees to create new ventures. The company set up an entrepreneurial training center as part of its severance support package; it provides exiting employees with one-on-one guidance on how to develop a business plan and obtain initial financing. In addition, Body Shop offers participants six months' use of a business center, which provides administrative and information technology for support, training grants, and ongoing mentoring (Feldman & Leana, 1994; Johnson, 1999).

Partnerships with Unions and Other Employee Organizations

In the case of large-scale layoffs in the manufacturing sector, organizations can work with unions and other employee organizations to mitigate against severe adverse consequences for communities. An excellent example of such collaborative efforts is the UAW-GM (United Auto Workers/General Motors) Human Resource Centers (Feldman & Leana, 1994). The national network of these joint human resource centers was established through agreement in the 1982 labor contract between GM and UAW. These resource centers provide skills testing by local vocational education programs, assistance in networking, one-on-one assistance from on-site counselors to find job leads, office support, and even general equivalency diploma education for workers wanting to obtain their high school diplomas (Feldman, 1988).

Other companies that have downsized have experimented with selling all (or parts) of the closing facility to current employees through employee stock ownership plans (ESOPs). These firms include Northwestern Steel and Wire Company, Republic Storage, Oremet, and Bliss-Salem. Such arrangements tend to be most effective (and long-lasting) when ESOPs are not used to replace fully funded pension plans and when participating employees are not required to pay the full cash value for the stock they receive (Leana & Feldman, 1992, 1995b).

Partnerships with Public Sector Organizations

Corporations that are downsizing can work with various public sector organizations to lessen the negative impact layoffs have on communities. A good example of such a partnership is the JOBS project on Long Island in the 1990s. Defense contractors like Grumman worked with the municipalities in Suffolk County (New York) and the business school at the State University of New York at Stony Brook to train displaced engineers for science-related jobs in growing high-tech firms (Wolf, Pufahl, Casey, & London, 1995). Other firms, such as IBM, Kodak, and Rockwell International, also have worked with local universities to retrain displaced engineers for jobs as secondary school and junior college math and science instructors (Kaufman, 1995).

Donations in Kind

The final type of corporate assistance we consider here is donations in kind to the community, particularly real estate and buildings. As major organizations close facilities and exit communities, they can display good corporate citizenship by donating real estate and vacant buildings to the municipalities they leave behind. For example, after the federal government shut down major military installations in California, it transferred 4,339 of its 5,449 acres to the Federal Bureau of Prisons and local airport authorities to build new prisons and new cargo facilities. RJR Nabisco donated several properties and buildings to Winston-Salem, North Carolina, when it moved its headquarters to Atlanta (Greene & Brooks, 1997; Wright, 1998).

Conclusion

This chapter has outlined the potential adverse consequences of downsizing for the spouses, children, friends, and communities of laid-off workers. Some negative spillover effects can be expected in most downsizings, but there are also moderating conditions under which these outsiders are most vulnerable to secondary negative fallout from unemployment. Corporations can lessen the collateral damage caused by layoffs by assisting the laid-off workers themselves or through creative relationships with other community-based institutions.

Even when implemented with the best intentions and best practices, restructurings, mergers, and divestitures can have some negative impact on employment opportunities for laid-off workers. Consequently, downsizings will continue to take their toll on family members, friends, and members of the community—individuals who did nothing to cause the layoffs but who nonetheless suffer some of their adverse consequences. For both academics and practitioners, more thoughtful attention to and empirical evaluation of corporate assistance programs to these broader networks is clearly warranted.

References

Altman, B. W. (1998). Transformed corporate community relations: A management tool for achieving corporate citizenship. *Business and Society Review, 102/103,* 43–51.

Barling, J., Dupre, K. E., & Hepburn, C. G. (1998). Effects of parents' job insecurity on children's work beliefs and attitudes. *Journal of Applied Psychology, 83,* 112–118.

Barling, J., Rogers, K. A., & Kelloway, E. K. (1995). Some effects of teenagers' part-time employment: The quantity and quality of work make the difference. *Journal of Organizational Behavior, 16,* 143–154.

Barling, J., Zacharatos, A., & Hepburn, C. G. (1999). Parents' job insecurity affects children's academic performance through cognitive difficulties. *Journal of Applied Psychology, 84,* 437–444.

Barrick, M. R., & Mount, M. K. (1991). The Big Five personality dimensions and job performance: A meta-analysis. *Personnel Psychology, 44,* 1–26.

Boudreau, J. W., Boswell, W. R., Judge, T. A., & Bretz, R. D., Jr. (2001). Personality and cognitive ability as predictors of job search among employed managers. *Personnel Psychology, 54,* 25–50.

Brett, J. M., Stroh, L. K., & Reilly, A. H. (1993). Pulling up roots in the 1990s: Who is willing to relocate? *Journal of Organizational Behavior, 14,* 49–60.

Bretz, R. D., Jr., Boudreau, J. W., & Judge, T. A. (1994). Job search behavior of employed managers. *Personnel Psychology, 47,* 275–301.

Brockner, J. (1990). Scope of justice in the workplace: How survivors react to coworker layoffs. *Journal of Social Issues, 46,* 95–106.

Brockner, J., Grover, S., Reed, T., DeWitt, R., & O'Malley, M. (1987). Survivors' reactions to layoffs: We get by with a little help from our friends. *Administrative Science Quarterly, 32,* 526–541.

Cascio, W. F. (1998). Learning from outcomes: Financial experiences of 311 firms that have downsized. In M. K. Gowing, J. D. Kraft, & J. C. Quick (Eds.), *The new organizational reality: Downsizing, restructuring, and revitalization* (pp. 55–70). Washington, DC: American Psychological Association.

De Meuse, K. P., Bergmann, T. J., & Vanderheiden, P. A. (1998). Corporate downsizing: Separating myth from fact. *Journal of Management Inquiry, 6,* 168–176.

De Meuse, K. P., Vanderheiden, P. A., & Bergmann, T. J. (1994). Announced layoffs: Their effect on corporate financial performance. *Human Resource Management Journal, 33,* 509–530.

Downs, A. (1995). *Corporate executions: The ugly truth about layoffs.* New York: AMACOM.

Dutton, G. (1998). Warming the cold heart of business. *Management Review, 86,* 17–20.

Eby, L. T., Allen, T. D., & Douthitt, S. S. (1999). The role of non-performance factors on job-related relocation opportunities: A field study and laboratory experiment. *Organizational Behavior and Human Decision Processes, 79,* 29–55.

Feldman, D. (1988). Helping displaced workers: The UAW-GM Human Resource Center. *Personnel, 55,* 34–36.

Feldman, D. C. (1996). The nature, antecedents, and consequences of underemployment. *Journal of Management, 22,* 385–409.

Feldman, D. C. (2000). Down but not out: Downsizing and its impact on underemployment. In R. Burke & C. Cooper (Eds.), *The organization in crisis: Downsizing, restructuring, and renewal* (pp. 188–201). Cambridge, MA: Blackwell Press.

Feldman, D. C., & Bolino, M. C. (1998). Moving on out: When will employees follow their organization during corporate relocation? *Journal of Organizational Behavior, 19,* 275–288.

Feldman, D. C., & Leana, C. R. (1994). Better practice in managing layoffs. *Human Resource Management, 33,* 239–260.

Feldman, D. C., & Leana, C. R. (2000). What ever happened to laid-off executives? *Organizational Dynamics, 29,* 64–75.

Feldman, D. C., & Turnley, W. H. (2001). A field study of adjunct faculty: The impact of career stage on reactions to non-tenure-track jobs. *Journal of Career Development, 28,* 1–16.

Fisher, S. R., & White, M. A. (2000). Downsizing in a learning organization: Are there hidden costs? *Academy of Management Review, 25,* 244–251.

Galuszka, P., & Dallas, S. (1998, December 21). Dreams begin to melt in an old steel town. *Business Week,* pp. 30–31.

Goffredson, L. S. (1981). Circumscription and compromise: A developmental theory of occupational aspirations. *Journal of Counseling Psychology, 28,* 545–579.

Goode, W. (1994). Why men resist. In A. Skolnick & J. Skolnick (Eds.), *Family in transition* (8th ed., pp. 137–148). New York: HarperCollins.

Gottfredson, D.C. (1985). Youth employment, crime, and schooling: A longitudinal study of a national sample. *Developmental Psychology, 21,* 419–432.

Greenberger, E., & Steinberg, L. (1986). *When teenagers work: The psychological and social costs of adolescent employment.* New York: Basic Books.

Greene, K., & Brooks, R. (1998, June 18). Winston-Salem relapses into white-collar funk. *Wall Street Journal,* pp. S2–S4.

Greenhalgh, L., Lawrence, A. T., & Sutton, R. I. (1988). Determinants of work force reduction strategies in declining organizations. *Academy of Management Review, 13,* 241–254.

Harrison, J. (1999). How charities may suffer after a deal. *Mergers and Acquisitions, 33,* 6–8.

Harvey, E. (1999). Short-term and long-term effects of early parental employment on children of the National Longitudinal Survey of Youth. *Developmental Psychology, 35,* 445–459.

Hochschild, A. R. (1989). *The second shift.* New York: Holt.

Hochschild, A. R. (1998). *The time bind.* New York: Holt.

Hoerr, J. (1988). *And the wolf finally came: The decline of the American steel industry.* Pittsburgh: University of Pittsburgh Press.

Jahoda, M. (1982). *Employment and unemployment.* Cambridge: Cambridge University Press.

Johnson, R. (1999). Body Shop: Giving support in all the right places. *People Management, 5,* 46–47.

Justice, B., & Justice, R. (1976). *The abusing family.* New York: Human Services Press.

Kaufman, H. G. (1995). Salvaging displaced employees: Job obsolescence, retraining, and redeployment. In M. London (Ed.), *Employees, careers, and job creation* (pp. 105–120). San Francisco: Jossey-Bass.

Kessler, R. C., Turner, J. B., & House, J. S. (1988). Effects of unemployment on health in a community survey: Main, modifying, and mediating effects. *Journal of Social Issues, 44,* 69–85.

Kinicki, A., & Latack, J. (1990). Explication of the construct of coping with involuntary job loss. *Journal of Vocational Behavior, 36,* 339–360.

Knowdell, R. L., Branstead, E., & Moravec, M. (1994). *From downsizing to recovery: Strategic transition options for organizations and individuals.* Palo Alto, CA: CPP Books.

Kobasa, S. C. (1979). Stressful life events, personality, and health: An inquiry into hardiness. *Journal of Personality and Social Psychology, 37,* 1–11.

Kokko, K., & Pulkkinen, L. (2000). Aggression in childhood and long-term unemployment in adulthood: A cycle of maladaptation and some protective factors. *Developmental Psychology, 36,* 463–472.

Krosnick, J. A., & Alwin, D. F. (1989). Aging and susceptibility to attitude change. *Journal of Personality and Social Psychology, 57,* 416–425.

Leana, C. R., & Feldman, D. C. (1992). *Coping with job loss: How individuals, organizations, and communities respond to layoffs.* San Francisco: New Lexington Press.

Leana, C. R., & Feldman, D. C. (1994). The psychology of job loss. In G. R. Ferris (Ed.), *Research in personnel and human resource management* (Vol. 12, pp. 271–302). Greenwich, CT: JAI Press.

Leana, C. R., & Feldman, D. C. (1995a). Finding new jobs after a plant closing: Antecedents and outcomes of the occurrence and quality of reemployment. *Human Relations, 48,* 1381–1401.

Leana, C. R., & Feldman, D.C. (1995b). Coping with job loss: The collective activism of community-based job creation and retention strategies. In M. London (Ed.), *Employees, careers, and job creation* (pp. 287–299). San Francisco: Jossey-Bass.

Loughlin, C. A., & Barling, J. (1998). Teenagers' part-time employment and their work-related attitudes and aspirations. *Journal of Organizational Behavior, 19,* 197–207.

Marks, M. L. (1994). *From turmoil to triumph: New life after mergers, acquisitions, and downsizing.* San Francisco: New Lexington Press.

Marks, M. L., & Mirvis, P. H. (1998). *Joining forces: Making one plus one equal three in mergers, acquisitions, and alliances.* San Francisco: Jossey-Bass.

Morris, J. R., Cascio, W. F., & Young, C. E. (1999). Downsizing after all these years: Questions and answers about who did it, how many did it, and who benefited from it. *Organizational Dynamics, 27,* 78–87.

National Center for Education Statistics. (1998, July). *Postsecondary financing strategies: How undergraduates combine work, borrowing, and attendance.* Washington, DC: U.S. Department of Education.

Newman, K. (1988). *Falling from grace: The experience of downward mobility in the American middle class.* New York: Vintage Books.

Newman, K. (1993). *Declining fortunes: The withering of the American dream.* New York: Basic Books.

Noer, D. M. (1993). *Healing the wounds: Overcoming the trauma of layoffs and revitalizing downsized organizations.* San Francisco: Jossey-Bass.

Opdyke, J. D., & Barta, P. (1998, February 25). As ranks of low-skilled workers swell, El Paso struggles for answer. *Wall Street Journal*, p. T1.

O'Regan, K. M., & Quigley, J. M. (2000, May–June). Spatial effects upon employment outcomes: The case of New Jersey teenagers. *New England Economic Review*, 41–58.

Schmitt, N., Sacco, J. M., Ramey, S., Ramey, C., & Chan, D. (1999). Parental employment, school climate, and children's academic and social development. *Journal of Applied Psychology, 84*, 737–753.

Shamir, B. (1986). Protestant work ethic, work involvement, and the psychological impact of unemployment. *Journal of Occupational Behavior, 7*, 25–38.

Shanahan, M. J., Finch, M., Mortimer, J. H., & Ryu, S. (1991). Adolescent work experiences and depressive affect. *Social Psychology Quarterly, 54*, 299–317.

Shellenbarger, S. (2000, January 12). An overlooked toll of job upheavals. *Wall Street Journal*, p. B1.

Steinberg, L. D., Fegley, S., & Dornbusch, S. (1993). Negative impact of part-time work on adolescent adjustment: Evidence from a longitudinal study. *Developmental Psychology, 29*, 171–180.

Stern, D., Stone, J. R., Hopkins, C., & McMillion, M. (1990). Quality of students' work experience and orientation toward work. *Youth and Society, 22*, 263–282.

Stroh, L. K. (1999). Does relocation still benefit corporations and companies? *Human Resource Management Review, 9*, 279–308.

Sutton, R. I., Eisenhardt, K. M., & Jucker, J. V. (1986). Managing organizational decline: Lessons from Atari. *Organizational Dynamics, 14*, 17–29.

Vanderheiden, P. A., De Meuse, K. P., & Bergmann, T. J. (1999). And the beat goes on: Corporate downsizing in the twenty-first century. *Human Resource Management Journal, 38*, 261–268.

Vinokur, A. D., van Ryn, M., Gramlich, E. M., & Price, R. H. (1991). Long-term follow-up and benefit-cost analysis of the JOBS program: A preventive intervention for the unemployed. *Journal of Applied Psychology, 76*, 213–219.

Wolf, G., Pufahl, J. M., Casey, J., & London, M. (1995). Engaging displaced employees in retraining and job creation. In M. London (Ed.), *Employees, careers, and job creation* (pp. 234–257). San Francisco: Jossey-Bass.

Wright, A. G. (1998). California's strong economy smoothes other conversions. *Engineering News Record, 241*, 3–4.

CHAPTER 10

Moving as the Markets Move
Planning for Resizing
Kathryn D. McKee
Nina E. Woodard

"The email looked harmless enough. Be at the Renaissance Austin Hotel in about an hour. The economy is bad. We can't afford to keep you so we're not. Hand in your badges on the way out. It was over in eight minutes. Dell's cuts illustrate both the abruptness of the downturn and the almost chaotic nature of today's layoff, even for companies trying to do it right. 'Layoffs are an admission we screwed up by overhiring. When things heat up quite a bit, we should take some pause'" (Cohen & Thomas, 2001). Given the unexpected economic volatility of the first two years of the twenty-first century, executives must learn to anticipate shifts in the business climate and then prepare to make adjustments in the shape of their workforces. The comment from the Dell executive alluding to the fact that the organization may have overhired is a telling observation about the need and competency for human resource (HR) planning.

How does an organization become or remain nimble, ready to move as the markets move and able to turn on a dime? How can an organization ensure it is flexible, stretching for opportunity, rearranging its staff to meet the changing requirements of the times? How does management react to instant changes in demand for products and services? How are product lines shifted, new ideas generated, and staff redeployed to ensure the organization retains its competitive edge and market position? What are the implications for people in organizations—people who come to work every day, eager for the opportunity to excel, loyal to the company, giving back in return for recognition and reward? What steps should be taken as shifts occur, when, and by whom? And why? This chapter is intended to help you find the answers to these questions.

An Approach to Planning

Using an HR planning approach that builds on the organization's business planning process can help protect against sudden and unplanned swings in staffing levels or aid in the execution of swift redeployments as was evident in the aftermath of the World Trade Center tragedy. Planning is a common business tool. Although there are sophisticated and complex processes available, the planning approach we have used in several business settings is a simple one that does not require an army of staff to make it work. It has four key thrusts:

1. An environmental scan
2. Identification of the business issues facing the organization
3. Development of courses of action the business will undertake to deal with the issues identified
4. Development of the HR plans and strategies to facilitate successful implementation of the changes in the business

Environmental Scan

An environmental scan facilitates the organization's examination of the external threats and opportunities impinging on it, as well as review its internal strengths and weaknesses. This is sometimes referred to as a SWOT (strengths, weaknesses, opportunities, and threats) analysis. This scan can be a lengthy, formal, research-based process, using national, regional, and local labor market information, as well as industry, market, and product trends. It can be derived through focus groups, or it can employ any combination of data-gathering techniques. We use a structured interview approach with the senior management team and their direct reports in small groups or one-on-one, whichever will be the more effective with the organization. We have provided two approaches to developing an environmental scan in Exhibit 10.1: a macro approach and a structured interview approach. The macro approach works well as part of a strategic planning process where the facilitator can help the group explore and probe for information quickly. The structured interview approach works well when there are fewer constraints on time, and the group can spend several sessions developing detailed information.

Identification of Business Issues

The second step in the planning process is to identify relevant business issues facing the organization. John Coutts, retired president of Peak Technologies, declared the organization is designed to accommodate the market: "You organize around it, and must change with it. The primary reason for resizing or restructuring an organization is profitability" [interview, June 22, 2001]. Many of the threats and opportunities facing an organization may be revealed during the development of its environmental scan. The identification of the specific problems an organization is facing now or in the immediate future will help determine priorities, as well as how, when, and where to begin to take action.

The business planning questions in Exhibit 10.2 provide structure for the senior team to examine the business climate. They usually build on the data collected during the environmental scan. When we were employed at First Interstate Bank, we would go off-site periodically for a day with the senior management team to update our environmental scan. Subsequently, we would come back and use it to analyze the business climate, market share, and product success and failure and then develop the business plan for the next one to three years.

Developing Business Courses of Action

Following the development of the environmental scan and review of business issues, the senior management team can begin to plot the strategic implications for the organization in resolving any or all of the issues identified and prioritized. For example, the team

Exhibit 10.1. Environmental Scan Approaches.

Macro Scan Questions for a Focus Group

Analysis of External Environment
- What are three forces favorable to the organization?
- What are three forces unfavorable to it?
- What are the three most important future external forces—favorable or unfavorable?

Analysis of Internal Environment
- What are our three key strengths as an organization (things we do well)?
- What are our three key weaknesses (things we do not do well)?

Macro Scan Questions for a Structured Interview

Analysis of External Environment
- What is happening with the economy in general?
  In the United States?
  In countries where you have operations?
  In countries whose economies could affect your operations?
- What is happening in your industry?
  How is your competition faring?
  What is happening in the industries that are part of your service and delivery chain?
- What is happening in your market segment or niche?
  What is your competitive edge? Are you retaining it?
  What new opportunities abound?
  Are you in control, or is the market in control?
  What about your product pricing?
  Can you gain an edge?
  What actions, if any, would be prudent for you to consider?
- Where does 80 percent of your business come?
  What economic factors might force changes in their buying power?
  What about demographics?
  What else should you be thinking about?

Internal Strengths and Weaknesses
- What do you do better than your competition?
  What is it about your people that allows you to outperform your competition?
- What are your values?
  How do you exemplify them?

Exhibit 10.1. Environmental Scan Approaches, Cont'd.

- How clear is your sense of direction?
- What are the good things about your culture?
- What competencies does your organization possess that will allow it to survive?
- What is the depth of your talent pool?
  What holes do you have in your pool?
- How strong is the management team?
  Have you allowed for succession?
- What doesn't work well in your organization?
  What will it take to fix it? Can it be fixed?
- If the competition is gaining on you, what internal issues may be causing your change in market position?
  What do you need to do to stop that?
- How do your culture and values effect your productivity?
- How does your decision-making process effect your productivity?

Exhibit 10.2. Identification of Business Issues.

- Is there an increased demand for current products or services?
- Are we adding new products?
- Will we be expanding to new markets?
- Will we need to add cross-border operations?
- If we undertake a critical review of the cost-income ratio, will we need to trim costs in:
  - Production?
  - Sales, advertising, or marketing?
  - Administrative staff?
  - Other areas of the business?
- Has there been a dramatic downward market or economic shift?
- Will we need to exit a line of business?
- Do we need to close operations in domestic or international locations?

may decide to increase spending in sales, manufacturing, operations, or marketing with consequent increases in staff. Or it may decide to cut costs to retain market position. There are implications for employees in either of these change scenarios. The HR executive can play devil's advocate in these sessions, reminding colleagues of the staffing, employee relations, and legal issues that may arise in each of the scenarios under discussion. It does not mean acting as the "personnel police." Rather, HR should facilitate a strategic discussion and decision-making process on the human side of the business.

The Americas Region of Standard Chartered Bank, headquartered in New York City, came to realize that its strategy of decentralizing certain banking operations to locate them closer to its regional corporate banking centers was too costly. After a thorough cost-benefit analysis, it was decided to centralize these operations in New York and Los Angeles. HR moved on several fronts simultaneously, developing severance packages, scripts for small group meetings, deployment of HR staff to each affected site, and outplacement services for affected employees. A list of frequently asked questions was devised and distributed to managers. We also dealt with real estate and relocation issues. We moved quickly once the business solution was decided, deploying our HR programs and allowing the people affected to leave the company with dignity. We helped them recognize that although the bank had made a tough business decision with severe impacts on people, we had given serious thought to the consequences on our staff. We did all we could to assist them in making transitions in their lives as smoothly as possible.

Another example of dealing with a business issue solving it with people comes from Harold J. Meyerman, former CEO of First Interstate Bank. He asserted, "Too often cost–cutting is solely top-down. In looking at innovative ways to cut expenses, at First Interstate Bank, we set up 'Tiger' teams and asked each team where they would cut costs. We took a bit of time and involved employees at all levels to find expense reduction possibilities, and they came up with some incredible suggestions. We also used these teams as an assessment tool and noted who the best performers on these teams were" [interview, June 20, 2001]. The long-term effect of this innovative approach to cost cutting was a tremendous boost in morale, team spirit, a strong sense of caring about the organization, and improved productivity.

Positioning Human Resource Leadership

HR leadership must take responsibility for moving expeditiously to facilitate the changes in staffing resulting from the business plan and develop the tactics necessary to make it operational. Therefore, it is important whenever HR reviews current HR plans, programs, or policies that they are analyzed in the context of how these plans will help or hinder the organization if it needs to change its staffing strategy. For example, implementing a benefit program that rewards longevity and seniority may run counter to the organization's need to be nimble and flexible.

Human resource leaders must have a keen eye for business imperatives affecting the organization and should be attuned to any economic and regional turbulence that may signal a change in direction. An example of an environmental signal is when labor unions decide to take on industries that have little or no union representation. With few exceptions, the banking industry is union free. The senior management in most banking systems refused to believe that such a thing could happen, until the Service Workers International Union decided to attempt to organize one of the bank card operations centers. Once this happened, it was amazing how fast CEOs became receptive to the Remaining Union Free Workshops we had been promoting. We conducted the workshops and remained union free.

Human resource leaders are the change masters who must take immediate action if there are signs of a problem on the horizon, leading change efforts, anticipating what change means, and shaping tomorrow. For example, the sudden success of the dot-com sector changed the way high-tech employees were recruited and paid. On-line recruiting became commonplace, and so did huge signing bonuses, enormous stock option grants, foosball in recreation rooms, and the like. In order to be competitive, other business sectors had to change their recruitment and compensation approaches to remain appealing to high-tech candidates. Then, almost as suddenly, the dot-coms became dot-bombs. Organizations had to change their employment strategies again, so they were not overrewarding newly hired employees. Swift changes like these require HR professionals to determine the consequences to their organizations quickly and lead changes to keep them current.

David Ulrich (1997), a noted academician and business consultant, has created a model that is helpful when examining the roles HR leaders can play in moving their organizations forward. The model also can serve HR leaders as an audit tool for measuring the success of the HR function in an organization. In the model, Ulrich describes four roles: strategic partner, administrative expert, employee champion, and change agent.

A strategic partner understands the business, can diagnose the organization, and design and build effective organizational structures. Human resources should be counted on to get the job accomplished and does not wait to be asked. The HR executive's ability to play this role and perform these tasks is critical to the success of both planning and executing effective staffing change strategies. The administrative expert acts as a relationship manager to clients, understands the technical side of HR, and believes in continual improvement. Maintaining close ties to the operating units allows HR to be effective in assisting affected managers to prepare their business cases for staff changes, their communications to affected employees, and working with those who survive the resizing efforts. The employee champion enables employees to control key decisions about how work is performed, as well as for them to know where the organization is going and why. A clear, fair, and equitable approach exemplified by HR leadership helps employees understand and buy in to the changes proposed. Finally, a change agent leads the change effort. Facilitating the development of the staffing strategies and their execution is where HR can shine. It must shape the vision and ensure that the people strategies employed fit the business case.

Aligning the Business Plan with HR Plans and Strategies

Business planning may result in changing the organization. There could be a layoff, a divestiture, a restructuring, a merger or acquisition, or a plant closing. The change required to support the business plan might have an impact on the number of people required by the various lines of business. If the number of employees increase or decrease, or if they are moved around within the organization, a carefully thought out HR plan is essential. For organizations facing staffing flux, the ability to attract new employees, retain them, and help them reach their potential is daunting. With the possible exception of automated steel rolling mills, people are a critical asset in organizations. They need care and feeding in order for the organization to flourish.

Employees should never be viewed as a wasting asset, that is, one that is used up in its entirety. If there is a need for a flexible workforce, that must be an important part of the HR philosophy, with a strategy for contingent staffing. All organizations will experience changes in staffing. It is important that the senior leadership give serious thought to the relationship between staffing and such business actions as these:

- Developing the existing lines of business
- Exiting current lines of business
- Entering new markets
- Adding new product lines
- Changing technologies
- Crossing new borders to enter markets
- Streamlining business processes

Questions that can aid this thought process are presented in Exhibit 10.3.

It is important to develop staffing approaches and action plans for each of the business strategies to be executed. Asking what im-

---

Exhibit 10.3. Questions to Aid in Analyzing the Impact of Business Planning on Staffing Strategy.

- How will this action affect our long-term strategy?
- What will this action buy us in the short term?
- How will we determine how many to add or terminate?
- How will we determine who to add or let go?
- Will we ever be on this path again? If yes, what precedents are we setting, and can we live with them?

---

pact the business strategy will have on recruitment, selection, staff reduction, and staff redeployment is the first step in developing the appropriate HR strategies to facilitate the success of the business plan. Asserts Harold J. Meyerman, "You can't human resource plan your way to prosperity, but you can use the HR function to raise strategic and tactical issues, and get to the heart of the people issues in these transactions. By balancing HR planning with efficiency, you can achieve greater profitability" [interview, June 20, 2001]. When he was CEO at First Interstate Bank, Meyerman had each of his executive committee members work together closely every time the bank faced the challenge of entering new markets with consequent increases in staffing or when it needed to downsize or exit a product area. Because of this closely knit effort, we in HR partnered effectively with our line colleagues to help them with strategies and tactics that resulted in well-thought-out changes with minimal disruption.

There are four major HR strategies to consider when aligning HR strategies to business plans. Planning questions for each of these that can facilitate analysis and planning are provided in Exhibit 10.4.

Strategy to Increase Staffing Levels

There may be a need to increase head count, or add new skill sets when developing the business, entering new markets, adding new product lines, changing technologies, crossing new borders, or streamlining business processes. If this is the case, HR strategies such as competency assessment and individual skills gap analyses, job postings, employee development, project assignments, or job shadowing can be implemented. In addition, external recruitment strategies such as job fairs, contract or part-time employment, and job sharing can be used.

Strategy for Redeployment

Employees may be redeployed, that is, promoted, demoted, or transferred throughout the organization, as a result of the business issues identified. Redeployment may occur when specific business units are eliminated, or when units may need staffing increases due to new products or achieving full market penetration.

Exhibit 10.4. Strategic Questions
Regarding Changes in Staffing.

Questions for Staff Increases

- What jobs? What skills? Where?
- What flexibility do you need in staffing levels?
- Will they be core jobs? Part-time? Contract?
- Are they permanent or temporary increases?
- Can or should the work be outsourced?
- How will you fill the jobs?
  - Internally?
    Can you promote from within?
    Do you have to train or develop current staff?
    Will you need to relocate staff?
  - Externally?
    Agencies and headhunters?
    Contract recruiters?
    Employee referrals?
    Job fairs?
    Internet or Web site?
- Are salary ranges and rates of pay competitive in the labor markets?
  - Do you need to conduct quick surveys?
  - Will there be incremental costs?
  - Will you need equity adjustments?
- Are there union issues?
  - Seniority or bumping?
  - Potential for arbitration?
  - Internationally—do you know enough about the local union to frame a strategic approach to them?
- Will increased demand for products and services require possible changes in locations?
  - Do you know the labor supply for the specific occupations needed in the potential new locations?
  - Do you know the availability and cost of housing at various socioeconomic levels?
  - Do you know the availability of quality K–12 schools?
  - Do you know the regional cultural differences if a domestic move?
  - Do you know the national cultural differences if an international move?
  - Do you know the adequacy and availability of public transportation?

Exhibit 10.4. Strategic Questions
Regarding Changes in Staffing, Cont'd.

- Do you have a relocation plan in place? What will it cost?
- Will there be a need for cost-of-living adjustments in the new area?

Questions for Redeployment

- Who will go where into existing jobs and why?
- What are the selection criteria?
- How should you match people to jobs?
- Should there be any incentive or retention pay to encourage people to move?
  - Are there geographical relocation or cost issues?
- Have you created job briefs and selection criteria for restructured jobs?
  - How will you fill the restructured jobs?
  - What are the selection criteria?
  - Will employees be allowed to opt in or out for selection?

Questions for Training and Development

- Do you have time to develop people for reassignment?
- Can you perform a cost-benefit analysis and make the case for internal development versus recruitment?
- Have you developed competency models for affected job families?
  - Do you have time to do a skills-gap analysis?
- Do you have time to put together effective development plans?

Questions for Reductions in Force

- How effectively will the executives make their selection decisions?
  - Do they need a briefing on decision making within workplace laws and regulations?
- Has the organization set a precedent in previous action, and is that process applicable in the current environment?
  - If it is, will it be more acceptable to the managers and employees because they are familiar with it?
  - If it is not, it will be important to explain how this process is different and why.
- Are there labor union contract stipulations?
- What selection criteria will be used?
- Who will be involved in the selection process?

**Exhibit 10.4. Strategic Questions
Regarding Changes in Staffing, Cont'd.**

- What role will HR play?
- Have you performed adverse impact calculations?
- Is a severance pay plan in place?
- Will you need transition (outplacement) counseling?
  - For what employee groups?
  - Are there any special situations?
- Do you need to set up career centers on site?
- Will you need retention or stay bonuses for certain key people?
- What are the cultural norms around bonuses?

Promotions and demotions also can occur on an individual basis or due to shifts in demand in certain business units or product lines. HR can use competency assessment and skills gap analyses, an opt-out program where employees self-select themselves out of consideration for a transfer to another unit, or job postings allowing employees to bid into other departments.

Human resources may be asked to assist in organizational or job redesign. Former CEO John Coutts provides a vivid experience he had when restructuring the workforce in his company:

> One time we restructured the entire company, and organized it around three market sectors. We went from nineteen hundred employees to nine hundred. Here is what we did. We closed the company for ten days and laid everyone off except the key decision makers. We worked sixteen hours a day for those ten days, organizing the company from the ground up. We used a draft system. We developed selection criteria; next, we force-ranked all employees by performance. We created three engineering functions to support each market sector instead of the previous two, so the heads of the engineering departments then selected their new teams. Each division head did the same thing. The marginal performers dropped to the bottom and were not retained. We rehired the nine hundred people selected and gave the rest their termination packages [interview, June 13, 2001].

Strategy for Training and Development

Harold J. Meyerman provides a thought-provoking view of the need for development of staff: "In looking at people, too often we don't take the time to assess where people could best be re-deployed; we assume they are too specialized, and can't move into something new, or in case of a merger where there are duplicate jobs, we don't always select the best people as it's easier to just cut the head-count" [interview, June 20, 2001]. The development of staff can be an effective resizing strategy as it provides a cost-efficient means for keeping known talent on board instead of recruiting new employees. The difficulty with this tactic is that it takes time, and the organization may not have the time for development because it needs to make immediate changes. If the organization has the time for training and development, it can support several business strategies, such as increasing existing lines of business, entering new markets, adding new product lines, crossing borders, and streamlining business processes.

Strategy for Reduction in Force (RIF)

An RIF is one of the most common techniques used to resize organizations. Although it is unclear whether they are effective in the long run, RIFs are a quick way to cut costs when there are volatile shifts in profitability, a need to exit products or markets, or sudden technology changes.

The first step in executing a smooth RIF is to have all affected managers prepare their business cases, that is, the compelling business reasons for making the changes. It is important for each manager to write the business case in his or her own words and outline what it means in terms of critical next steps. This exercise helps ensure that managers support the RIF and that they have a clear understanding of how their plans support the organization's need for swift action. A second reason for preparing these business cases is to ensure all managers have taken applicable laws and regulations into consideration.

We have observed that some managers perceive they are being placed in an untenable position and will be unable to maintain work efficiency and quality with fewer staff. They also have stated that the financial support package is not sufficient and have requested that management be more generous. When this is the case, their ability to work through staff change is negatively affected, and they have difficulty supporting the path that the senior leadership has decided is necessary. The attitudes and request for changes must be addressed by the top decision makers, so that the managers throughout the organization truly are committed to the changes.

Closing a Facility or Line of Business

There are times when business requires the closure of facilities or winding down lines of business (Savage, 2002). This is basically a RIF, with several additional issues to be considered:

- Determine if the federal Worker Adjustment and Retraining Notification (WARN) Act will be triggered. In general, the WARN Act requires any employer of one hundred or more employees to give sixty days' written notice before laying off or terminating fifty or more of its employees. There are substantial fines and penalties for not giving adequate notice. If notice cannot be given, the employees affected must be given sixty days' back pay.
- Determine if you will be relocating people to other facilities or business units. Business unit heads, along with HR professionals, need to examine who will be offered the opportunity to move and be careful that protected groups of employees (under Title VII of the U.S. Civil Rights Act, Age Discrimination in Employment Act, and any applicable state laws) suffer no disparate treatment.
- Ascertain if there are any special situations requiring exceptions to termination (for example, employment agreements or contracts) and determine what course of action to take.
- Determine if there are any special regulatory issues involved (such as antitrust or reviews by industry regulators), and build these into planning. In regulated industries, this analysis is especially critical because the regulatory review process may cause delays in plans.
- Examine whether there may be complaints on such tort issues as detrimental reliance (for example, "I relied on what you told [or promised] me when you hired [or promoted] me, and it

was to my detriment"). The covenant of good faith and fair dealing is another consideration (for example, "Was what I relied on in good faith and fair, or will your action break that covenant?"). Fraudulent inducement also needs to be examined (for example, "You induced me to join this company [take the promotion, relocate, and so forth] and the offer [or promise] was fraudulent").

• Ascertain whether you will need to retain certain people for short or long periods of time to make the close of the business smooth. You may need to design retention or stay bonus plans that give recipients an amount of money at the front end of the close and the rest once the deal is completed.

• Examine whether it is appropriate to provide outplacement and transition counseling service, set up a career center, or hold a job fair. We made outplacement counseling a cornerstone of all our RIF efforts. When the number of employees to leave warranted, we set up job fairs and invited local employers that were hiring to set up a booth or a table. The employees who attended were grateful we took these extra steps to help them in their transition to another employer.

There may be some additional external issues that require attention, such as the potential adverse impact on the local economy, dealing with angry citizens, or unfriendly media. For example, when First Interstate Bank found it was necessary to close branches in small communities, extra effort was given to public relations explaining why the branch was selected for closure. This approach helped cool off angry citizens and customers, as well as minimize press rhetoric.

Divestitures, Mergers, and Acquisitions

A divestiture, merger, or an acquisition takes on a life of its own. The acquiree will be required to provide enormous amounts of information to the acquirer. Furthermore, it may not be a partner in deciding what will happen to its staff. For example, the acquiring company may plan to place its existing management team in charge of the acquired business. It may not be interested in hearing anything about the quality of the team being replaced. Consequently, it is difficult to participate on the team. This situation requires the HR leader to rise above the fray and continue to be a professional.

A climate of anticipation (and not anxiety) is critical to the success of the divestiture, merger, or acquisition. It requires HR to communicate, communicate, and then communicate some more. The HR staff needs to help facilitate the redeployment of its employees to the acquirer or vice versa.

Sometimes changes are not without difficulties. When Standard Chartered Bank acquired businesses in New York and Connecticut, some of the employees who were acquired had just been relocated to Connecticut. The acquiree had paid some significant incentives to encourage employees to move from Manhattan. There were continuing unresolved issues from that move, such as pending incentive payments and pending car loans and leases that the acquiree had undertaken to subsidize the employees. Ultimately, many of the details were not discovered until HR began making offers of employment to their employees. Then all of these open issues surfaced. We learned how to resolve them quickly, even daily.

Although employees are critical to the process, they should not be allowed to dictate inappropriate terms. Several employees did not want to accept jobs with us. We recommended they not come, but their manager insisted. Special deals were negotiated with them, and the situation created internal inequities. In the long run, these employees did not stay. Nevertheless, the damage created by this special handling of their packages was difficult to overcome. Although everything was supposed to be accomplished under the restrictions of utmost secrecy, many employees soon knew the basic facts.

A merger, acquisition, or divestiture is more complex than other forms of resizing and requires a detailed planning process.

Preparation

Be clear on which organization is going after whom and why. Establish a crisis management team immediately. This type of effort will require a large team through all phases of the action. Develop best- and worst-case scenarios; understand and be ready for the reality of employee anxiety and its impact on productivity. In addition, watch for unwanted turnover, and gather information on how employees feel.

Cultural Considerations

Be clear on the values and beliefs of your organization (that is, the words and behaviors that drive your culture). Determine the values and beliefs of the other organization (the words and behaviors that drive its culture). Understand your political culture, power relationships, teamwork, and employee attitudes of respect. What is your management structure: Is it hierarchical, a web, or a matrix? Understand how your structure differs from the other side. Understand your technical culture: Is it corporate, divisional, or subsidiary? Know your strategies and your organization's decision-making style and those of the other side. Understand the markets you serve, the products and services sold to your clients and customers, and how they may differ from the other organization. Understand your information technology (IT) and its sophistication. Be able to understand the IT and sophistication level of the other side.

Communication

Understand your attitude toward communication and that of the other side, and determine if they are compatible. Develop the overall strategy and plans for action, and determine which each side will communicate. Discuss considerations for all other stakeholders, and what, when, and how you will communicate to them.

Employee Relations

Ask about transition management. If you use change management programs, will they be different for survivors and victims? Be clear on how the other side feels about this. Know what job search preparations you will put in place. Decide what you plan to do about outplacement and what stress management approaches you might use. Again, attempt to coordinate what the two participating companies do.

HR Policies

Decide if you will you use your policies, theirs, or an integration of both companies' policies. This process is a time-consuming but critical step. Consider putting a team together of HR policy specialists from each side to undertake this task.

Assessment of Talent

Both sides will develop lists of key employees for now, during, and after the close. Determine how they will be assessed. Will it be top down, or will employees self-select in or opt out? We have used competency models for critical jobs and then matched employees' performance as well as the skills, knowledge, and abilities they had demonstrated against the requirements of the jobs for which they were being considered. In some cases, we allowed the employees to assess themselves against the job competency models, and they could opt in for consideration or opt out and take the severance packages offered.

Preparing for Due Diligence

Several critical questions must be answered in the due diligence phase. Exhibit 10.5 presents a checklist for due diligence. Each of these questions is designed to provide the HR member of the due diligence team with data that can uncover potential liabilities that the acquirer will want to analyze.

Transition Teams

It is critical to decide early in the process who will be on the teams and who will be in charge. Unfortunately, this decision frequently is not addressed, and both sides end up with too many generals, no direction, and much frustration on the part of those charged with making things happen. Human resources should facilitate the integration process, ensuring there are leadership, vision, and direction.

Be clear on the agenda and who will set it. Determine how disputes will be resolved. Set up a schedule, and be clear on where and when the team will meet. It is important that decisions be

Exhibit 10.5. Human Resource
Questions for Due Diligence.

Employee Relations Issues

- Are there pending or recent lawsuits, agency charges, or audits?
  - What were the results?
- Are there any recent internal audits of human resources?
  - What were the results?
  - What changes were requested?
  - Is a copy of the management letter available?
- Are there any special consulting agreements with ex-employees or vendors?
  - What are their terms?
  - What are the consequences of terminating them?
- Are there any international employee issues?
  - What is their nature, consequence, or resolution?
- Is there any concerted activity now or in the recent past?
  - What happened?
  - What promises were made to stay union free?
- Are there any employment contracts or special salary and benefit agreements?
  - What are their terms?
  - What are the consequences of terminating them?

Compensation and Benefits

- How are compensation and benefits philosophies the same or different?
- What impact can this have on the compensation program going forward?
- What about incentive compensation? How do the plans work? How do they differ?
- What about vacation pay liabilities?
  - Will this be a deal point?
  - What strategy may be implemented to pay off the liability?
- How are payroll systems compatible? What system do they use? Which will be used by the merged entities? What systems support will be needed to implement a change?
- What benefit plan data will you need? Examples: copies of summary plan description, booklets, certificates for all plans; 5500s and all other government reporting; pension valuation reports for last three

**Exhibit 10.5. Human Resource
Questions for Due Diligence, Cont'd.**

to five years; IRS determination letters; welfare plan employee
census data; policy anniversary dates; special arrangements, if any;
benefit plan premium contribution rates; eligibility periods; plan
summary data; retirement plan funding and contribution rates;
investment reports, retirees by plan, reportable events, partial plan
terminations? Reportable events? Frozen plans? All of these data are
important in analyzing and evaluating plan similarities and
differences, as well as financial, legal, and regulatory risk. If any of
the terms delineated above are unfamiliar, ask your benefits advisor
for assistance.

- Are there any special plans for senior executives?
  - What are their terms?
  - What are the consequences of terminating them?
- Details of the last payroll audit. This is important for determining
  any financial or legal risk.

---

made regarding whether the transition and integration team assignment will be full time or part time. We recommend it be a full-
time assignment. There are too many details necessary to be
executed for a successful change to simply view it as a part-time
role. Determine how rumors will be stopped. Consider installing a
telephone hot line or a Web site.

Watch for the "victor-vanquished syndrome" ("We acquired
you, so we won and you lost!"). This attitude has a chilling effect
on bringing people together. In the Standard Chartered Bank
(SCB) acquisition of parts of First Interstate, many First Interstate
executives ended up in senior positions with their new employer.
The SCB employees did not understand this, and many of them
declared, "But we acquired you. Why are you in charge?" It took
months to bring the two groups together. In some cases, a sense of
teamwork never developed.

International Resizing Efforts

Working on international staffing issues requires the same delicate
efforts and communications campaigns as any other resizing action plan. Obviously, they require regulatory compliance and legal

assistance in every affected location. This complexity adds a great amount of time to planning and executing the integration. In addition, there are cultural differences to consider. People from another country are not necessarily going to see things the way you do or understand verbal or cultural nuances in the same way you do.

We hear time and time again, "We are different here; this won't work because of our special culture [or ethnicity, or something else]." Actually, the heart of any change process is meeting the individual needs of people. Regardless of nationality or culture, employees around the world have many of the same universal needs: to know what is happening, how it will affect them, and what they are expected to do next.

From our experiences of working on four intercountry acquisitions, we do not believe that local people should be left to manage change and people integration issues. A team of select external or very senior internal company consultants should drive the changes. Local managers are going through all the difficulties of personal change. Their frames of reference are limited by what they know and see. They also are concerned about their own futures. Typically, they are stuck in the old paradigms and unable to accept support or assimilate new ideas critical to the process of change. Naturally, the local managers should be involved. However, the outside expertise should carry weight in making final decisions.

The Impact of Resizing on Other HR Programs

Depending on the specific resizing activity, there may not be any impact on current HR programs, plans, or policies. For example, if your organization had implemented previous resizing activities, your current HR programs may suffice. However, if this is your first resizing experience and the organization has no idea how to proceed, you will need to move swiftly to develop approaches for aspects such as retention or stay bonuses, severance plans, outplacement activities, transition management, and employee counseling.

It is important that resizing implications have been included in the philosophy and execution of policies for recruitment, compensation, benefits, employee-labor relations, and termination. Inevitably, questions arise on relocation programs, continuation of benefits, salary and bonuses due, and performance management.

Develop answers to these questions as soon as possible. For example, some managers use an RIF as an excuse to get rid of poor-performing employees who have not been counseled or warned about their unsatisfactory performance. Any of these unresolved grading, performance, and salary increase issues would surface loudly. This section should serve as a warning to ensure your performance management system is functioning as designed to ward off these problems.

John Coutts asserted, "Communication is key. You can't communicate enough. It is critical to the success of the change. Without it, you have organizational trauma, which can have a tremendous negative impact on the organization, and it never recovers" [interview, June 13, 2001]. Obviously, communication is a vital component of any resizing initiative. Outlining the strategies and actions to be taken in easy-to-understand terms is the first and most essential step. The initial definition of the change will serve as a cornerstone for all future communications.

Resizing research reveals that employees are looking for information to be delivered in person by their immediate supervisors (Larkin & Larkin, 1996). Executive road shows and presentations are important for establishing the top management perspective. However, follow-up conversations and information sharing are preferred to come from employees' managers.

Information must be written in easy-to-communicate "bites" and be complete with anticipated questions. Putting as much information in writing and circulating it as early in the process as possible goes a long way toward keeping rumors from running rampant. Continual updates conveniently available to every level of the organization are the backbone of a communications program. All stakeholders must be informed: customers, vendors, regulators, board of directors, managers, and employees. Each must receive targeted communication documents and kept apprised on an ongoing basis. The role that individual line managers play is crucial. They should be armed with as much information as possible and receive immediate updates. The importance of their ability to be in touch with their constituents and convey daily messages with conviction should not be underestimated.

Communications must be as comprehensive as possible. They should be reinforced by believable action and be consistent and in clear language. Certain key truths should be communicated in every written communication, so that the messages become clear to all stakeholders over time. Exhibit 10.6 provides a checklist of questions to help formulate a communications approach.

Change implies acceptance, moving on to some version of business as usual. However, gaining acceptance and buy-in is the most important element for success. Once the activities associated with resizing begin, there are exponential changes in work patterns. Precise details of who, what, where, when, and how need to be clearly articulated. How you accomplish this task is a critical part of communications planning.

Exhibit 10.6. Questions for Formulating a Communications Campaign.

- Meeting with all management?
- Notifications to the press?
- Notifications to regulators?
- Letters and booklets?
- Small group meetings
  - Scripts for managers and supervisors?
  - Run-throughs?
- Videoconferencing for long-distance staff?
- E-mails?
- Hotlines for employees?
- Meetings with union officials?
- Preparation of Frequently Asked Questions
  - Be as comprehensive as possible in answering all the questions you can identify. Even if they are not all published, they form the frame of reference for all involved in the project. This is a critical step.
  - It is sometimes thought best to hold back sensitive questions; however, that does not keep them from being asked. Putting the difficult information into print makes it easier to stick to a course of action and easier for employees to begin to accept.
  - The language and attitude of the answers need to be critically reviewed by legal and regulatory experts to ensure that they will not create a bigger issue.

The employees of First Interstate Bank surmised that something was up when several of them happened to be in an elevator with a group of British people who were talking among themselves. When they all exited the elevator on the executive floor, the executive team was asked within minutes what was going on with these unusual visitors. No matter what answers we gave them, employees were skeptical and cynical, and the rumors started immediately. They were remarkably accurate.

Conclusion

Resizing an organization may be a one-time event or an ongoing facet of remaining competitive in an ever-changing environment. At First Interstate Bank and continuing on with Standard Chartered Bank in the United States, we resized the organization almost every year as the demands of the business required. We entered new lines of business with consequent increases in staff, and downsized or exited other lines of business. We moved as the markets moved.

Resizing organizations is a constant process, and employees must learn to cope. Human resource executives are the agents of change in organizations and never should be laissez-faire about this aspect of what they do. The following guidelines can be helpful for annual budget and economic forecasting exercises. They can assist HR and the rest of the senior team in positioning the organization successfully to deal with whatever the economic fates deliver:

• Ensure that you understand your external environment and the economic factors with an impact on your business in the short and long terms. Perform an environmental scan at least every two years, and more often if your organization is in a fast-changing industry.

• Make sure your HR philosophy, policies, and programs are closely aligned with business strategy. This does not mean HR policies change annually, but the philosophy that underlies them may change. Changing compensation practices quickly to attract and retain high-tech employees reflects a corporate value of flexibility.

- Business realities may force you to reassess your values and philosophy in order to remain competitive. For example, IBM changed its practice of no layoffs when its market position fell apart in the 1990s.
- Develop the ability to understand and articulate what worst-case and best-case actions may be necessary if budgets are exceeded or not met. If the business environment is changing or prospects for the next fiscal year are superb or dismal, are you prepared to resize if necessary?
- Your internal communications program needs to be ready for any eventuality. Ensure that it is strong enough to combat the inevitable rumor mill through innovative and swift techniques for getting your messages out.

Resizing is not a simple task. However, if the HR leader and the other members of the senior management team take the time to build a philosophy of trust and the strategies to support that philosophy, action planning and subsequent results can be successful.

References

Cohen, A., & Thomas, C. B. (2001, April 16). Inside a layoff. *Time Magazine.*

Larkin, T. J., & Larkin, S. (1996, May-June). Reaching and changing front-line employees. *Harvard Business Review,* pp. 95–104.

Ulrich, D. (1997). *Human resource champions.* Boston: Harvard Business School Press.

Savage, E. S. (2002). Chapter 11 plant closings. *California Labor Law Digest, 1,* 353–362.

How to Implement Organizational Resizing

Roger D. Sommer

For many executives, conducting a layoff is about as undesirable as undergoing major dental work. Consequently, these mass cutbacks may be referred to as the "root canal of management." No one wants to undergo a root canal, but if you must have it done, you want the dentist to be fully competent. The same is true with major resizings. This chapter addresses the many issues that surround resizing, how to implement it correctly, and the consequences of not doing it right.

In the past, some managers might have asserted: "What's the big deal? You tell them to clean out their desk or toolbox, and they leave. It's over with, you get back to work, and then go about your business!" Such is not the case today. The "big deal" is that we are dealing with employees' lives. By eliminating their employment, we are not only inflicting a major economic blow, but we are affecting their self-esteem, their family's security, and their relationships with their former coworkers (Kalifon, 1995; Noer, 1997). Furthermore, we operate in a litigious society and in a workplace bounded by complex laws at the federal, state, and local levels. Consequently, management must proceed with knowledge and caution—just as the endodontist does in skillfully executing that root canal we have been delaying.

Consider All the Stakeholders

Downsizings, divestitures, and plant closings all have distinct and special considerations. However, what is common to each situation is that a variety of stakeholders will be significantly affected. Each party will react to what is happening by making adjustments, seeking to control the process, minimize it, or even stop it. These reactions depend on how directly the individual stakeholders are affected by the resizing and how much control they can reasonably exercise over the ensuring developments (see Table 11.1).

Employees

Based on my experience in dealing with hundreds of employee terminations, both mass downsizings and individual firings, the most obvious stakeholder is the employee. Employees generally

Table 11.1. Summary of Stakeholder Concerns.

Stakeholder	Concerns
Employees	Continued employment, pay and benefits, loss of coworkers, working harder, trust of management, uncertainty
Executives and managers	Job loss, career concerns, compensation issues, employee treatment, departmental productivity
Board of directors	Need to be informed, fiduciary responsibility
Labor union	Loss of members, contract enforcement, decreased dues, possible negotiation issues
Customers	Ability to deliver, quality issues
Vendors	Loss of orders, credit worthiness, future relationship uncertainty
Governmental agencies	Laws followed, assistance needed
Community leaders	Community's reputation, loss of taxes, unemployment, media attention
Investors	Stock prices

experience fear of the unknown and concern over their continued employment and the prospect of obtaining new positions. Those employees leaving the organization may experience feelings of sadness over lost relationships, and those remaining often have a feeling of guilt since they were spared job loss. Depending on past communications from upper-level management, employees may feel betrayed by the rosy pictures painted by executives or by silence from the top when communications is needed most.

Executives and Managers

Executives and managers determine the need for the resizing and implement it. Some may be affected themselves. If so, their concerns are similar to those of their employees. If they are not designated to leave the organization, it does not mean that they are unaffected. Numerous fears and anxieties may cross their minds. What will be the impact on their careers and their chances for advancement? Do they agree with the actions being taken? Would this be a good time to consider other employment options? What will happen to bonuses and stock options? Such questions and concerns need to be addressed in a factual and caring manner. Now is not the time to distract or lose key players who may believe that the resizing will adversely affect their careers.

Labor Unions

The employees of the organization being resized may or may be represented by a labor union. If they are, the union has a vital interest in how its members are treated. Organized labor will insist that the contract provisions regarding seniority and layoffs be strictly followed. Union leaders and members alike need to be assured that employees not in the bargaining unit also will participate in the reduction. As a practical matter, the loss of dues income may be a concern. Depending on the severity of the resizing, the union may be entitled to bargain over the effects of the cutbacks (severance pay, group insurance continuation, and similar member safeguards).

The Community

The importance to the community will depend on the size of the company and the extent of resizing relative to the population of the community or that of the neighborhood in which the facility is located. The concerns of community officials frequently center on unemployment, the impact on tax rolls, and the assistance given employees who are departing the organization. These officials need to be fully informed of developments, in advance if possible. Community leaders need to be kept abreast of downsizing announcements so they can prepare their responses. Economic conditions change. Sometime in the future, the company may want to seek approval for expansion plans or other conditions. People tend to have long memories.

Vendors and Customers

Among the other parties affected by a resizing are the vendors to the organization. Depending on the magnitude of the resizing, suppliers will be concerned about the volume of future business they can expect. In addition, the credit worthiness of the firm may be questioned. It should be noted that suppliers might express their concerns to another class of stakeholders: the customers. Moreover, customers frequently question the company's ability to deliver the products or services as scheduled and with the quality expected. Depending on the availability of alternative suppliers and the closeness of the relationship with the resizing firm, customers may reexamine this relationship or shift orders to other suppliers.

Divestitures

Divestitures represent the sale of the entire organization or a portion of it. Consequently, they often have a greater impact on employees than do mass layoffs or plant closings due to the protracted nature of most divestitures and the uncertainty it generates on all levels. Uncertainty starts the minute word gets out that the company or the facility is for sale. Rumors abound in the absence of specific information. Frequent questions include: Which companies are the potential buyers, and what are their reputations in such circumstances? What will happen to the employees and the management team? Will the new company shut down this facility? What will happen to my pay and benefits if I stay? What will become of my chances for promotion? What will happen to my job and me? Managers too may worry about the viability of the new organization, its corporate culture, and the loss of ties with the organization. There are no quick answers, and uncertainty may last for six months to a year. Productivity suffers, and rumors flourish (De Meuse & Tornow, 1990; Noer, 1993).

Although typically the identity of the potential buyers is closely guarded, employees are resourceful. When an employer I previously worked for was for sale and the unknown buyer was visiting the facility, enterprising employees checked the wing identification on the unmarked corporate jet and quickly determined the name of the corporation. Word traveled swiftly throughout the organization. The identity of the buyer can have a calming effect, or it can have the opposite impact. If an investment firm is the buyer, there is more uncertainty since it is assumed that the company will be resold at some future date. If the buyer has a reputation as a good corporate citizen, it may allay some employee fears.

Impact on Employees

Frequently, there is uncertainty whether the buyer will honor future contracts and whether the buyer will be acceptable to the customer. In the case of an asset sale, the new buyer is not obligated to take the employees. Sometimes the new owners require all current employees to reapply for the jobs they already hold, taking a physical exam and a drug test. Only individuals who successfully pass these requirements remain as employees under the new ownership.

Given these and other such hurdles, what should top management do during this lengthy period of time? These leaders need to identify key managers and employees whom it cannot afford to lose and then take care of them. Options for retention include contracts, stay or retention bonuses, golden parachutes, and enhanced separation packages.

Communications

Effective communications are vital to the success of the divestiture. Employees should be kept informed about the status of negotiations and any other information that management can legally and prudently share. Top management can accomplish this through bulletin board announcements, memos, "town hall" or "all-hands" meetings, as well as electronic media. Questions should be anticipated and provisions made to answer them on an ongoing basis. First-line supervision can be an effective ally in rumor control. If there is a labor union in the facility, the union's local leadership must be informed about the pending sale. The timing of this notice may vary. In some instances, management may decide to inform the union as soon as the decision to sell is made. In other instances, the seller may keep negotiations secret until the buyer's representatives are visiting, and it becomes obvious that something is pending. In either situation, the union must be given a reasonable amount of time in which to enter negotiations with the seller over issues such as the pension plan, health benefits, and vacation and holiday pay. Depending on the labor-management relationship, notification can be helpful in stopping rumors.

Ultimately, the buyer will place a value on the facility and its employees, who represent the intellectual capital of the firm. While this analysis and evaluation will not constitute a guarantee of continuing employment, employees need to be encouraged to maintain a high level of productivity, demonstrating their commitment and value to the buyer.

Facility Closings

Facility closings, traumatic to a variety of stakeholders, are an increasingly common fact of business life. The term *plant closings* applies to more than the traditional industrial manufacturing operation. The "plant" could be a distribution center, a sales office, a hospital, or any number of facilities that are deemed to be no longer economically viable at the location. The closing could be relocation to another city, state, or country. In general, the impact on stakeholders is virtually the same.

Community Issues

Depending on the size of the closing entity relative to the population of the community, civic officials fear the impact on tax assessments, local unemployment, and the reputation of the city as a place to locate or expand a business. In an attempt to minimize this impact, management should cooperate with the community by holding job fairs and inviting interested potential employers to interview affected workers. In addition, advertisements can be placed in newspapers in select communities listing the types of job categories being cut. Federal funds may be available in cooperation with the state unemployment service for interview training, retraining for different job skills, and similar services that will assist displaced employees. Ultimately, a goal should be to lessen the impact on the community.

Labor Unions

Typically, incumbent unions are not entitled to negotiate the decision to close a facility. Nevertheless, they have a legitimate right to enter into negotiations with management over the effects of the closing decision. The company frequently is faced with demands for severance pay, health insurance extension, transfer rights, reemployment assistance, and other issues. This requirement to negotiate with the union is an illustration of the economic interests of another stakeholder and the need for management to anticipate and plan for this eventuality.

Management Issues

From the time the closing is announced until the last employee leaves, management is confronted with a variety of challenges. Operations must continue on some scale, customer needs must be satisfied, and key employees must be retained. The typical response is to award stay bonuses to a select group of managers and severance pay and other inducements to production employees who agree to remain until they are no longer needed.

Timing

An important issue is to determine when the closing will actually occur. I was involved in the closing of an avocado packinghouse. The employees were informed of the closing date and made their individual plans accordingly. Management had timed the last day based on the end of the avocado harvesting season. Unfortunately, the avocados to be packed that season were still on the trees, and it was difficult to estimate how many green avocados remained among the thick green leaves on the trees. The result was that the crop exceeded estimates. The final day for packing subsequently had to be revised several times. Rather than seeing these changes in a positive manner (since the paychecks would continue longer than anticipated), the employees were uniformly displeased. They wanted to get on with their "post-avocado" lives. This story illustrates the difficult role for management to correctly anticipate the needs of stakeholders and structure the best outcomes under the circumstances.

Employees

Whereas the selection of those to be terminated in a complete facility closing is different than it is with a mass layoff, the sequence of who goes first versus who stays longer can present another major problem for management. Anger among the affected employees is not uncommon. Employees may react negatively toward perceived favoritism in the sequence of departures. Although sabotage is rare, employees can think of other ways to get back at management. In one case, a group of disgruntled employees caught in a downsizing set up a Web site to name and criticize individual members of management, encouraging other employees to vent their feelings about what was perceived to be uncaring treatment by management.

Media

Media attention often follows the closing notice, and often it is not very friendly. Obviously, management must be prepared to tell its story of why the closing was necessary and what efforts it is putting forth to help employees and the community recover. Lack of careful planning can portray management as uncaring.

From the time the closure is announced until it is completed, management has the responsibility to communicate its story honestly to the various stakeholders. While this communication effort may take different forms for various stakeholders, the goal is to obtain as favorable an audience as possible. Such an effort will allay fear of the unknown for employees and seek their cooperation in maintaining production until the closure is brought to an orderly conclusion. If conducted properly, this communication effort may gain a sympathetic, or at least a neutral, hearing among other interested groups. Once again, preparation is the key.

In one instance, a two-hundred-employee plant in a city of several hundred thousand residents was slated to be closed by a firm headquartered in another state. As the human resource executive who announced the closing was leaving the plant for his return flight, he was surprised when confronted by a microphone, a reporter, and a rolling television camera. His assumption that the closing of a relatively small plant in a large city would go unnoticed obviously was wrong. This story illustrates the need to anticipate and plan for stakeholder reactions to a negative event.

Sound advice about disseminating negative news, such as a plant closing, is contained in the following *Los Angeles Times* article (Vaughn, 2001):

> The public's first impression of how your company handles misfortunes will be long lasting, said Michael Kempner, chief executive of the MWW Group, a New Jersey based crisis communications and public relations firm. "As you learn and verify information, have your spokesperson disseminate it quickly. You're battling rumors that spread with lightning speed on the Internet, and you're up against 24-hour news cable channels. Respond straightforwardly and factually. As the public relations adage goes, 'Tell the truth, tell it all, tell it fast.' The public perceives techno babble, legalese and euphemistic spins for what they are: avoidance strategies" [p. W1].

Mass Layoffs

The general understanding of the term *mass layoff* is that a large number of employees are going to lose their jobs, typically all at the same time. Clarification of terms is appropriate here. A layoff implies a temporary cessation of employment with an expectation of recall, as with seasonal employment or cyclical business periods. The classic example is with unionized employees whose recall rights are spelled out in detail. Technically, the resizing that results in the termination of employees is not a layoff. Typically, when an organization resizes, there is no expectation of reemployment; hence, the emphasis is on such matters as severance pay and outplacement assistance. Instead of a layoff, the action taken when an organization resizes is a termination of employment. Resized employees are not being fired, as is so often reported in the press. An employee is considered fired when there is some level of wrongdoing or lack of performance. This is not the case with a mass reduction in force. Consequently, resizing is not a layoff or a firing; resizing results when a group of employees lose their employment.

To the affected employees, the terminology that management uses makes little difference. The action can be called a restructuring, downsizing, delayering, right-sizing, or any of the other terms frequently used to describe this situation. Whatever word is used, they have lost their position and need to find another one.

The press has reported numerous stories of how *not* to inform employees that their positions are being eliminated. A classic example occurred in one large company when employees were notified to report for a meeting in either Conference Room A or Conference Room B. Those who entered Room A were told that their jobs were eliminated and to pack their personal belongings immediately. Those in Room B were informed that they were not terminated. This message was followed by a pep rally atmosphere and then an admonition to return to work. Moreover, there was an obvious security presence since computer access was frozen for those departing employees. Not too surprisingly, the company experienced a wide range of operational problems soon after.

Even a respected consulting firm can run into difficulties in carrying out a reduction. Murray (2001) stated that "some of the 400 PricewaterhouseCoopers LLP consultants who received pink slips in January [2001] had posted complaints on Internet message boards about a lack of communication from partners, their short notice, and the indignity of being escorted out of the building the same day." Other companies have resorted to e-mail to deliver the bad news. The same article cites Amazon.com as having chosen this method when telecommuters could not attend a meeting where the job cuts were announced.

How to Resize

While there are differences among a plant closing, a divestiture, and a mass layoff and their effect on stakeholders, it is useful to consider the commonality among them. Each action will cause (1) uncertainty and fear of the unknown among employees, (2) a desire for current, factual information among all stakeholders, (3) managerial awareness of and consideration for all individual stakeholder concerns, and (4) appropriate assistance in making the transition. A wise management team will recognize these issues and attempt to accommodate all stakeholders in the planning process and the execution of its plans.

There is a better way to deliver such a sensitive and important message as job loss than that noted in the *Wall Street Journal* article. In the following sections, we examine the how to implement a resizing from the time the decision is made to resize to well after employees have been notified.

Planning for the Resizing

As is often is the case, resizing should start with planning. If operational considerations allow it, two months is not an unusual time frame to prepare for a significant downsizing. Typically, upper-level management determines the extent of the reduction. Most often it is expressed as a percentage of the workforce, an absolute number (for example, two hundred employees will have to go), or the amount of dollars that need to be cut from the payroll. This figure forms the basis to start the planning process. If at all possible, management should avoid serial terminations (small cutbacks spaced weeks or months apart) rather than one large downsizing that is well thought out. With repeated job cuts, morale suffers, and employees fear that cutbacks will become a way of life within the organization. There is an old aerospace joke that an optimist is someone who brings his lunch to work on Friday. Clearly, serial terminations are a situation to be avoided through careful planning.

Management needs to develop a statement outlining why this course of action is necessary and what outcomes may result. The rationale for the downsizing is communicated to employees who are leaving and those who are staying, to the press, to customers, to the investment community, and to other stakeholders.

Decisions have to be made about which geographical locations will be affected, what functional departments will be downsized or spared, and to what extent. In addition to human resources, the CEO or unit head, along with his or her direct reports, are involved in making these strategic decisions. This task is not an easy one. The overriding consideration must be the ability of the organization to move forward after the reductions have been completed. Will the reductions be in overhead expense only, or will line departments be reduced? At what organizational levels will the cuts take place? Will across-the-board cuts be mandated, or will they be selective? It is critical to remember that the goal of any downsizing activity is not simply to cut expenses but to make the organization more competitive in the marketplace. A plan needs to focus on what the organization will look like and how it will operate after the downsizing occurs.

Criteria for Selecting Which Jobs to Eliminate

With these questions answered, management next needs to determine the criteria for selecting which jobs will be eliminated. Depending in part on the corporate culture, the criteria used frequently are a combination of job performance evaluations, the type of work remaining to be performed, and seniority. These factors need to be as objective as possible in order to protect the organization from legal and governmental challenges. Employees leaving and remaining must perceive that management was fair when determining which employees will be let go and which ones will stay.

Job Performance

Job performance implies that the organization has fairly, objectively, and systematically evaluated the contributions of employees and selected those individuals for dismissal who are least effective. Recent articles have addressed the pros and cons of classifying employees into A, B, C or similar groupings based on their job performance (Greenwald, 2001; Shirouzu & White, 2001). At the time of reductions, the C's would be the first to be considered for termination.

Ranking employees in dissimilar positions, even within the same department, is an extremely difficult task. Furthermore, the ratings given on an employee's annual performance appraisal form can vary greatly across employees depending on the leniency or harshness of the supervisor providing the ratings. Nevertheless, a large number of companies appear to use such an approach when selecting employees to terminate.

Work Remaining

Another selection factor is the work remaining to be performed. Companies shift focus and may move from manufacturing hardware to software, for example. In this instance, some employees hired previously with hardware capabilities may not be interested in or able to develop software skills. Assuming they had been offered the requisite training, these employees would be vulnerable in a layoff situation since they would not be capable of performing the work remaining.

Seniority

Aside from employees covered by union contracts where seniority is the primary determinate of layoff selection, length of service often is a factor in downsizing. While some managers may question why employees who have worked the longest are entitled to stay while less senior employees are terminated, employees generally regard seniority as a fair selection factor. Overall, it appears that seniority is used as a tie-breaker in some companies, a major determinant in other companies, and completely ignored in others. Generally, juries are not sympathetic toward organizations that terminate older, longer-service employees while continuing to employ younger and more recently hired employees.

Refining the List

Once a tentative list of employees slated for termination has been developed, it needs to be refined with demographic data. Typically, age, race, sex, tenure, departments affected, and any other special data that could cause a legal challenge are collected. Additional information, such as whether the selected employee has a worker's compensation claim, is subject to the Americans with Disabilities Act, or has an employment contract, also needs to be collected. Management has an obligation to determine whether these special circumstances are grounds for removal from the list of those slated for termination. Human resource staff should carefully review this list. Are favorite employees of certain managers being kept even though they meet the criteria for termination? Is selection being used as an excuse for not managing employees? Are protected classes of employees on the list more frequently than the majority employees? In other words, is there an adverse impact against protected classes of employees?

The next step is a review by legal counsel who specializes in employment law. It is not uncommon for the initial names of employees selected for termination to be changed prior to the termination date. There are many reasons for these last-minute additions and subtractions, but they require legal review to protect the organization from a potential lawsuit.

Timing

Once the final list has cleared the scrutiny, it is time to select the termination day. The utmost sensitivity is required. I know of situations where December 23 was chosen as the date because the company wanted to "get it over with" before the end of the year. Why would an organization terminate employees immediately before a holiday season? Reasons I have been given range from (1) no budget for them in the new year, (2) it is a "loss year" anyway, so take the layoff costs in the down year to start off afresh next year, and (3) it was a last-minute edict from top management. Other executives have asserted that there is no good time for a layoff. Consequently, if the company waited until January to terminate, those employees affected might have run up big holiday expenses. Obviously, these reasons by management ignore the negative impact that preholiday terminations have on those employees separated and those remaining. It is a short-run solution to a problem that may engender long-term negative consequences in terms of employee loyalty, commitment, turnover, and productivity. Some more

enlightened corporations have a policy that there will be no reduction in force between early November and the start of the new
year. There also are other religious and special holidays to consider
before selection of the date.

What day of the week to terminate employees is best? Some organizations favor a Friday, but that leaves those terminated with no
support and a weekend to develop anger and despair. Selecting
Monday creates an apprehensive weekend for managers who must
deliver a difficult message. In addition, there may be developments
over the weekend within the firm or the nation that could have an
effect on selecting Monday. This leaves Tuesday through Thursday
as the most likely days of the week to give notice. The actual day
chosen will depend on operational considerations and issues such
as whether a four-day workweek is common in the organization.

There is a further refinement to timing. What time of the day
is best? The hour selected should have the least impact on the normal operations of the organization. If employees are in different
time zones, the time selected to start the process should be coor-
dinated. Employees working evening shifts are usually notified as
soon as they start work because they may have heard the bad news
from day shift friends.

Media Communications

Prior to the announcement, it is important to appoint a spokesperson to be responsible for media contact. All communication external to the company should be through this person. Rumors
spread with lightning speed on the Internet, so it is important to
get the company's story out quickly and factually. This point pre-
supposes a press release by the downsizing company. If the company is publicly held, actions taken that could affect the share price
must be considered. The best advice is to tell the truth, tell it all,
and tell it fast. The same advice applies to internal communication
with employees.

If the organization is publicly held and the resizing is of significant proportion, it must be announced. Privately held firms do
not have to make such a disclosure, but the reaction of banks or
other financial institutions could be of equal importance in terms
of existing lines of credit, loan covenants, and their ongoing relationship with the downsizing company.

Managerial Considerations and Training

Some top executives assume that managers accept the necessity for resizing, agree with it, and are fully capable of delivering the unpleasant message. They are wrong on all counts. Managers often have close ties with their employees. They might not see the strategic necessity for planned terminations or may not be entirely supportive of the actions to be taken. The company risks a "they made me do it" attitude that can be conveyed to the affected employees. It is important that managers buy into the reasons behind the resizing and the selection process. Top management should not simply assume that this understanding and support are automatic. The solution is gaining their support as to the logic behind the actions to be taken and then train the managers in how to deliver the message.

Meeting with managers is important for a number of reasons. Typically, managers are apprehensive about how to inform employees that their jobs have been eliminated. Furthermore, the managers are coping with organizational change, and it is stressful for them. What is the impact on their positions and career paths? Upper-level management must communicate why the terminations are necessary and how the company will benefit in the long run. If an outplacement consulting firm has been retained, its consultants can be called on to conduct this meeting. They will acknowledge the concerns of managers and employees to be terminated and then go through a step-by-step process of how the meeting will be conducted.

This meeting has secondary advantages. In addition to training managers in how to notify employees of job loss, invariably there is a review of the entire process. Issues such as security, timing, communication, and possible problem situations surface. Decisions are made by the group. At the conclusion of the meeting, all participants will have a greater feeling of confidence that the plan will be implemented with a minimum of surprises.

Although the substance of the meeting with the notifying managers will vary with circumstances and corporate culture, the session generally includes an explanation of the reasons behind the staff reductions by top management. These reasons may be supplemented by a written explanation available for use by managers during their sessions with terminating employees. Training may include an audio or videotape. These training aids feature the overall do's and don'ts of giving notice. Often, scenarios illustrate how to (and how not to) conduct a termination meeting (see Exhibit 11.1).

The Role of Human Resources

The human resource (HR) department plays a key role during mass layoffs. Ultimately, it is charged with the responsibility of successfully implementing the reduction. Success is defined in this way:

- The cutbacks take place as scheduled.
- There are no security breaches.
- The list of those leaving passes legal review.
- Termination meetings are carried out with sensitivity.
- Communication is handled effectively.
- The dignity of departing employees is maintained.

To achieve this success, the HR department needs to operate in strict secrecy. Lists of employees designated for termination are restricted to a few employees. HR works with the department managers to develop their layoff lists and secures approval from the executive in charge. HR should develop a master schedule of the individual and group termination meetings, attending select meetings as needed. Its representatives explain the termination benefits to leaving employees, as well as field questions and complaints. In addition, HR may have a key role with internal and external communications as appropriate. Depending on the size of the cutbacks and the company unit being affected, these stakeholders may include members of the board of directors, key customers, financial institutions, the union (if applicable), and community officials.

Personal Security

Various security issues need to be considered. Although the chance of violence on the part of departing employees is rare, it is possibility. At a cement plant several years ago, blue-collar employees thought that they were attending a safety meeting when in actuality they were told that they were being laid off. They reacted angrily to this trickery, and before long, hard hats were flying about the room. The HR manager retreated quickly, leaving it up to me,

Exhibit 11.1. Agenda for Training Managers on How to Conduct a Termination Meeting.

A. Scenario: Need to explain why the reduction is necessary.

B. Objectives of the notification meeting
1. Reduce impact on employees and their emotional reaction
2. Preserve employees' dignity
3. Deliver an unpopular message
4. Avoid litigation
5. Preserve future relationships
6. Limit adverse public relations

C. How to deliver the message
1. In private—never at a meal
2. Neutral conference room preferred
3. Rehearse the actual words to be used; get to the point quickly
4. Go from the general scenario to the specific; explain the reasons for termination
5. Display a serious demeanor
6. Brief meeting—ten minutes is normal
7. Termination decision is final and not subject to negotiations
8. Address company assistance available
9. Listen to employee reaction; be calm; anticipate "Why me?" questions
10. Repeat the message as necessary to ensure understanding
11. Explain next steps in the termination process
12. Offer personal support as appropriate

D. Play videotapes and audiotapes (if available) dramatizing various employee reactions that may ensue.

E. Role-play: Managers alternately deliver and receive a termination message to another manager.

F. Review all aspects of the notification day:
1. Times of day to start and finish notifications
2. Manager-employee notification meeting schedules
3. Consider security issues: software, documents, facility access, and badges
4. Review impact on operations
5. Role of HR, outplacement consultants, governmental assistance agencies, employee assistance plan
6. Special cases (for example, absent employees, car pools, out-of-town employees, shift workers)
7. Postnotification meetings
8. Communication to stakeholders, both internal and external

G. Questions and answers

as the outplacement consultant, to explain the benefits of the reemployment workshop in which they were entitled. A check later revealed that a vending machine had been kicked in, and gunshots were fired at the guard shack (fortunately equipped with bullet-proof glass).

I was involved in another situation where sales employees across the country were called to what they believed was a routine sales meeting, only to be informed that they were being terminated. Although their reaction was not violent, it was an employee relations disaster for the remaining employees who heard about this treatment.

The moral of these stories is that management must be truthful and sensitive to the feelings of the departing employees. Employees have long memories of how they were treated on their last day. More important, the remaining employees are watching. If they perceive that their coworkers were treated poorly, their attitudes and performance will be adversely affected. Personal security on the day of notification can be addressed by having a plain-clothes security officer in the facility. All notifying managers should know the extension number of security in the event help is needed. It is not recommended that uniformed security officers escort departing employees out of the building.

There are other security issues to be addressed. These include intellectual property, company property (such as laptop computers), company credit cards, and computer security. The chances of sabotage and theft diminish when management preserves the dignity of its departing employees. Some managers rationalize that employees given notice are good people and will not suddenly turn against their employer. In contrast, some employers are concerned about individual employees whom they may judge to be disgruntled. Their computer access is ended before notification, whereas other employees who are deemed to be trustworthy retain access after notice is given. How to handle the computer access situation is a management decision that balances risk with trust. The decision to grant or not to grant access is particularly important if the notified employees do not immediately exit the facility.

In one situation, a terminated systems administrator hacked into the computer system and published user IDs, passwords, and secret company information on public chatrooms (Conlin, 2001).

This same author reported that the FBI estimates the cost of the average insider attack is \$2.7 million and recommended terminating computer access immediately before notice is given. Another situation to avoid was one related to me by a laid-off employee. He stated that he knew he was about to be terminated before actually being informed because he could not log into his computer network that morning. There are better ways to let an employee know that his services are no longer needed.

Employee Notice Considerations

Another question is how much time should elapse between an employee's notice of termination and his or her last day of work. It should be stressed that the Worker Adjustment and Retraining Notification (WARN) Act requires sixty days' advance notice to every affected employee. This notice must be in writing and individually given to the employee. If it is not, the organization is subject to governmental fines and employee back pay. Obviously, there are certain conditions required for this act to be enforced (for example, a company must employ one hundred or more individuals). Aside from a layoff triggering the WARN Act, the number of days before departure varies widely. One employee expressed how pleased she was that she was given notice. This enabled her to finish projects, say good-bye to associates, and begin preparations for a new position. Other organizations want those employees notified to be off the premises within hours, never to return again. In general, employees resent being given a surprise notice and a quick departure. Management should decide this issue in keeping with its corporate culture and practice.

Invariably, there are special situations to consider—for example:

- How does the company notify employees who are on vacation or sick leave?
- What about employees in remote locations or working at home?
- How does a company notify employees on all three shifts simultaneously?
- What should a company do if it operates plants in a number of different time zones around the world?

- What if the driver of the company car pool is terminated?

Management needs to plan for and decide the best way to handle these cases. Normally, notice should be given in person, as opposed to e-mail or by telephone, even if the notification must be delayed or a special meeting arranged. Many organizations hire taxicabs to ensure car-pooling employees a ride home.

Notification Day Specifics

Eventually, the day of notification comes. The advance planning and preparation will make the day run more smoothly. Nevertheless, the act of informing employees requires careful scrutiny. The following points should be considered.

Timing

Plans have been made, managers have been trained, and select stakeholders have been notified. Now, the day has arrived to give notice to employees whose jobs have been eliminated. It is recommended that a specific time be established, and each department begin its notifications simultaneously. Often, the hour selected is in the morning, depending on minimal interference with operations. Ideally, all notification meetings will be one-on-one. When a large number of employees need to be notified, some organizations deliver the message on a small group basis for blue-collar and nonexempt employees. Regardless of the specific time selected or whether the notice is given individually or in a group setting, a goal is to preserve the dignity of employees who are leaving. The manner in which terminations are conducted greatly affects the likelihood of future lawsuits being filed by the dismissed employees. Furthermore, it sends a very strong message to surviving employees that management cares about its workers. If another job cut needs to be implemented later, these employees recognize that they too will be treated with respect and dignity.

Delivering the Message

The actual meeting with employees being terminated should be held in private, preferably in a neutral setting such as a conference room. A representative from HR may be present if trouble is anticipated. The meeting should be brief, perhaps as short as ten minutes. The only message being delivered is the employee's termination. This meeting is not the time for a debate or rehash of past problems. The decision must be labeled as final and not subject to negotiation. Managers must be prepared to answer the most common question: "Why me?"

An employee who is being told of job termination typically hears about half of what is said, so repetition is helpful. It is a good idea to give the employee a one-page written document highlighting the key points to remember (for example, that vacation pay is included in the final pay check, what to do with company property, and termination benefits). Typically, affected employees go through several stages that may include denial, anger, fear, loss of self-confidence, and a desire to negotiate. The five-stage model of grieving developed by Elizabeth Kübler-Ross (1969) can be extremely helpful in knowing what emotional phases an employee may experience. Managers who are sensitive to these stages can conduct these meetings more effectively.

It is suggested that the manager use an outline of points to address with the employee to ensure that he or she does not forget something important. This termination meeting frequently is a very emotional and difficult time for the manager as well as the affected employee. It is very easy for the manager to neglect covering a vital aspect. A brief script provided to all managers who are involved in this process also will help ensure uniformity in the information that is given to the terminated employees.

Termination Benefits

When the notification meeting is completed, employees will want to know what benefits they are entitled to receive. Typically, an HR representative will meet with employees individually or in small groups after the meeting with the departmental manager and explain the benefits outlined in their personal packets. These benefits include the final paycheck, vacation pay, health insurance coverage, severance pay (if applicable), and any other programs for which they are eligible. Finally, checkout procedures will be addressed, including the return of badges, keys, and other items of company property. If the company uses a termination agreement or some form of legal release waiver, it is explained at this meeting.

When a large number of employees are leaving, the organization may contract with an outplacement firm to set up a career center. This center is a special area set aside on the employer's premises or off-site to offer a wide array of counseling services, secretarial support, Internet access and telephone lines, open jobs lists, as well as other means to support the former employees in their job search. Local employers may be invited to come on-site to interview the terminated employees. These services are expensive but can demonstrate to individuals leaving that their former employer is concerned about their welfare and is willing to spend money to help them find new employment. In addition, such actions send strong signals to surviving employees that management cares.

Personal Property

Management needs to determine how employees' personal property will be removed. In order to preserve the dignity of departing employees, many companies give them a choice. They either can pack their things immediately after notification (which can be a humiliating experience to do in front of other employees), or they can be offered an opportunity to return after hours or on a weekend to collect their personal items. Provisions should be made to be sure that company property is not taken along with their personal belongings.

The Posttermination Meeting

When an organization arranges for outplacement services for an executive or manager, it is common to have the outplacement consultant meet with the terminated employee immediately after the notification meeting (see Exhibit 11.2). As the notifying manager leaves the room and the consultant enters, it is difficult to predict what to expect. The terminated employee can be in tears (both men and women), sitting in stunned silence, display anger and bitterness toward the consultant, or refuse to meet altogether. At other times, it can be a businesslike meeting with little emotion displayed. One of the most unusual sessions that I encountered began with a whoop of joy from the terminated employee. It was ten o'clock in the morning, and he pointed out that he had planned to quit at noon. Now he was eligible for several months of severance pay.

Exhibit 11.2. Outplacement Consultant and Terminated Employee Meeting.

A. Purpose
1. Gauge emotional state of candidate
2. Sounding board as neutral third party; listen
3. Explain role of outplacement services available
4. Arrange services

B. Typical Meeting
1. Typically individual meetings but could be in a group setting
2. Starts after employee notification; in private without company representatives present
3. Introduction and explanation of the role of the consultant
4. Listen to employee reactions and concerns; address the issues raised as appropriate
5. Proceed based on employee emotions and willingness to listen
6. Explain outplacement services provided and make arrangements to start the program
7. End meeting when the employee is ready; average meeting time is about twenty minutes, but can vary widely

C. Debrief management in general but maintain employee confidentiality

A more typical session begins with a surprised employee who puts on a brave front. The role of the consultant is to focus the employee's thoughts toward the future rather than on the past. The employee needs to be reassured that the organization will provide significant assistance in helping him or her get through the period of unemployment and actively locate a new job. The meeting may be brief if the manager was blindsided and totally unprepared for this development. One time I spent ninety minutes with a manager before he was judged able to drive home safely. The common thread is to listen, give assurance, and start the person on the road to the next position.

Legal Release Waiver

Many employers do not offer outplacement consulting or enhanced severance benefits unless departing employees sign a release waiver. The release form stipulates that in consideration for these services and increased benefits, the employee relinquishes the right to sue the employer for unjust termination, age discrimination, or other causes. In order for such a waiver to be legally valid, there are specific ways in which the release must be worded and signed. Organizations are advised to seek employment law counsel if the use of releases is contemplated.

Severance Pay

A recent survey of severance payments given by organizations revealed that the most common practice was one week of severance pay per year of service (Hirschman, 2001). Payments ranged from less than one week per year of service to more than a month per year. Although law in the United States does not require severance payments, many employers offer them when the termination is not for cause (that is, performance-related causes). The formula of one week per year of service often is supplemented by a minimum payment, particularly for managerial employees. Companies also frequently include a maximum severance payment.

Meeting with the Remaining Employees

Once the notifications have been completed, it is recommended that each departmental manager hold a meeting with the remaining employees to explain what has happened and why. It is important that these employees are told that notifications are over for now. Given the unpredictable nature of business, managers should never indicate that downsizing will never happen again. Many senior-level executives have given such assurances, only to have to preside over another reduction in force in the future.

Communicating with the Media

If plans call for a press release or other media contact, the time to do it is on the day of notification. It is important to identify one employee who will serve the role as media spokesperson. This approach will help ensure that a consistent message is given. The designated spokesperson must be readily available to answer questions and put forward management's position in a factual manner. In one case, a union president was the source of information that was significantly different from the position of the company. The issue centered on the offer by the company to reemploy workers at another site thirty miles away and how much seniority would be granted employees who accepted the offer. After lengthy negotiations were completed, a settlement was reached that was satisfactory to both sides. However, it would have been preferable not to argue the positions in the press.

After the Notification

Management at all levels in the organization needs to be readily available to answer questions and meet individually with concerned employees. Depending on the severity of the resizing and the corporate culture relative to its communication style, this special accessibility may last days or weeks. Communication may be face-to-face, by e-mail, videoconferencing, or other means. An 800-number hot-line can be set up, either on an anonymous basis or for employees with specific questions or comments. The nature of the communication tools used is not as important as their availability. After such a major organizational event, some managers have a tendency to stay in their offices and tend to business as usual. The only problem is that it is not business as usual for concerned employees. They need answers and reassurance that only management can provide.

A good example of how to communicate to employees during the layoff process was noted in a *Wall Street Journal* article regarding the 3Com Corporation (Murray, 2001). At 3Com, a three-stage plan was developed, including early notification of the upcoming reductions. Prior to the cutbacks, on-site meetings were held at all locations explaining why the resizing was necessary. The remaining employees received e-mails directly from the CEO; department heads carefully explained the decision to terminate about 10 percent of the workforce. Throughout the process, 3Com sent weekly updates on the cost-cutting plan, established an e-mail account by which employees could talk to the chief executive (anonymously if they wanted), and encouraged them to seek counseling if they needed it through the company's employee assistance program.

Beyond the departmental meetings after notification, management should consider whether workshops should be held for the remaining employees. Variously known as "survivor training" or a "recommitment session," these meetings are conducted by a skilled facilitator. They offer employees a safe opportunity to express their emotions, which may range from guilt for not being selected for termination to anger and resentment because of the increased workload that remains. If they are successfully performed, these sessions help the survivors understand why there were reductions, how the organization must proceed to remain viable, and how their individual roles contribute to the future success of the company.

Finally, the management team should convene at an appropriate time to review what has transpired and evaluate the effectiveness of the notification process. Any unusual problems need to be addressed, along with a review of what procedures went well and what should be done differently next time. Because managers are major stakeholders who have been through a difficult period, there needs to be a reassurance of their future role in the organization. Acknowledgment of their contributions in the resizing effort also should be given.

Conclusion

Why should companies spend significant funds on those whom have been terminated? Obviously, money already is a concern, or management would not be laying off employees to cut expenses. Perhaps companies could spend their financial resources more wisely elsewhere. Nevertheless, it could be argued there are good business reasons for implementing any resizing effort ethically, humanely, and compassionately. First, the manner in which the organization conducts terminations sends a powerful signal to surviving employees about how they will be managed in the future. The length of time it takes an organization to recover can be greatly shortened by an effective downsizing process. Second, the likelihood of future lawsuits is significantly reduced when employees are treated with respect and dignity. Third, the economy will turn around in the future. Sooner or later, the company will need to hire additional staff. Those employees who left will have long memories regarding how they were treated on the way out. Organizations can benefit by bringing back those experienced former employees it was forced to terminate. Moreover, the recruitment of new employees will be easier if the company has engendered a reputation of treating its employees well.

The steps for implementing a significant resizing in an organization are (1) the deliberate crafting of an initial plan, (2) the careful development of the list of those employees to be terminated, (3) the delivery of the message, (4) ongoing communications throughout the process, and (5) reemployment assistance. An effective organizational resizing has the following characteristics:

- Stakeholders accept the reasons for the action.
- No laws were violated.
- The reductions were managed well in the eyes of all employees—those staying and those remaining.
- The dignity of the affected employees was preserved.
- There were no lawsuits or adverse judgments.
- The organization was able to become more competitive in the marketplace.

In short, management showed concern that it was influencing the lives of its employees, customers, venders, and investors and took the steps necessary to carry out the resizing in an effective manner.

Management has an obligation to implement resizings successfully for all stakeholders. Central to a successful resizing is the development and implementation of an overall plan designed to preserve the dignity of all stakeholders affected and enhance the competitiveness of the organization. This objective is what stakeholders expect, and this is what management must deliver.

References

Conlin, M. (2001, July 30). Revenge of the nerds. *Business Week*, p. 40.

De Meuse, K. P., & Tornow, W. W. (1990). The tie that binds—Has gotten very, very frayed. *Human Resource Planning, 13*, 203–213.

Greenwald, J. (2001, June 18.). Rank and fire. *Time Magazine*, pp. 38–40.

Hirschman, C. (2001, April). The kindest cut. *Human Resources Magazine*, pp. 49–53.

Kalifon, M. (1995). *My daddy lost his job and mom doesn't work there anymore.* Los Angeles: Cedars-Sinai Medical Center.

Kübler-Ross, E. (1970). *On death and dying.* New York: Collier Books.

Murray, M. (2001, March 13). Stress mounts as more firms announce large layoffs but don't say who or when. *Wall Street Journal,* pp. B1, B12.

Noer, D. M. (1993). *Healing the wounds: Overcoming the trauma of layoffs and revitalizing downsized organizations.* San Francisco: Jossey-Bass.

Noer, D. M. (1997). *Breaking free: A prescription for personal and organizational change.* San Francisco: Jossey-Bass.

Shirouzu, N., & White, J. B. (2001, July 9). Ford may change white-collar job-rating system. *Wall Street Journal,* p. A14.

Vaughn, S. (2001, April 29). No crisis of confidence for those prepared for the worst. *Los Angeles Times,* pp. W1–W2.

CHAPTER 12

Revitalization After Resizing

Mitchell Lee Marks

Organizational transitions do not have abrupt endings. Some employees encounter immediate and substantial change, but others wait months or even years until the full impact affects their departments or jobs. Then these changes invariably produce reverberations that ripple through the organization. Often, things seem to get worse before they get better: employees who survive a downsizing or divestiture find themselves thrust into an even more stressful and drawn-out period of struggling to meet business objectives in an environment of chaos and confusion. Survivors mourn the loss of former coworkers and mentors and cope with getting work done with fewer resources. However, if the process is well managed, over time employees develop new perceptions, revise work expectations and career aspirations, and adapt to new realities.

Resizing can be an opportunity for personal and organizational renewal. Importantly, moving on after a resizing is not a return to the way things used to be. Rather, it entails setting sights on something more than what was prior to the transition. On a personal level, it means more self-confidence that one can endure, survive, and, indeed, thrive during a period of transition. On a group level, it means more empathy for what all involved are going through in moving from the old to the new. And on an organizational level, it means more effective and creative ways in which to get work done.

Adapting to life after a resizing is never easy for people. This chapter shows how the employee adaptation process can be facilitated in organizations that have resized. I label this process organizational revitalization—the set of activities that sustain the desired postresizing organization by resuscitating individual employee spirit, team performance, and organizational effectiveness. Revitalization may involve modifications in perceptions, practices, policies, and processes. In Kurt Lewin's terms, it is the "refreezing" step that reinforces desired changes in the organization and its people (Lewin, 1947).

The Need for Revitalization After Resizing

After resizing, first and foremost, people need to cope with the loss before being able to accept a new state. Letting go of the old before accepting the new is a perfectly normal human dynamic. If you think otherwise, consider how religious institutions acknowledge the need to let go of the old before accepting the new. Putting the spiritual dimension aside, religions have formal processes to help people deal with death and the loss of loved ones. Wakes and funerals are expressly designed to help individuals mourn and accept the loss of a loved one, so that they can move on with their lives. Some individuals never accept the loss of loved ones and never move on with their lives. Others deal with the loss, experience a middle ground of confusion and anxiety, and then get on with accepting new realities.

Transition consultant William Bridges (1991) says it concisely: beginnings start with endings. Just like mourning the loss of a loved one, employees have to cope with and adapt to the loss of their pre-resizing expectations and attitudes. Loss is in the eye of the beholder and may include the deflated perceptions of job security, career aspirations, relationships with mentors or coworkers who have departed from the organization, status and perks that had come with a position, or the assumed psychological work contract between employer and employee (Marks, 1994). This implies the loss of the status quo: accustomed behavioral routines (how to get things done in the organization) and attitudinal assumptions (the cause-and-effect relationships that people develop based on their experiences in a work organization). This disruption from the status quo, even when it is a change for the better, requires psychological adaptation and adds to the stress of experiencing a resizing.

Second, revitalization is needed because most downsizings, plant closings, divestitures, and similar transitions are very difficult events to manage and always produce some unintended consequences (Marks & Mirvis, 1998). While many resizings are outright mismanaged, even the best-planned and most carefully managed organizational transitions have some negative fallout. (See Chapter One for a review of employees' behavioral and attitudinal responses to surviving a resizing.)

A third reason for a revitalization effort after resizing is more positive: a formal revitalization program provides an opportunity to use the event as a stimulus for desired organizational change (Marks, 2003). Staying with Lewin's unfreezing-changing-refreezing model of organizational change, the resizing itself can be an unfreezing event. A downsizing, divestiture, or plant closing jars people, changes relationships, redefines work team composition and goals, and disrupts behavioral norms and accustomed ways of doing things. It also opens the door to think about what organizational life after the transition could be like. That which makes a resizing so stressful for people—its potential to separate them from their favorite projects, tasks, mentors, coworkers, perks, and ways of doing things—concurrently provides the benefit of unfreezing people. A resizing also has the potential to open up organization structures, systems, strategies, programs, and processes for review and enhancement.

The opportunities in revitalizing after resizing are almost limitless. Leadership can articulate and work to develop organizational enhancements such as greater attention to internal and external customer service, better relations across divisions and departments, or better use of technology. In addition to its content, the process of defining and achieving organizational enhancements after resizing can result in a number of important benefits:

- *Resuscitating the human spirit*—reenergizing burned-out employees, creating a high level of aspiration, focusing people on future possibilities, and increasing individuals' capacity to act

- *Renewing human resources*—strengthening the pay-for-performance link, improving selection systems, and investing in training and development
- *Enhancing work methods*—nurturing creativity, developing problem-solving skills, embracing experimentation, and increasing appropriate levels of risk taking
- *Living the vision*—rallying people around an inspiring vision, clarifying group mission, determining operating guidelines appropriate for the resized organization, and helping people prioritize competing demands by focusing them on what really matters now
- *Promoting organizational learning*—raising up learning opportunities, rewarding learning from mistakes, and increasing upward, downward, and lateral communication

The Problem of Executive Inattention

Many times, executives deny or ignore the necessity of a formal process for helping employees and teams regroup and rebound from a difficult transition. Some executives like to believe that resizing survivors are ready to roll up their sleeves and get down to work. A few even communicate that survivors should be "grateful" to have retained positions in the postresizing organization. However, the real consequences are quite different. Survivors of resizings experience the broad range of psychological and behavioral reactions that begin with rumors of impending change, continue through the weeks and months of transition planning and implementation, and linger long after the dust settles. Executives must come to see that how they manage resizing and its aftermath has a lasting impact on employees' perceptions of the organization and expectations for its future. The work of revitalizing after a transition begins with accepting that there is unintended human and business fallout from transition, understanding these consequences, and acting as proactively as possible to recover from them.

The legitimacy of the need for revitalization may be denied by those with the capacity to authorize programs to accelerate recovery. While human resource professionals and first-line supervisors witness the pain being experienced by employees (along with the resulting distraction from performance), executives, concerned about the future, overlook the need to let go of the old before accepting the new. Many managers are blinded by their personal agenda of submerging themselves in the resized organization quickly. They want to impress new leaders or reduce their personal vulnerability in the event of another round of downsizing. They hold on to a fallacy of getting people's behavior in line by putting their noses immediately to the grindstone and producing operational results. The hoped-for acquiescence, however, invariably is blocked by human anxieties and concerns.

Executives also may question the expenditure of money on a revitalization program when the organization has endured a painful pruning of costs. Employees sometimes echo their doubts, like the administrative assistant who asked her CEO during a lunch break at a postdownsizing grieving program, "How can you justify spending money on this hotel room, lunch for everybody, and an outside facilitator when we just laid people off and you told us we have to find even more ways of cutting costs?" The CEO gave an exemplary reply:

> While it has been a painful decision to terminate some employees, and the other financial sacrifices we have to make are substantial, we will never cut back on investing in our employees. The competition is only getting stronger out there, and if we want to be a survivor in this industry, our people have to get stronger too. We have come here today to help you cope with your feelings about where we have been and what we are going through, but also to help you identify how to be more successful as individual contributors in the future. This is only going to help us become a more competitive organization, and I always will pay for that.

There is another key reason that the need to revitalize after resizing often is ignored. Senior executives typically have made progress in letting go of the old before others in the organization have begun their adaptation process. They may have been involved in secret negotiations prior to a plant closing or sale of a division, deliberated the need for a downsizing, or pondered the cultural implications of resizing well before the transition was announced to the overall organization. In short, they have several months' head start in the process of psychologically rejecting the old and adapting to the new.

As Figure 12.1 shows, those at the top levels in an organization begin their process of letting go of the old and accepting the new well before employees at other levels. Senior executives, with the most at stake, often have the most intense reactions to a transition. They adapt to change and mourn their losses through what typically is a private process, but one that nonetheless consumes personal attention and time. Significantly, however, their adaptation process is accelerated by the high degree of control they enjoy relative to others in the organization. Senior executives are the architects of the transition; they understand why change is needed and where it is headed. All other members of the organization have much less influence and a lot more uncertainty when it comes to adaptation.

By the time executives at the top of the organization are looking ahead to new realities, people lower in the hierarchy are only beginning or, at best, are in the middle of their adaptation process. In large organizations, resizing implementation may not ripple down to the lowest levels for quite some time. Many employees do not experience their first wave of transition-related change—and thus do not begin their adaptation process—until senior executives have put the old behind them and are well on their way to accepting the new. Just as lower-level employees are beginning to contend with holding on and letting go, senior executives frequently repress memories of the pain and confusion of leaving the

Figure 12.1. Adaptation to Transition by Hierarchical Level.

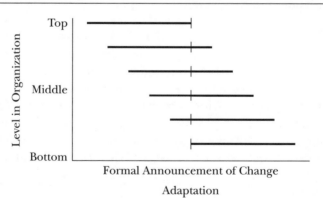

Formal Announcement of Change

Adaptation

old behind. Consequently, they are unsympathetic to others' needs for holding on. Having let go of the past, they are concerned with the future. Either because they are impatient to move on or because they refuse to consciously accept the pain of their own personal transition, executives sometimes forget that a new beginning requires ending the old. Despite employees' ongoing need to assess and cope with transition-related changes, senior management comes to the point where it has had enough talk of divesting, downsizing, or closing and declares the transition is now "over" even as employees are in the midst of their adaptation to new personal and organizational realities.

The Process of Adaptation

Individual adaptation to transition occurs through three phases: letting go of the old, dealing with the neutral zone, and accepting the new (Bridges, 1991). Throughout these phases, every person and organization encounters forces for maintaining the status quo and forces for growth and change. These forces tend to operate counter to each other, with a constantly shifting balance. Early on, the maintenance forces predominate and are expressed in outright resistance to change or, at best, the absence of a will to act. Over time, the growth forces tend to dominate and provide the necessary impetus for adaptation.

In the letting-go phase, the individual comes to terms with the reality that the old organizational order is ending or has ended and they must identify new perceptions and behaviors. Employees discover that some of their valued ways of coping are no longer successful. Intellectually, they recognize the need for improvements in work processes; emotionally, however, they are frightened by the specter of change. Frequently, the individual hopes to exert some control through politicking and positioning. Eventually, however, the person learns that conventional coping mechanisms do not succeed at fending off the forces for change, nor does wishful thinking. The emotional experience that accompanies these changes is one of bitterness, confusion, and mourning for the old ways of working.

The second phase of adaptation is dealing with the neutral zone when the organization is no longer what it was but not yet what it will be. Many managers I have worked with describe this as the "twilight zone"—a dark and scary time when the security of the old is gone but the comfort of a new organizational order is not yet set. This is a time of experimentation and learning new mental models, cause-and-effect relationships, and ways of doing things. From an organizational perspective, this is a critical period when either desired attitudes and behaviors can be reinforced or when undesirable perceptions and ways of doing things become the norm.

Finally, the individual arrives at the third phase of accepting the new. More than just the weakening of forces for the status quo, arrival at this phase implies a strengthening of the forces for change and growth. The employee embraces the new organizational order: it is understood and accepted, and it becomes a beacon for navigating out of the neutral zone and guiding action toward organizational goals. On a personal level, the employee operates in the here and now and begins to look ahead to new realities.

After accepting the new postresizing organization, employees grow more comfortable with their position in it. They begin to modify their self-image and develop a renewed sense of worth. New mental models are developed, delineating both expectations and limitations in the organization. As sense is made of the postresizing organization and as employees see they can cope with it and understand how they can succeed in it, anxiety and depression lesson. Employees figure out what they can accomplish in the revitalized organization and what their available resources are. They now are ready to move forward to achieve both personal and organizational aspirations.

Letting Go of the Old: The Venting Meeting

Interventions to facilitate letting go have two objectives: (1) to help individuals come to terms with the loss of the attitudes and behaviors that were appropriate for the pre-resizing organization but are not aligned with the new realities of the postresizing organization and (2) to prepare employees for the rigors of moving through personal and organizational transition. A versatile activity to help people loosen their grip on the old and prepare for the new is the venting meeting. By raising awareness and accelerating learning, this meeting heightens people's understanding of how they are dealing with their individual adaptation. The venting meeting facilitates letting go by helping people along the three steps of coming to terms with loss (Tannenbaum & Hanna, 1985):

- *Consciousness raising.* The meeting alerts employees to common patterns of organizational and individual reaction to transition and, in particular, the personal adaptation process. This shows that reactions to loss are to be expected following a transition and acquaints employees with the sequence of letting go of the old, dealing with the neutral zone, and accepting the new. The goal is to help employees acknowledge intellectually what they are personally holding on to and to help them become aware of their reasons for doing so.
- *Reexperiencing.* The reasons for and implications of holding on become truly understood only when they are expressed experientially. Talking through where they have been and what they are experiencing as a result of the resizing helps employees bring their feelings to a conscious level. This is typically an emotional and highly charged process, in contrast to the more intellectual level at which initial consciousness raising occurs.
- *Mourning.* The psychological process of letting go is completed through an active mourning of what is being left behind: old ways of seeing and doing things, lost hopes and expectations, and the loss of what was once satisfying, meaningful, or simply familiar. Sometimes this mourning is accompanied by remorse—a sense of guilt for time wasted or the work situation that could have been but may not ever be. Yet it also instills a sense of renewal and rebirth and an acceptance for what lies ahead. From the most primitive to the most modern cultures, there always has been a recognized need for rituals to carry individuals from one phase of life to another. Mourning is a key facilitating ritual in the process of letting go of the old and accepting the new, at the organizational as well as at the individual level. Some firms hold symbolic funerals and wakes to mourn the loss of the old and ready people for life after resizing.

Benefits of a Venting Meeting

A venting meeting provides many benefits to a workforce recovering from a resizing. First, it validates the experiences of employees who are coping with loss in their personal situation and adapting to the death of the old organizational reality. The mere acknowl-edgment from the organization that there is a need to mourn le-gitimizes the emotions and feelings employees experience as they cope with loss and change. Second, the venting meeting gives peo-ple guidance for dealing with and moving through an uncomfort-able experience. It is a visible forum in which a group of people comes to see that holding on to the old, although normal and nat-ural, is a maladaptive response to the new organizational realities. The venting meeting is a turning point at which people let go of anger and blame and take personal responsibility for accepting their situation in the resized organization.

Third, bringing people together to share in the venting meet-ing establishes a bond among members of the group. The tendencies to turn inward during times of crisis, to constrict com-munication, and to restrict involvement are replaced by a reach-ing out to each other as members of a community. Fourth, the venting meeting accelerates the pace at which people let go. Group members are at once providers and receivers of support and cop-ing strategies. Finally, the venting meeting clarifies and confirms to those who may be stuck in denial that something is being lost. The dramatic scene of watching others acknowledge that the old order has ended weakens enduring forces for maintaining the sta-tus quo.

Venting is distinct from complaining. Complaining is blaming, while venting raises up, legitimizes, and works through feelings. Employees who work through the stages of consciousness raising, reexperiencing, and mourning are better prepared to accept new realities and move forward. For a workforce that is banged up and burned out after a resizing, a venting meeting is a forum for heal-ing and renewal.

The meeting also helps people come to terms with ambiguous organizational endings. If the organization ceased to exist, then the individual members could begin a process of mourning and letting go. When an organization's structure dies but its identity lingers through a resizing, this is a less obvious transition. The mourning component of the venting meeting transforms what might be perceived as a lingering hope for survival of the status quo into a finite experience of death—an event that can be dealt with, adapted to, and eventually moved on from.

Design Considerations for the Venting Meeting

Several factors must be considered in designing a venting meeting, especially when prevailing conditions in a resizing (such as restricted communication and heightened tension and stress) result in reduced levels of trust and openness in the organization. Design factors include issues pertaining to what should be covered in the program's content and who should be invited to participate.

Learning Methodology

In a venting meeting, consciousness raising initially occurs through presentations or pre-session readings. This is reinforced during the reexperiencing and mourning steps through discussions, role-plays, and simulations. When designing a venting meeting, a decision needs to be made whether the target audience will respond best at the intellectual or emotional level or some combination of the two.

Although an emotional reckoning is important to the reexperiencing process, the members of a work team may initially be very uncomfortable with expressing their feelings to a group of peers. In this case, the most that should be expected from a meeting is some consciousness raising and perhaps written (as opposed to spoken) activities such as having people write down their behaviors, emotions, and perceptions in response to the resizing and note their feelings about the organization. At the very least, this experience gives people insight into the extent to which they have moved through the adaptation process. Often, however, the need to vent will take over, and a spontaneous and energetic expression of feelings will ensue. This occurred in a consumer products firm that acquired a major competitor and subsequently experienced a reduction in force to deal with redundant positions. It seemed that everybody had something to be upset about: lead company managers, who for three years running had been told that merit pay increases would be minimal due to weak results, were angry about the high price paid for the target and the generous employment contracts given to its executives; acquired managers resented the arrogant attitude of their counterparts from the lead company; and everyone was turned off by the highly political staffing process and the top-heavy organization that resulted (all senior executives were retained following the merger, while deep cuts were made at middle and lower levels to meet cost savings targets).

Senior executives recognized the cynicism and distrust lingering in the organization for months after the integration supposedly was over. However, they scoffed at the notion of what they assumed would be a "touch-feely" venting session. Instead, they consented to sponsor a series of "Rebuilding After the Merger" training workshops for middle managers. The workshops were promoted with no mention of venting or letting go in the course description or objectives. Knowing of the managers' strongly negative feelings about the merger and subsequent downsizing, the workshop facilitator sought to create an environment of trust and openness during the session. In each of the twenty sessions, the floodgates opened and emotions poured forth. Considerable anger was directed at the leadership and with the staffing. Even people who did not speak up during the session benefited from their attendance. One manager who was quiet said to the facilitator afterward, "I thought it was only me who felt this way. It really surprised me that all these people feel the same way. I was worried something was wrong with me, because no one ever talks about this stuff."

After about ninety minutes, a collective sense came over the group that venting by itself would not change their situation. Rather than wait for senior executives to manage the revitalization process, these middle managers realized that they would have to take responsibility for leading recovery in their work areas. This phenomenon was replicated in each of the twenty sessions. After the first few sessions, the company grapevine talked up the venting aspect of the program, and attendees at later sessions came with some expectations for venting. To senior management's credit, they did not attempt to terminate or alter the remaining sessions. The chief financial officer later said, "Hey, if that's what people need to do, then that's what they need to do."

Degree of Confrontation

Substantial resistance to open discussion may hinder the purpose of a venting meeting, even when senior leadership wholly endorses the meeting. Consequently, the proper degree of confrontation to elicit the optimum amount of venting is another design consideration. (Confrontation here refers to an encounter, as in confronting facts, not a clash or showdown between two parties.) The most purely relevant—and thus most confrontational—level is that of data collected from the client organization itself. These data may take the form of findings from interviews conducted with employees to determine their feelings about the transition, results from an employee attitude survey, or archival data such as financial reports or personnel records. Data drawn from the organization are the most powerful way to confront the presence of resizing fallout within an organization and its people, countering such classic sources of denial as the resistance underlying statements like, "Let me tell you why things are different with us . . ." Data collection has some up-front costs in terms of time and money, but data collected from the organization may be the most potent way to grab people's attention and accelerate their involvement in a venting meeting.

Despite a history of outstanding financial results, a financial services firm headquartered in New York City never capitalized on chances to cross-sell across product areas. The CEO and other members of the firm's executive committee hoped to use a restructuring of business units and concurrent reduction in force as an opportunity to promote behavior change in the organization. Management targeted the firm's trading group as ripe for producing greater profitability through aggressive cross-selling. In this group, conflict historically raged between product managers and relationship managers—the product managers cared only to get the deal done and move on to the next customer, while the relationship managers protected long-term associations with their customers. Despite previous structural and attempted cultural changes, managers continued to play by the old rules. The executive committee sought assistance in getting the managers to abandon their old behaviors and attitudes and accept new ones aligned with cross-group cooperation. One component of the plan to facilitate letting go was a venting meeting. "These are New York City traders we are talking about," warned one member of the executive committee in response to the proposed meeting, "They will run right back to the trading floor if they feel their time is being wasted."

To get at the issues quickly, the venting meeting was designed to be highly confrontational. Interviews were conducted with a sample of traders from each business unit, and a summary of key findings was presented at the beginning of the meeting. Direct quotes from the interviewees clearly showed agreement with the concept of cross-selling, but also revealed the stubbornness of old behaviors. "Look," commented one trader in his interview, "I know the firm will make more money if we sell multiple products to the same customers, but I don't see what's in it for me." "I don't know those guys in the other product area, and I'm not about to bring them to see one of my customers," reported another. Moreover, unreserved comments by product and relationship managers about each other were reported to the group. Product managers regarded relationship managers as "out of touch with reality" and "lazy." Relationship managers described product managers as "willing to sell their grandmothers to make a deal." Captured by the intensity and relevance of the data, not one of the meeting attendees left the ensuing venting session to return to the trading floor.

A lower level of confrontation is the dissemination of war stories from other organizations. These stories can be colorful and relate well to the situation in the client organization; managers are especially attentive to how others before them have grappled with revitalization after resizing. The facilitator must carefully guide the group from an examination of transition dynamics elsewhere to a discussion of what is gong on within their organization and what is going on among themselves. When anecdotes from other organizations are being served up, it is critically important that they pertain to the specific kind of resizing experienced by managers in the audience. People coping with the aftermath of, say, the closing of a division want to hear about other closings. Otherwise, they will perceive the sessions as generic or irrelevant and throw up an added barrier of resistance.

Ceremonies

Ceremonies are powerful tools for bonding people who are recovering from a resizing and accepting the changes confronting them. A variety of ceremonies have been used in conjunction with venting meetings. Many build on the theme of death and involve burials or wakes. Others celebrate the "good old days" left behind through such techniques as placing items in time capsules. One utility I worked with used a downsizing as an opportunity to promote a culture change toward more entrepreneurial and risk-taking behaviors than had prevailed historically in the organization.

An internal HR manager created a display that featured the Grim Reaper taking away "deceased" behaviors and a diapered baby delivering the new behaviors.

A ceremony is not a surrogate for venting. Rather, it is a dramatic method for marking the transition from old to new. In organizations where the target audience is deeply uncomfortable with confronting issues in a public forum, a ceremony can emphasize the need to let go of the old at a lower level of emotional risk. However, executives who regard ceremonies as too exotic sometimes reject them out of hand. The choice of whether to integrate a ceremony into a venting meeting agenda depends on the prevailing organizational culture and climate.

Attendees

A few important rules guide the decision of who should attend a venting meeting. One rule is never to have people and their direct superiors in the same session. Employees will have difficulty expressing their deepest feelings if their boss is looking at them from across the room. This is not meant to deride the work of leaders who have built trust across hierarchical levels, but it is prudent to err on the side of creating as safe an environment as possible for people to speak up in venting meetings. (The exception to this rule is the top team in an organization: the senior executive and his or her direct subordinates. In senior teams with sufficient trust and maturity, the venting meeting can be successfully conducted with the team leader and members together in the session.)

If the superior has a genuine interest in understanding what subordinates are thinking and feeling, this need can be satisfied through the offer of an anonymous summary of key points made during the meeting. The report also can include any ideas that may have been discussed in the session for facilitating the revitalization process within the work group, including what resources or support are needed from leadership. Another option, if the participants consent, is to invite the superior to attend the final half-hour of the meeting to hear a summary of the issues raised by the group. Again, this should be an anonymous report in which only summaries of the group's work are presented.

Another rule is to make the session voluntary. No one should be forced to attend a venting meeting, and once the meeting has begun, no one should be put on the spot and compelled to participate. Even those who remain silent in a venting meeting often report vicarious benefits from hearing how others are dealing with the adaptation process.

Facilitator

The meeting facilitator needs to be someone whom the attendees see as credible and will protect their confidentiality. The facilitator also needs to be well versed in group dynamics, able to draw out attitudes and emotions, contend with individuals who dominate, know when to push the group further and when to back off, and treat the people and the process with the utmost respect. In most organizations, trained external facilitators are used to conduct venting meetings. The leaders of these organizations recognize that the assurance of confidentiality and skillful leadership are essential ingredients if a venting meeting is going to succeed at its objective of helping people let go of the old.

I have worked with a variety of organizations where external consultants have facilitated the initial set of venting meetings and then turned the process over to internal resources. Typically, these are human resource professionals with expertise in group process facilitation. However, I have trained people ranging from plant managers to directors of marketing in leading venting meetings. At one small company, the CEO successfully led several venting meetings after I initiated the process.

For the benefits of the venting meeting to be realized, the organizational community must regard it as a safe milieu for expressing their deepest and truest feelings. In organizations that sponsor a series of meetings, the impressions brought back and discussed through informal channels by attendees of the first few sessions will strongly influence whether other employees regard the meetings as something to look forward to or something of which to be wary. Therefore, most organizations use external professionals to facilitate initial sessions, if not the entire set of meetings.

Venting Meeting Agenda

A venting meeting can range in length from one hour to a few days, and it can be scheduled on an ongoing basis or as a one-time-only event. After a downsizing, lunchtime brown bag venting meetings were sponsored for acquired airline employees. Following an internal restructuring that included a reduction in force in a telecom giant, a single three-day off-site meeting was designed to help people let go of the old and begin accepting the new.

Exhibit 12.1 provides a menu for preparing the venting meeting agenda. Not all components are intended to be used in all meetings, either because of their poor fit with the organization's culture or time constraints. The full agenda typically requires two days of work but can be expanded to three days if strong holding-on forces are anticipated. Alternatively, the meeting can be condensed to one day or less if components like the mourning ceremony or the feedback session with senior management are dropped.

Set the tone and atmosphere of the venting meeting early on by clarifying the meeting's purpose and objectives, establishing the facilitator's credibility, and loosening up people through an icebreaking exercise. Icebreakers such as asking people to draw their current feelings about organizational life on a piece of paper or to describe them as a food or television program succeed at getting people to open up and participate. Subsequently, raise awareness of the adaptation process through a presentation that educates attendees on organizational transitions and their impact on employees. This kind of presentation validates what employees have been experiencing during and after the resizing, which in turn gives the session and facilitator credibility and brings people's energy and interest into the process.

The presentation typically is met with considerable head nodding and verbal confirmations of how the discussion applies to the attendees' situation. In some cases, the attendees may be bursting to let out their feelings in an emotional and energetic catharsis. In others, a more conservative approach is taken by conducting a breakout group activity that serves as a segue between the consciousness-raising and reexperiencing components of the meeting. The intention is to build up employees' comfort level with the venting process; people in a small group typically feel more at ease and more responsible to contributing to the group discussion. Consequently, attendees are assigned to small groups to identify and prioritize the issues from the presentation that are the most pertinent to their personal situation. A lively exchange usually ensues and continues until the facilitator persuades the members to return to the full group.

Exhibit 12.1. Venting Meeting Agenda.

I.   Introduction
   • Meeting objectives
   • Facilitator's background
   • Icebreaking exercise

II. Presentation on organizational and individual responses to transition

III. Breakout group assignment
   • Identify key issues affecting this transition
   • Prioritize issues for discussion

IV. Full group meets
   • Breakout groups report lists of high-priority issues
   • Consensus developed regarding key issues for discussion

V.   Discussion of key issues

VI. Mourning ceremony

VII. Presentation on guidelines for managing self and subordinates during revitalization after resizing

VIII. Individual assignment
   • What I can do to facilitate revitalization
   • What the company needs to do to facilitate revitalization

IX. Breakout group assignment
   • Consolidate "what I can do" and "what company can do" lists

X.   Full group meets
   • Breakout groups report lists
   • Consolidated lists prepared

XI. Feedback session with senior management
   • Review of lists with questions of clarification
   • Commitment to next steps

In the full group, each breakout group reports its list of high-priority issues. The full group achieves consensus regarding the key issues in this particular transition and organizes them into a set of discussion items to guide the reexperiencing portion of the meeting. Now comes the emotional highlight of the venting meeting: a facilitator-led discussion that addresses salient issues weighing on the minds of employees. Precisely following the consensus list of items is less important than letting the group go where it wants with the discussion. Invariably, one issue will bleed into the discussion of another. The depth of the discussion will vary according to the skill of the facilitator and the openness of the group. The full reexperiencing step rarely occurs at one meeting. Still, the facilitator may take advantage of the presence of the group and conduct a mourning ceremony to facilitate bonding, supportiveness, and acceptance of the end of the old organizational realities among the attendees.

In addition to covering the three steps of the letting-go process, the venting meeting may include a module that readies people for their responsibilities in the postresizing organization. This forward-looking preparation typically addresses a common request by senior leadership to finish the meeting on a positive note. Although the mourning process itself may end in a celebratory fashion, much like a traditional Irish wake, the notion of grieving retains a negative stigma in most organizational cultures. To help people look forward and feel optimistic about their chances for success, the venting meeting can include a segment on preparing for life in the new organization.

After a symbolic pause in the meeting, a break, or lunch, the focus turns toward the future, with guidelines for managing the recovery period following resizing. In meetings involving nonsupervisory employees, this could be in the form of suggestions for managing oneself. Typically, these guidelines include some mix of tactics for continuing the work of letting go and adapting to the new organizational realities. When the meeting involves participants who manage other people, guidelines for managing subordinates during the revitalization period are presented along with those for managing oneself. An individually focused exercise to get people to distinguish between areas they can and cannot control prevents attendees from fixating on matters beyond their influence.

Finally, the full group makes summary lists of individual and organization actions that can be taken as part of revitalization.

These lists should be reported to senior leadership as a first step in using the data collected in the meeting to aid the revitalization process. If time permits and the climate is appropriate, the venting meeting can conclude with a scheduled appearance by members of senior leadership to hear the findings firsthand from participants. This symbolizes leadership's genuine interest in what people have to say about what they have gone through and where they are headed, and it lets executives hear the issues in employees' own words and with their emotions attached.

Prepare executives for this portion of the meeting by reminding them that this is the attendees' meeting and not theirs. Their role is to be active listeners during the reporting-back session—first showing empathy for where the attendees have been and what they are experiencing, and then conveying that they heard the employees' ideas about how the company could help manage revitalization after resizing. Alternatively, summaries of the work produced in the venting meeting can be presented to senior leadership in a written report following the meeting.

Dealing with the Neutral Zone: Monitoring and Communicating

Employees who let go of their attachment to the old have not yet completed their adaptation after a resizing. They must contend with the awkward period of feeling out new methods, roles, and relationships. This reignites stress and uncertainty but is a critical—and creative—step in revitalization.

The neutral zone is a time when the organization is no longer what it was prior to the resizing but not yet what it can become following the transition. If well managed, the neutral zone sees the easing of forces for the status quo and strengthening of forces for the new. As such, facilitation during the neutral zone is built around communication to clarify what is being abandoned and what is being adopted. This includes upward communication to monitor transition and downward communication to reinforce the new and strengthen forces for desired change.

Monitoring people as they struggle through the neutral zone can be achieved through common methods for conducting employee research. These include questionnaires, one-on-one interviews, focus group interviews, and observations. The content of the employee research should focus on whether employees understand the business and personal opportunities in the postresizing organization and what is needed to align their individual contributions to work team and overall organizational performance.

Following the last in a series of plant closings, senior executives at a manufacturing firm launched a formal revitalization program. Working with an external consultant, internal human resource professionals conducted a series of focus group interviews to monitor how employees viewed the emerging organization and their readiness to contribute to it. The focus group interviews were structured around a few key questions:

- To what extent do you have the information you need to do your job well at this time?
- To what extent do you see personal opportunity in the resized organization?
- To what extent do you see a new and better organization emerging?
- What cultural characteristics are predominating in the resized organization?
- What makes you feel optimistic or pessimistic about the new organization?

The standards of good organizational communication apply to the neutral zone (for example, send timely, consistent messages using multiple methods). There are no right or wrong methods of communication during the neutral zone; use whatever works for the organization and its people. However, messages about the promise of the new organization should be repeated and reinforced through multiple media, including written, electronic, and in-person communications.

The manufacturing firm launched a biweekly transition newsletter, sent periodic letters to employees' homes, printed packets to equip managers and supervisors with appropriate answers to employees' questions, created a Web page with transition updates and information, sponsored town hall meetings, and rewarded superiors for holding small group meetings with their work teams. Through all these outlets, some constant themes were reinforced:

- A clear and compelling argument for why the status quo is no good
- An equally clear and compelling vision for a new and better postresizing organization
- Ground rules and desired culture norms for the new organization (including commitment to communication)
- The process for getting from the status quo to the desired organization
- Setting a tone for the neutral zone, including setting expectations for things like inevitable mistakes being made and the need for people to cut one another some slack during the process

Managing the neutral zone requires the solid application of good change management practices. The delicacy comes in the execution of these standard practices. Managing the neutral zone in a manner that contributes to weakening forces for the status quo and strengthening forces for desired change requires adequate resources to monitor and communicate during the period following resizing; attention must be paid to time, staff, and budget. The organization will not reorient itself by accident, and people will not automatically embrace new practices and perspectives congruent with the new organizational order while abandoning the ones that served them well prior to resizing. Monitoring and communication provide the feedback and detail required to stay on track to attain the desired organization. Almost as important, these efforts demonstrate senior leadership's acknowledgment of the adaptation process and the need to manage revitalization following resizing. As a result, during the neutral zone, leadership has the opportunity to model the communication and feedback norms it wants to characterize the postresizing culture.

Accepting the New: Bringing Vision to Life

For a workforce that is letting go of the old and contending with the confusion of the neutral zone, a well-articulated vision of where the organization is headed plays an important role in revitalizing employee spirit after a painful transition. Vision makes it easier for people to let go of their grasp on the status quo and instills a sense of confidence that they and their organization can manage through the neutral zone. When coupled with guidelines for desired values and behaviors, vision directs employee actions in line with the desired postresizing organization. However, most efforts to communicate corporate vision and subsequently direct employee behavior miss the mark. In the typical scenario, a CEO takes his team off site to hash out a vision statement. On returning home, an article appears in the company newsletter heralding the arrival of the new vision, a video is made to explain the vision in detail, and plaques are ordered so that all employees can have a constant reminder of the vision hovering above their desk or work area. The CEO and other senior executives then get back to running their business.

Employees want to learn more about the vision, how it will be attained, and precisely how they can contribute to achieving it as the organization rebounds from a resizing. To convey an adequate degree of precision, middle managers and direct supervisors must reiterate and reinforce the CEO's statement of vision. Employees prefer face-to-face communication on matters of organizational change to other styles, and while senior executives must set the tone in communicating direction, employees want to hear directly from their immediate superiors (Ackley, 1992). Unfortunately, middle managers are themselves often unclear about the vision and, following a resizing, often put a higher priority on producing business results than on contributing to organization change and development. First-line supervisors are even further in the dark about the vision and how it will be attained. Although newsletters, intranets, videos, and plaques are important supplements to face-to-face communication, they are not substitutes for the personal touch that employees seek to revitalize them after a resizing. Moreover, without any involvement in the development of the vision statement or the plan to roll it out, managers and supervisors tend to be cynical about the promise of a vaguely worded statement, threatened by the changes it suggests. With no sense of ownership of or stake in the vision, they resist rather than support its attainment.

Eventually, the CEO gets some kind of feedback that indicates that people are not clear about where their organization is headed and have increasingly lost faith in leadership's ability to move the organization forward. This feedback may be in the form of findings from an employee attitude survey, persistent nudging from a consultant or human resource director, or disappointing financial results. This typically frustrates the CEO. "Haven't I already told the people the vision?" asks the baffled leader. Yes, perhaps, but the CEO's message and intentions have not been brought to life.

Living the Vision

Statements of vision in and of themselves do little to restore faith, create hope, or generate the motivation to act in an organization recovering from a resizing. To facilitate revitalization, the vision must jump off the paper on which it is printed. It must become animated and integrated into people's actions on the job, not merely be spoken about or pointed to. The process of aligning employee behavior with the desired postresizing organization is called *living the vision*.

Figure 12.2 represents a model for living the vision through activity up and down the organization. It is built from the vision of senior leadership at the top of the organization, but it requires the support of each level from the bottom up. This activity at all levels engages people in living the vision. Senior leadership articulates a clear direction for the organization; managers and supervisors in the middle link business unit mission statements with the corporate vision and develop guidelines for employee behavior. In work groups, employees translate the vision, mission, and operating guidelines into day-to-day operating practices. This process involves employees in aligning their work with the new organizational order and provides answers to the prominent question of how they can contribute to overall organizational success. Finally, working back up the pyramid, supervisors and managers review proposed new ways of approaching work to ensure they support the mission and vision and to provide coordination across work areas.

Living the vision succeeds at rebuilding employee spirit following a resizing for a number of reasons:

- *High credibility.* Living the vision directly addresses employees' questions such as, "Where is this organization headed?" and "How do I align my work accordingly?"

Figure 12.2. Model for Living the Vision.

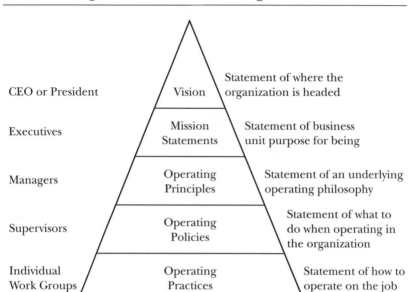

- *High validity.* Changes in work procedures are based on employees' own recommendations for aligning work with the vision, not some consultant's suggestion or some program's prescription.
- *High involvement.* Care is taken each step of the way to ensure genuine support for suggested revisions before the process engages the next level.
- *High relevance.* The vision is linked with people's daily work situation.

These qualities contrast with common approaches to abiding by vision statements. Visions can wither if people feel they must read tablets of stone passed down from above. Allowing people some participation in developing initial vision statements, subsequent mission statements, and operating guidelines can help boost energy and enthusiasm in the postresizing organization. This involvement provides the emotional glue that holds together the various parts of the organization and complements the strategic and financial plans in revitalizing after resizing. And, no small matter, it engages people close to the work in recommending and adopting new on-the-job behaviors.

Articulating Vision

Vision statements need not be elegant. In fact, the simpler they are, the easier they are to communicate and the more accessible they tend to be for translation into on-the-job behaviors. Frequently, vision statements include core values that should accompany efforts to attain the vision. Values represent what the organization believes in and how people should work with and treat one another. They are the attitudes that subtly sanction or prohibit behaviors on the job.

The process through which the vision statement is developed is as important to revitalizing people after a resizing as the content of what it says. The extent to which an organization's vision is supported by top executives is an early test of how the vision will be received through the ranks and of how facilitative it will be in aligning people and their work with the new desired organization. If people at the top of an organization do not understand or support the vision, then most certainly neither will people at the middle and lower levels.

The case of a retail sales conglomerate shows how support for the process can be built concurrently with the crafting and communication of the vision. The firm experienced multiple waves of downsizing, store closings, and restructurings as part of an effort to close unprofitable locations while attempting to centralize decision making and rein in autonomy from business units. A consultant conducted one-on-one interviews with the CEO and business unit presidents to identify issues, concerns, and priorities related to business direction and vision. At an off-site meeting with the executives, the consultant reported the interview findings and facilitated a discussion to align their perspectives about the desired end state for the restructured firm. Key concerns of autonomy versus centralization were addressed head-on and examined through rounds of give-and-take discussion. As the CEO put it, "We now have a vision that is not just a bunch of words, but something that each of us has influenced, really believe in, and commit to achieving." Anything short of a consensus among the top team would have foiled implementation in the business units.

Translating Vision into Mission

Once articulated at the very top of an organization, the vision should be tested at the next level of management before it is announced to the overall workforce. As with the top team, if people at this level cannot understand and support the vision, rolling it out to the rest of the organization will only spell failure. At the retailer, a management forum brought together the senior teams of each business unit to hear the CEO present the draft of the vision. In small groups, executives generated questions about the vision and its implementation. Some discussion of semantics and other relatively minor matters ensued, but the group soon endorsed the vision as something they could and would support in their units. Subsequently, each team met and adapted the vision into mission statements for their business units. A mission statement is the business unit's direction and purpose for being, including what distinguishes it from the competition. One specialty retailer in the conglomerate's portfolio came up with a mission of "contributing to the [conglomerate company's] overall financial success by being recognized as the premier source of moderately priced women's sportswear." The team also prepared work plans to pave the way for moving the vision and mission statements through their organization and soliciting employee involvement and feedback.

Only after plans were set for bringing it to life in the business units was the vision communicated throughout the retail conglomerate. This countered the tendency for vision statements to be rolled out amid fanfare, only to fade away as people's behaviors remained consistent with the old organizational realities. The vision communication strategy addressed how to involve people in translating the vision into on-the-job behaviors along with the promotion of the vision statement itself.

Translating Vision and Mission into Operating Principles

The next step in living the vision is to translate statements of corporate vision and business unit mission into operating principles to guide individuals' work on the job. Middle managers in each business unit meet to determine two important aspects of this process. First, they develop operating principles based on the mission statement. Operating principles are statements of an underlying operating philosophy. These are general guidelines, not unyielding instructions, on how to approach work and align it with the company's direction. In one of the retailer's business units, managers developed an operating principle that "we will be recognized by our customers for being responsive to their needs." Second, the managers determine how to continue the process of living the vision into the next levels of the organization. They develop work plans within their work areas to solicit employee input in clarifying operating policies and procedures that reinforce the unit's mission statement and corporation's vision. The managers review the plans with their superiors, make necessary revisions, and implement the plan.

In the case of the retailer, part of the implementation plan was to develop an internal resource group to help middle managers, supervisors, and employees align their work with the vision. In each business unit, a small group of line managers—selected for their mix of generalist business skills, process orientation, and excellent communication skills—were taken off-line and given one-year assignments as resource specialists. After receiving training, these resource specialists assisted managers in ways like gathering work-related data and writing clear operating principles.

Being a large organization, the retail conglomerate replicated the involvement of middle managers at the next lower level. Their charge was to translate operating principles into operating policies. Again, their work was submitted for review at the level above before being communicated to subordinates. In the retailing unit, an operating policy of "regularly survey customers to assess their satisfaction with current products and service, and to determine their changing needs for the future" was aligned with the operating principle of being recognized by customers as being responsive to their needs. In smaller or flatter organizations, it may not be necessary to separate the tasks of developing operating principles and policies. Rather, they can be combined in the work of middle managers.

Translating Operating Principles and Policies into Operating Practices

Next, the operating principles and policies need to be translated into operating practices: statements of how to operate on the job. Employee groups, usually integrated work teams, meet to discuss the corporate vision, business unit mission, and operating principles and policies to ensure their understanding. A manager from the business unit attends an initial meeting to explain the rationale underlying the operating principles and policies and solicit feedback regarding their relevance and applicability to work activities. Then employee teams meet regularly to identify new operating practices that align work behaviors with the operating principles and, ultimately, the mission and vision. Recommendations for matters like eliminating unnecessary work or proposing new ways of approaching tasks are prepared for presentation to and review by supervisors and managers. Periodic meetings are held to review employee recommendations and ensure that proposed modifications to work activities support the mission and vision and are economically and technically feasible.

In the retail unit, employee groups recommended many ways in which the operating principle of "we will be recognized by our customers for being responsive to their needs" and the operating policy of "regularly survey customers to assess their satisfaction with current products and services, and to determine their changing needs for the future" could be brought to life. These suggestions ranged from cashiers taking the time to solicit feedback from customers after transactions to the development of a customer satisfaction questionnaire.

Operating practices are not rigid rules to be followed in an uncompromising manner. Rather, they are suggested guidelines for behavior on the job. In the retail stores, for example, if cashiers saw that customers were in a hurry, they would not bother them with questions about service standards. And although there is great license for creativity in developing operating practices, employee groups need clear statements of vision, mission, and operating principles to define the boundaries within which that license operates. This direction provides a context within which work teams can design practices that are likely to receive approval from the organization's regular decision-making authority.

Work groups require support in conducting the work of aligning behaviors with the vision of where the organization is headed. Training programs help enhance data collection, work analysis, and problem-solving skills among group members, as well as alerting them to common inhibitors to group decision making. Work groups need information—such as specifics about business plans and goals, performance results, technical capabilities, and competitive insights—if they are to develop recommendations that win approval from their superiors. Sometimes work groups gather this information up front in the operating practice development process; other times, it comes as a result of discussion and analysis in meetings with superiors to review recommendations. At the retailer, resource specialists offered their assistance to any work team needing an extra set of hands to procure information, collect data, interview technical experts, or simply serve as a sounding board to test propositions.

The process of living the vision breeds confidence and revitalizes the organization. It gets people to understand how their contributions on the job are aligned with the greater vision and mission of their workplace. As a result, employees move beyond a mind-set of recovering from resizing and start developing a self-reinforcing capacity for creativity and renewal on the job. This is living the vision to its fullest. Like an individual who pursues continuous improvement, the organization living the vision does not content itself with hitting a target or reaching a threshold of improvement. Rather, it sets forth on a journey toward ever-increasing improvements in competitiveness and work life quality.

Moving On

Resizing has a negative, not merely neutral, impact on employee behaviors and attitudes. People are adaptive, however, and can work through the unintended consequences of downsizings, closings, and divestitures. Organizations that have downsized can facilitate this adaptation process by helping people let go of the old, contend with the neutral zone, and accept the new.

With a workforce that has relinquished its grip on the past and is ready to grab on to the new, executive leadership and managerial action can combine to develop a context for revitalization after resizing. When the direction, values, and other components of the desired vision are articulated, employees can participate in designing and implementing practices that align their individual and group activities with postresizing realities. The precursor to moving on after resizing is acknowledging and actively addressing the need to let go of the old. This is the normal and natural process of human adaptation to change and transition—a process that the leadership must recognize and address in order to help an organization and its people revitalize after resizing.

References

Ackley, D. (1992, August). The secret of communicating bad news to employees. *Communication World,* pp. 27–29.

Bridges, W. (1991). *Managing transitions.* Reading, MA: Addison-Wesley.

Lewin, K. (1947). Frontiers in group dynamics. *Human Relations, 1,* 5–41.

Marks, M. L. (1994). *From turmoil to triumph: New life after mergers, acquisitions, and downsizings.* San Francisco: New Lexington Press.

Marks, M. L. (2003). *Charging back up the hill: Workplace recovery after mergers, acquisitions, and downsizings.* San Francisco: Jossey-Bass.

Marks, M. L., & Mirvis, P. H. (1998). *Joining forces: Making one plus one equal three in mergers, acquisitions, and alliances.* San Francisco: Jossey-Bass.

Tannenbaum, R., & Hanna, R. W. (1985). Holding on, letting go, and moving on: Understanding a neglected perspective on change. In R. Tannenbaum and others (Eds.), *Human systems development* (pp. 95–121). San Francisco: Jossey-Bass.

CHAPTER 13

The Hidden Costs and Benefits of Organizational Resizing Activities

Anthony F. Buono

The early part of the twenty-first century has produced headlines and articles in the business section of newspapers and popular press that have a vintage 1980s flavor: "Layoffs and attrition after the merger, compounded by a subsequent earnings crash that prompted a management shake-up, restructuring and further cuts, have whittled ABC Company's workforce by 21 percent." "HIJ Corporation, struggling to reposition itself in a changing market, yesterday said it would cut 2,000 jobs, or a quarter of its global workforce." "XYZ Inc., in its largest internal organizational change to date, has merged its commercial and consumer personal computer operations into a single business unit, reducing head count in that area by 15 percent."

While such cutbacks were a routine part of corporate life during the late 1980s through the mid-1990s, when 85 percent of Fortune 1000 companies initiated major workforce reductions (Hitt, Keats, Harback, & Nixon, 1994), the latter part of the 1990s was characterized by significant growth, dot-com mania, and the belief that the U.S. economy had entered a golden age of commerce. How quickly things can change, as consumer demand, especially for high-technology products, began to wane. As a result, a large part of corporate America, with an intriguing blend of old economy–new economy consensus about the future, seems to have reverted to the belief that the most appropriate response to reduced demand is to shrink flexible resources, particularly a firm's human resources. During the first quarter of 2001 alone, a wide array of companies across the United States laid off more than 100,000 employees a month (Butterfield, 2001). In the wake of the September 11, 2001, terrorist attacks on the United States, downsizing strategies quickly reverberated from the airline and hospitality industries, through the high-tech world, and into literally every industry imaginable. A recent survey by Bain & Company found that nearly 40 percent of U.S. business executives interviewed saw layoffs as a quick solution and part of their strategy for confronting any economic slowdown (Ackerman, 2001). Intense global competition, investor impatience and an increasingly nervous Wall Street, seemingly capricious decisions by consumers, rapidly shifting technologies, the volatile transition from the dot-com revolution to "dot-bomb" realities, and deregulatory pressures have all precipitated significant organizational changes as companies continue to struggle to enhance performance, cut costs, and try to survive. At the same time, growing stakeholder pressures and demands for quality and outstanding customer service have magnified the pressures companies are under to perform. Consequently, many organizations seem caught in a permanent restructuring process, routinely displacing and rehiring large segments of their workforces through what appears to be a revolving-door set of policies (McKinley, Zhao, & Rust, 2000; Naik, 1998).

Organizational Resizing

As the preceding chapters have underscored, there is a decided difference between sheer downsizing and the essence of organizational resizing. From an analytical vantage point, the distinction between downsizing—a proactive, intentional management strategy to respond to current marketplace conditions—and decline—an involuntary erosion of an organization's resource base (Freeman & Cameron, 1993)—is especially relevant in the context of resizing decisions. For many organizations struggling with demanding and hypercompetitive markets, downsizing is closely linked with traditional cost-cutting measurements in an effort to revitalize slumping business. The conventional approach has been along the lines of "binge and purge" firms that quickly hire and just as quickly fire employees when economic times shift (Andresky Fraser, 2001). Such quick-fix orientations, which are typically poorly planned and badly managed, rarely bring about the expected improvements in company performance. In fact, these so-called fixes often end up as a high-cost rather than low-cost strategy (De Meuse, Bergmann, & Vanderheiden, 1997; Mishra, Spreitzer, & Mishra, 1998; Mroczkowski & Hanaoka, 1997; Perry, 1986). Such downsizing decisions significantly and abruptly alter existing organizational arrangements, violating fundamental psychological contracts, and precipitating high degrees of stress and a range of dysfunctions for the individuals involved, as well as the organization itself (Buono, 1995; Buono, Bowditch, & Nurick, 1987; De Meuse, Bergmann, & Lester, 2001).

Resizing, in contrast, is based on the ideal that organizational restructuring and the reallocation of resources have less to do with immediate market conditions, especially compared to the downsizing decisions of the 1980s and early 1990s (Mroczkowski & Hanaoka, 1997), than the emerging longer-term realities of business and industry conditions. Many of the corporate shifts we have been witnessing are driven by the pace of change—change that is occurring at such a phenomenal rate that a growing number of companies, especially those in indeterminate industries where success is always difficult to predict (Sutherland, 1981), are finding it difficult to keep up. Consequently, an increasing number of companies are positioning themselves for a long-term strategy of improving supply-chain efficiencies, outsourcing key functions, and consolidating manufacturing and services in an effort to enhance their competitiveness and overall profitability. Instead of simply reacting to recent market changes or short-term reassessments of the marketplace by quickly shedding resources, these decisions appear to be an increasing part of a longer-term plan to make the business more flexible and adaptable to rapidly changing marketplace realities.

Thus, rather than traditional approaches to downsizing, the focus of resizing is to ensure that the firm is in a stronger position to respond to such rapid shifts and transformations. Instead of using downsizing targets to drive the redesign of work processes and organizational structure, resizing begins with redesign efforts.

When downsizing and cost reduction drive work-related redesign, downsizing is the primary goal. When a redesign strategy and long-term performance improvement are the driving forces, the primary goal is to change the way work is accomplished, literally redefining what work is important (Freeman, 1999; Mirvis, 1997). The underlying belief is that such continuous adaptation, rather than staggered layoffs and traditional approaches to downsizing, is the key to arresting decline (Sutton, Eisenhardt, & Jucker, 1986). As research has suggested, in leading firms, resizing means far more than simply paring down human resources. It requires a new, shared vision of the future of the organization, driven and supported by organizational redesign, retraining, and redeployment of organizational members. It is a clearly articulated mission and strategy that are not only understood but owned by organizational members (Greenhalgh, McKersie, & Gilkey, 1986; Hitt et al., 1994; Mirvis, 1997; Walton, 1986). The challenge for management is to capture such advantages and benefits while minimizing the myriad of costs associated with such change. Indeed, what appear to be the new, immutable rules of our current work environment (for example, expectations of a sixty- to seventy-hour workweek, zealous loyalty, and fanatical devotion to the job) can quickly take their toll on our families, our organizations, our communities, and ourselves.

The Hidden Costs of Downsizing and Resizing

As we have witnessed with the wave of downsizing decisions over the past decade, some organizations clearly carried it out better than others. Numerous organizational experiments with right-sizing (Applebaum, Simpson, & Shapiro, 1987; Greenhalgh et al., 1986; Hitt et al., 1994; Sutton et al., 1986) have underscored that it is virtually impossible to prevent all of the pain and loss associated with such change regardless of how carefully and thoughtfully key decisions are enacted. However, many organizations exacerbate the problem, needlessly inducing the exit of talent, literally pushing key employees out of the organization, and falling increasingly out of step with their environment. The curtailment of internal career opportunities, undifferentiated retention strategies, and the resulting unbalanced workloads all contribute to an increased sense of frustration, discontent, and alienation within the organization, inducing talented employees to take advantage of their marketability and potential options (Rosenblatt & Sheaffer, 2001). Therefore, an underlying key in thinking through effective resizing decisions is to understand the challenges and consequences this strategy can have at the individual, organizational, and societal levels. Some of these outcomes are readily apparent and clearly visible, but others are far more latent and covert in nature.

At the Individual Level

While the notion of free agent managers (Hirsch, 1987) and "e-lancers" (Carr, 1999) is readily embraced by *Fast Company* and similar business publications, research suggests that the majority of organizational members would prefer to stay with their companies for longer, not shorter, periods of time (Labbs, 1999). For the majority of people in the workforce, the idea of a truly freewheeling economy, with business professionals embracing the resultant turbulence, easily moving from project to project and company to company without hesitation, is currently more theory than fact (Carr, 1999). While predictions suggest that in the near future virtually all organizations will resize, attempting to ensure sufficient flexibility and agility to be able to respond to rapidly changing environmental conditions, such change can have very different overtones for the individuals involved (Cameron, Dutton, & Whetten, 1998; Conference Board, 1998; Halal, 1993; Jacoby, 1999; Sennett, 1998).

Erosion of the Psychological Contract
The psychological bond between an organization and its members—the beliefs that people have about the reciprocal obligations between them and their organization—has long been suggested to lay at the foundation of employment relationships (Etzioni, 1961; Kotter, 1973; Levinson, Price, Munden, Mandl, & Solley, 1962; Schein, 1965). The waves of corporate restructuring and downsizing experienced over the past two decades, however, have begun to make it increasingly unclear as to exactly what organizations and their members owe one another (De Meuse & Tornow, 1990; Morrison & Robinson, 1997). To a large extent, the turbulence and resulting uncertainty that companies face today have made it difficult for management to fulfill all of the promises and obligations made to their members. A disconcerting result is the growing perception

among a large number of employees that organizations are reneging on their promises, and the terms of their psychological contracts are being violated (De Meuse et al., 2001; McLean Parks & Kidder, 1994; Morrison & Robinson, 1997; Sims, 1994).

This sense of violation, which carries a strong emotional component, leads to a range of feelings and reactions ranging from initial disappointment, frustration, and distress to outright anger, resentment, and bitterness of betrayal by the organization (Morrison & Robinson, 1997). As a result, employee trust toward the organization is undermined, job and organizational satisfaction plummet, and intention to remain even among valued members wanes, causing people to reduce their efforts, withhold contributions, or exit the organization (Rousseau, 1995; Robinson & Morrison, 1995; Robinson & Rousseau, 1994). Especially in extreme cases of violation, research has shown that the underlying sense of betrayal can induce employees to seek revenge or retaliation against their employer (Buono & Bowditch, 1989; Greenberg, 1990).

While explicit violations of the psychological contract can readily lead to such volatile reactions, there also are more insidious realities that reflect basic changes in the nature of the employer-employee relationship. As companies increasingly focus on corporate goals that reflect short-term realities, such as daily stock prices and quarterly profit margins, organizational members too focus more and more on their immediate job needs and career possibilities (De Meuse et al., 2001; Hymowitz, 2001; Noer, 1997). The result is an organizational world in which employees come to believe that it no longer matters if they are "good" corporate citizens, looking out for their own self-interest rather than focusing on broader organizational needs and realities. Once such communal agreements are undermined, employee morale, dedication, and loyalty can rapidly decline. Yet these employee attributes are the very essence of what is needed to guide leaner organizations through turbulent times.

The Loss of Attachments

On a more subtle level, the resizing revolution also is linked to changing psychological orientations and shifting attachments that we create as human beings. Sociologist Richard Sennett (1998) suggests that while the capability to continually shift to meet marketplace demands may be quite beneficial at the organizational level, the resultant breaks in attachments (what he refers to as the "ability to let go") have far more ominous repercussions at the individual level. Firms that are constantly in flux may be increasingly flexible and adaptable, but that also means that their members will have to constantly give up their attachments, whether to a person, a place, or a company.

The ideal of being flexible at the strategic level inevitably translates into the need for flexibility at the individual level. However, the ability to let go of an existing product, customer base, or work unit is far different from the ability to let go of personal attachments and links with those around us. While transition management experts talk of the need to prepare us to let go of the old and embrace the new (Bridges, 1991), there still is a lingering sense that the new possibilities will be in existence for a foreseeable future. With constant change envisioned for organizations, concerns reflect an emerging organizational nexus where people are part of ever-shifting coldly utilitarian networks rather than enduring, nurturing organizational communities (Carr, 1999; Sennett, 1998).

As jobs themselves change to "fields of work," a latent byproduct is a shift away from a long-term perspective, focusing more fully on short-term realities (see Jacoby, 1999). Sennett (1998) suggests that the loss of such a long-term focus erodes our ability to view ourselves in a narrative, to see continuity in our lives. While the ability to reinvent oneself is often played up as filled with opportunities and invigorating changes, it also means that the context our experiences have provided us with is literally erased. The result is an increasingly disconnected workforce that defines success on far more personal than organizational terms.

Survivor Guilt

Researchers examining the effects of downsizing initiatives and layoffs have found that one of the most painful losses that individuals have to contend with is the loss of valued coworkers (Feldman & Leana, 1989). The survivor syndrome among those who remain with the downsized organization is basically characterized by feelings of guilt for surviving the layoff and anxiety due to the insecurity created by the threat of future layoffs (Applebaum & Donia, 2000; Brockner, 1992; Brockner, Grover, O'Malley, Reed, & Glynn,

1993; Brockner, Grover, Reed, & DeWitt, 1992). As a result, the underlying sense of trust, empowerment, and control among organizational survivors often suffers (Mishra et al., 1998), especially when downsizing activities occur gradually, leaving remaining employees in a perpetual state of suspense (Feldman & Leana, 1989). Unless there is significant assurance and support given to these individuals, these survivors wonder who will be next and if they will join the forced exodus. Moreover, as research has indicated, withdrawal behavior among a person's relevant others in a social network readily increases the individual's propensity to leave as well (Krackhardt & Porter, 1986; Sandell, 1999). As a coping strategy, many of these individuals quietly begin looking for a position elsewhere, further undermining morale, organizational commitment and citizenship behavior, and productivity (Brockner et al., 1992, 1993).

Compounding the problem, due to overly severe cutbacks in personnel, organizations are often forced to place survivors in positions that they are ill prepared to handle. Although on-the-job training and trial-and-error approaches can ameliorate this problem, it typically takes far more time for such adjustments than anticipated, mistakes are often costly, and downsized training programs typically mean that survivors are unlikely to get the support they need in a timely manner (Hitt et al., 1994). Furthermore, research suggests that survivors frequently do not believe that top management sufficiently cares about employee needs, and trust in the competency of the senior management team often is called into question (Noer, 1995; O'Neil & Lenn, 1995). From an organizational vantage point, the underlying perception is that continuing employees are expected to work harder, being grateful that they still have their jobs (Applebaum & Donia, 2000). Unfortunately, the resultant organizational culture is one of looking after one's own needs rather than a more collaborative one, focused on coaching, guiding, and assisting colleagues and coworkers.

Stress and Health

Workplace transitions can be extremely traumatic, involving significant levels of stress on the individuals involved. The lives of downsizing victims are literally turned upside down, as financial pressures, the loss of fringe benefits such as health insurance, the breakdown of social relationships, and lowered self-esteem contribute to high levels of stress and health-related problems. Those individuals keeping their jobs—the survivors—also experience significant tension and pressure. While research suggests that managers can begin to ameliorate much of the stress and strain associated with such changes by limiting the expansion of work demands and ensuring that organizational members perceive greater control over their immediate environment (Moyle & Parkes, 1999), the reality is that in resized organizations, there are far greater psychological pressures on fewer employees to do the same amount of, if not more, work. The result is a culture of overwork, as corporations seem increasingly dependent on squeezing increased amounts of work from fewer people supported by fewer resources (Andresky Fraser, 2001), which further exacerbates the work-related stress, overload, and burnout that organizational members experience (Kets de Vries & Balazs, 1997; O'Neil & Lenn, 1995).

The ramifications of such pressures are significant. A recent study by the Families and Work Institute found that employee perceptions of being overworked are directly related to making mistakes on the job, feeling anger toward their employers, resenting coworkers who may not appear to be working as hard, and looking for new jobs outside the organization. Even more disconcerting is that these individuals also report being more likely to neglect taking care of themselves, noting difficulties with sleeping and related psychosomatic maladies (see "The Negative Effects of Overwork," 2001). Similarly, other studies have found significant relationships between downsizing-based work pressures and increases in depression, sickness absence rates, the prevalence of smoking and alcohol consumption, substance abuse, related ill-health symptoms (such as loss of appetite, fatigue, strokes, and heart attacks), marital problems, and impaired social network support (Cartwright, 2000; Ferrie, Shipley, Marmot, Stansfeld, & Smith, 1998; Kivimaki, Vahtera, Pentti, & Ferrie, 2000).

While much of the attention during downsizing initiatives is placed on displaced lower-level organizational members and the need to recapture the trust and commitment of survivors, a hidden problem concerns upper-level managers themselves, who often become withdrawn, abrasive, narcissistic, apathetic, or depressed (Kets de Vries & Balazs, 1997; Mishra et al., 1998; Perry, 1986). The resultant health-related strains on this critical group can be significant, especially if executives become increasingly isolated and detached as they wrestle with difficult decisions and develop a myopic focus on achieving short-term organizational outcomes. Because supportive top management behavior—empathy, accessibility, and the ability to clearly articulate a vision—is suggested as one of the key determinants that guides successful downsizing initiatives, this concern goes well beyond the ramifications these problems can have for the health of these individuals. Stressed-out executives, often seen as "executioners" by those around them (Kets de Vries & Balazs, 1997), can unwittingly undermine the very qualities that they need for long-term competitive success and advantage by undermining trust and disempowering key organizational members.

At the Organizational Level

Many observers argue that in today's hypercompetitive environment, a company's human capital (that is, its intellectual assets) is the only truly sustainable source of competitive advantage and growth (Barney, 1997; Conner, 1991; Labbs, 1999). Yet in many instances, downsizing organizations find that they lose far more of the wrong people and critical institutional memory than they anticipated (Cascio, 1993; Mirvis, 1997). Although part of the attraction associated with downsizing is to free the organization of poor performance and inefficiency, it appears that talented, skilled employees—the ones with clear options and opportunities—are often the ones to bail out of a downsizing organization voluntarily. As Levine's "free exiter" predicament (1979) underscores, the organizational members most needed to tackle the challenges facing the new organization are the ones who tend to leave. The premature and early departure of such qualified individuals exacerbates the problems that the organization is facing, often inhibiting recovery and accelerating the firm's decline (Bedeian & Armenakis, 1998).

While common downsizing tactics such as voluntary early retirement programs and across-the-board reductions often provide companies with a seemingly quick way out, the result often is the loss of talented individuals whose knowledge, skills, and abilities are needed by the organization as it prepares itself for future operations.

In fact, as some companies have found, it is problematic to control who takes advantage of early retirement offers due to legal constraints. Consequently, more people than are targeted frequently choose to leave, and companies are forced to rehire the people who just "retired" on a contract basis because of a shortage of critical skills (Applebaum et al., 1987; Hitt et al., 1994). As a result, organizations can unintentionally create significant voids in their overall talent pool and knowledge base if such tactics are poorly implemented and too many of the wrong people are eliminated. These firms then find an unexpected increase in the use of temporary workers and overtime, often rehiring displaced workers as consultants, leading to higher costs, which are compounded by greater-than-anticipated severance payouts (Mirvis, 1997).

Declining Performance

Downsizing has become a fact of life even in financially healthy companies. The underlying belief appears to be that despite longer, frenzied workdays, a new, lean regime will result in a sharper, more agile, highly competitive organization. Yet while this cost-cutting mantra may result in more efficient organizations, they appear to be far less effective (DeMarco, 2001). Although some research suggests that corporations that undertook workforce reductions during the past decade have experienced improved short-term financial performance (Wayhan & Werner, 2000), it appears that such improvements are difficult to sustain over the long term. All too often, what might look like inefficiency on the surface (often referred to as downtime or organizational slack) may be a critical part of organizational members' ability to innovate, adjust, and change. Companies can become overly efficient, trimming so much slack that they risk losing the agility and ability to exchange important information and shift directions that were part of the strategic intent guiding the change. Such downsizing, especially those using nonprioritized implementation tactics, often creates situations where key knowledge, skills, and abilities are lost, inflicting undetected damage on the learning and functioning of the organization (Fisher & White, 2000).

The resultant danger is that many companies are becoming more efficient without really becoming better, with the overall size of the underlying risk far more difficult to determine than the loss of individual expertise and talent. Survivors easily can become hesitant to commit their energy to an organization that shows a lack of loyalty to its members. Yet even if attitudes among survivors are favorable toward the organization, research suggests that these individuals often are so overworked and overburdened that they are unable to spare the effort required for new challenges and innovation (Thomson & Millar, 2001). As a number of studies indicate, productivity, profitability, and efficiency indicators suggest very little difference among downsizing and nondownsizing organizations (Cascio, Young, & Morris, 1997; De Meuse et al., 1997; Dougherty & Bowman, 1995; Mentzer, 1996; Morris, Cascio, & Young, 1999), with some organizations even less profitable after downsizing than they were prior to the reductions (Cascio, 1998; De Meuse, Vanderheiden, & Bergmann, 1994; Palmer, Kabanoff, & Dunford, 1997).

An illustration of the loss of effectiveness and declining performance is reflected by trained hazmat professionals (that is, organizational members who handle and manage hazardous materials). Prior to September 11, 2001, the role these individuals played was not very visible, and they were particularly vulnerable to downsizing initiatives, a reality that can compromise basic organizational safety and well-being (Currie, 1999; Perron & Shanley, 1999). The responsibilities and activities of these individuals are typically hard to quantify in terms of productivity and cost-of-service delivery. Rather than dealing with tangible outcomes, such as sales revenues or return on investment targets, hazmat professionals are judged more on what does not happen (such as a spill or an industrial accident). It is hard to quantify the cost of what might have happened if a safety compliance manager was not assigned to a particular job. Yet in downsizing, the issue of how a company should measure its exposure to risk against any budget allocations for ensuring compliance often is neglected. Thus, effective resizing decisions must ensure that important organizational activities and outcomes (such as plant safety) are not compromised, so that ordinary process upsets do not significantly undermine organizational effectiveness and become major catastrophic events (Perron & Shanley, 1999). While cutbacks and downsizing-based cost-containment strategies clearly shrink the organization, they do not necessarily make it more efficient or profitable over the long term.

An Amoral Compass

Another repercussion from an overarching focus on efficiency and cost containment is an insidious subordination of organizational ethics to performance (McKinley et al., 2000), where the scope of moral judgment is reduced and an enhancing market value becomes the all-encompassing organizational goal (Brockner et al., 1993). The results of such downsizing-related initiatives often manifest in short-term thinking and an impoverished sense of meaning (Solomon, 1999), which can readily undermine an organization's ability to deal with the imprecise nature of moral dilemmas in an era of rapid globalization and change (Hosmer, 1995).

As employment relationships and their underlying psychological contracts are redefined as private contractual relationships, the accountability that employers and employees feel they have toward each other is reduced (Van Buren, 2000). Because the ability of an organization and its members to determine and accept their accountability and responsibility lies at the foundation of ethical management (Toffler, 1986), this shift creates a void contributing to what might be thought of as an amoral orientation. In essence, organizational members stop thinking (either intentionally or unintentionally) about the ethics of their business decisions (Carroll, 1987). The problem is that most unethical and illegal acts emerge from incremental processes and decisions based on past practices and unforeseen future events and executed as part of the normal, everyday responsibilities of organizational members who spend most of their lives in entirely legal and ethical activities. As downsizing reduces the accountability that employees and their organizations have to each other, the resulting moral rules in use become sufficiently lax that the broader ethical ramifications of different decisions, policies, and activities are never explicitly examined (Jackall, 1988).

Declining Morale and Organizational Citizenship

Numerous studies indicate that most downsizing efforts fail to meet the basic goals of reduced costs and improved performance and profits. One of the most significant factors associated with such failure is the decline in employee morale and commitment (Allen, Freeman, Russell, Reizenstein, & Rentz, 2001; Glassberg, 1978;

Luthans & Sommer, 1999; Mirvis, 1997) and the resulting resistance to change (Buono, 1995). In fact, a recent survey by the Carlson Marketing Group and the Gallup organization found that of the major changes faced by organizations, downsizing had the most negative effect on employee morale (Salopek, 2000). The resulting reactions can manifest in withdrawal behaviors ranging from productive high performers voluntarily bailing out of the organization, to employees symbolically "resigning" while staying on the job (that is, simply going through the motions of working), to countercultural wars where employees literally fight the organization's plans and directions (Buono & Bowditch, 1989; Carpenter, 1995).

While giving the appearance of a type of democracy of pain, across-the-board cutbacks tend to have a demoralizing impact on organizations and often cut into areas that should be expanding rather than contracting. To organizational members, the underlying message appears to be that it no longer matters if the employee contributes to organizational goals or is a good corporate citizen. As loyalty, dedication, and hard work seem to be cast aside, the willingness of organizational members to work for the good of the organization and support coworkers outside their immediate work unit similarly begins to erode (Chen, Hui, & Sego, 1998; Luban, 2001). Collegiality declines as employees see themselves as possible competitors for existing jobs, and the willingness to go above and beyond the call of duty, one of the hallmarks of organizational citizenship behavior (Neuman & Kickul, 1998), quickly deteriorates. Thus, the level of dedication, commitment, and willingness to take on additional responsibilities that downsized organizations require is lacking.

Weakened Organizational Learning

Rather than viewing training and development as a priority in downsizing strategies, in many organizations training resources are typically the first budget that is cut. Consequently, opportunities for organizational members to develop the requisite knowledge, skills, and abilities to deal with the challenges they will face as the organization moves forward are constrained (Weakland, 2001). However, the full dysfunctional impact of downsizing on organizational learning is far more extensive.

Organizations can be conceptualized as a series of networks in which interrelationships across organizational members generate and disseminate information leading to knowledge creation and organizational learning. The loss of individuals, and the concomitant loss of knowledge they held, reduces the quality and value of information held by the organization, especially tacit knowledge that is rarely retained elsewhere in the organization (Fisher & White, 2000). Traditional downsizing efforts frequently disrupt a company's network of relationships—between employees, between teams of employees, and between employees and key stakeholders—literally destroying the organization's existing memory and memory capacity, vital foundations for future growth and creativity (Dougherty & Bowman, 1995; Fisher & White, 2000; Mroczkowski & Hanaoka, 1997). Such downsizing decisions can unwittingly precipitate dramatic changes in the informal organization, creating structural holes where links to unique sources of information are no longer present (Susskind, Miller, & Johnson, 1998) and literally tearing apart deep-seated patterns of interaction and knowledge sharing among organizational members (Fisher & White, 2000).

A related factor undermining the level of information flow necessary for true organizational learning concerns the role that anxiety and mistrust play in limiting knowledge sharing. In situations where downsizing appears to be an ever-present reality, a latent threat exists that communicated information might strengthen the job-retention position of a colleague, often at the expense of the individual initially sharing the information (Thomson & Millar, 2001). As a result, organizational members are far more likely to guard rather than share important information as knowledge hoarding becomes intertwined with increasing one's power and influence base.

Declining Customer Satisfaction

Especially for service companies, downsizing is related to significant reductions in customer satisfaction (Mroczkowski & Hanaoka, 1997). A growing body of research suggests that a significant relationship exists between employee attitudes and important organizational outcome measures, including customer attitudes and related financial criteria (Lundby, Fenlason, & Magnan, 2001). The basic tenet underlying this causal link is that employee attitudes drive their behavior and that customers experience these attitudes and behaviors either directly, in the case of service organizations, or indirectly, through the quality of goods they purchase. Because employee satisfaction, whether it is influenced by or is a determinant of service quality (Heskett, Jones, Loveman, Sasser, & Schlesinger, 1994; Rucci, Kirn, & Quinn, 1998; Wiley, 1996), influences their behavior and performance, plummeting morale and disenchantment following downsizing activities make it less likely that such important organizational outcomes as customer satisfaction, loyalty, and revenue growth will be realized. Downsizing initiatives also can break down communication and information sharing, potentially limiting the flow of informal information (tacit knowledge) about how to handle certain customers or suppliers (Hilsenrath, 2001).

Organizational Reputation

Although there is a tendency to use job cuts as a short-term response to economic turbulence, a layoff decision can have long-term repercussions for the image and reputation of the organization. Firms that are perceived to use downsizing to increase an already adequate profit margin risk developing a negative reputation (Van Buren, 2000). The media openly question the wisdom of such decisions, running headline stories on corporate "killers" and "executioners," often with pictures of chief executive officers (CEOs) alongside the number of layoffs undertaken by their firms. Implicit in many of these stories are links between such mass firings and CEO compensation, suggesting that top executives continue to receive huge bonuses for putting people out of work (Boroshok, 2001; Van Buren, 2000), which further contributes to a negative image of these companies and their senior management. Even small businesses, which in the past have resisted the pressures to downsize, are creating resentment by trimming their workforces (Bailey, 2001), which will make it difficult for them to reattract workers in more prosperous economic times.

Once a company begins to develop a negative reputation, it is extremely difficult to improve its image. Advertising campaigns aimed at enhancing public awareness and the reputation of such firms often are seen as little more than public relations gimmicks (Alsop, 2001). Because the reputation of a company is an important factor in how people relate to that organization—from the willingness of consumers to purchase its products, to the attractiveness of the company as a place to work—a negative image can take its toll on a company for years, even decades (Alsop, 2001; Dunham, 2001).

Rampant downsizing decisions also appear to be contributing to a growing movement among labor activists, especially in industries where there has been little unionization initiative. In Seattle, for example, the ongoing cutbacks in e-commerce and the telecommunications industry have prompted the Washington Alliance of Technology Workers to focus more of its attention on organizing employees at Amazon.com and Microsoft (Shadid, 2001). Both companies enjoyed stellar reputations during the economically prosperous 1990s, but recent cutbacks have begun to raise questions about the true values of the companies, giving union activists the opening for which they have been looking.

At the Societal Level

The continued emphasis on organizational retrenchment through cutbacks, serial layoffs, and downsizing initiatives is undermining the traditional social contract that the business system has had with the workforce and its surrounding communities (Cooper, 1997; Dudley, 1994; Murray, 1995; Watson, Shepard, & Stephens, 1999). Many critics contend that the social contract—the reciprocal assumption that successful companies will provide continuing employment for competent organizational members—is eroding as firms that are seen as profitable continue to lay off employees regardless of their performance. Many companies are perceived as closing profitable operations in search of greater profitability elsewhere. The results reflect the increasingly tenuous nature of modern employment, where community obligation is undermined and many of the ties that bind the larger society are disrupted (Donaldson & Dunfee, 1999; Miller, 2001).

Downsizing often has significant dysfunctional effects on individuals losing their jobs, a problem magnified at the societal level as the number of downsizing victims grows. Marriages, families, and communities are all vulnerable to the devastating effects of mass layoffs, especially as rising unemployment creates even greater pressures on those losing their jobs. Poorly managed downsizing initiatives further contribute to discontent and disillusionment with our business system and a growing cynicism that is further associated with general increases in withdrawal and aberrant behavior, to the point of overt violence in the workplace (Griffin, O'Leary-Kelly, & Collins, 1998; Kanter & Mirvis, 1989; Robinson & Greenberg, 1998).

A Detached Citizenry

Social critics suggest that the rush toward continuous change and continual flexibility in our organizations contributes to a pervasive sense of irony in our lives. The resultant "ironic" person, as eloquently captured by Sennett (1998), is one who engages in "deep acting" rather than genuine behaviors that promote cohesion and community. The cost of continually letting go of the attachments we have, which is the essence of the resized, flexible organization, contributes to a mentality of withdrawal and detachment. A situation surfaces where we do not take ourselves sufficiently serious to question, much less challenge, existing power arrangements and relationships. An outcome is an unwitting adoption of what might be thought of as a postmodern worldview. It is a mentality that might accurately capture the realities of downsized organizations but offers little in the way of creating a meaningful narrative regarding our lives in the workplace (Leana, 2000).

Given the traditional role of work as a central life interest in our society (Anderson, 1964; Morse & Weiss, 1955), the resulting void contributes to increased cynicism, social distance, and emotional detachment among a growing number of people as they struggle with the loss of their jobs, their positions, and, for many, their identity in what feels like an anchorless world. Thus, a significant portion of the population appears to be retreating from idealism and involvement in favor of the virtue of being realistic in an increasingly impersonal, detached society (Kanter & Mirvis, 1989; see also Reichers, Wanous, & Austin, 1997).

Executive Health and Weakened Organizational Contributions to Society

Some observers argue that executive health is a key factor in safeguarding the wealth of a nation, since top management is directly linked with organizational success and, by extension, the creation of wealth (Quick, Gavin, Cooper, & Quick, 2000). While the pressures and demands of leading a corporation carry their own burdens and related health risks, this stress can be exacerbated by the transition-based difficulties associated with organizational resizing initiatives. Resizing can further disconnect key executives, who are already isolated due to the confidentiality requirements of their jobs, which can have a further impact on the financial and emotional well-being of a company and undermine its contributions to the larger society (Quick et al., 2000; Worrell, Davidson, Chandy, & Garrison, 1986).

The Benefits of Resizing: Goals, Objectives, and Challenges

The downsizing era has created a myriad of problems and associated costs in an effort to shore up short-term performance. The ideal underlying resizing, in contrast, is to move an organization to a new state of well-being, concentrating on seeking an appropriate size and organizational focus rather than on how much to cut. The underlying challenge is a far more difficult task than simply restoring the firm to its previous healthy state. Key foci that are part of this process concern organizational competence (ensuring appropriate know-how and expertise), connection (the sense of belonging and involvement that people develop through interaction with peers, bosses and the organization as a whole), and commitment (the psychological contract that binds the individual and the organization together; Caplan & Teese, 1997). The goal should be to align workforce reductions with concomitant changes in organizational structure, roles, and responsibilities. Rather than viewing such change as a short-term fix, a key challenge is to integrate resizing decisions into a thoughtful, well-crafted, credible vision that clarifies how the requisite changes will revitalize the firm, ensuring that it keeps pace with environmental change, creating or restoring competitive advantage (Mishra et al., 1998).

In an era of rapid technological change, resizing is often crucial for organizational survival, especially for companies faced with technological innovations in production processes or products that abruptly alter basic industry dynamics (Anderson & Tushman, 1990; Edwards, 2000). Because such technological discontinuities can accelerate the obsolescence of worker skills and capabilities, organizations are faced with the decision to reskill or downsize their workforce. Some of these changes are competence enhancing, allowing the organization to build on existing techniques and skills to improve organizational performance. Competency-destroying discontinuities, in contrast, create a different reality where organizational survival depends on concomitant changes in the application of and response to the new technology, which often included reallocating resources, reengineering work processes, and resizing organizational functions (Tushman & Anderson, 1986). Especially if radically changing technologies require fewer workers to produce equivalent or even greater amounts of output, a reduction in force is necessary to avoid an uneconomical, inflated workforce. Failing to resize in such environments can readily place the organization at a competitive disadvantage, since the cost of maintaining unnecessary workers and functions creates a substantial drain on the organization's resources (Edwards, 2000).

It is important to remember that many of the negative outcomes associated with downsizing are related to poorly planned and poorly implemented programs that attempt to use a reduction in force as a short-term fix for longer-term organizational problems. However, organizational resizing initiatives do not have to be unduly painful. By taking a holistic approach to creating and implementing appropriate strategies to guide the process, organizations can improve the probability of creating a healthy, committed workforce and successful organization. By building on our understandings of the limitations of traditional approaches to downsizing, resizing can present a number of benefits at the individual, organizational, and societal levels.

At the Individual Level

The focus of resizing on developing new skills and investing in organizational members bodes well for those individuals and groups that remain a critical part of the organization. While much of the attention on downsizing is placed on the negative impact that such change can have on individuals and their careers, a critical element of resizing is identifying and nurturing talent, building leadership and change-related skills, and empowering these individuals with the appropriate authority and responsibility to make job-related decisions (Hitt et al., 1994). As organizations reframe the change from mere downsizing to a true corporate transformation, organizational members are provided with the prospect of embracing and developing new learning opportunities and innovative work practices (Kets de Vries & Balazs, 1997).

Enhanced Opportunities and Personal Growth

Ironically, the opportunity to improve one's position can be greater during organizational downturns than it is during periods of high growth and confidence. For survivors, the uncertainty and ambiguity that accompany the resizing process and its concomitant changes can be disorienting and anxiety provoking. However, that same uncertainty also creates opportunities for these individuals, opening challenging projects and assignments that may not have been available prior to the change (Rothman, 2001). If organizations work with survivors to help them conceptualize and understand the challenges that face them and their changing spheres of influence and control, managers can facilitate their employees' assessments of and willingness to seek out new opportunities (Buono & Nurick, 1992). Indeed, transformational leaders, with the right mix of visionary and charismatic leadership skills, can energize organizational members around the notion that the resizing was not only a necessary response to the realities of the marketplace but an opportunity to improve work-related processes and individual contributions (Marks, 1994). By helping survivors to differentiate between what they can and cannot control, organizational members can experience personal growth and renewal by focusing their energies on areas where they can exert influence.

Enriched Jobs

While traditional downsizing decisions are typically made by a handful of upper-level executives, resizing decisions, especially those assessing alternative work processes and redesign possibilities, demand the broader involvement of a range of organizational members. Planning for a resizing strategy may still be initiated by top management, but much of the analysis, formulation, and implementation must be performed by other members of the organization, individuals, and task forces that can provide the requisite insight and devote the necessary time and attention to these activities (Walton, 1986).

One of the concerns associated with downsizing reflects the unbalanced workloads that can result from such retrenchment, as organizations assign fewer employees to perform larger shares of the work (Marks, 1994). Organizational members, however, can see such change as a challenge. Increasing levels of responsibility can motivate employees *if* the change is viewed as enriching their work lives. Organizational members frequently respond very well to the challenges associated with meaningful change and an upsurge in vertical responsibilities. Although the underlying goal of the organization might still be to accomplish more with less, by having a select group of highly skilled, well-trained, and committed employees, resized organizations provide their members with greater levels of autonomy, authority, and opportunity. Consequently, employees in these organizations can feel more empowered and become more adept at problem solving, decision making, and innovation (Applebaum & Donia, 2000; Frazee, 1996). Difficulties ensue when the additional work is perceived as little more than job enlargement, a mere extension of the initial tasks for which their downsized coworkers were previously responsible (Rosenblatt & Sheaffer, 2001). Thus, it is essential that role clarification—where each employee's new role, responsibility and workload are assessed and communicated—is part of the resizing process (Kets de Vries & Balazs, 1997).

One of the lessons that has emerged from experiences with downsizing is that employees need more skills and technology training to handle larger workloads and changes in goals and methods successfully (Hornestay, 1999). Developing employees as part of a resizing strategy is crucial in order to build the essential skill sets needed to support the new organization. The underlying ideal is to create a new organizational mind-set where employees are engaged in continuous learning in search of innovative workplace practices supported by the skills and capabilities necessary to carry out these initiatives (Kets de Vries & Balazs, 1997).

At the Organizational Level

Resizing is more closely aligned to the idea of organizational reinvention (Carr, 1999) and re-creation (Nadler, 1988) than reducing organizational head count. When a company resizes, it essentially reinvents and recreates itself to be in a better position to deal with the competitive realities of the marketplace. The guiding mentality is that flexibility and change are no longer options but rather requirements for success (Carr, 1999). The underlying perspective entails radical departures from past practices and traditional ways of carrying out business decisions. Outcomes often include a retrained, more flexible workforce, upgraded technology to facilitate performance, reduced costs and enhanced economic efficiency, and improved productivity (Applebaum & Donia, 2000; McKinley et al., 2000). Thus, resizing emphasizes cutting layers or levels in the organization, decentralizing decision-making processes, and reducing the time necessary to gain approval for implementing new ideas and innovations (Hitt et al., 1994). Whether the specific outcome is an internal merger of different departments or work units, the centralization of support units, reduced organizational levels or work units, outsourcing of major functions, or a reconfiguration of staff specialists, the results are based on systematic organizational analysis rather than the mere reduction of the number of individuals in particular jobs (Freeman, 1999; Nienstedt, 1989).

Flatter Organizational Structures

As centralized, multilayered organizations resize, a guiding determinant of successful resizing is the identification and elimination of unnecessary and wasteful work processes and tasks. Organizational analysis should focus on the appropriateness of the existing structure (for example, managerial control, reporting relationships, and organizational layers), the identification of redundancies and overlaps in managerial and work-related functions, the new organizational structure, and excess positions in that new structure (Applebaum & Donia, 2000). By eliminating needless organizational layers and roles, the new, flatter organization that emerges from this process is often more flexible and better able to respond to marketplace needs, since greater autonomy and responsibility are delegated to organizational members (Mathys & Burack, 1993). Flattening organizations in this manner also can translate into improved communication flows, with increased information sharing within and between departments and work units (McClelland & Wilmot, 1990).

Strengthening Core Competencies

A growing number of companies are resizing with the intent of strengthening their core competencies and protecting key areas such as research and development, customer support, and the sales force in anticipation of future growth and development. Although the need to control expenses may still underlie such retrenchment decisions, a goal should be to ensure that the core competencies and strengths of the organization are enhanced. One of the ways to facilitate such decisions is through an audit of the organization's human resources. By developing a focused profile of the organization—which might include such categories as business unit, functional group, occupational specialization, technical expertise, and location—the unique needs and contributions of different subgroups can be identified (Bargerstock, 2000). By measuring current and anticipated service levels, the organization can then develop an action plan for the requisite realignment and reductions. Similarly, through a careful analysis of the social networks in different departments and work units, managers can identify how communication and innovation patterns in the organization function (Fisher & White, 2000). While there are a myriad of concerns related to the application of such prescriptions, understanding the ways in which organizational members interact with each other and contribute to organizational processes and objectives enables organizations to make more informed decisions that strengthen rather than undermine employee attitudes and capabilities.

Team Orientation

One of the ramifications of resizing to a flatter organizational structure is a resulting emphasis on teamwork and collaboration. In a lean environment, collaborative interactions across different functions and organizational levels become increasingly important (Hitt et al., 1994; Mirvis, 1997). Decentralizing decision making and responsibility and integrating functional expertise at the team level also can have a number of benefits: broadening jobs, responsibilities, and spans of control; enhancing motivation; creating more flexible coordination and control systems; and creating a more adaptable organization where people feel valued. As decisions are made at lower levels, influence is based less on positional authority than on the individual's knowledge, skill, and ability base, which further enhances the role of organizational members (Walton, 1986).

Work teams also can serve as a focal point for recovery and revitalization following organizational resizing (Marks, 1994). Teams, in essence, can be thought of as the new link between the individual and the organization. Team members can experiment with new work methods and explore organizational learning possibilities, testing to see if the resized organization and its management truly are dedicated to long- as well as short-term goals. The resulting sense of team and openness helps people envision the possibility of creating a larger pie if they were to work together (Mishra et al., 1998). This team orientation enhances commitment to organizational goals, builds competence in solving problems, broadens capabilities for self-management, and in general facilitates a willingness to collaborate with key stakeholders, both internal and external (Walton, 1986).

While this type of delayering and team-based initiative can have a myriad of benefits for an organization, it is still important to be wary of reducing middle management layers to the point where the company is endangering a future shortage of top management talent (Hitt et al., 1994). Many organizations draw executive-level talent from the middle ranks of the company. Consequently, a drastic shortage of these individuals could hamper longer-term growth and development. Moreover, team effectiveness in resized organizations is, to a large extent, still dependent on the initial structure and guidance provided by middle management. While a team orientation requires these individuals to redefine their roles—for instance, becoming more customer focused and holistic in recommending service improvements that are consistent with the process ownership by the team (Winchell, 2001)—management support is still needed to ensure long-term success.

Enhanced Organizational Commitment

Although the idea that resizing can result in higher levels of organizational commitment might not be readily apparent, the manner in which organizations formulate and implement these strategies sends out clear signals about the value they place on their human resources. Senior-level managers can instill a sense of confidence and belief in the organization by proceeding with care and sensitivity, ensuring that all organizational members are treated with fairness, dignity, and respect. An underlying key is to ensure that departing employees are treated with compassion while emphasizing a commitment to establishing a strong future for the company and its remaining employees. Tangible signs of such caretaking—outplacement counseling and job placement efforts, stress management and coping-with-change workshops, and appropriate severance packages and financial planning workshops—provide clear messages to victims and survivors that the company values its human resources. Venting meetings that allow survivors an opportunity to grieve, focusing on what was and what will be, also are useful in rebuilding a foundation for trust and commitment (Marks, 1994; Young & Brown, 1998).

If the reasons for resizing the firm are made very clear to organizational members, managers may be able to minimize many of the negative reactions associated with downsizing (Mone, 1997). For example, by explaining that the resizing strategy eliminates only jobs and functions that were rendered obsolete by relevant technological and industry and market changes, managers signal to their remaining workers that they do not need to fear becoming victim to another round of downsizing (Edwards, 2000). Open and honest communication can prevent or dispel rumors, and it signals to organizational members that upper management is aware of what is happening, is in control, and is concerned about the impact of its decisions on employees (Applebaum & Donia, 2000; Noer, 1995). In contrast, giving false hope to employees, raising expectations that are likely to be shattered by foreseen cutbacks and retrenchment plans can have dire long-term consequences (Kets de Vries & Balazs, 1997).

Involving organizational members in the decision process also can make them feel valued and supported, enhancing their commitment to the organization. By communicating the need to realign the organization with the competitive realities of the marketplace and asking for employee input, proposed solutions can serve to empower organizational members (Applebaum & Donia, 2000). For example, Weakland (2001) reports on a manufacturing firm that established teams of employees from all organizational levels to challenge organizational practices, policies, and procedures and recommend changes. Team-based suggestions included outsourcing key tasks, negotiating new contracts with internal and external vendors, changes in work-related processes, and a related downsizing plan that was perceived as fair and accepted by organizational members. Especially in highly technical areas, the people actually performing the work often have the best insight on where to cut jobs and responsibilities (Perron & Shanley, 1999). Where staff cuts are deemed necessary, involuntary separations often can be avoided through a combination of careful planning, managed attrition, reduction of overtime, retraining, and reassignment of organizational members (Umiker, 1999). These steps are crucial, especially when a resizing organization might be faced with hiring new people with a critical skill set in the wake of terminating other organizational members.

Involving key employees in the decision-making process, delivering the bad news in person rather than using impersonal and indirect approaches (such as pink slips and memo notifications), providing clear and honest explanations, and ensuring consistency in determining where cuts will be made reflect the values of the organization. Some firms are even modifying their employee appraisal and compensation systems, including stock option and gain-sharing programs not previously available, to emphasize the survivors' stake in the new organization (Freeman, 1999; Weakland, 2001). By looking at the ramifications of resizing from both the organization and the employee perspective, the pain that departing employees experience can be minimized, while preparing survivors for the new responsibilities and challenges they will face.

Broader Stakeholder Orientation

Effective resizing strategies reflect an assessment and consideration of the needs of an array of stakeholders, from displaced employees and organizational survivors, to customers, investors, and surrounding communities (Buono & Bowditch, 1989, 1990; De Meuse et al., 1997; Mishra et al., 1998). Indeed, since corporate downsizing can adversely affect employees and surrounding communities, the emphasis of resizing on long-term value creation is an important element of community development and corporate citizenship (Vidaver-Cohen & Altman, 2000). Such stakeholder orientations, as opposed to a sole focus on shareholders, attempt to assess and balance the competing claims that surround resizing decisions. This realization can help organizations to determine and articulate the reciprocal nature of these relationships and their underlying ramifications for strategic decisions, further facilitating the creation and maintenance of a desirable organizational image and reputation (Scott & Lane, 2000).

At the Societal Level

As organizations resize and technology continues to change both the focus and locus of work, workdays themselves are likely to become more flexible and work location less important. Some observers suggest that the emerging networked economy will provide workers with more control over their lives, especially in terms of where people choose to live and how they allocate their time (Carr, 1999). As people gain greater self-control over managing their own careers (Nicholson, 1996), one outcome could be a reconnection with the larger society as people attempt to replace traditional work-related ties with those aimed at their communities and social institutions. Hall (1996, p. 10) suggested that the career path "to the top" is beginning to be replaced by the path "with a heart."

Clearly, there are numerous uncertainties that workers must face in the resized business world. Unlike previous generations where present success typically translated into future successes, what we produce at a particular point in today's world is no guarantee of future achievement. As we move from project to project, assignment to assignment, and organization to organization, we continually face the possibility of failure. However, as Carr (1999) points out, while this dynamic may be true, the actual penalty for failure is far lower than it has been in the past. Many dot-com entrepreneurs, for example, wear their failed companies as badges of honor, viewing an unsuccessful venture as a platform for growth and learning. While many assessments of the repercussions from the wave of corporate downsizings experienced during the late 1980s and early 1990s point to the human toll, a significant number of these individuals realized they had to take control over their own lives (Luban, 2001). The result was a burst of entrepreneurial energy, creating truly innovative and dynamic companies that have created many sources of new jobs and career opportunities (London, 1996; Schein, 1996).

As organizational members adapt to the realities of a resized business world, people will need to take more and more control over their own careers. The focus will increasingly be placed on employability rather than employment, continuous learning rather than past accomplishments, partnering skills and collaboration rather than traditional command and compliance directives, and self-governance skills rather than an overreliance on hierarchy and organizational rules (Allred, Miles, & Snow, 1996; Hall, 1996; Nicholson, 1996). While these changes will help people become more self-reliant, organizations can also minimize the need for gut-wrenching, sporadic downsizing decisions through effective resizing. Effective resizing strategies minimize the negative effects on both workers and the companies' surrounding communities, which often are negatively affected by widespread layoffs and resulting uncertainties (Edwards, 2000).

Some companies also are beginning to experiment with innovative ways to resize while supporting displaced workers. Cisco Systems, for example, has been cited as one of the first major corporations to pay downsized employees partial salaries while they work for charitable organizations (Davis, 2001). Although many of these employees earn only about one-third of their former salary during this time, they still receive company benefits and related support. These individuals have not been given any guarantees that they will be rehired, but they are considered internal candidates for new positions when they become available, and for some, their involvement in social institutions has opened new career paths. Similarly, in the wake of the economic disruption exacerbated by the September 11 tragedy, there does appear to be an awakening of attention for the need for retraining and greater social support for individuals caught up in the realities of a downsized world. As specific industries, such as the airline and hospitality industries, are resizing their operations and shifting foci as they adapt to the new realities, support networks such as the Commonwealth Corporation and Rapid Response are providing workers with retraining and financial support (Jordan, 2001).

Although resizing decisions can be very tough on specific individuals in the short term, they tend to be beneficial over the long run for a far larger number of people and organizations, creating a stronger foundation for sustainable economic and societal growth and success. By minimizing the upheaval and disruption that traditional downsizing strategies have created, restraining from using workforce reductions as a cookie cutter strategy and making only changes that truly strengthen the organization (Edwards, 2000), organizations can enhance their role as engaged corporate citizens (Marsden, 2000).

Conclusion

Over the long term, successful companies will be the ones that can effectively align their business goals with marketplace demands and consumer needs as well as the needs, aspirations, and commitment of their workforce. A truly strategic approach to resizing requires ongoing analysis of the organization's direction with a focus on the future, the firm's fit with the larger environment, and the actions and skills required to ensure that the organization accomplishes its objectives. Such continuous alignment mandates careful analysis and incremental processes, based on gradual and meticulous planning rather than approaching such change in a quick-fix fashion. Effective resizing initiatives must be part of a long-term, well-planned strategy rather than a shortsighted attempt to reduce costs and boost profits (Applebaum & Donia, 2000; Mirvis, 1997; Mroczkowski & Hanaoka, 1997). However, once the decision is made, it is just as important to ensure expeditious implementation with full consideration for the emotional responses of departing employees and the training and developmental needs of survivors (Applebaum & Donia, 2000; Umiker, 1999). Keeping the prospect of ongoing layoffs dangling over the heads of survivors creates a climate of fear and distrust and contributes to organizational paranoia that feeds productivity declines to the point of potential paralysis (Kets de Vries & Balazs, 1997).

Clearly, there is no one set of prescriptions that is a perfect fit for all organizations. Rather, effective resizing should be thought of as a continuous rather than an episodic, discrete event (Kerber,

2001; Kets de Vies & Balazs, 1997; Weick & Quinn, 1999). Managers must not only engage in an ongoing process of reconfiguring the organization to function effectively in the present, they also need to prepare the organization to do so in the future as well (Hitt et al., 1994). Companies can build a solid foundation on which to build the new organization by using multiple communication channels to ensure that organizational members are fully informed about the problems that contributed to the resizing decision and the wider plan that is linked to the firm's long-term potential (Greenhalgh et al., 1986; O'Daniell, 1999). Yet the pressures to resize the organization, engaging in significant restructuring, reengineered jobs, and reengineered processes often are sufficiently significant that organizations often move far faster than they think, acting in much more of a reactive than proactive manner.

Although there are definite benefits that can be achieved, organizational resizing is a high-risk strategy, though clearly necessary. The alternative to thoughtful resizing efforts is a reactive, wholesale binge-and-purge mentality (Rosenwald, 2001). Hence, the key is to ensure that such decisions are informed and rational, based on long-term strategic assessments, and focused on specific business goals rather than head count reductions (Edwards, 2000; Mroczkowski & Hanaoka, 1997). Emphasis should be placed on organizational redesign efforts that focus on eliminating low value-added tasks and a redeployment of existing personnel into higher value-added tasks. As this chapter has noted, key considerations are (1) employee involvement and participation in the diagnosis and planning processes, (2) full and honest disclosure of assessments and plans, (3) broad outplacement assistance for those being laid off, (4) increased retraining initiatives and related supports for survivors, and (5) a focus on organizational renewal, rebuilding morale, reestablishing trust, and reformulating a basic foundation for performance enhancements and revitalization. As Feldman (1990) has suggested, open and honest information about the changes and the reasons behind them, a recommitment to survivors where they are ensured of their status with the company, and ongoing support through assistance and feedback mechanisms are crucial to successfully addressing and managing the concomitant disruption that accompanies such change. Rather than focus on a single activity or a single set of concerns, managers must take a broader, holistic view of the organizational dimensions touched by resizing strategies and prepare themselves to juggle a number of processes and activities simultaneously (Freeman, 1999).

Resizing is a stressful strategy for all organizational members, managers and employees alike. Nevertheless, if it is conducted in a thoughtful, well-planned manner, greater levels of trust, commitment, and employee empowerment can create sources of competitive advantage for the organization.

References

Ackerman, J. (2001, February 11). Survey finds layoffs seen as quick fix. *Boston Globe*, p. H2.

Allen, T. D., Freeman, D. M., Russell, J.E.A., Reizenstein, R. C., & Rentz, J. O. (2001). Survivor reactions to organizational downsizing: Does time ease the pain? *Journal of Occupational and Organizational Psychology, 74*, 145–164.

Allred, B. B., Miles, R. E., & Snow, C. C. (1996). Characteristics of managerial careers in the twenty-first century. *Academy of Management Executive, 10*(4), 17–27.

Alsop, R. (2001, February 7). Survey rates companies' reputations, and many are found wanting. *Wall Street Journal*, pp. B1, B6.

Anderson, N. (1964). *Dimensions of work: The sociology of a work culture.* New York: McKay.

Anderson, P., & Tushman, M. (1990). Technological discontinuities and dominant designs: A cyclical model of technological change. *Administrative Science Quarterly, 35*, 604–633.

Andresky Fraser, J. (2001). *White-collar sweatshop: The deterioration of work and its rewards in corporate America.* New York: Norton.

Applebaum, S. H., & Donia, M. (2000). The realistic downsizing preview: A management intervention in the prevention of survivor syndrome (Part I). *Career Development International, 5*, 333–350.

Applebaum, S. H., Simpson, R., & Shapiro, B. (1987). The tough test of downsizing. *Organizational Dynamics, 16*(2), 68–79.

Bailey, J. (2001, November 6). Small businesses do what big firms have done—Cut jobs. *Wall Street Journal*, p. B2.

Bargerstock, A. S. (2000). The HRM effectiveness audit: A tool for managing accountability in HRM. *Public Personnel Management, 29*, 517–527.

Barney, J. B. (1997). *Gaining and sustaining competitive advantage.* Reading, MA: Addison-Wesley.

Bedeian, A. G., & Armenakis, A. A. (1998). The cesspool syndrome: How dreck floats to the top of declining organizations. *Academy of Management Executive, 12,* 58–63.

Boroshok, J. (2001, September 4). Wretched times for the worker. *Boston Globe,* p. D2.

Bridges, W. (1991). *Managing transitions.* Reading, MA: Addison-Wesley.

Brockner, J. (1992). Managing the effects of layoffs on survivors. *California Management Review, 34*(2), 9–28.

Brockner, J., Grover, S., O'Malley, M. N., Reed, T. F., & Glynn, M. A. (1993). Threat of future layoffs, self-esteem, and survivors' reactions: Evidence from the laboratory and the field. *Strategic Management Journal, 14,* 153–166.

Brockner, J., Grover, S., Reed, T., & DeWitt, R. (1992). Layoffs, job insecurity and survivors' work effort: Evidence of an inverted U relationship. *Academy of Management Journal, 35,* 413–425.

Buono, A. F. (1995). Moral corporate cultures in a downsized, restructured world. In W. M. Hoffman & R. E. Frederick (Eds.), *Business ethics: Readings and cases in corporate morality* (pp. 226–233). New York: McGraw-Hill.

Buono, A. F., & Bowditch, J. L. (1989). *The human side of mergers and acquisitions: Managing collisions between people, cultures and organizations.* San Francisco: Jossey-Bass.

Buono, A. F., & Bowditch, J. L. (1990). Ethical issues in merger and acquisition management: A human resource perspective. *SAM Advanced Management Journal, 55*(4), 18–23.

Buono, A. F., Bowditch, J. L., & Nurick, A. J. (1987). The hidden costs of organizational mergers. In A. Larocque, Y. Bordeleau, R. Boulard, B. Fabi, V. Larouche, & A. Rondeau (Eds.), *Psychologie du travail et nouveaux milieux de travail* (pp. 313–333). Quebec: University of Quebec Press.

Buono, A. F., & Nurick, A. J. (1992). Intervening in the middle: Coping strategies in mergers and acquisitions. *Human Resource Planning, 15*(2), 19–33.

Butterfield, B. D. (2001, April 15). Layoffs blindside region. *Boston Globe,* pp. E1, E6.

Cameron, K. S., Dutton, R. I., & Whetten, D. A. (Eds.). (1998). *Readings in organizational decline.* Cambridge, MA: Ballinger.

Caplan, G., & Teese, M. (1997). *Survivors: How to keep your best people on board after downsizing.* Palo Alto, CA: Davies-Black Publishing.

Carpenter, T. (1995). Corporate anorexia: Downsizing's darker side. *Business First, 12*(7), 34–37.

Carr, N. (1999). Being virtual: Character and the new economy. *Harvard Business Review, 77*(3), 3–7.

Carroll, A. B. (1987). In search of the moral manager. *Business Horizons, 30*(2), 7–15.

Cartwright, S. (2000). Taking the pulse of executive health in the U.K. *Academy of Management Executive, 14*(2), 16–23.

Cascio, W. F. (1993). Downsizing: What do we know? What have we learned? *Academy of Management Executive, 7*(1), 95–104.

Cascio, W. F. (1998). Learning from outcomes: Financial experiences of 311 firms that have downsized. In M. K. Gowing, J. D. Kraft, & J. C. Quick (Eds.), *The new organizational reality: Downsizing, restructuring and revitalization* (pp. 323–340). Washington, DC: American Psychological Association.

Cascio, W. F., Young, C. E., & Morris, J. R. (1997). Financial consequences of employment-change decisions in major U.S. corporations. *Academy of Management Journal, 40,* 1175–1189.

Chen, X., Hui, C., & Sego, D. J. (1998). The role of organizational citizenship behavior in turnover: Conceptualization and preliminary tests of key hypotheses. *Journal of Applied Psychology, 83,* 922–931.

Conference Board. (1998). Organizing the corporate HQ: An HR perspective. *HR Executive Review, 6,* 18–22.

Conner, K. R. (1991). A historical comparison of resource-based theory and five schools of thought within industrial organizations economies: Do we have a new theory of the firm? *Journal of Management, 17,* 121–141.

Cooper, M. (1997, July 14). A town betrayed: Oil and greed in Lima, Ohio. *Nation,* pp. 7–9.

Currie, J. V. (1999). Downsizing, rightsizing, resizing, . . . capsizing? *Logistics Management and Distribution Report, 38*(5), 40.

Davis, K. A. (2001, September 3). Laid-off Cisco workers give nonprofits a helping hand. *Boston Globe,* p. C4.

DeMarco, T. (2001). *Slack: Getting past burnout, busywork, and the myth of total efficiency.* New York: Broadway Books.

De Meuse, K. P., Bergmann, T. J., & Lester, S. W. (2001). An investigation of the relational component of the psychological contract across time, generation and employment status. *Journal of Managerial Issues, 13,* 120–118.

De Meuse, K. P., Bergmann, T. J., & Vanderheiden, P. A. (1997). Corporate downsizing: Separating myth from fact. *Journal of Management Inquiry, 6,* 168–176.

De Meuse, K. P., & Tornow, W. W. (1990). The tie that binds—Has become very, very frayed! *Human Resource Planning, 13,* 203–213.

De Meuse, K. P., Vanderheiden, P. A., & Bergmann, T. J. (1994). Announced layoffs: Their effect on corporate financial performance. *Human Resource Management, 33,* 509–530.

Donaldson, T., & Dunfee, T. W. (1999). *The ties that bind: A social contracts approach to business ethics.* Boston: Harvard Business School Press.

Dougherty, D., & Bowman, E. H. (1995). The effects of organizational downsizing on product innovation. *California Management Review, 37*(4), 28–44.

Dudley, K. (1994). *The end of the line: Lost jobs and new lives in post-industrial America.* New York: Basic Books.

Dunham, K. J. (2001, March 14). Companies approach layoffs with kinder, gentler strategy. *Asian Wall Street Journal,* p. N7.

Edwards, J. C. (2000). Technological discontinuity and workforce size: An argument for selective downsizing. *International Journal of Organizational Analysis, 8,* 290–308.

Etzioni, A. (1961). *A comparative analysis of complex organizations.* New York: Free Press.

Feldman, D. C., & Leana, C. R. (1989). Managing layoffs: Experiences at the *Challenger* disaster site and the Pittsburgh steel mills. *Organizational Dynamics, 18,* 52–64.

Feldman, L. (1990). Duracell's first aid for downsizing survivors. *Security Management, 34,* 123–124.

Ferrie, J. E., Shipley, M. J., Marmot, M. G., Stansfeld, S. A., & Smith, G. D. (1998). An uncertain future: The health effects of threats to employment security in white-collar men and women. *American Journal of Public Health, 88,* 1030–1036.

Fisher, S. R., & White, M. (2000). Downsizing in a learning organization: Are there hidden costs? *Academy of management review, 25*(1), 244–251.

Frazee, V. (1996). When downsizing brings your employees down. *Personnel Journal, 75,* 126–127.

Freeman, S. J. (1999). The gestalt of organizational downsizing: Downsizing strategies as packets of change. *Human Relations, 52,* 1505–1541.

Freeman, S. J., & Cameron, K. S. (1993). Organizational downsizing: A convergence and reorientation framework. *Organization Science, 4*(1), 10–28.

Glassberg, A. (1978). Organizational response to municipal budget decreases. *Public Administrative Review, 38,* 325–332.

Greenberg, J. (1990). Employee theft as a reaction to underpayment inequity: The hidden cost of pay cuts. *Journal of Applied Psychology, 75,* 561–568.

Greenhalgh, L., McKersie, R. B., & Gilkey, R. W. (1986). Rebalancing the workforce at IBM: A case study of redeployment and revitalization. *Organizational Dynamics, 14,* 30–47.

Griffin, R. W., O'Leary-Kelly, A., & Collins, J. M. (1998). *Dysfunctional behavior in organizations: Violent and deviant behavior.* Stamford, CT: JAI Press.

Halal, W. E. (1993). The transition from hierarchy to . . . what? In W. E. Halal, A. Geranmayeh, & J. Pourdehnad (Eds.), *Internal markets: Bringing the power of free enterprise inside your organization* (pp. 27–51). New York: Wiley.

Hall, D. T. (1996). Protean careers of the twenty-first century. *Academy of Management Executive, 10*(4), 8–16.

Heskett, J. L., Jones, T. O., Loveman, G. W., Sasser, W. E., & Schlesinger, L. A. (1994). Putting the service-profit chain to work. *Harvard Business Review, 72,* 164–174.

Hilsenrath, J. E. (2001, February 21). Many say layoffs hurt companies more than they help—"The evidence is very weak" that downsizing boosts productivity. *Wall Street Journal,* p. A2.

Hirsch, P. (1987). *Pack your own parachute: How to survive mergers, takeovers, and other corporate disasters.* Reading: MA: Addison-Wesley.

Hitt, M. A., Keats, B. W., Harback, H. F., & Nixon, R. D. (1994). Rightsizing: Building and maintaining strategic leadership and long-term competitiveness. *Organizational Dynamics, 23*(2), 18–32.

Hornestay, D. (1999). The human factor. *Government Executive, 31*(2), 39–43.

Hosmer, L. T. (1995). *The ethics of management.* New York: McGraw-Hill.

Hymowitz, C. (2001, November 1). In the lead: Poor layoff payouts lower staff morale. *Wall Street Journal,* p. 25.

Jackall, R. (1988). *Moral mazes: The world of corporate managers.* New York: Oxford University Press.

Jacoby, S. M. (1999). Are career jobs headed for extinction? *California Management Review, 42,* 123–145.

Jordan, R. (2001, October 9). Reaching out to laid-off workers. *Boston Globe,* p. D4.

Kanter, D. L., & Mirvis, P. H. (1989). *The cynical Americans: Living and working in an age of discontent and disillusion.* San Francisco: Jossey-Bass.

Kerber, K. W. (2001). Change in human systems: From planned change to guided changing. In A. F. Buono (Ed.), *Research in management consulting: Current trends in management consulting* (pp. 145–170). Greenwich, CT: Information Age Publishing.

Kets de Vries, M.F.R., & Balazs, K. (1997). The downside of downsizing. *Human Relations, 50*(1), 11–50.

Kivimaki, M., Vahtera, J., Pentti, J., & Ferrie, J.A.E. (2000). Factors underlying the effect of organizational downsizing on health of employees: A longitudinal cohort study. *British Medical Journal, 320,* 971–975.

Kotter, J. (1973). The psychological contract: Managing the joining-up process. *California Management Review, 15,* 91–99.

Krackhardt, D., & Porter, L. (1986). When friends leave: A structural analysis of the relationship between turnover and stayers' attitudes. *Administrative Science Quarterly, 31,* 50–55.

Labbs, J. (1999). The new loyalty. *Executive Excellence, 16*(2), 13.

Leana, C. R. (2000). Review of *The corrosion of character* by Richard Sennett. *Academy of Management Review, 25,* 252–253.

Levine, C. H. (1979). More on cutback management: Hard questions for hard times. *Public Administration Quarterly, 39,* 179–183.

Levinson, H., Price, C., Munden, K., Mandl, H., & Solley, C. (1962). *Men, management, and mental health.* Cambridge, MA: Harvard University Press.

London, M. (1996). Redeployment and continuous learning in the twenty-first century: Hard lessons and positive examples from the downsizing era. *Academy of Management Executive, 10,* 67–79.

Luban, R. (2001). *Are you a corporate refugee? A survival guide for downsized, disillusioned, and displaced workers.* New York: Penguin Books.

Lundby, K. M., Fenlason, K. J., & Magnan, S. M. (2001). New directions in linking research: Employee satisfaction as an outcome or predictor? In A. F. Buono (Ed.), *Research in management consulting: Current trends in management consulting* (pp. 127–142). Greenwich, CT: Information Age Publishing.

Luthans, B. C., & Sommer, S.M. (1999). The impact of downsizing on workplace attitudes: Differing reactions of managers and staff in a health care organization. *Group and Organization Management, 24*(1), 46–70.

Marks, M. L. (1994). *From turmoil to triumph: New life after mergers, acquisitions, and downsizing.* San Francisco: New Lexington Press.

Marsden, C. (2000). The new corporate citizenship of big business: Part of the solution to sustainability. *Business and Society Review, 105*(1), 9–26.

Mathys, N. J., & Burack, E. H. (1993). Strategic downsizing: Human resource planning approaches. *Human Resource Planning, 16*(1), 71–85.

McClelland, V., & Wilmot, D. (1990). Lateral communication as seen through the eyes of employees. *Communication World, 7*(12), 32–35.

McKinley, W., Zhao, J., & Rust, K. G. (2000). A sociocognitive interpretation of downsizing. *Academy of management review, 25,* 227–243.

McLean Parks, J., & Kidder, D. (1994). `Til death do us part . . .: Changing work relationships in the 1990s. In C. L. Cooper & D. M. Rosseau (Eds.), *Trends in organizational behavior* (pp. 112–133). New York: Wiley.

Mentzer, M. S. (1996). Corporate downsizing and profitability in Canada. *Canadian Journal of Administrative Sciences, 13,* 237–250.

Miller, R. A. (2001). The four horsemen of downsizing and the tower of Babel. *Journal of Business Ethics, 29,* 147–151.

Mirvis, P. H. (1997). Human resource management: Leaders, laggards, and followers. *Academy of Management Executive, 11*(2), 43–56.

Mishra, K., Spreitzer, G. M., & Mishra, A. (1998). Preserving employee morale during downsizing. *Sloan Management Review, 39,* 83–95.

Mone, M. A. (1997). How we get along after the downsizing: Post-downsizing trust as a double-edged sword. *Public Administration Quarterly, 21,* 309–336.

Morris, J. R., Cascio, W. F., & Young, C. E. (1999). Downsizing after all these years: Questions and answers about who did it, how many did it, and who benefited from it. *Organizational Dynamics, 27*(3), 78–87.

Morrison, E. W., & Robinson, S. L. (1997). When employees feel betrayed: A model of how psychological contract violation develops. *Academy of Management Review, 22,* 226–256.

Morse, R., & Weiss, N. (1955). The function and meaning of work and the job. *American Sociological Review, 20*(1), 191–198.

Moyle, P., & Parkes, K. (1999). The effects of transition stress: A relocation study. *Journal of Organizational Behavior, 20,* 625–646.

Mroczkowski, T., & Hanaoka, Y. T. (1997). Effective rightsizing strategies in Japan and America: Is there a convergence of employment practices? *Academy of Management Executive, 11*(2), 57–67.

Murray, M. (1995, May 4). Amid record profits, companies continue to lay off employees. *Wall Street Journal,* p. A1.

Nadler, D. (1988). Organizational frame bending: Types of change in the complex organization. In R. H. Kilmann and others, *Corporate transformation: Revitalizing organizations for a competitive world* (pp. 66–83). San Francisco: Jossey-Bass.

Naik, G. (1998, March 5). Telecom deregulation in Britain delivered a nice surprise: Jobs. *Wall Street Journal,* pp. A1, A8.

The negative effects of overwork and related stress. (2001). *HR Focus, 78*(11), 9.

Neuman, G. A., & Kickul, J. R. (1998, Winter). Organizational citizenship behaviors: Achievement orientation and personality. *Journal of Business and Psychology,* 263–264.

Nicholson, N. (1996). Career systems in crisis: Change and opportunity in the information age. *Academy of Management Executive, 10*(4), 40–51.

Nienstedt, P. R. (1989). Effectively downsizing management structures. *Human Resource Planning, 12,* 155–165.

Noer, D. M. (1995). *Healing the wounds: Overcoming the trauma of layoffs and revitalizing downsized organizations.* San Francisco: Jossey-Bass.

Noer, D. M. (1997). *Breaking free: A prescription for personal and organizational change.* San Francisco: Jossey-Bass.

O'Daniell, E. E. (1999). Energizing corporate culture and creating competitive advantage: A new look at workforce programs. *Benefits Quarterly, 15*(2), 18–25.

O'Neil, H. M., & Lenn, D. J. (1995). Voices of survivors: Words that downsizing CEOs should hear. *Academy of Management Executive, 9*(4), 23–34.

Palmer, I., Kabanoff, B., & Dunford, R. (1997). Managerial accounts of downsizing. *Journal of Organizational Behavior, 18*, 623–639.

Perron, M. J., & Shanley, A. (1999). If downsizing is inevitable, do it right—or risk huge liability nightmares. *Chemical Engineering, 106*(7), 97–98.

Perry, L. T. (1986). Least cost alternatives to layoffs in declining industries. *Organizational Dynamics, 14*(4), 48–61.

Quick, J. C., Gavin, J. H., Cooper, G. L., & Quick, J. D. (2000). Executive health: Building strength, managing risks. *Academy of Management Executive, 14*(2), 34–44.

Reichers, A. E., Wanous, J. P., & Austin, J. T. (1997). Understanding and managing cynicism about organizational change. *Academy of Management Executive, 11*(1), 48–59.

Robinson, S. L., & Greenberg, J. (1998). Employees behaving badly: Dimensions, determinants and dilemmas in the study of workplace deviance. In C. L. Cooper & D. M. Rousseau (Eds.), *Trends in organizational behavior* (Vol. 5, pp. 1–30). New York: Wiley.

Robinson, S. L., & Morrison, E. W. (1995). Organizational citizenship behavior: A psychological contract perspective. *Journal of Organizational Behavior, 16*, 289–298.

Robinson, S. L., & Rousseau, D. M. (1994). Violating the psychological contract: Not the exception but the norm. *Journal of Organizational Behavior, 15*, 245–259.

Rosenblatt, Z., & Sheaffer, Z. (2001). Brain drain in declining organizations: Toward a research agenda. *Journal of Organizational Behavior, 22*, 409–424.

Rosenwald, M. (2001, March 25). When Cisco speaks, dictionaries open. *Boston Globe*, p. J2.

Rothman, J. (2001). Livable layoffs. *Software Development, 9*(11), 47–50.

Rousseau, D. M. (1995). *Psychological contracts in organizations: Understanding written and unwritten agreements.* Thousand Oaks, CA: Sage.

Rucci, A. J., Kirn, S. P., & Quinn, R. T. (1998). The employee-customer-profit chain at Sears. *Harvard Business Review, 76*(1), 82–97.

Salopek, J. J. (2000). Survey says. *Training and Development, 54*(1), 14.

Sandell, R. (1999). Organizational life among the moving bandwagons: A network analysis of dropouts from a Swedish temperance organization, 1896–1937. *ACTA Sociologica, 42*(1), 3–15.

Schein, E. H. (1965). *Organizational psychology.* Upper Saddle River, NJ: Prentice Hall.

Schein, E. H. (1996). Career anchors revisited: Implications for career development in the twenty-first century. *Academy of Management Executive, 10*(4), 80–88.

Scott, S. G., & Lane, V. R. (2000). A stakeholder approach to organizational identity. *Academy of Management Review, 25*(1), 43–62.

Sennett, R. (1998). *The corrosion of character: The personal consequences of work in the new capitalism.* New York: Norton.

Shadid, A. (2001, February 18). Letting go: Analysts—Many firms are slashing jobs to please Wall Street. *Boston Globe,* pp. E1, E4.

Sims, R. (1994). Human resource management's role in clarifying the new psychological contract. *Human Resource Management, 33,* 373–382.

Solomon, R. C. (1999). *A better way to think about business: How personal integrity leads to corporate success.* New York: Oxford University Press.

Susskind, A. M., Miller, V. D., & Johnson, D. (1998). Downsizing and structural holes: Their impact on layoff survivor' perceptions of organizational chaos and openness to change. *Communication Research, 25* (1), 30–63.

Sutherland, J. (1981). *Systems: Analysis, administration and architecture.* New York: Van Nostrand.

Sutton, R. I., Eisenhardt, K. M., & Jucker, J. V. (1986). Managing organizational decline: Lessons from Atari. *Organizational Dynamics, 14*(2), 17–29.

Thomson, N., & Millar, C. C. (2001). The role of slack in transforming organizations. *International Studies of Management and Organization, 31*(2), 65–83.

Toffler, B. L. (1986). *Tough choices: Managers talk ethics.* New York: Wiley.

Tushman, M., & Anderson, P. (1986). Technological discontinuities and organizational environments. *Administrative Science Quarterly, 31,* 439–465.

Umiker, W. (1999). The essentials of compassionate downsizing. *Health Care Supervisor, 17*(4), 63–69.

Van Buren III, H. J. (2000). The bindingness of social and psychological contracts: Toward a theory of responsibility in downsizing. *Journal of Business Ethics, 25,* 205–219.

Vidaver-Cohen, D., & Altman, B. W. (2000). Corporate citizenship in the new millennium: Foundations for an architecture of excellence. *Business and Society Review, 105*(1), 145–168.

Walton, R. R. (1986). A vision-led approach to management restructuring. *Organizational Dynamics, 14*(4), 4–16.

Watson, G. W., Shepard, J. M., & Stephens, C. U. (1999). Fairness and ideology: An empirical test of social contracts theory. *Business and Society, 38*(1), 83–108.

Wayhan, V. B., & Werner, S. (2000). The impact of workforce reductions on financial performance: A longitudinal perspective. *Journal of Management, 26,* 341–363.

Weakland, J. H. (2001). Human resources holistic approach to healing downsizing survivors. *Organization Development Journal, 19*(2), 59–70.

Weick, K. E., & Quinn, R. E. (1999). Organizational change and development. *Annual Review of Psychology, 50,* 361–386.

Wiley, J. W. (1996). Linking survey data to the bottom line. In A. I. Kraut (Ed.), *Organizational surveys: Tools for assessment and change* (pp. 330–359). San Francisco: Jossey-Bass.

Winchell, T. E. (2001). Successfully using teams to assist in structural realignments or downsizing initiatives. *Public Personnel Management, 30,* 261–268.

Worrell, D. L., Davidson, W. N., Chandy, P. R., & Garrison, S. L. (1986). Management turnover through deaths of key executives: Effects on investor wealth. *Academy of Management Journal, 29,* 674–694.

Young, S., & Brown, H. N. (1998). Effects of hospital downsizing on surviving staff. *Nursing Economics, 16,* 258–262.

CHAPTER 14

Organizational Adaptability
Rethinking the Resizing Process
Jessica L. Saltz
Philip H. Mirvis

Stage 1: Downsize. Stage 2: Right-size. Stage 3: Capsize.

Most references to sizing in the business world have a pejorative connotation. For instance, *downsizing* often translates into "dumb-sizing" through mindless layoffs. *Right-sizing* refers mostly to closures, divestitures, and other staff reductions. *Upsizing* is a new label for palliatives aimed at maintaining morale among employees who have been spared the ax. The opening slogan captures the end result of resizing efforts in many companies. Unfortunately, such efforts seldom do very much to keep a sinking ship afloat. In this chapter, we take a more optimistic look at resizing and consider how organizations can ease the pain of changing their size and ultimately improve through the process. Our thesis is that more adaptable organizations handle resizing better than their less adaptable counterparts.

Elements of Size

Size has several meanings in organizations. With respect to the workforce, size often refers to the absolute number of people on staff (rather than assets, sales, market value, and the like, which also can measure a firm's size). Thus, most talk about sizing refers to how that total shrinks or grows through hiring, voluntary departures, and layoffs.

Other elements of size are of equal or even more importance. One area of interest, for example, concerns the relative size of units, layers, and other groupings in a company. There are many studies on ratios between line employees and staff, between supervisors and direct reports, and between managerial, exempt, and nonexempt groups, as well as the implications for different types of firms (Porter & Lawler, 1968). Human resource specialists find it useful to compute relative staffing, salary, and promotion rates for various occupational, racial, and gender segments in their firms. Different configurations give an organization a different shape and character. There also are more qualitative dimensions of size to consider. For example, a firm may be "top heavy" with senior executives or "bloated" with middle managers, and its workforce may be "fat and happy" versus "lean and mean."

In this chapter, we consider two separate dimensions of size. The first element, organization size, refers to the absolute number of people employed by an organization. The second, organization shape, reflects the distribution and grouping of employees within a company. This dimension also includes people connected to a firm as contractual or contingent labor and even as a supplier or strategic partner. Certainly, size and often shape change as an organization resizes itself.

Organizational Adaptability

There are basic requirements for adaptability having to do with an organization's structure, culture, and people. In the case of structure, these include optimal levels of differentiation (to observe boundary conditions) and integration (to formulate and implement a response). Adaptability also is enhanced by having roles and rules that allow for appropriate levels of communication and enable work units to self-design a response to change situations. These structural features are involved whenever an organization changes its size and shape.

An adaptable culture, in turn, includes values and norms that support a flexible structure and processes that promote both continuity and change among people and in relation to the business environment. Culture can be a bane or boon to resizing and is surely affected by the results. Finally, an adaptable organization has optimal diversity among its people overall and has a significant proportion who can cope with uncertainty and change. We now take a closer look at adaptability in structure, culture, and people in terms of resizing and reshaping an organization.

Organizational Structure

An organization's structure defines the distribution of units and positions within it and how these different parts are related (James & Jones, 1976). Structure dictates who works with whom, for whom, doing what, and so forth. Although observers vary on what they consider to be the most germane dimensions of structure, most include role definitions, the division of labor and authority, and boundary relationships.

An adaptable structure enables a company to observe, report, and quickly respond to changes in its environment. Different structural arrangements, in turn, argue for units of a different size and shape. For instance, structural differentiation recognizes diversity in an organization's environment and allows units to get closer to distinct opportunities and threats. With respect to size and shape, this typically translates into smaller business and work units, operating under decentralized authority, and with the capacity to respond to situations with great flexibility. Integration, by comparison, favors larger scale, often features centralization, and standardizes more activities. It reduces the costs of gathering and assembling information and of launching and coordinating a response.

Finding the optimal mix of differentiation and integration is a constant challenge for companies. To move quickly and efficiently between the two, many companies rely on temporary structures, have employees work on multiple tasks, and develop a capacity for their workforce to band together and disband without a lot of fuss. In practice, this translates into the 3Rs of resizing and reshaping an organization: restructuring, retraining, and retention.

Changing the number of employees in a firm, whether up or down as the need dictates, is no guarantor of success. More important is the management and grouping of the human capital of an enterprise, that is, the accumulated value of employees' knowledge, experience, skills, and abilities that contributes to the attainment of an organization's goals (Knowledge Workers, 2001). Many authors have documented the point that a firm's strategies, and even its processes, products, and services, can be copied quickly by its competitors (Lawler, 1994). By comparison, the know-how and experience of employees cannot be so readily imitated and thus provide a more sustainable source of competitive advantage.

Resizing affects not only head count but also the value of human capital in an organization. Reductions in force typically subtract from human capital, even when poor performers are removed. The problem is that most companies lose not only individual knowledge but also collective human capital in downsizing.

We contend that an adaptable organization maintains more of its human capital with a reduction in force than a less adaptable firm does. One place to see this is in the results of downsizing in the United States during the 1990s. The evidence is clear that many firms undertook across-the-board cutbacks and emphasized getting higher-paid people off the payroll (De Meuse, Bergman, & Vanderheiden, 1997; Marks, 1993). As a result, business units and staff departments suffered comparable reductions regardless of their strategic significance and value added. Furthermore, there was scant accounting of employee performance in layoff decisions; often, a disproportionate number of mature workers departed with early-retirement packages, robbing firms of organizational memory and depriving younger workers of seasoned mentors. In many instances, the most marketable and valued surviving employees then voluntarily jumped ship, and yet another round of layoffs followed.

By comparison, firms that downsized effectively did so with strategic intent and underwent some form of restructuring. These firms reported fewer problems with their downsizing and far more favorable human and financial results (Marks, 1993). In turn, they complemented their resizing efforts by retraining many more of their employees for new jobs and emphasized retaining their top talent (Mirvis, 1997). These 3Rs—restructuring, retraining, and retention—all have a bearing on the structure of an adaptable organization.

Restructuring

On the matter of absolute size, adaptable companies strategically restructure their business units. For example, rather than making broad-based cutbacks, Tenneco adopted a strategy of shrink-and-grow, reducing head count aggressively in units and functions where opportunities for growth were limited and maintaining and often adding staff in areas with brighter prospects. Firms that have followed the dictums of reengineering typically streamlined work flows, reduced staff in noncore work areas, and outsourced in functions where human capital was not a distinct source of competitive advantage for the firm. American Express, Hewlett-Packard, Microsoft, Procter & Gamble, and many other large organizations outsource activities that in the past would have been accomplished by their human resource and public relations departments. Siemens Business Services, a wholly owned subsidiary of Siemens AG, has announced an outsourcing agreement whereby AT&T will manage its information technology network. Strategic alliances and joint ventures between firms are more dramatic means of resizing and reshaping organizational structure to gain competitive advantage.

Another structural change involves delayering. General Electric, as one storied example, successfully eliminated between three and eight layers of management in its various businesses and saw its rates of productivity grow. Atlas Copco, the parent company for Rental Service Corporation, plans to remove layers of management that are reportedly slowing the company's ability to react to change. The rationale for delayering is that it forces upper management to focus on strategic, longer term needs and empowers subordinates down the line to take charge of their work.

We also believe that companies can more successfully resize when they have an adaptable organization structure. One such structure, identified by Handy (1989), is in the form of a shamrock with three "leaves" of employees. The first leaf consists of full-time core employees who are committed to the organization and its success. It is essential for organizational survival. Managers, technicians, and professionals populate this leaf. The second leaf encompasses people who fulfill specific needs of the organization. They typically are outside contractors that perform tasks that are not a primary focus of the organization. This saves firms some funds and gives them more flexibility to change contractors or eliminate the work. The third leaf is composed of contingent and temporary workers. These part-time or temporary workers perform a variety of tasks, such as clerical and technical support, and act as a buffer for the core employees of the organization.

This shamrock structure rearranges a firm's labor force into internal and external labor markets. These two workforces meet different organizational needs. The internal employees (first leaf) provide for stability and continuity and are seen as firm-specific resources. The external labor pool (the second and third leaves) increases organizational flexibility. An organizational structure composed of these distinct yet complementary labor forces offers new options for resizing. Typically, companies want to increase the human capital of core employees, imbue them with the firm's vision, and draw on their historic knowledge and familiarity with past practices. By comparison, external work assignments and arrangements can be altered more quickly and with less disruption than internal ones (Davis-Blake & Uzzi, 1993). And because employment contracts with external contractors and contingent labor are typically short term, these workers can be let go without threatening the company's reputation or stability (Osterman, 1988).

How commonplace is the three-leaf structure? It depends on the industry segment. Fortune 500 companies, for example, often spend liberally on specialized high-end consultants and outsource many of their back-office functions. They also maintain a large proportion of core employees. High-tech firms and dot-coms, by comparison, keep their core relatively small and rely more on contracts, alliances, and joint ventures to get the work out.

It is clear that a labor market is developing in line with this new organizational form. One new form of contract employment is the interim manager, who typically provides clients with short-term coverage for a functional area or a specific project (Inkson, Heising, & Rousseau, 2001). Organizations using these self-employed managers gain the skills needed for an activity or temporary role without making a longer-term employment commitment. On a broader scale, temporary employment agencies like Manpower can literally rent a workforce to a firm to produce a product or deliver a service. Manpower has been among the fastest-growing employers in the United States.

Retraining People

Adaptable firms resize effectively by retraining their surviving employees, as well as by reorienting their overall training philosophy. Hall and Mirvis (1995) argue that training employees for a specific position is not appropriate in today's turbulent business environment. Resizing, when accompanied by restructuring, often changes the mix of work in a firm and the knowledge and skills that an employee needs to be successful. Continuous learning enables employees to more effectively perform the changing assignments often associated with a shakeup of roles and responsibilities.

Continuous learning gives employees confidence to constantly acquire new skills. Firms like Corning, Kodak, and Dow Chemical maintain skill banks that track employee development and encourage employees to learn by challenging them with special projects and varied work assignments. This model of continuous learning increases the adaptability of the organization because employees can be successfully moved in and out of different positions as a firm changes its size and shape. Furthermore, employees who are let go in the process should be more attractive job candidates given their ability to acquire new skills.

Interestingly, the case has been made that continuous learning also may prevent some downsizing in companies. The argument is that firms gain a competitive advantage based on the broader skills of their workforce and ability to redeploy human assets more rapidly and at less cost. Although few companies provide lifetime employment security today, Hewlett-Packard, Herman Miller, and selected others have made a commitment to regularly relocate displaced employees rather than hire in from the outside as long as employees develop and maintain a broad skill set. These firms have implemented smaller reductions in force than other comparable firms in their industry and have become a magnet for top talent.

Retaining Talent

Although all employees contribute to an organization's total human capital, certain workers are more valuable than others, and during a resizing, these key employees are critical to the success of the firm. However, they also are often the most marketable and may be easily attracted to employment opportunities elsewhere. Adaptable companies make a point of holding on to top talent even as less valuable employees are let go.

Organizations have managed to differentiate and retain top talent through a variety of practices. For example, large firms like PP&G, Unilever, and Honeywell have special programs aimed at high-potential employees and groom them with key assignments and senior mentors. IBM, Compaq, the Big Five accounting firms, and other leading high-tech and professional firms have technical career ladders that provide individual contributors with recognition and pay increases commensurate with those offered to people moving up the managerial career ladder. Taking a different tack, SAS Institute focuses on helping its people balance the competing pressures of work and family. It provides flextime, part-time employment options, low-cost day care, and on-site fitness facilities (Stein, 2000).

These efforts help to ensure that a company retains the talent needed to cope with problems and exploit opportunities as they arise—at least more so than competitors.

Other Forms of Adaptable Restructuring

New kinds of career ladders and flexible work arrangements are themselves a form of adaptable restructuring. Indeed, studies find that companies that develop them also are likely to retrain their employees and restructure themselves regularly in the light of changing circumstances (Mirvis, 1997).

At the other end of the workforce, companies are resizing and reshaping themselves through ranking systems. General Electric, Ford, and other firms now rate their employees as A, B, or C performers and insist that the bottom segment either improve or leave. This rank-and-yank system, while in principle aimed at increasing a firm's human capital, has experienced less satisfactory side effects. At Ford, for example, older workers are more likely to be ranked as C, and the company has been hit with several lawsuits. Other firms have seen rankings marred by bad judgment and petty politics.

Organizational Culture

Adaptable organizations use the 3Rs to maintain and productively use human assets even as units shrink and grow. However, flexible structures are only part of the answer to adaptability. Companies also need adaptable cultures and employees.

Schein (1992) defines culture as "a pattern of shared basic assumptions that the group learns as it solved its problems of external adaptation and internal integration, that has worked well enough to be considered valid and, therefore, to be taught to new members as the correct way to perceive, think, and feel in relation to those problems" (p. 12). For our purposes, an adaptable organizational culture does not emphasize change for its own sake; adaptability is not the equivalent of changeability. Rather, an adaptable culture carries learnings and experiences that guide correct changes. One characteristic is a predilection for proactive, not reactive, responses to the marketplace.

Denison and Mishra (1995) stress the importance of an organization's ability to make necessary changes while maintaining the core identity of the firm. They define an adaptable culture as one that balances the need for making changes and trying out new ideas with maintaining the organization's core values and goals. A body of research demonstrates a positive, significant relationship between an adaptive culture and organizational performance (Christensen & Gordon, 1999; Kotter & Heskett, 1992; Denison & Mishra, 1995).

It may help to think of structure as the anatomy of a firm and culture as its physiology. Culture is what animates structure and brings the organization to life. For example, even as differentiation moves activity to an organization's boundaries, it is the culture that dictates whether a firm sees problems or opportunities. In the same way as integration pulls things together, culture influences whether action is cooperative or conflictual. An organizational structure can be no more or less flexible than is deemed valid and acceptable in a company culture.

Company cultures are modified from the outside in as a changing environment dictates new actions, and the business either adapts or not. However, cultures also are changed from the inside out as people depart along with organizational memory. One profound kind of reshaping in organizations relates to the demographic makeup of the workforce. When members leave a company, its corporate culture and subcultures are affected. This is especially true when older employees who have a long and deep knowledge of the organization and its history and lore are let go (Mirvis & Hall, 1996).

Sometimes a disproportionate segment of older workers depart a company because of its type of business (such as downsizing in a mature industry) or because of actions taken relative to roles and positions (such as delayering or outsourcing). In other situations, older employees are specifically singled out for early retirement. Some companies facing a reduction seem to view younger employees as more valuable than the stereotypical inflexible, slow, older worker. It should be noted, however, older employees are culture carriers and play an important role in an organization's ability to use corporate culture as a source of competitive advantage. Using our frame of reference, adaptable organizations recognize this culture-carrying function and are cautious about losing older employees.

Resizing affects an organization's culture. When employees are let go, they carry the company culture out the door. Employees who remain (the survivors) often develop more negative attitudes about their company, whose culture may be changing as a result of downsizing activity.

Organizations with adaptable cultures are able to deal successfully with survivor sickness and maintain at least some cultural continuity (Noer, 1993). They do so not only by retraining and retention programs, but also by rebuilding and strengthening their culture during and after the resizing process. This means revisiting and revising basic assumptions about how things work in the company and transmitting and inculcating new messages, values, and norms. This process might be called reculturation.

Dealing with Survivor Sickness

Organizations with adaptable cultures recognize that before they can begin to rebuild a new organization, the anger, sense of loss, and uncertainty felt by the remaining employees must be addressed. Mirvis and Marks (1991) recommend that employees be allowed to grieve the loss of valued coworkers and customs abandoned as a result of cutbacks. This grieving process allows not only for mourning but also for venting anger, expressing cynicism, and challenging more senior managers on whether they have "walked the talk."

In turn, there may be a need to resocialize employees in new ways of doing business. Organizational socialization, which encompasses the processes through which an employee learns about and adapts to a new situation (Chao, O'Leary-Kelly, Wolf, Klein, & Gardner, 1994), is most pronounced for newcomers in a company. However, socialization can occur whenever an individual takes on a new role or responsibility or experiences life changes that alter how he or she works (Feldman, 1989; Morrison & Hock, 1992; Van Maanen, 1976, 1984).

Schein (1992) suggests that socialization is necessary whenever an employee experiences change on any of three specific dimensions: (1) functional, which involves moving from one area of an organization to another; (2) hierarchical, representing a change in power or status; and (3) inclusion, which concerns how central an individual is to the workings within his or her work unit or team. Employees involved in resizing may face changes in all three of these dimensions.

Mergers and acquisitions and other combinations often join companies with different business models and organizational structures. Employees who previously worked in a staff function, for instance, may have to move into a line-of-business function following a merger. In turn, some individuals may be further removed from the perceived power center, as when companies institute dual head offices or find that their formerly decentralized position has been centralized. Finally, acquired employees may find themselves part of a combined team that operates according to the rules and regimens of their acquirer.

Organizations with adaptive cultures use a myriad of acculturation methods to combat survivor sickness and cope with changes in work designs and norms (Noer, 1993). Relevant techniques range from creating mission statements and new employee contracts to enacting new cultural stories and rituals. For example, when AT&T's Communications and Information Systems divisions internally merged, the head of the newly created Network Operating Group was concerned about survivor sickness and how to develop cooperation and a sense of group identity among the employees (Marks & Mirvis, 1992). He arranged for a reorientation retreat in which employees from both of the combined units openly discussed their different approaches to conducting business and participated in team-building exercises. The retreat ended with an exercise in which the employees ceremoniously let go of their worries and fears about the merger and graduated to membership in the new work team. By taking the time to discuss employees' concerns and feelings about organizational changes, companies can increase the likelihood that their employees will remain committed, loyal, and productive.

Reculturation

Organizations with adaptable cultures recognize the importance of reculturation as they change their size and shape. Reculturation takes on special significance when members of task forces or work groups are chartered with rebuilding their business and cultures. Many companies have empowered task forces and work teams to manage changes in their business. Marks (1993), for example, cites several instances where teams planned and executed downsizings and then developed practices to help heal the sense of loss and rebuild the work culture.

Changes in strategy are another occasion for reculturation. Companies that turn work over to suppliers to form joint ventures or alliances or that choose to distribute through franchisers change their size and shape, as well as experience change in their corporate culture. Typically, this involves a turnover in management and often a changeover in staff. Techniques such as a goals-and-roles exercise, where business units redefine their goals in the light of new strategies and employees renegotiate their roles and responsibilities, help in building a new organizational culture.

Changes in the composition of a workforce also require attention to culture. The entry of many more women into companies and increasing numbers of nonwhite workers at all levels in companies influence the prevailing company culture. Many firms like to think of themselves as multicultural and as valuing diversity. This message is communicated to employees and external stakeholders regularly in companies like IBM and businesses like Benetton. Changes in image and identity contribute to changes in organization culture (Hatch & Schultz, 2001).

Employees

Structure and culture concern macrolevel dimensions of an organization. We propose that it is time to consider how individual employees affect an organization's ability to cope successfully with the changes associated with resizing. In this regard, Champy (1995) suggests that many restructuring efforts are troubled because they fail to pay attention to the needs and capabilities of employees. We next consider what makes for adaptable employees and how their adaptability bears on company resizing.

Resizing often challenges employees with new tasks and different roles within their organization. An adaptable organization is composed of flexible structures and a responsive culture. It also has a workforce that copes effectively with ambiguity and uncertainty and is capable of responding quickly to change. Research has demonstrated that certain personality variables affect people's ability to cope with change and are brought into play in resizing (Kobasa, 1982; Judge, Thoresen, Pucik, & Welbourne, 1999).

One personality characteristic associated with coping skills is an internal locus of control. People with an internal locus of control believe that they have control over their work environment and are responsible for their success in that environment (Rotter, 1966). This feeling of control increases their self-confidence and helps them cope with the stress associated with the change (Judge et al., 1999). More broadly, research demonstrates a strong relationship between an internal locus of control and successful adaptation to change (Kobasa, 1982; Lau & Woodman, 1995; Callan, Terry, & Schweitzer, 1994).

Psychological hardiness is another personality trait associated with adaptability. Hardiness is a composite of three dispositions: a sense of control, commitment, and challenge (Kobasa, 1979). Within this framework, control represents a feeling of being an influential participant in life events rather than a helpless, passive observer. Commitment is a feeling of involvement as opposed to alienation in life events. And challenge is described as an awareness of continual change throughout one's lifetime and a belief that these changes are not to be feared or avoided but rather to be seen as opportunities for individual growth. Research shows that hardy individuals feel more in control and optimistic when faced with a stressful experience than their less hardy counterparts (Rhodewalt & Agustsdottir, 1984). Hardy individuals also appear to be less stressed by changes in their work environment (Rush, Schoel, & Barnard, 1995).

Various other personality variables also appear to influence the adaptability of an employee. For instance, open-mindedness is associated with adaptability, as is self-esteem (Folkman, Lazarus, Gruen, & DeLongis, 1986; Ashford, 1986; Callan et al., 1994). Self-efficacy or the faith in one's capabilities to organize and execute a course of action also appears to play a role in how employees respond to critical career experiences such as job loss and career changes (Holmes & Werbel, 1992; Stumpf, Brief, & Hartman, 1987). Judge and his colleagues (1999) reported a positive relationship between people's self-esteem and self-efficacy and their ability to cope with organizational change.

Based on these personality traits, Lau and Woodman (1995) contend that an individual's change schemata shape perceptions of and reactions to organizational changes. Three dimensions form a change schema according to Fiske and Taylor (1984). Beliefs about causality, the first dimension, provide a frame of reference for why the changes are occurring. The second dimension, valence, refers to the importance placed on changes. And inferences, the third dimension, refer to predictions made about how the changes will affect an individual. Through a change schema, personality characteristics such as locus of control, self-efficacy, and hardiness factor into how people perceive a resizing effort in their companies, gauge their vulnerability and the consequences, and develop a coping strategy.

Recruiting and Selecting for Adaptability

Because one factor affecting the success of resizing is the workforce, organizational leaders are well advised to pay attention to individual adaptability when recruiting and selecting employees. Psychological measures of locus of control, hardiness, self-efficacy, and other factors in adaptability are well established and in use by many organizational psychologists. More complex selection tools, such as the Birkman and the Life Orientations instruments, purport to measure people's temperament under normal and high-stress situations. In addition, surveys such as the one developed by De Meuse and McDaris (1994) assess an individual's reaction to change.

Adaptable companies make use of such instruments and personality tests not only for purposes of hiring but also for subsequent reselection and placement when it comes to job rotation, promotion and development, and reassignment following organizational changes. Two instruments that are useful to an organization during resizing were developed by Pulakos, Arad, Donovan, and Plamondon (2000) and Ployhart, Saltz, and Mayer (2001). Pulakos and her colleagues developed a taxonomy of adaptive performance that identifies aspects of adaptable behavior that different jobs require. For example, a particular position might be described as requiring employees who can learn new work tasks and technologies or are able to cope with uncertainty. Ployhart, Saltz, and Mayer (2001) took this a step further by developing a self-report scale (called ADAPT) that measures an employee's strength on each of the aspects in Pulakos et al.'s taxonomy (2000). During resizing efforts, organizations can use this taxonomy to identify the skills and abilities that an employee will need. An organization that includes an instrument such as ADAPT as part of its selection system will be able to match adaptable employees to the jobs that demand those skills.

Besides personality tests, assessment centers, simulations, and other means of quantifying adaptability, firms also rely on managerial and peer judgment in placing employees following a resizing effort. For example, in its acquisitions, General Electric often brings executives from the two sides together to review the resumés of managers and key staff, rank them based on past performance, potential, and values, and then conducts the equivalent of a player draft in placing them in new positions.

Developing Adaptability

A large body of research has shown that the best source of development is the job itself (Hall & Mirvis, 1995). One means of accelerating this real-time learning is through participation in projects emphasizing adaptive skills. For example, action learning programs at 3M, Ford, and Motorola have used a variety of formats to incorporate personal development into work projects. In most of these applications, workers operate on project teams, which build their skills in managing complex relationships. Included as part of the learning program are 360-degree feedback, teamwork and leadership skill training, and change management concepts.

Looking ahead, we project that just as the product life cycle is shortening in many industries, so too will the career cycle of many employees. The implication is that companies need to find new ways of maintaining career adaptability not only for chronologically older workers but also for the much larger group of employees at an advanced career age. One way to promote this is to have employees move in and out of their organizations by working in core areas for a time, taking a job in a supplier company or consulting firm, working as an individual contractor on selected projects, and then returning to the fold as a senior core contributor.

Furthermore, adaptable companies may have more options where to redeploy aging workers. Given that corporations will have closer relationships with supplier plants, distributors, and other firms on their second leaf, it is possible that the movement of older workers to these organizations could become part of a phased retirement career plan. Indeed, it is not hard to imagine companies using these firms much like the farm system in professional baseball, drawing in young people after they have gained some seasoning and sending back older workers who might serve as mentors and coaches in addition to performing day-to-day chores.

Goals of Organizational Adaptability

We have proposed that organizations with an adaptable structure, culture, and workforce will more successfully manage the process of resizing than less adaptable organizations. Its essence can be captured by the psychological term *alloplastic*, which refers to the ability to make changes in response to external conditions while maintaining one's underlying character (Nicholls, 1985).

Hall (1993) proposed that an adaptable organization could be characterized as a "3F organization." The 3Fs stand for free, fast, and facile. Free represents autonomous units of an organization that have the ability to respond to their specific market segments. Fast describes the organization's ability to respond swiftly to changes in the environment. The third F, facile, is defined as an organization's capability of learning from experience and applying the lessons to new situations.

Although we agree that an adaptable company must have the characteristics of a 3F organization, it also needs counterbalancing traits that retain its underlying character. We suggest that the three Fs be balanced with the three Cs of connection, consideration, and coherence. In response to Hall's free dimension, we propose that an adaptable organization also is characterized by connection, defined as an association or relation. While an adaptable organization relies on the freedom of units and people to respond to changes in the environment, it needs to maintain connections between them and to its customers, shareholders, and other stakeholders.

Connection is extremely important during periods of organizational change. The resizing process often is associated with a great deal of confusion and uncertainty for all individuals affected by the changes. As organizational departments and units change with the resizing, it is critical that these components share information with each other so that all elements of the organization are aware of the changes taking place. Customers and shareholders also are affected by resizing and face uncertainty as they question how the changing organization will continue to meet their needs and expectations. Adaptable organizations provide information to their customers and shareholders during all stages of the resizing process.

This connectivity is especially important when companies come unexpectedly into the public eye. The interactivity offered by the intranets and the World Wide Web allows for multiway dialogue among companies, employees, and external stakeholders. The upsides and downsides of the proposed merger of Hewlett-Packard and Compaq can be tracked in both company-sponsored and independent Web sites.

We have made the argument that an adaptable organization makes the right changes. Hall's "fast" dimension implies that the organization will respond quickly to changed conditions. We add to this point the need for an organization to consider changes in the environment carefully and respond only to those that warrant change. Consideration, our second C, implies taking careful account of all circumstances associated with a change in size or shape to avoid error or unfavorable consequences.

The experiences of Exide Corporation demonstrate the difficulties of shifting work responsibilities and people as the firm switched from a geographic- to a product-based organization. No sooner had Exide formed its product structure than it reversed itself to accommodate a large geographically organized acquisition. Mirvis (1997) calls for the development of "flexfirms," where staffing and structure, and the rearrangement of time and space, are fast and fluid.

However, flexibility is only part of the adaptive equation. Adaptable organizations also need to consider carefully how to resize and reshape themselves correctly. For instance, when layoffs are required, it behooves firms to maintain their core group of adaptable employees, while letting go of those who are less adaptable and able. Adaptable organizations consider what skills and knowledge are required of employees in redesigned roles and positions and staff these jobs accordingly.

Furthermore, turnover should be viewed as positive, not negative, in the adaptive corporation. Of course, there always is a risk that adaptable companies, having continuously enriched the skills and experiences of their employees, will lose them before these investments have been recouped. In that sense, firms that do not invest in people but pay top dollar for talent would seem to be free riders. Our feeling is that, on the contrary, firms that carefully consider employee development are more likely to retain talented people, reduce the ranks of the less able, and are attractive to eager-to-learn people of all ages.

The last C, coherence, means being logically integrated or consistent. This dimension addresses the need for the organization to maintain its strategic intent and cultural integrity as it changes. In the past decades, retailer Sears has changed directions countless times, downsized and redirected staff, lost its clear identity for customers, demoralized its workforce, and neared bankruptcy. No amount of talk—inside the company and in public advertisements—could clarify what was going on. By comparison, Caterpillar's smooth segue into a line of boots and clothing has been a smashing success. The company coherently extended its brand and its culture into a new arena and source of revenues.

Lessons Learned

Adaptable organizations are better suited to meet the demands and challenges associated with resizing an organization. In this light, we believe that companies should treat increased adaptability as a goal of their resizing efforts. With regard to organizational structure, it suggests that organizations adopt a more flexible structure, such as the three-leaf shamrock, that provides more freedom to rearrange work units and employee groupings. At the same time, maintaining a sense of connection is equally crucial. Attention to the 3Rs of restructuring, retraining, and retention can help on both counts as companies resize and reshape themselves.

An adaptable organization must have an adaptable culture. An important component of this culture is to acknowledge and address survivor sickness. Many company cultures favor speed. Equal attention, in our view, should go to a consideration of the impact of change on company culture. An emphasis on resocialization and reculturation following resizing is warranted.

Finally, we emphasize the importance of hiring and correctly placing adaptable employees throughout the organization. Taking steps to assess an individual's adaptability and develop it in the workforce makes it easier for companies to handle change. Adaptable people are more facile at handling change. At the same time, they also are able to situate themselves in changed circumstances more effectively and create a level of coherence for themselves, their coworkers, and whomever they work or communicate with in their business and community.

Adaptable organizations may face just as much environmental turbulence as other firms. They will not be able to avoid many of the pains of resizing. However, we believe that they will be more likely to respond to needed changes and will have the structural, cultural, and employee resources to do so more efficiently and effectively.

References

Ashford, S. J. (1986). Feedback-seeking in individual adaptation: A resource perspective. *Academy of Management Journal, 29,* 465–487.

Callan, V. J., Terry, D. J., & Schweitzer, R. (1994). Coping resources, coping strategies and adjustment to organizational change: Direct or buffering effects? *Work and Stress, 8,* 372–383.

Champy, J. (1995). *Reengineering management: The mandate for new leadership.* New York: HarperCollins.

Chao, G. T., O'Leary-Kelly, A. M., Wolf, S., Klein, H. J., & Gardner, P. D. (1994). Organizational socialization: Its content and consequences. *Journal of Applied Psychology, 79,* 730–743.

Christensen, E. W., & Gordon, G. G. (1999). An explanation of industry, culture, and revenue growth. *Organization Studies, 20,* 397–422.

Davis-Blake, A., & Uzzi, B. (1993). Determinants of employment externalization: A study of temporary workers and independent contractors. *Administrative Science Quarterly, 38,* 195–223.

De Meuse, K. P., Bergmann, T. J., & Vanderheiden, P. A. (1997). Corporate downsizing: Separating myth from fact. *Journal of Management Inquiry, 6,* 168–176.

De Meuse, K. P., & McDaris, K. K. (1994). An exercise in managing change. *Training and Development, 51,* 55–57.

Denison, D. R., & Mishra, A. K. (1995). Toward a theory of organizational culture and effectiveness. *Organization Science, 6,* 204–223.

Feldman, D. C. (1989). Socialization, resocialization, and training: Reframing the research agenda. In I. Goldstein (Ed.), *Training and development in organizations* (pp. 376–416). San Francisco: Jossey-Bass.

Fiske, S. T., & Taylor, S. E. (1984). *Social cognition.* Reading, MA: Addison-Wesley.

Folkman, S., Lazarus, R. S., Gruen, R. J., & DeLongis, A. (1986). Appraisal, coping, health status, and psychological symptoms. *Journal of Personality and Social Psychology, 50,* 571–579.

Hall, D. T. (1993). *The new "career contract": Wrong on both counts.* Boston: Boston Executive Development Roundtable, Boston University School of Management.

Hall, D. T., & Mirvis, P. H. (1995). The new career contract: Developing the whole person at midlife and beyond. *Journal of Vocational Behavior, 47,* 269–289.

Handy, C. (1989). *The age of unreason.* Boston: Harvard Business School Press.

Hatch, M. J., & Schultz, M. (2001, February). Are the strategic stars aligned for your corporate brand? *Harvard Business Review,* pp. 128–134.

Holmes, B. H., & Werbel, J. D. (1992). Finding work following job loss: The role of coping resources. *Journal of Employment Counseling, 29,* 22–29.

Inkson, K., Heising, A., & Rousseau, D. M. (2001). The interim manager: Prototype of the twenty-first-century worker? *Human Relations, 54,* 259–284.

James, L. R., & Jones, A. P. (1976). Organizational structure: A review of structural dimensions and their conceptual relationships with individual attitudes and behavior. *Organizational Behavior and Human Performance, 16,* 74–113.

Judge, T. A., Thoresen, C. J., Pucik, V., & Welbourne, V. P. (1999). Managerial coping with organizational change: A dispositional perspective. *Journal of Applied Psychology, 84,* 107–122.

Knowledge Workers. (2001). http://www.knowledgeworkers.com/ human_capital_solutions.cfm.

Kobasa, S. C. (1979). Stressful life events, personality and health: An inquiry into hardiness. *Journal of Personality and Social Psychology, 37,* 1–11.

Kobasa, S. C. (1982). Commitment and coping in stress resistance among lawyers. *Journal of Personality and Social Psychology, 42,* 707–717.

Kotter, J. P., & Heskett, J. L. (1992). *Corporate culture and performance.* New York: Free Press.

Lau, C. M., & Woodman, R. W. (1995). Understanding organizational change: A schematic perspective. *Academy of Management Journal, 38,* 537–554.

Lawler, E. E. (1994). From job-based to competency-based organizations. *Journal of Organizational Behavior, 15,* 3–15.

Marks, M. L. (1993). Restructuring and downsizing. In P. H. Mirvis (Ed.), *Building the competitive workforce.* New York: Wiley.

Marks, M. L., & Mirvis, P. H. (1992). Rebuilding after the merger: Dealing with "survivor sickness." *Organizational Dynamics, 21,* 18–32.

Mirvis, P. H. (1997). Human resource management: Leaders, followers and laggards. *Academy of Management Executive, 11,* 2, 43–56.

Mirvis, P. H., & Hall, D. T. (1996). Career development for the older worker. In D. T. Hall & Associates (Eds.), *The career is dead—long love the career: A relational approach* (pp. 278–296). San Francisco: Jossey-Bass.

Mirvis, P. H., & Marks, M. L. (1991). *Managing the merger.* Upper Saddle River, NJ: Prentice Hall.

Morrison, R. F., & Hock, R. R. (1986). Career building: Learning from cumulative work experience. In D. T. Hall (Ed.), *Career development in organizations* (pp. 236–274). San Francisco: Jossey-Bass.

Nicholls, J. R. (1985). An alloplastic approach to corporate culture. *International Studies of Man and Organization, 14*(4), 32–63.

Noer, D. M. (1993). *Healing the wounds: Overcoming the trauma of layoffs and revitalizing downsized organizations.* San Francisco: Jossey-Bass.

Osterman, P. (1988). *Employment futures: Reorganizations, dislocations, and public policy.* Oxford: Oxford University Press.

Ployhart, R. E., Saltz, J. L., & Mayer, D. M. (2001). *ADAPT: Development and construction validation of a measure of individual workplace adaptability.* Working manuscript.

Porter, L. W., & Lawler, E. E. (1968). *Managerial attitudes and performance.* Homewood, IL: Irwin.

Pulakos, E. D., Arad, S., Donovan, M. A., & Plamondon, K. E. (2000). Adaptability in the workplace: Development of a taxonomy of adaptive performance. *Journal of Applied Psychology, 85,* 612–624.

Rhodewalt, F., & Agustsdottir, S. (1984). On the relationship of hardiness to the Type A behavior pattern: Perception of life events versus coping with life events. *Journal of Research in Personality, 18,* 212–223.

Rotter, J. B. (1966). Generalized expectancies for internal versus external control of reinforcement. *Psychological Monographs: General and Applied, 80,* 1–28.

Rush, M. C., Schoel, W. A., & Barnard, S. M. (1995). Psychological resiliency in the public sector: "Hardiness" and pressure change. *Journal of Vocational Behavior, 46,* 17–39.

Schein, E. H. (1992). *Organizational culture and leadership* (2nd ed.). San Francisco: Jossey-Bass.

Stein, N. (2000, May 29). Winning the war to keep top talent. *Fortune,* pp. 132–138.

Stumpf, S. A., Brief, A. P., & Hartman, K. (1987). Self-efficacy expectations and coping with career-related events. *Journal of Vocational Behavior, 31*(1), 91–108.

Van Maanen, J. (1976). Breaking in: Socialization to work. In R. Dubin (Ed.), *Handbook of work, organization, and society* (pp. 67–130). Skokie, IL: Rand McNally.

Van Maanen, J. (1984). Doing new things in old ways: The chains of socialization. In J. L. Bess (Ed.), *College and university organization: Insights from the behavioral sciences* (pp. 211–247). New York: New York University Press.

CHAPTER 15

Quicker, Faster, Cheaper, Smarter
Resizing Organizations, Resizing Employees

Kenneth P. De Meuse
Mitchell Lee Marks

I feel I gave thirteen years of my life for this company and I got paid well and had great benefits. All these years we were told it was the people who made the difference in our workplace. All of a sudden we are just numbers.

LAID-OFF TIRE WORKER

Today, we are demanding much more from our employees. They must continue their skill growth, be receptive to cross-training, be responsive to customer service, and be an active member of a team. If employees are unwilling to do this, they have diminished value.

TOP EXECUTIVE IN A LARGE UTILITY

It was a typical cold, crisp, winter morning in America's heartland. The air was frigid, and snow heaped in high banks along the roadside. Yet there was a quiet serenity as the moon cast its mystic glow on the snow-covered fields as Jim drove to work that day. This day was special; it was his forty-sixth birthday. Jim was a foreman at a meatpacking plant in northern Wisconsin, the industry that gave the Green Bay Packers its name. Jim was proud of the fact that he worked his way up the organizational ladder. He had only a high school diploma but attended night school and went to every supervisory seminar the company made available. His first job was on the killing floor, then a promotion to leadman, then supervisor, and now foreman. The company had been good to Jim during his twenty-four years of employment; he was able to raise five children, save enough money to invest in a couple of duplexes, and looked forward to retiring in about fifteen years. Jim was particularly proud of the fact that he had his own office.

When Jim arrived at work that morning at 6:30, there was a short message on his desk that his boss wanted to see him. As Jim walked to his boss's office, he wondered if his boss had a birthday surprise for him. However, Jim immediately sensed something was wrong when he was curtly asked to sit down. His boss revealed that the plant was not meeting its projected profit margins. Operations had to be streamlined, costs needed to be cut, and efficiency increased. His boss called it "corporate restructuring," or "reengineering," or maybe "right-sizing." Jim could not remember. All he knew was that he was stripped of his supervisory duties and responsibilities effective immediately. He was reassigned to the assembly line; his new job was removing hoof nails from cow's feet. His $45,000-plus salary was replaced with what he had made nearly twenty years ago. Moreover, there was a caveat: in three months, his performance would be reevaluated and if he was not performing up to par, he would be terminated. (Refer to Chapters Two and Four for personal stories of organizational resizing.)

Organizations, and individuals who work in them, are experiencing the greatest transformation in the history of business. Top executives, managers, and employees at all levels are being required to work smarter, change faster, and do more with less. A myriad of techniques are being employed to make organizations more competitive in today's global marketplace. Corporate mergers, Total Quality Management (TQM), self-managed work teams, ISO certification, cell manufacturing, employee empowerment, and open book management are just a few strategies being implemented by management as companies resize and reposition themselves to meet the needs of the dynamic global economy.

Today's organizational environment requires managers and nonmanagers at every level to change the way they have traditionally worked. Although it may seem sad to see employees struggle to find their identity in this chaotic work world, it is equally sad to watch thousands of companies go bankrupt because their management failed to respond effectively. Change is a fundamental law of nature. Charles Darwin once wrote that "it is not the strongest of species that survive, nor the most intelligent, but the one most responsive to change." To be successful today and tomorrow, organizations and their members will have to continuously change, flex, and adapt as the marketplace adjusts and then readjusts. We can complain bitterly, argue that it is not fair, or nostalgically long for the way the workplace once was, but it will do no good. In this new workplace, resizing is not an option but a necessity. The question is not whether one should or should not resize but how to resize. How do we resize organizations and their members with minimal pain, while capitalizing on the gain that comes with change, growth, and evolution?

In this book, we have explored the concept of corporate restructuring and downsizing. We suggested that the term *organizational resizing* be used in order to avoid the emotional baggage that the term *corporate downsizing* engenders. Furthermore, corporate downsizing is strongly rooted in the 1990s as American business and industry shed tiers of management and excess employees who accumulated through decades of complacency. The global marketplace now requires companies of every size, location, and product and service line to resize, remold, and reshape themselves on an ongoing basis. Let us not delude ourselves: organizational resizing is not a temporary state. It will not simply be a difficult month, quarter, or year, and then things will settle down and we can catch our breath. Success requires ongoing resizing at both the organizational and the individual levels.

Each chapter of this book has focused on a different facet of the resizing puzzle. In this concluding chapter, we examine the new realities facing organizations and organizational members today and into the future. We then offer some advice for organizations and employees with regard to this resizing mandate.

New Realities Facing Organizations and Their Members

Organizations and their members need to grapple with seven new realities.

Reality 1: The Disappearance of the Stable Workplace

During each business day of the 1990s, approximately two thousand jobs were eliminated at U.S. plants, factories, and offices. During 2000 and 2001, the rate accelerated to more than five thousand jobs per business day. Participating companies read like a Who's Who list of American corporations—IBM, Sears, AT&T, Boeing, Procter & Gamble, GM, Citicorp, Shell, Xerox. No industry or employee level appeared to be immune (see Chapter One). Obviously, when jobs disappear, employees disappear. In other words, coworkers, mentors, and protégés go; friends and colleagues move on. Surviving employees become concerned about the security of their jobs. Frequently, the remaining employees are asked to do more work, performing tasks that were accomplished by employees no longer there. Furthermore, employees are being cross-trained to perform jobs in a variety of classifications in order to develop a more flexible labor pool of workers. On top of these internal issues, product lines are changing faster and faster as customers demand new products, cheaper products, higher-quality products, and quicker response times. Taken as a whole, these events are creating a workplace that is much less predictable, comfortable, and stable than in the past.

Reality 2: The Disappearance of the Traditional Job and the Traditional Employee

Many of our grandparents followed a similar career path: they tended to work in the same large organizations, located in the same relatively large city, their entire lives. Their jobs were fragmented, relatively narrow in scope, unskilled, and repetitive. This work world consisted of regular hours and strictly prescribed job duties with little power or authority. Pay was determined by annual job appraisals and strict job classification systems.

Today, fully 25 percent of the workforce is composed of part-time, temporary, or contract employees (Reynolds, Masters, & Moser, 1998). In some respects, companies have moved from using employment agencies to secure employees to using outplacement firms to remove employees. Most employees are required to be multiskilled, cross-trained, flexible, and readily adaptive to an ever-changing work environment. Employee empowerment programs, such as TQM and open book management, demand that individuals latch onto power and make sound business decisions. Technology is an important element in nearly all jobs today. Moreover, the movement toward group work and team-oriented behaviors dictates that employees support, communicate, facilitate, and process information in ways very foreign to our grandparents. In most ways, today's workplace, jobs, and employees bear little resemblance to the ones thirty or forty years ago.

Reality 3: The Erosion of the Traditional Employer-Employee Relationship

In 1956, William H. Whyte wrote a fascinating book entitled, *The Organization Man*. In it Whyte described a corporate America in which an employee invested "himself" completely into "his" company, working fifty- to sixty-hour weeks, going on the road whenever and wherever needed, relocating on a minute's notice. In return, the employer provided a good job with good pay and benefits, granted annual merit increases, and provided ample opportunity for advancement. The employee gave unquestioned loyalty, and the employer offered continuous financial security. It was a cradle-to-grave mentality (De Meuse, Bergmann, & Lester, 2001; De Meuse & Tornow, 1990).

This employer-employee relationship provided order, stability, and predictability. However, this relationship does not (and cannot) exist any longer—in the United States or any other country of the world. Today, employee layoffs and corporate restructuring are common. We live in an era of decreased job security and short career ladders. In addition, we live in a period of increased individual leisure time, increased family demands, and rampant job and career mobility. The work environment is weaving a new, dynamic employer-employee relationship based on self-reliance, independence, and mutuality that accommodates both sexes and integrates a mosaic of races, heritages, needs, values, and individual differences (see Table 15.1). This evolving new work agreement offers new roles, responsibilities, and opportunities for each party (see Chapter Five).

Table 15.1. The Old and New Employer-Employee Relationship.

Employee's Responsibilities	Employer's Responsibilities
The old relationship	
Fair day's work	Fair day's pay
Sustained good work	Continued employment
Quality work	Praise and recognition
Extra good work	Advancement
Organizational loyalty	Job security
The new relationship	
Focus on personal needs	Focus on corporate goals
Career and self-development	Corporate survival and growth
Seek legal protection if wronged	Seek legal protection if wronged
Self-reliance	Self-reliance

Reality 4: The Obsolescence of Military Management

Effective managers in the past used a directive, almost dictatorial style of supervision. Management made all the important decisions. For example, managers directed, organized, planned, budgeted, and judged all activities related to their department. Employees were expected to comply readily with their orders, not make waves, and show blind loyalty to their boss and the company. In many ways, this style of supervision was an extension of the military training many managers had experienced during World War I and the Korean and Vietnam wars. Even the managerial nomenclature that evolved suggested a unilateral approach (for example, "span of *control*" rather than "span of *support*," "hired *hand*" as opposed to "*multiskilled* team member").

In today's business environment, we can no longer pay premium wages simply for "do-it-my-way, muscle-only" work. Employees need to add value and creativity, providing brain activity in their jobs. They must be expected to show initiative, be flexible, communicate solutions (as well as problems), be multiskilled, and

**Table 15.2. The Changing Role
of Management and Employee.**

The Past	The Present
The manager	
Directed	Coaches
Organized	Facilitates
Planned	Delegates
Judged	Supports
Budgeted	Involves
Controlled	Empowers
The Administrator	The Change Agent
The employee	
Followed orders	Shows initiative
Did not make waves	Questions status quo
Showed blind loyalty	Shares problems and solutions
No input in decisions	Adds value
Little cross-training	Multiskilled
Male oriented	Diversity conscious
The Organization Man	The Team Player

demonstrate an ability and willingness to change. Consequently, managers today also must change. The old militaristic paradigm fostered compliant, docile, complacent employees. For employees to be effective organizational members today, managers need to facilitate rather than direct, support rather than judge, and empower rather than control (see Table 15.2).

Reality 5: The Obsolescence of Hierarchical Control

Related to the loosening of control on the managerial level is the reduction of control on the structural level. Organizations are becoming flatter, more decentralized, and more responsive to their external and internal customers' needs. At one point, organizational hierarchies created a three-tier model. At the top level were the senior executives who made all the strategic decisions. They possessed all the organizational power, had the most status, and received high salaries and numerous perks. Colloquially speaking, we can refer to them as the thinkers of the organization. At the lower level of the organization were the doers. The doers were the employees who made the product or serviced the customer. Those employees actually built the ships, manufactured the cars, assembled the computers, sold the merchandise. In between the thinkers and doers were the controllers. The controller's job was to make sure the doers did what the thinkers said they should be doing. Today, organizations still need these three roles performed. Thinking, controlling, and doing are critical to the functioning of any company. However, rather than separate individuals performing each role, all three roles need to be performed by every organizational member. Each employee needs to be held simultaneously responsible for thinking, controlling, and doing. This approach is what self-managed work teams are all about.

Reality 6: The Changing Role of Management and Team Membership

In the past, managers managed, and workers worked. Managers were expected to direct, organize, plan, budget, hire, and fire. In short, they were responsible for controlling all activities within their department. In contrast, workers were expected to follow orders, not make waves, show blind corporate loyalty, respect the status quo, and listen without asking questions. American companies can no longer operate under such a system. Labor in the United States (and in many other countries of the world) is very costly. We can no longer pay premium wages simply for muscle activity. Employees also need to provide brain activity in their work. As a senior-level executive asserted, "It used to be once you were hired, that was it! Companies would never ask you to leave. Moreover, your job was so comfortable you did not want to leave. Management had very limited expectations for employees in the past. That has changed. Today, we are demanding much more from our employees. They must continue their skill growth, be receptive to cross-training, be responsive to customer service, and be an active member of a team. If employees are unwilling to learn new skills, they have diminished value." Today's manager (a team leader) must serve the role of coach, facilitator, and supporter. In short, managers need to empower team members rather than control subordinates. The distinction between manager and worker needs to become more blurred.

Reality 7: The Importance of Walking the Talk

You are the manager for Pat Kelly, a computer applications specialist with Luther Software. Pat was asked to give an early-morning presentation to a prospective client in a distant city. At the last minute, Pat decided to travel a day early so that he could spend an evening with the client. The meeting and presentation went extremely well, and he garnered a substantial contract for your company. However, when Pat returned from his trip, there was a $205 hotel bill for the night prior to his client presentation on his expense account. Company policy states that any lodging expense above $100 must be approved beforehand by a manager. Which of the following three alternative courses of action would you take?

Alternative A: You would reluctantly approve the hotel expense in full after discussing the situation with Pat and noting the special circumstances. You also would make sure he submitted a supplemental memo explaining the details, as well as stressing it should not happen again.

Alternative B: You would double-check the policy, and if so, would approve only $100 for the hotel room—despite Pat's contention that the hotel was the only one with vacancies in the area and that his staying there helped him land the account.

Alternative C: You would view the company policy as a general guide only. You would be much more interested in what Pat accomplished during his trip. You would happily approve the entire amount and commend Pat for his initiative.[1]

In today's work world, we casually speak of TQM, self-managed work teams, and employee empowerment, managerial techniques that have been cited frequently as crucial to the future success of business (Colenso, 2000; French & Bell, 1999; Pfeffer, 1998). Nevertheless, when managers are required to support employee behaviors congruent with those techniques, they often fail to do so (or are very uncomfortable doing so). Managers frequently resort to espousing company policy as a means of controlling employee behavior (alternative B), when what clearly is needed are trust, flexibility, and reinforcement of employee creativity and risk taking (alternative C).

Many organizations try to legislate employee performance through rules, policies, and procedures rather than motivate employee commitment by providing a nurturing, caring work environment. One of the most rules-bound organizations in the world is the U.S. federal government. This same organization is one of the most strongly criticized for fraud, political corruption, inefficient operations, and poor employee performance. In tomorrow's workplace, less dependence on rules and more dependence on individual discretion, ability, and trust are needed.

Suggestions for Enhanced Organizational Performance

Daryl Conner made an interesting observation in his book, *Managing at the Speed of Change* (1996). He reported that the vast majority of organizational change efforts failed due to poor implementation procedures used by management. In his research, he asked two simple questions: (1) Was the proposed change a good idea? That is, did it make good business sense for the organization to implement it? (2) Was the change implemented well? That is, did management do a good job preparing employees for the impending change, communicating it, involving employees in the process, and so on? He found that 80 percent of the time, the proposed change was a good idea. However, he reported that only 10 percent of the time did management do an effective job implementing it (see Figure 15.1).

Throughout the academic literature, authors historically have reported that organizations have done a poor job implementing and evaluating change efforts (Bastien, Hostager, & Miles, 1996; Brockner, Davy, & Carter, 1985; Choi & Behling, 1997; De Meuse & Liebowitz, 1981; Kotter, 1995; Porras & Robertson, 1992; Waclawski & Church, 2002; also see Chapters Three, Six, Seven, and Eight of this book). In 1966, noted industrial/organizational psychologist Marvin Dunnette published a seminal piece contending

**Figure 15.1. An Examination of
Organizational Change Efforts.**

Was it a good idea?

		No	Yes
Implemented Well?	No	10 percent	70 percent
	Yes	10 percent	10 percent

Source: Adapted from Conner (1996).

that executives frequently get caught up in the "fashionability" of organizational development efforts without fully understanding the underlying dynamics of implementation. It appears as though top executives simply expect all organizational levels to comprehend the change concept, embrace it, and then change their behaviors accordingly. If only it was that easy. For organizational resizing programs to be effective, the following guidelines should be followed:

- *Employees need to be prepared in advance for the impending change.* Frequently, top management has been contemplating such changes for months, sleeping on it, discussing it, analyzing it, and then rehashing it yet again. They should not simply expect other employees to embrace the new approach readily and change their behaviors, forgetting that they have taken several months to get to this point.
- *Involve employees in the resizing process.* An old adage of management is that on-the-job employees are much more knowledgeable with the inner operations of their work than are office-bound managers. Certainly, that point may be true. However, another major benefit of involving employees in the change process is to give them a sense of control over their workplace. Rosabeth Moss Kanter once wrote that "change is perceived as a threat when done to you, but an opportunity when done with you."

- *Open, honest, frequent communication with all employees is critical to the success of any resizing effort.* One cannot overestimate the importance of effective communication in organizational change process. With that point in mind, we offer ten guidelines in Exhibit 15.1.

- *Create an inspiring long-term vision, but implement it in small steps.* Employees need a general direction by which to rally around. They will need to know where the company is going, why is it going there, and how can they help it get there. Furthermore, management must be patient. Resizing efforts should be implemented gradually, and goals and time frames should be reasonable. Although it may be tempting to want to get back to business as usual, resizing takes time. Remember that most change efforts fail due to implementation problems, not because the idea was bad (Conner, 1996).

- *Management must address the emotional side of the resizing process.* It is natural for employees to feel apprehensive, frustrated, confused, and angry about many changes in the workplace. It is unrealistic (and unwise) to pretend that those feelings do not exist or that management should focus only on employee performance. Managers and supervisors at all levels should acknowledge such concerns, openly discuss them, and brainstorm solutions as to how to resolve them.

Throughout this book, many additional guidelines on implementing organizational resizing can be found. In Chapter Ten, McKee and Woodard specifically address the process of planning for resizing. In Chapter Eleven, Sommer makes numerous recommendations for implementing resizing. And in Chapter Twelve, Mitch Marks examines various approaches on how to revitalize the organization after resizing. Finally, Saltz and Mirvis present a number of interesting observations with regard to organizational adaptability and the resizing process (Chapter Fourteen).

The congruence among different organizational resizing efforts also needs to be taken into consideration by management. In many companies, employees are being restructured, reengineered, and right-sized and generally being asked to do more with less. Simultaneously, they are being exposed to TQM approaches and employee empowerment programs, and being placed into self-managed work teams. It could be argued that these organizational

Exhibit 15.1 Managerial Guidelines for Effective Communication During Organizational Resizing.

1. *Recognize that communication will assume a larger role during times of organizational resizing.* Take time to work through the questions and concerns of employees, customers, vendors, and family members. They will have lots of questions and naturally will turn to you as the manager.

2. *Be positive.* It does no good to complain, blame, and fight the change every step of the way. If plausible, take an advocacy role in selling the resizing to your employees. Focus their attention on the new opportunities being created in the organization.

3. *Be honest.* Even if the truth hurts. Even if the truth is that a lot of employees will be laid off. In such cases, individually meet with employees who will be terminated and inform them that all existing commitments will be honored, and a fair severance package will be provided, and ask them to stay on for a while to help ease the transition.

4. *Do not promise that things will remain the same.* Most employees will not believe you anyway. Those individuals who do will later insist that you lied or misrepresented things to them. Instead, explain that there will be changes and that there likely will be some problems for a while. However, reassure them that every effort will be made to consider the interests of every employee and keep them as well informed as possible of forthcoming changes.

5. *Keep the promises you do make.* When you do make a personal commitment or go on public record, be as good as your word. There is a tremendous need for you to instill confidence and develop a high degree of credibility. Do all that you can to enhance the trust level in your organization. If reversals of decisions do occur, follow up immediately with your employees.

6. *Talk specifics whenever you can.* The work environment already is full of ambiguity and apprehension. Do not add to it. Use direct, straightforward language, repeat things, clarify, and ask if there are questions. It is important to put key decisions in writing to enhance understanding.

7. *Do not feed the rumor mill.* Be acutely aware of the effect of your comments and actions, even in routine conversation. Employees will read things into almost everything you do and say. A careless wording or casual remark can fire up yet another rumor.

8. *Listen with a third ear.* Be keenly aware of implied meanings and hidden agendas. Deal with the total message (for example, the

Exhibit 15.1 Managerial Guidelines for Effective Communication During Organizational Resizing, Cont'd.

nonverbal and verbal, what is not said as well as what is said, what is implied as well as what is actually spoken).

9. *Remember the customer.* It is very natural (and normal) to get so focused on internal organizational issues and problems that you neglect the customer base. Customers also will have lots of questions and concerns. Savvy competitors will try to lure your disgruntled customers to their businesses.

10. *Overcommunicate.* It is critical to provide more communication than usual during times of organizational resizing. Maintain closer-than-normal contact with your employees and customers. Everyone becomes increasingly hungry for information during times of uncertainty.

---

interventions are contradictory in nature. On one hand, management appears to be saying to employees, "We value you," "We need you," "You are an integral business partner," and "You are an asset." On the other hand, management's actions might suggest that employees are expendable; they are not needed and are viewed as an expense.

The popular press, as well as academic literature, proclaim that the current work environment of mixed signals has led to employee confusion and uncertainty (at best) and distrust, fear, and anger (at worst). Reports suggest that the relationship between employers and employees is waning. A recent Watson Wyatt Worldwide survey found only 39 percent of employees trust senior leadership in U.S. companies ("Top managers more untrusted," 2002). Moreover, there was a significant decline from 2000 to 2002 in both the percentage of employees who say they have confidence in the job being done by senior management and the percentage who believe their companies conduct business in an honest and ethical manner. Organizational pundits allege that a growing cynicism is emerging between employer and employee and that trust, respect, and support may be at an all-time low. The media attention to the accounting scandals of Arthur Andersen, the financial collapse of Enron and WorldCom, and the alleged mismanagement of Tyco and Waste Management, among others, has contributed to the credibility gap between top management and lower-level employees in many companies. It would seem that top management must take an active role in reestablishing trust. Management must help employees envision a more profitable workplace, empower employees to take an active role in developing it, and reward them accordingly. Congruency in resizing efforts is a step in that direction.

Advice for Organizational Members

Every year, hundreds of books are published to assist individuals in everything from diet and exercise to financial health. And every year, numerous books are written by successful entrepreneurs who offer their pearls of wisdom on how to be successful in today's business world. Bill Gates recently wrote *Business @ the Speed of Thought* (1999) and outlined eleven rules students should learn in school. Harvey Mackay published his entertaining novel a few years ago about swimming with the sharks without being eaten alive. Each year job advice books are published by such divergent authors as Sam Walton and Al Dunlap. In addition, *Fortune, Business Week,* the *Wall Street Journal,* and other publications publish articles on how employees can effectively cope (or thrive on) the current business environment. All of those materials are informative and provide some unique perspectives that may be helpful for some people. (Refer to Chapters Nine and Thirteen for additional recommendations.)

In some ways, it seems trivial for us to attempt to provide some additional insight in a single chapter. Consequently, we offer only one. Reflect on your life over the past ten to fifteen years. How many of you have a cell phone (or several phones)? How many of you have one or more computers at home? How many of you own a CD player? How many of you have a house cleaning service? How many of you own a second home, a boat, or an RV? The point is that we as individuals and we as families continuously change. We purchase new products as technology improves. We buy new merchandise as our family needs fluctuate. On a daily basis, we buy and sell and discard products and services. Is it not appropriate for our companies to do the same? Market demands, competitive pressures, governmental laws, and consumer expectations constantly require companies to resize their operations. In many ways, it is no different from your reshaping your life as your needs change. In fact, your buying behaviors may be partially responsible for the resizing that is implemented in your organization.

Conclusion

Here are a few statistics to contemplate:

- In 1911, USX was one of the biggest corporations in the world. Where is it today?
- Approximately 70 percent of the largest companies in 1955 no longer existed in 1996.
- Only three of the top ten firms in the world in 1972 remain in the top ten today.
- Montgomery Ward, Woolworth, Compaq, Enron, the Los Angeles Rams, the floppy disk, GTE, Oldsmobile, the Sears and Roebuck catalogue: all are part of the history of American commerce.
- The average life expectancy of a large industrial corporation is approximately forty years, or the equivalent of the life span of a Neanderthal man (Mische, 2001).

It takes more than quality products, a good location, low prices, sound financial performance, and size to be a great company. It takes ongoing change. Consumer expectations will continue to increase; governmental regulations will come and go; technology and competition likely will escalate. Remember that tomorrow someone will be quicker, faster, cheaper, and smarter. Resizing provides an opportunity for organizational renewal and individual employee development. It offers organizations and their members an opportunity to begin anew, shore up their weaknesses, and reevaluate their strengths. Resizing is not an option; it is a mandate. Its success largely depends on how it is implemented. Percy Barnevick, CEO of Asea Brown Boveri, once asserted, "In business, success is 5% strategy and 95% execution" (Mische, 2001, p. 7). When it comes to resizing an organization, those numbers may not be far off.

Note

1. The scenario was adapted from Kolb, Osland, and Rubin (1991).

References

Bastien, D. T., Hostager, T. J., & Miles, H. H. (1996). Corporate judo: Exploiting the dark side of change when competitors merge, acquire, downsize, or restructure. *Journal of Management Inquiry, 5,* 261–275.

Brockner, J., Davy, J., & Carter, C. (1985). Layoffs, self-esteem, and survivor guilt: Motivational, affective, and attitudinal consequences. *Organizational Behavior and Human Decision Processes, 36,* 229–244.

Choi, T. Y., & Behling, O. C. (1997). Top managers and TQM success: One more look after all these years. *Academy of Management Executive, 11,* 37–47.

Colenso, M. (Ed.). (2000). *Kaizen strategies for improving team performance: How to accelerate team development and enhance team productivity.* Upper Saddle River, NJ: Prentice Hall.

Conner, D. K. (1996). *Managing at the speed of change: How resilient managers succeed and prosper where others fail.* New York: McGraw-Hill.

De Meuse, K. P., Bergmann, T. J., & Lester, S. W. (2001). An investigation of the relational component of the psychological contract across time, generation, and employment status. *Journal of Managerial Issues, 13,* 102–118.

De Meuse, K. P., & Liebowitz, S. J. (1981). An empirical analysis of team-building research. *Group and Organization Studies, 6,* 367–378.

De Meuse, K. P., & Tornow, W. W. (1990). The tie that binds—Has become very, very frayed! *Human Resource Planning, 13,* 203–213.

Dunnette, M. D. (1966). Fads, fashions, and folderol in psychology. *American Psychologist, 21,* 243–252.

French, W. L., & Bell, C. H., Jr. (1999). *Organization development: Behavioral science interventions for organizational improvement* (6th ed.). Upper Saddle River, NJ: Prentice Hall.

Gates, B., with Hemingway, C. (1999). *Business @ the speed of thought: Using a digital nervous system.* New York: Warner.

Kolb, D. A., Osland, J. S., & Rubin, I. M. (1991). *Organizational behavior: An experimental approach* (5th ed.). Upper Saddle River, NJ: Prentice Hall.

Kotter, J. P. (1995). Leading change: Why transformation efforts fail. *Harvard Business Review, 73*(2), 59–67.

Mackay, H. (1996). *Swim with the sharks without being eaten alive: Outsell, outmanage, outmotivate, and outnegotiate your competition.* Westminster, MD: Fawcett Columbine.

Mische, M. A. (2001). *Strategic renewal: Becoming a high-performance organization.* Upper Saddle River, NJ: Prentice Hall.

Pfeffer, J. (1998). *The human equation: Building profits by putting people first.* Boston: Harvard Business School Press.

Porras, J. I., & Robertson, P. J. (1992). Organizational development: Theory, practice, and research. In M. D. Dunnette & L. M. Hough (Eds.), *Handbook of industrial and organizational psychology* (2nd ed., Vol. 3, pp. 719–822). Palo Alto, CA: Consulting Psychologists Press.

Reynolds, L. G., Masters, S. H., & Moser, C. H. (1998). *Labor economics and labor relations* (11th ed.). Upper Saddle River, NJ: Prentice Hall.

Top managers more untrusted. (2002, August 4). *Eau Claire Leader-Telegram,* p. 1D.

Waclawski J., & Church, A. H. (Eds.). (2002). *Organization development: A data-driven approach to organizational change.* San Francisco: Jossey-Bass.

Whyte, W. H., Jr. (1956). *The organization man.* New York: Simon & Schuster.

Name Index

Subject Index